John Bell Hood

Stephen M. Hood

The Rise, Fall, and Resurrection of a Confederate General

SB

Savas Beatie

California

Hood, Stephen M.
John Bell Hood: the Rise, Fall, and Resurrection of a Confederate General / Stephen M. Hood. — First edition.
    pages cm
Includes bibliographical references and index.
ISBN 978-1-61121-140-5
1. Hood, John Bell, 1831-1879. 2. Generals—Confederate States of America—Biography. 3. United States—History—Civil War, 1861-1865—Biography. 4. United States—History—Civil War, 1861-1865—Campaigns. I. Title.
    E467.1.H58H66 2013
    355.0092—dc23
    [B]
    2013010919

First edition, first printing

SB
Published by
Savas Beatie LLC
989 Governor Drive, Suite 102
El Dorado Hills, California 95762

Phone: 916-941-6896
(E-mail) sales@savasbeatie.com
(Website) www.savasbeatie.com

Savas Beatie titles are available at special discounts for bulk purchases in the United States by corporations, institutions, and other organizations. For more details, please contact Special Sales, P.O. Box 4527, El Dorado Hills, CA 95762, or you may e-mail us at sales@savasbeatie.com, or visit our website at www.savasbeatie.com for additional information.

Printed in the United States of America.

To General John Bell and Anna Hood and their descendants,
living and dead, who, with dignity and grace, endured so much, for so long.

John Bell Hood Personal Papers

General John Bell Hood in a previously unpublished photograph, circa Richmond early 1864, before he left to command a corps in the Army of Tennessee.

Table of Contents

Preface
by Stephen Davis   x

Foreword
by Thomas J. Brown   xii

Introduction   xxxi

Chapter 1
John Bell Hood: The Son and the Soldier   1

Chapter 2
Robert E. Lee's Opinion of John Bell Hood   11

Chapter 3
Jeff Davis, Joe Johnston, and John Bell Hood   19

Chapter 4
The Cassville Controversy   46

Chapter 5
The Battles for Atlanta: Hood Fights   53

Chapter 6
Desperate Times, Desperate Measures: The Tennessee Campaign   69

Chapter 7
John Bell Hood: Feeding and Supplying His Army   89

Chapter 8
Frank Cheatham and the Spring Hill Affair   112

Table of Contents *(continued)*

Chapter 9
John Bell Hood and the Battle of Franklin   131

Chapter 10
The Death of Cleburne: Resentment or Remorse?   169

Chapter 11
John Bell Hood and the Battle of Nashville   176

Chapter 12
The Army of Tennessee: Destroyed in Tennessee?   200

Chapter 13
Did John Bell Hood Accuse His Soldiers of Cowardice?   208

Chapter 14
A Callous Attitude: Did John Bell Hood "Bleed His Boys"?   227

Chapter 15
John Bell Hood and Frontal Assaults   235

Chapter 16
Hood to His Men: "Boys, It is All My Fault"   242

Chapter 17
John Bell Hood and Words of Reproach   249

Chapter 18
Words of Praise for John Bell Hood   261

Chapter 19
John Bell Hood: Laudanum, Legends, and Lore   267

Table of Contents *(continued)*

Afterword
by Eric Jacobson   291

Appendix 1
Excerpt from *Advance and Retreat*   293

Appendix 2
"An Eloquent Tribute to the Memory of the Late Gen. J. B. Hood"   300

Appendix 3
Jefferson Davis on Joe Johnston: Excerpt to the Confederate Congress   303

Bibliography
314

Index
324

Maps and photos have been placed throughout the book
for the convenience of the reader.

Preface

The time is right for Sam Hood's book. Another way of looking at it is, my, what we have learned since the Civil War's Centennial fifty years ago.

No, I'm not thinking about Clive Cussler's discovery of the wreck of the Confederate submarine *H.L. Hunley* in 1995. Nor David Blight's discovery, in the Harvard University archives, of African-Americans' first decoration day in May 1865 for deceased Union POWs at Charleston's Race Course prison, which he announced in *Race and Reunion* (2001).

I'm thinking about the realization that in the last fifty years Confederate General John Bell Hood deserves a better shake by Clio, our Greek muse of history. Every now and then a major figure of the past merits a re-examination and fresh appraisal by the writers of history. That's because historiography— the very act of writing history—takes on trends built by previous writers, and even the most conscientious practitioners of the art may absorb ideas and opinions expressed in earlier books and monographs. Such has been the shifting historiography of General Hood.

There is no disagreement over the first half of Hood's Confederate war record in Virginia, where he rose from first lieutenant to major general. At the time of his severe wounding at Gettysburg, Hood was widely regarded as one of Lee's best division commanders. Wounded again at Chickamauga, with his right leg amputated, Hood was lionized in Southern society. At the request of General Longstreet and Secretary Seddon, and with President Davis' warm approval, Hood was promoted to lieutenant general.

It was when Hood became a corps commander in the Army of Tennessee, in early 1864, that historians began to differ over his merits as Confederate general. When he was promoted to temporary rank of general and placed in charge of the Army of Tennessee, Southerners at the time and students of the war since have quarreled about Hood's qualification for this huge responsibility. The loss of Atlanta, the disastrous repulse at Franklin and humiliating rout at Nashville created such a tragic record of failure that critics of Hood have virtually taunted Jeff Davis with "we told you so."

Sam Hood addresses this trendy literature here, commendably pointing out "factual errors, inaccurate and misleading paraphrasing of primary sources, and apparent concealment of historical facts." On the other hand, in the past few decades there has appeared at least a small bookshelf which might be called "Hood's scholarly rehabilitation/work in progress."

Whether Sam's keen eye and sharper pen lead to a better shake for Hood at the bar of history will be anyone's guess. For now, I invite you to join Sam in taking a fresh look at John Bell's Hood historical record.

You're in for a fine read.

Stephen Davis
Atlanta, Spring 2013

John Bell Hood
and the Lost Cause

The path to the destruction of John Bell Hood's historical memory began with his official report, submitted to Richmond a few months before the end of the war in February of 1865. In particular, Hood in his report sharply criticized Joseph Johnston's battlefield conduct, claiming it led to great waste in men and material along with a gradual demoralization of the troops. Johnston's consistent policy of strategic withdrawal in the face of the enemy, with its vain hope of luring Sherman into a trap, had worn the men down, Hood believed.

Hood declared that he "was placed in command under the most trying [of] circumstances"[1] and went on to state that "the army was enfeebled in number and in spirit by a long retreat and severe and apparently fruitless losses."[2] Here "fruitless" refers to Johnston's seeming reluctance to fight a decisive battle or to defend Atlanta. By engaging in a Fabian strategy of a fighting withdrawal, Johnston had given up more than one hundred miles of territory, and by finally crossing the Chattahoochee River he had sacrificed the last natural barrier between Georgia's capital and the enemy. Hood also noted that during

---

1 *The War of the Rebellion: A Compilation of the Official Records of the Union and Confederate Armies,* 128 vols. (Washington, DC, 1880-1901), Series 1, vol. 38, pt. 3, 636, hereafter cited as OR. All references are to Series 1 unless otherwise noted.

2 Ibid.

Johnston's tenure the army "had dwindled day by day in partial engagements and skirmishes."[3]

Some of Hood's comments are open to debate. For example, Johnston undoubtedly fought battles. The distinction, later made by Hood in his memoirs, however, is that Johnston failed to fight a general battle. Writing in the aftermath of his promotion and ascension to command of the Army of Tennessee and its total defeat at Nashville, Hood may well have felt bitter about being placed in such a tenuous position and, by February 1865, with the Confederacy on the threshold of its demise, perhaps regretted that he had accepted the job. His report elicited a threat of legal action from Johnston, and more importantly it motivated the proud Virginian to begin writing his own memoirs. Historian Brian Miller writes that this event "serves as the onset of Hood's postwar memory construction."[4] Johnston attacked Hood in his postwar memoirs. When Hood wrote to defend himself, however, Lost Cause Johnston supporters (such as former generals Cadmus Wilcox and James Chalmers) joined in with negative comments of their own.

Hood fought this battle mostly alone, as few chose to risk their own reputations by going up against the Southern Historical Society writers, based in Richmond after its move from New Orleans.

Immediately following the war, Hood moved to Louisiana and settled in New Orleans, where he began building himself a place in the postwar world. He concentrated on business and charitable works involving wounded veterans, widows, and orphans funds. He also took an active part in early efforts by the Southern Historical Society, established in the Louisiana capital, to help the South come to terms with its heavy losses, serving most notably as vice president of the Lee Monument Association in 1870. Hood also reestablished a connection with his former famous command, the Texas brigade, attending its first reunion held in Houston in 1872. In sum, by involving himself with public works and acting as a constructive citizen, he rebuilt feelings of self-worth shattered by the war and established a positive reputation for himself in New Orleans.[5]

---

3   Ibid.

4   Brian C. Miller, *John Bell Hood and the Fight for Civil War Memory* (Knoxville: University of Tennessee Press, 2010), 203.

5   Ibid., 178-179.

Hood responded to critical content in Johnston's memoirs and quickly began work on his own. Miller writes that Johnston "made Hood the scapegoat, ridiculed his military actions, and deflected any possible blame for his own failure at Atlanta."[6] Johnston's writings proved dry and overly technical and did not sell well. The work had critics, including a reviewer for the *New Orleans Daily Picayune*, who observed, "There are hyenas in human form who stand ready to tear open the grave of the buried past and whet their insatiable appetites for revenge upon the slain heroes . . . and spit their venom on those who survive."[7] Had Hood been able to step back, ignore Johnston's ill-selling memoirs, and continue his charitable works, the controversy may well have died, but the Kentuckian was unable to ignore what he considered to be an attack on his honor.

A profound shift in the construction of Civil War history occurred when the Southern Historical Society relocated to Richmond, Virginia, in 1873, where Southern nationalists from the Old Dominion, led by Jubal Early, built upon romanticized Lost Cause ideology and aimed to re-create the Old South. Most importantly for Hood, Early's group sought whipping boys for defeat. Residents of New Orleans complained that their historical society had been hijacked, and could have further claimed that the newly managed Southern Historical Society failed to represent the entire South.

Early's Virginians elevated themselves and their own state. Virginius Dabney, a well-known author and journalist of the day crowed: "We Virginians modestly admit our superiority to citizens of all other American states."[8] Historian Thomas Connelly, a Tennessean, wrote that Lost Cause architects "sought the best of both worlds—to be sorrowful, reluctant lovers of the Union who were dragged into the secessionist camp."[9]

The Virginia coalition used the Lost Cause to ease the region through hard times by memorializing the Southern war effort. Among its central tenets, the battle of Gettysburg became the crucial turning point of the war; the "high water mark of the Confederacy." Southerners argued that the Confederacy succumbed because it ran up against not superior civilization and military

---

6   Ibid., 203.

7   Ibid., 201.

8   Thomas Connelly and Barbara Bellows, *God and General Longstreet: The Lost Cause and the Southern Mind* (Baton Rouge: Louisiana State University Press, 1982), 39.

9   Ibid., 41, 199-200.

strength but to overwhelming numbers and an unfair industrial advantage. Convenient villains such as "Lee's old war horse," James Longstreet, and John Bell Hood shared blame for the loss in Pennsylvania.[10]

Hood was assessed partial blame for Gettysburg, but more significantly, also for the Confederate defeat in the West, with the battle of Franklin symbolic of his overall failed performance.[11]

"Old Jube" Early and his Virginia cohorts controlled virtually all of the South's literary output from 1865 to 1876, the period historically known as Reconstruction. The most important Lost Cause organ consisted of a large collection of articles and writings that came to be known as *The Southern Historical Society Papers*, but other publications including *Confederate Veteran, Our Living and Our Dead,* and *Southern Bivouac* also played important roles in reconstructing the history of the war. In these periodicals, Southern authors exerted herculean effort in an attempt to explain the crushing defeat they had suffered in the Civil War. Since Virginians largely controlled the information apparatus, a complimentary national stereotype emerged featuring a "moonlight and magnolias" interpretation of plantation society with gallant cavaliers galloping across the landscape, breathless belles anxiously awaiting their return, and happy and contented slaves praising their master's generosity.[12]

Lost Cause writers transformed Robert E. Lee from a dependable and inspirational military leader into a Confederate deity symbolic of Southern virtue. They made it possible for him to evolve from a Southern hero to inclusion within the national pantheon of military leaders where he could stand among such legendary figures as George Washington and Andrew Jackson. Through skillful manipulation "Marse Robert," who had been modest in life, became all that glittered in Southern chivalry after death. This process reached completion with the unveiling of a massive statue of Lee in Richmond on May 29, 1890.

---

10 Miller, *John Bell Hood*, 178-179.

11 Connelly and Bellows, *God and General Longstreet*, 23-25.

12 Ibid., 21; Gaines Foster, *Ghosts of the Confederacy: Defeat, the Lost Cause and the Emergence of the New South* (New York: Oxford University Press, 1987), 6; Thomas Connelly, *The Marble Man: Robert E. Lee and his Image in American Society* (Baton Rouge: Louisiana State University Press, 1977), 68.

Lost Cause artists possessed the power to enhance reputations and to wreck them.[13] Casting about for support and eager to castigate Hood for his actions, Joe Johnston sought out a loyal former subordinate, Benjamin Franklin Cheatham.

Cheatham, who had named his son after Johnston, expressed willingness to help in this new campaign. Perhaps he should not have been so willing to assist in denigrating Hood. After all, Hood had the opportunity to remove him from command following Spring Hill and Franklin but had held back. On December 8 and 9, 1864, Hood wrote to Secretary of War James Seddon concerning Cheatham, a corps commander under Hood. His first message withdrew an earlier recommendation that Cheatham be promoted, while the second requested someone to replace him in command. In a third communication, however, he withdrew the removal, stating that though Cheatham had made mistakes, he felt he could learn from them and should remain in command of his troops.

In the immediate wake of events in Tennessee, Cheatham should have understood his mistakes and realized that others did as well. In the postwar years, especially with Lost Cause advocates seeking scapegoats, Cheatham may have calculated in supporting Johnston, the Virginian, over Hood, the Kentuckian. After all, the Old Dominion coalition had momentum on its side and must have looked like a winning combination. In heaping blame on men such as Longstreet and Hood in far-away Louisiana, Cheatham, Johnston, Early, and others could exorcise their own demons, transferring their own failings onto others.[14]

Hood's memoirs *Advance and Retreat*, published a year after his untimely death in 1879, directly contradicted the creators of the Lost Cause myth, which sought to glorify certain ex-Confederates (mostly Virginians like Generals Lee and Johnston) and vilify men like Generals Longstreet and Hood. In other words, Hood's accounting did not fit "within the collective memory being constructed across the South."[15] Though he would have preferred to leave his story to the "unbiased historians of the future," Hood believed that those

---

13 David W. Blight, *Race and Reunion: The Civil War in American Memory* (Cambridge, MA: The Belknap Press/Harvard University Press, 2001), 267.

14 *OR* 45, pt. 3, 659, 665; Miller, *John Bell Hood*, 204.

15 Miller, *John Bell Hood*, 205.

writers would be unable to do him justice as Johnston had already prejudiced his case.[16]

Hood listed the reasons for the failure in Tennessee: "The unfortunate affair at Spring Hill, the short duration of daylight at Franklin," and the lack of Trans-Mississippi cooperation from Kirby Smith.[17] Hood also offered a harsh assessment of his predecessor, asking, "Since [Johnston] fought not a single general battle during the entire war of Secession, what just claim has he to generalship?" He further insisted that "had General Johnston possessed the requisite spirit and boldness to seize . . . various chances for victory, which were offered to him, he never would have allowed . . . Sherman to push him back one hundred miles in sixty-six days, into the very heart of the Confederacy."[18] Brian Miller concluded that though Hood "was not perfect, he certainly was no Joe Johnston."[19]

Hood's case was hurt by his untimely death from yellow fever in 1879. At the time, his memoir remained unpublished and P. G. T. Beauregard took on that responsibility as part of an effort to raise money for the Hood orphan fund. *Advance and Retreat* gives a strong impression of being incomplete and reads like a rough draft. It appears that Hood became distracted by Johnston's ravings, which caused Hood to meander away from his main purpose (to write a cogent memoir) and instead write a chapter titled "Reply to General Johnston," which takes up 80 pages and turned the book into a polemic.

Though much of the well-researched information contained in "the reply" could have been useful if employed in other areas, the argument with Johnston had no place within the book. Hood instead could have used his memoir as a platform to explain his experiences and actions. In this way, he could have answered much of the criticism directed against him and preempted much of what came in the future. *Advance and Retreat* would also have become a valuable historical document, but as it stands, it is frustratingly incomplete. We have no way of knowing whether or not Hood would have chosen, or been advised, to edit or modify what he had written.

16 Ibid.

17 John Bell Hood, *Advance and Retreat* (Secaucus, NJ: Blue and Gray Press, 1985), 304.

18 Ibid., 316.

19 Miller, *John Bell Hood*, 208.

Some modern Atlanta Campaign historians tend to side with Hood, at least in saying that opportunities existed for Johnston to seriously injure Sherman's army and greatly delay its advance into Georgia. Had Johnston attacked Sherman's vulnerable supply line with more determination, for example, he may have postponed the conquest of Atlanta until after the crucial 1864 United States presidential election. Basically, the strategy of attack on Sherman's railroad came down to an argument between Johnston, Jefferson Davis, and Braxton Bragg. The latter two contended that Johnston had sufficient cavalry to accomplish the task, rather than employing Nathan Bedford Forrest's horsemen, who busied themselves turning back Federal raids into Mississippi, which Johnston wanted. Historian Richard McMurry writes, "This impasse continued all through the remaining weeks of Johnston's command. As with the winter discussion of strategy for 1864, Johnston in Georgia and Davis in Richmond were unwilling or unable to trust each other. Nothing was decided on; nothing was resolved; nothing was done."[20] Sometime toward the end of May, Johnston came to believe, despite his inability to halt Sherman's advance, that "appearances to the contrary—his efforts had been a great strategic success."[21] A great part of this delusional optimism came from grossly overestimating Sherman's losses. For example, Johnston's chief of staff wrote glowingly on May 30, "We have thus far succeeded in making . . . [Sherman] pay three of four [casualties] for every one of ours . . . if we can keep this up, we win."[22] Even in his memoirs Johnston made the ludicrous claim that he had inflicted 60,000 casualties on Sherman while sustaining fewer than 10,000 losses.[23]

Lost Cause artists who strove to stigmatize Hood ignored or minimized these facts. The more Hood wrote in reply to Johnston's criticisms, the more they responded in kind toward him. Unfortunately for Hood, his memoirs were not published until after his death. At the end of a steamy New Orleans summer, Hood fought his last battle, this time against yellow fever, following his wife, Anna Marie, and eldest daughter Lydia to the grave on August 30,

---

20 Richard McMurry, *Atlanta 1864: Last Chance for the Confederacy* (Lincoln: University of Nebraska Press, 2000), 98-99.

21 Ibid., 96.

22 Ibid.

23 Joseph E. Johnston, *Narrative of Military Operations Directed During the Civil War*, (New York: Da Capo Press, 1990), 356-357.

1879. His last wish had been that the Texas brigade veterans take care of his ten orphaned children. Following his wife's passing on the twenty-fourth, members of his old brigade had written to him, stating in conclusion, that though "the pall of sadness has fallen on you and yours. Your old comrades share your poignant grief."[24]

The ever critical Southern Historical Society compressed its obituary of Hood into a few words: "The death of General John B. Hood . . . is announced just as we are going to press, and we have only space to say that another gallant soldier, true patriot and highly atoned gentleman has fallen at the post of duty." Though Jubal Early gave a brief speech in General Hood's memory in November of that year, it is notable that his words did not appear within the papers.[25]

In striking contrast, national newspapers displayed more sympathy and recounted Hood's career in greater detail. The *Chicago Tribune* stated: "At dawn this morning, Gen. John B. Hood, the distinguished Confederate Chieftain, breathed his last . . . Gen. Hood's malady was the result of over-anxiety and care, watching at the bedside of his devoted wife. He truly dies of a broken heart."[26] Though the *New York Herald* often echoed critical voices, it also stated that "Hood's thorough knowledge of the 'trade of war,' and his force of character . . . courtesy and judgment . . . impressed officers and men alike with a sense of his fitness for command."[27] Closer to home, scribes wrote in even more complimentary terms. The *New Orleans Times* commented: "It has been said . . . that he led his men into appalling perils, but . . . it must [also] be remembered that it was his fortune to participate in battles that were essentially desperate and that the humblest of his soldiers was never asked to go where he could not see his general also." The writer concluded by stating that following the war Hood had developed into a "good citizen [and] honorable businessman."[28]

The most complimentary analysis came from New Orleans's largest paper, the *Daily Picayune*. Its writer not only stated that Hood would "always rank

24 Miller, *John Bell Hood*, 220.

25 Ibid., 225.

26 Ibid., 222.

27 Ibid., 222.

28 Ibid., 223.

among the bravest and most chivalric of . . . Confederate leaders," but directly addressed controversy about his appointment to command the Army of Tennessee, by affirming, "Hood's splendid field record was eminently that of a fighting general," and, in a swipe at Johnston, "That was what the department deemed was needed—fighting." The *Daily Picayune* writer finished with a tribute to the general's memory, stating, "Hood was known to everyone in this city, and by everyone respected and admired." He had a "quiet dignified manner," an "amiable expression of countenance," a "genial disposition," and a "well-informed mind." Underlining all of this praise, the obituary declared that "The very soul of honor and knighthood lived in that shattered frame."[29]

In contrast, Southern Historical Society writers assailed Hood after death for contributing to Confederate defeat. As previously mentioned, according to the Lost Cause, Gettysburg stood as the "high water mark" for the South. Following that battle, so it was argued, Confederate fortunes had nowhere to go but down. Brian Miller writes that "Hood's role at Gettysburg dominated conversation for several decades following the war."[30] Hood had favored a turning movement around Little Round Top, rather than a direct assault, which he thought would prove successful in routing the Union position and less costly in terms of casualties. Cadmus Wilcox was convinced that Hood's three "inquiries about a change of attack delayed the entire advance of the Confederate force." In other words, Wilcox blamed the attack's ultimate failure on Hood, and his analysis appeared in the *Southern Historical Society Papers* in 1878. In truth Hood's questioning of Lee's orders formed only a small part of many large problems encountered by Confederates on that hot July afternoon.[31]

The most outrageous claim blamed Hood for Sherman's March to the Sea. Following the fall of Atlanta, Hood withdrew from Georgia into Tennessee with the aim of liberating Nashville, thus compelling Sherman to return to the defense of Kentucky and perhaps Ohio. Ignoring the fact that Hood's plans for the Tennessee Campaign had been developed in concert with President Davis and Generals Bragg and Beauregard, the society chose to stigmatize Hood alone, insisting that "the movement of General Hood, ill-advised and pregnant

29 Ibid., 223-224.

30 Ibid., 212.

31 Ibid., 212.

with disaster, left the State of Georgia fairly open to a Federal advance."[32] This analysis also ignored the very real possibility of Confederate success had Hood been able to reach the Tennessee capital sooner than he did. It is also an "analysis" carried out largely with the aid of historical hindsight and a full knowledge of how badly things turned out in the end, rather than taking into account the Confederacy's precarious position and hopes for success at the time.

If someone should be "blamed" for the March to the Sea, it should rightly be Sherman. After all, it had been his responsibility, given by General Grant, to corner and destroy Hood's Army of Tennessee. As we know, Sherman tired of the chase, petitioned Grant to be allowed to march on Savannah, and left George Thomas in charge of affairs in the Volunteer State. Moreover, using our own historical hindsight, we can see that Hood had almost no chance of defeating Sherman's great army in 1864 or any other year. Kennesaw Mountain historian Dennis Kelly remarked, "Even if the South had Alexander the Great and Napoleon Bonaparte . . . it would not have been able to stop Sherman."[33]

In the process of denigrating Hood, Southern Historical Society writers also improved the reputations of favored Confederate commanders such as Nathan Bedford Forrest. With Hood conveniently in his grave, former Army of Tennessee cavalry general James Chalmers claimed that had Forrest been in command at Spring Hill instead of Hood, Schofield would never have gotten away. Chalmers disregarded the fact that on the night of November 29 at Spring Hill Hood specifically asked Forrest to block the Franklin Pike, but for various reasons he failed to do so. Instead Forrest spewed forth "volumes" of impotent wrath at other Confederate commanders the following morning. How well would Forrest have done commanding a full army? Since his best previous experience was at cavalry corps level, and his only command of infantry ended in failure at Selma, Alabama, in the closing weeks of the war, we will never know. Similar questions have been raised in a somewhat different context about Stonewall Jackson. Forrest may not have been any better equipped for the

---

32 Ibid., 212-213.

33 Stephen Davis essay "A Reappraisal of the Generalship of John Bell Hood in the Battles for Atlanta," in Theodore P. Savas and David A. Woodbury, eds., *The Campaign For Atlanta and Sherman's March to the Sea* (Campbell, CA: Savas Woodbury Publishers, 1992), 82.

additional responsibility than John Bell Hood. To argue otherwise is simply to engage in counterfactual debate.[34]

Miller writes that as late as 1959 the Southern Historical Society published remarks from the *Confederate Congressional Record* from 1865, employing Hood as the culprit for failures by Johnston. The Tennessee congressman Henry Foote complained bitterly that "the Army of Tennessee had been rudely deprived of its noble and gallant leader, General Johnston," and that since Hood had taken command "there had been nothing in that quarter but an avalanche of misfortune." What Foote failed to mention, however, is that by this time in the war, the Confederacy as a whole was experiencing an "avalanche of misfortune." Whoever had command in the West would wind up as a scapegoat, regardless of their previous accomplishments. By inserting this critique among its writings, the Southern Historical Society thus managed to stain Hood's reputation in the *Confederate Congressional Record*.[35]

The Southern Historical Society constructed a blueprint for Hood, built by historians, particularly from 1940 onward. Three writers from Tennessee stand out as particularly dominant: Stanley Horn, Thomas Connelly, and James Lee McDonough. Wiley Sword, though not a Tennessean, joined this group of anti-Hood scribes in 1992 with publication of *The Confederacy's Last Hurrah*. In recent years, Hood has experienced something of a renaissance, with writers such as Richard McMurry, Russell Bonds, Eric Jacobson, and Stephen Davis taking a more nuanced view. An important question is: Was the Lost Cause-promoted derisive image of General Hood universal in the immediate postwar years?

After time spent in Texas during the 1850s, and experience with the men of the Texas brigade, Hood wanted to make his home in the Lone Star state following the war. Financial realities, however, dictated otherwise. He did visit Texas and the men of his old command several times, primarily to take part in veteran activities. The *San Antonio Herald* editorialized on one of these occasions: "It does our heart good to welcome back . . . after an absence of over four years, this truly great and gallant officer, soldier and gentleman." The writer noted sympathetically that Hood's "manly form has been hacked and pierced until it is now shorn of some of it fair proportions." Despite this, the

34 Miller, John Bell Hood, 213.

35 Ibid., 213.

correspondent remarked, "The general is in fine spirits and the full enjoyment of his health."[36]

The Texas brigade, with Hood as its leader, stands out among Civil War combat units. Whenever Robert E. Lee needed decisive action to tip the scales of battle, Hood's men were often employed as shock troops. Examples include Gaines's Mill, Second Manassas, Sharpsburg, and Gettysburg. After riding over the ground upon which the Texans made their attack at Gaines's Mill, Stonewall Jackson exclaimed, "The men who carried this position were soldiers indeed!" This was high praise from Jackson, known to be sparing in his compliments.[37] Dr. Harold B. Simpson writes that "the Hood-Texas brigade combination . . . was a great fighting machine, one of the best produced in America."[38]

Moreover, Richard McMurry remarks that "Hood led the brigade . . . [in] a series of engagements that won for it a reputation unmatched in Civil War annals."[39] The men felt a particular affection for their commander. Infantryman Tine Owen of the Fourth Texas Infantry (Hood's first command), for example, reacted with disappointment to news that his new baby brother had been named "William Travis" instead of "John Hood."[40]

The Texas Brigade Association, established in 1872, aimed to preserve the memory of its commander and his men. Though active in group affairs, Hood found himself restricted by financial and health concerns and attended only two reunions. At the first, held in 1872, many veterans saw their old leader for the first time since Chickamauga. There Hood found himself "greeted with great enthusiasm . . . [and] called to the chair by acclamation."[41] At Hood's second and final reunion in 1877, held in Waco, the general found his speech "constantly interrupted by the cheers of old comrades," and "heavy applause."[42]

36 Ibid., 176.

37 Harold B. Simpson, *Hood's Texas Brigade*, vol. 2 (Fort Worth, TX: Landmark Publishing, 1999), 126.

38 Ibid.

39 Richard McMurry, *John Bell Hood and the War for Southern Independence* (Lincoln: University of Nebraska Press, 1982), see Introduction.

40 Owen Letters, March 15, 1862, in Simpson, *Hood's Texas Brigade*, vol. 3, 91.

41 Ibid., Simpson, *Hood's Texas Brigade*, vol. 2, 158.

42 Ibid., 160.

One month prior to Hood's death, on July 9, 1879, members at the reunion held in Palestine, Texas, passed a resolution guaranteeing him free transportation to all future reunions.[43] Harold Simpson comments that heavy financial losses had left Hood in dire circumstances, not helped by the yellow fever epidemic that struck New Orleans the previous year, and that these circumstances motivated the association's resolution. Following Hood's death, at a special meeting in Houston on September 13, 1879, members put forth plans to offer help to the Hood orphans. In the end, the Texas brigade Association involved itself in the welfare of their late general's children for 20 years.[44] The 1887 reunion, held at Austin, displayed dramatic evidence of enduring affection for Hood. One speaker, Major Howdy Martin, after thrilling his audience with an account of Texan exploits at Gettysburg, where Hood had been severely wounded, displayed the general's frock coat, whose "bloodstains and . . . missing sleeve [gave] mute evidence to . . . sacrifice offered." Overcome with emotion, the old soldiers crowded around the speaker's platform, many with tears in their eyes, and "sacredly touched the garment, some even kissing it and clasping it to their breasts."[45]

Joseph Johnston's memoirs had been in circulation since 1873 and Lost Cause architects had been chipping away at Hood's reputation almost from the end of the war, yet this made no difference to Texans who had fought under Hood in the East and at Chickamauga. These men had seen greater casualty rates than those suffered by the Army of Tennessee, including Gaines's Mill, where losses stood at 40 percent or more. That battle included a frontal assault on fortified enemy positions, yet it represented a definitive victory and had been ordered by General Lee. The Texas brigade fought with Hood at a time when Confederate hopes had been high. Gaines's Mill represented one of a series of battles that drove Unionists out of Virginia while Tennessee, on the other hand, happened in the autumn of the Confederacy's existence. The men of the Texas brigade remembered their battles differently than did the Texans who marched through the cruel Tennessee winter of 1864. In short, anyone who had been in command at that time, even Joe Johnston, would likely have been made a scapegoat.

---

43 Ibid., 161.

44 Ibid., 161-162.

45 Ibid., 169.

Richmond Examiner editor and original Lost Cause historian E. A. Pollard wrote that Hood had "a lion's heart and a wooden head." Other Southern Historical Society writers alleged that Army of Tennessee soldiers commonly referred to their general as "Old Woodenhead,"[46] thus easily attaching a derogatory label on Hood, insulting his intellect. Yet implications about Hood's intelligence "appear to be retrospective," originating from a campaign led by postwar Lost Cause and pro-Johnston partisans."[47] From such techniques, one does not need to travel far to come upon Wiley Sword's *The Confederacy's Last Hurrah*. Clearly, "historians" of the Jubal Early school wanted Hood to be not only the scapegoat for Confederate disaster in the West, but a stupid man as well. This is too often the portrait painted by modern historians, in particular Horn, Connelly, McDonough, and Sword. The Lost Cause dominated early perceptions and it continues to influence historical output concerning the Civil War, assigning specific roles to actors in America's great national tragedy.

అ   ఆ

The historical roles that Civil War actors would play became clear in the years following the conflict. In many cases a man's funeral reflected his place within the hierarchy of wartime leadership. Sometimes this occurred by design and other times because of circumstances in their lives. George Thomas, due to his solid performance and pivotal role in the Northern victory, and Robert E. Lee, because of his recognized position as the premier general of the Confederacy, both passed from life with dignified ceremony and national publicity. By contrast John Bell Hood's end-of-life observances were more subdued. At the time of his death in 1879 the seeds of blame for the Kentuckian had been planted, saddling him with the mantle of scapegoat, not only for Gettysburg but also for the Southern defeat in the West. A victim of poverty caused by a severe yellow fever epidemic, Hood exited life's stage in quiet obscurity.

---

46 Russell Bonds, *War Like the Thunderbolt: The Battle and Burning of Atlanta*, (Yardley, PA: Westholme Publishing, 2009), 77. According to Bonds, he was unable to find any contemporary records that describe or even suggest that Hood was nicknamed "Old Woodenhead" by his troops.

47 Ibid.

Nine years earlier on the rainy morning of March 28, 1870, newly appointed United States Army Pacific Division commander General George Thomas sat down in his San Francisco office to respond to a letter that had appeared in the *New York Tribune* on March 12, questioning his generalship in defeating Hood. The anonymous letter claimed that Tennessee had been saved not at Nashville but two weeks earlier at Franklin, thus crowning John M. Schofield as the real victor over Hood.[48] Although on March 19 another letter was published defending Thomas, the public exchange upset the principled Unionist Virginian.

Worn by the war and upset over the aggressive assault on his reputation, Thomas suffered a fatal stroke while writing his reply. The government almost immediately went into high gear planning the funeral of one of its great commanders. Although William T. Sherman wanted Thomas buried at West Point, the Virginian's wife, upset at the treatment her husband had received from U. S. Grant and Schofield, insisted that the general rest in her family's private plot in a Troy, New York, cemetery. The government provided a special train to take Thomas's body from the Pacific coast to New York and a poignant ceremony was held at the start of the general's final journey. Thomas's biographer Francis F. McKinney described the event:

> At 6:30 a.m. on March 30 the coffin was put aboard the Oakland ferry and, as the little steamer left the San Francisco dock, the first of fifty-four minute guns [one for each year of his life] sounded from the fort on Alcatraz Island. Anchored in the stream, her hull hidden by the fog drifting through the Golden Gate, Her Britannic Majesty's frigate Zealous answered Alcatraz gun for gun. At Oakland Point, the coffin was placed in a special car and at 8 a.m. started for Troy, New York.[49]

But what of Thomas's place in history? That he had been one of the war's most able commanders stood without doubt. Although his military abilities and personal character were praised by his subordinates, colleagues, and even the Confederates who opposed him, Thomas's legacy—like John Bell Hood's—would be largely defined by others.

---

48 Robert P. Broadwater, *General George H. Thomas: A Biography of the Union's Rock of Chickamauga* (Jefferson, NC: McFarland and Co., 2009), 230.

49 Francis F. McKinney, *Education in Violence: The Life of General George H. Thomas and the History of the Army of the Cumberland* (Chicago: Americana House, 1991), 471-472.

During the 1880s and 1890s a clique of four men aspired to control northern Civil War memory: U. S. Grant, William Sherman, Philip Sheridan, and John Schofield.[50] Just as the Southern Historical Society did in the former Confederacy, these prominent former Federal commanders each rose to positions of great postwar political or military power in the United States government; Grant as president, Schofield and Sherman as generals-in-chief, and Schofield as secretary of war. All worked to ensure their own high places in American history, sometimes accomplished at the expense of others and thus many Civil War historians have come to accept the view of Thomas as a solid, dependable commander, but at times could be slow and needed prodding from his more talented superiors Grant and Sherman.

Six months after Thomas's death, another Civil War leader, Robert E. Lee, died in Lexington, Virginia, where he had been serving as president of Washington College (now Washington and Lee University). Cadets from nearby Virginia Military Institute filled an important role in the funeral ceremonies, guarding the general's body the night before. One of the young men selected for that prestigious duty, William Nalle, wrote to his mother giving details of the sad event:

> All business was suspended . . . all over the country and town, and all duties . . . suspended at the institute . . . all the black crepe and similar black material in Lexington was used up at once, and they had to send to Lynchburg for more. Every cadet had black crepe issued to him, and an order was published . . . requiring us to wear it as badge of mourning for six months.[51]

An account of the funeral in the October 21, 1870, *Lexington Gazette* described the congregation as "vast and impressive . . . the deepest solemnity pervaded the entire multitude." Lee's exalted position in Southern society was acknowledged even before his deification by Lost Cause strategists. A veteran recalled Lee as "the grandest thing in all the world to us . . . we trusted him like a providence and obeyed him like a god."[52]

---

50 Benson Bobrick, *Master of War: The Life of General George H. Thomas* (New York: Simon and Schuster, 2009), 334.

51 www.vmi.edu/archiv. Virginia Military Institute Archives, "The Funeral of General Robert E. Lee," 1-2; William Nalle letter, "The Funeral of General Robert E. Lee," March 4, 2011.

52 Ibid.

Nine years later in New Orleans another of the South's most prominent generals, in contrast, received but an obscure and abbreviated ceremony. Only a few friends accompanied John Bell Hood's wooden casket down empty streets from Trinity Episcopal Church to Lafayette Cemetery No.1, while a hastily assembled local militia group provided a military touch.[53] No matter the cause of death it seems that Hood had been chosen by fate and circumstance to fill the role as one of the scapegoats for the South's defeat.

Hood had not been the borderline "psychotic" who associated valor with casualty figures and he certainly had not been stupid.[54] His historical reputation appears to have been defined by forces beyond his control. After achieving noteworthy successes with Robert E. Lee during the war's early years he later took command of the Confederacy's great western army at a time when Southern fortunes were rapidly approaching their nadir and despite his best efforts, he failed.

When the war ended, Hood worked to build a new life by doing good work. He found a home, a wife, children, and community respect in New Orleans. During that time he was confronted by the Lost Cause men of Virginia who endeavored to designate his position in history. Until his death he fought against this new opponent, striving to defend himself by explaining—in his own words—his role in the war. Even after his death the revisionists of history kept at their work.

John Bell Hood: The Rise, Fall, and Resurrection of a Confederate General attempts to correct historical wrongs done to both Hood the man and the soldier, overturn the labels, and reveal how dominant individuals and groups have influenced history. George Thomas had faith that one day history would do him justice and his wish has been largely fulfilled in recent years. As an illustration, in the mid-2000s, the Civil War magazine *North & South* featured an article titled "Top Ten Generals," in which a panel of experts ranked Thomas fourth among all commanders, blue and gray. One of the panel's historians even placed Thomas ahead of William Sherman.[55]

A similar feature that appeared on the popular internet site Civilwarinteractive.com in 2005 illustrated the enigma of Hood's career as

53 McMurry, *John Bell Hood*, 203; Richard O'Connor, *Hood: Cavalier General* (New York: Prentice-Hall, 1949), 278.

54 Connelly, *The Army of Tennessee*, 431.

55 *North & South* magazine, vol. 6, number 4.

perceived by the modern Civil War history community. In a poll of the ten best and ten worst Civil War generals, only one—John Bell Hood—appeared on both lists. "John Bell Hood, 1862-63" was listed as a "best" general while "John Bell Hood, 1864" appeared on the "worst" list.

For Hood things are improving, but at a slow pace. Brian Miller's recent book *John Bell Hood and the Fight for Civil War Memory* examines the historical treatment of the general, revealing many inaccuracies and biases against Hood. Likewise author Eric Jacobson courageously ignored myth and orthodoxy in his recent book *For Cause and For Country: A Study of the Spring Hill Affair and the Battle of Franklin*, providing Civil War scholarship an unfiltered and unbiased presentation of those events, which have come to define Hood's enigmatic career.

Much remains to be done. The *Southern Historical Society Papers* is a gold mine of information for historians when it comes to men like Hood and Longstreet whose stories—one hundred and fifty years later—remain largely untold.

The battle for historical objectivity won't be won without a struggle. Leopold von Ranke, one of the founders of modern source-based history, urged us to strive to write history *wie es eigentlich gewesen ist* ("how it essentially was").[56] In practical terms, this is probably impossible as too many barriers stand between past events and the present. Historians, however, should try to get as close as they can. After all, it is this effort that separates us from writers of fiction. History, like a well-tended garden, requires some regular maintenance—weeds must be removed so that flowers can be seen at their best advantage.

Put another way, as Civil War historian Bruce Catton once observed, there are times when history needs upgrading.[57]

Thomas J. Brown

---

56 Bjanepr.Wordpress.com.

57 Bruce Catton review of McKinney's *Education in Violence*, www.home.earthlink.net/~one plez/majorgeneralgeorgehthomasblogsite/id35.html.

Victoria Portrait.

S. ANDERSON, PHOTO,   183 CANAL ST, NEW ORLEANS, LA,

A previously unpublished postwar
photograph of John Bell Hood.

John Bell Hood Personal Papers

"God alone knows the future, but only an historian can alter the past."

— *Ambrose Bierce*

Introduction

It's a shame a book like this even has to be written. Some reviewers might call it a hagiography of General Hood and say that it lacks balance. In fact, this book does not require balance because it represents the balance that is missing from most modern books and articles that have been published about Hood and his tenure as commander of the Army of Tennessee.

Most new readers of Civil War history will likely reach for one or more of the widely read and influential books about Hood as their introduction to the man and his generalship. My wish is that they read this book in conjunction with others, for these pages intentionally present only the quotes, comments, and excerpts I have accumulated in more than ten years of study and research that support Hood and his decisions with the Army of Tennessee. And therein rests the "balance" mentioned earlier, because the words and comments of Hood's critics are well-chronicled in the works of authors such as Thomas Connelly, James McDonough, Wiley Sword, and many others whose books and articles are largely cleansed of interpretations and references to historical records that shine a positive light on Hood's reputation.

This may strike some as difficult to believe. I assure you, the chapters awaiting you will disabuse you of this belief. Those who have read some of these authors who have written on Hood and the Tennessee Campaign will wonder whether they are reading about the same general. During the early decades of the twentieth century, when good Civil War scholarship relied on the *Official Records of the War of the Rebellion* in conjunction with letters, diaries, and memoirs, authors often disregarded the Lost Cause version of Hood the Butcher and typically portrayed him for what he had been: a highly successful young brigade and division commander who impressed his men and superiors alike and excited the general public. A warrior promoted to corps command in 1864 and then to lead an army; an idealistic leader who sacrificed half his body attempting (but ultimately failing) to do what was nearly impossible.

In appreciation for the maimed Confederate hero, the Andrew Female Academy in Cuthbert, Georgia, was converted in 1864 to a military hospital and named Hood Hospital in honor of the Army of Tennessee's commander who led the attempt to defend Atlanta. After the war, Hood was appointed president of the Southern Hospital Association for Disabled Soldiers and was frequently honored with landmarks, places, and children named for him. In addition to Fort Hood, the U.S. Army base in Texas, there is a Hood County, Texas, and a John B. Hood Middle School in Dallas. Manassas, Virginia, has a Hood Road. In Cohutta, Georgia, near Dalton, there is a John Bell Hood Drive, and a Hood Avenue in Atlanta, and General Hood Road in Ft. Oglethorpe, Georgia. Even in Nashville—the epicenter of the modern anti-Hood universe—landmarks abound, including General Hood Trail and Hood's Hill Road in Nashville, Hood Place in Oak Hill, and Hood Drive in Brentwood, near Franklin. A former governor of Alabama was named Forrest Hood "Fob" James, Jr. It is highly unlikely that anything or anyone would have been named after John Bell Hood had today's version of his reputation existed during the decades immediately following the war.

It is interesting to note that in 1885, John Bell Hood's brother William moved to—of all places—Nashville, Tennessee, where in 1897 he married a Nashville woman named Mary Jane Brewer. (William's first wife had died in 1888.) They remained in Middle Tennessee for the rest of their lives. William died in Warren County, Tennessee, in 1906 and is buried near the town of McMinnville. It is fair to say that John Bell Hood's brother would never have moved from his ancestral home in central Kentucky to Nashville and married a local woman if the disdain for the general asserted by today's authors existed in the immediate postwar era.[1]

---

1 Genealogical files of the John Bell Hood Historical Society, in possession of certified genealogist Ms. Gail Lamer of Savannah, Georgia.

John Bell Hood's wife, Anna Marie Hennen, of New Orleans was the great-granddaughter of James Robertson, the "Father of Tennessee" and founder of the city of Nashville in 1784. Would Anna's family of society-conscious New Orleans lawyers have approved the courtship and marriage of their daughter in 1868 to a man as despicable as the John Bell Hood of the late twentieth century? These few examples (and the many more to follow) demonstrate that John Bell Hood had a very different reputation during and immediately after the Civil War than what modern Civil War literature has led so many to believe.

Unfortunately, by the middle of the twentieth century, the second and third generation of Civil War books came to rely more and more on the opinions and facts (often biased and erroneous) of earlier authors rather than simply the historical record written by the men and women who lived it. For example, a 128-page book about Confederate Texas troops in the Tennessee Campaign published in 2002 contains some 325 endnotes, of which only 16 are based upon the *Official Records*. The same book cites John Bell Hood detractor Wiley Sword's *Embrace an Angry Wind: The Confederacy's Last Hurrah* 35 times.[2] Although some letters, memoirs, and diaries are cited, nearly 2/3s of the author's sources are simply earlier books, many of which are highly biased and themselves weakly grounded in contemporary historical data on many key issues. Thousands of Civil War books have been published by professional and amateur writers alike. Sadly, many of them incestuously recycle the findings and perspectives—often filtered and inaccurately paraphrased—of previous writers. "History repeats itself," wrote English historian Philip Guedalla in 1920. "Historians repeat each other."[3]

It is much easier to write a monograph or article based largely on the contents of secondary sources (i.e., previously published material written by non-participants). No complete and accurate history can be written without grounding it in primary sources. Before something in an earlier book or article can be cited, it is the writer's responsibility and duty to use every reasonable means possible to confirm its sources. This is especially true when the assertions are essential to an important issue or allegation. Unfortunately, too many authors routinely cite other writers whose own words are frequently inaccurate or erroneous. Worse yet, some authors even assert the opinions of

2 John R. Lundberg, *The Finishing Stroke: Texans in the 1864 Tennessee Campaign* (Abilene, TX: McWhiney Foundation Press, 2002).

3 Christopher Morley, *Modern Essays* (New York: Harcourt, Brace, 1921), 278.

earlier authors as "facts." Do this often enough, book after book, and the general reading public will come to view these opinions as historical truth.

Although John Bell Hood became a target of the Lost Cause architects in the late nineteenth century, the destruction of his reputation parallels his increasingly negative portrayal in four major books about the Army of Tennessee and Hood's Tennessee Campaign published between 1929 and 1992: Thomas Hay's *Hood's Tennessee Campaign* (1929), Stanley Horn's *The Army of Tennessee* (1941), Thomas Connelly's *Autumn of Glory* (1971), and Wiley Sword's *Embrace an Angry Wind: The Confederacy's Last Hurrah* (1992). It is difficult to find a book or article about the Civil War in the Western Theater published after 1992 in which these publications do not appear extensively in the source notes. These books, then, will appear extensively in the pages that follow. On the other hand, critical references to the generally accurate and objective three major Hood biographies—Richard O'Connor's *Hood: Cavalier General* (1949), John Dyer's *The Gallant Hood* (1950), and Richard McMurry's *John Bell Hood and the War for Southern Independence* (1982)—are largely absent from this study.

Two modern writers, Dr. Brian Craig Miller, author of *John Bell Hood and the Fight for Civil War Memory*, and Thomas Brown, the author of a thesis on the general entitled *John Bell Hood: Extracting Truth from History*, argue persuasively that Hood was targeted by the Lost Cause myth makers to be the virtual James Longstreet of the Western Theater. This, in turn, made Hood the all-purpose scapegoat for the destruction of the Confederacy's primary Western army. Miller and Brown assert that the besmirching of Hood began when former Southern General Dabney Maury's influential Southern Historical Society moved from its initial headquarters in New Orleans (Hood's postwar home) to Richmond, Virginia. The last two commanders of the Army of Tennessee, both of whom led the army to defeats in 1864 and 1865, were Joseph Johnston and John Bell Hood. The former, however, was a native Virginian, so the Lost Causers (led primarily by Virginians) turned their vitriol against the latter.[4]

While this theory has merit, my research also revealed that many of the early anti-Hood authors were Tennesseans. Of course this could be merely coincidence, but it is worth noting that the earliest Hood critics in Civil War

---

4   Brian Craig Miller, *John Bell Hood and the Fight for Civil War Memory* (Knoxville: University of Tennessee Press, 2010); Thomas Brown, Master's Thesis, *John Bell Hood: Extracting Truth from History*, in the possession of the author.

literature were Stanley Horn, followed in succession by Thomas Connelly and James McDonough—all of whom are/were Tennessee natives or who were at some point residents of Middle Tennessee, the site of the Army of Tennessee's defeats in its final major campaign.

In 1929, before these Tennessee authors set pen to paper, Thomas Hay (of New York) wrote the following on John Bell Hood:

> The strong force of Hood's character yielded an influence that no oratory could command and he passed his days, after the war, refined by sorrow, purified by aspiration, strengthened through self-reliance, and made gentle by an earnest faith in things unseen. He was genial, generous, and indulgent toward others and severe to himself. His aims were prompted by noble desires and in politics his ideals for democratic action were high. With all his limitations, which he recognized, as well as his powers, he commands our admiration and respect.[5]

For reasons difficult to understand, Hay's Hood the Confederate hero (a man who in 1929 was deserving of our admiration and respect) had by 1992 transformed into Wiley Sword's "fool with a license to kill his own men," and to economist, actor, and author Ben Stein's "horrifyingly misguided soul [who was] the most destructive American of all time" in 2006. Writing only a few years after the release of Sword's book historian Steven Woodworth said of the almost hysterically negative portrayals of Braxton Bragg and Hood, "Some recent accounts of these two hapless generals lead the reader to wonder not why they held command of an army but rather why they were not in an insane asylum."[6]

This study details many examples of factual errors, inaccurate and misleading paraphrasing of primary sources, and the apparent concealment of historical facts. I am reluctant to believe that multiple errors of fact by an author

5   Thomas R. Hay, *Hood's Tennessee Campaign* (Dayton, OH: Morningside Bookshop Press, 1976), 42.

6   Wiley Sword, *Embrace an Angry Wind: The Confederacy's Last Hurrah: Spring Hill, Franklin, and Nashville* (New York: HarperCollins, 1992), 263. This same title was published in paperback the following year as *The Confederacy's Last Hurrah: Spring Hill, Franklin, and Nashville* (Lawrence: University Press of Kansas, 1993); Ben Stein, "Cellphones in Flight? This Means War!" *New York Times* online, March 26, 2006; Steven Woodworth, *Civil War Generals in Defeat* (Lawrence: University Press of Kansas, 1999), 3.

relating to the same subject (Hood) are intentional; yet, it is equally difficult to credit these mistakes as an accident when factual errors accompany persistent misleading paraphrasing of letters, reports, journals, and other contemporary sources that completely mischaracterize the words of Hood and his supporters in and out of the army.

Some authors influence the perception of their readers by engaging in what I like to call sourcing sleight-of-hand, which includes some or all of the following:

1. Making factual statements without providing a source;

2. Making a factual statement and providing a source that has no relationship whatsoever to the "factual" statement;

3. Offering long complete verbatim quotes from sources that support the author's viewpoint or argument, but abbreviating quotes from witnesses whose testimony weakens the author's viewpoint or argument;

4. Inaccurately paraphrasing or distorting the context of a primary source;

5. Inserting an un-sourced assertion of fact into a paragraph containing multiple factual statements supported by correct sourcing.

Sometimes the best way to expose these unethical or sloppy methodologies is to provide the full quote of an eyewitness, which can run to many paragraphs. The advantage is that it not only offers what these witnesses said or wrote in their own words, but it allows readers to fully grasp the context of entire quote. I have always been much more interested in an eyewitness's own words than how an author chooses to paraphrase him or her—especially agenda-driven authors.

The documentary film *The Battle of Franklin: Five Hours in the Valley of Death* offers an example of No. 3 (above). Hood's name is mentioned in the hour-long film 54 times, making him by far the most prominent character of the entire production. The film's script heavily relies upon verbatim quotes from Franklin veterans and other witnesses. Of the 58 veteran/eyewitness quotes cherry-picked by the producers of this film, however, General Hood accounts for precisely three. One of his quotes concerns his relationship with his fiancée, which is unrelated to anything else in the film, while his other two quotes are followed immediately by derisive comments from the narrator.[7]

More appalling is the selective disclosure of historical evidence. Many Hood critics routinely fail to include material that contradicts their thesis or anti-Hood viewpoint. The American Historical Association, Statement on Standards of Professional Conduct, insists that historians "should report their findings as accurately as possible and not omit evidence that runs counter to their own interpretation." Unfortunately, nearly every book written on Hood and the Tennessee Campaign routinely includes just such omissions. One example is when both pro-Hood and anti-Hood comments appear in the same primary source material, and sometimes within the same page or paragraph. So often in these cases, only those portions critical of Hood are reproduced for the reader. Courts don't ask witnesses to swear to tell the truth; they demand witnesses swear to tell the whole truth. Regretfully, too many writers toil under no such constraints.[8]

Unfortunately, the word "hagiography" (defined as "a worshipful or idealizing biography") has no antonym. I use "malportrayal" to refer to an intentionally malicious portrayal of a character designed to destroy his or her legacy and compromise the accuracy of historical events. "Malportrayal" doesn't exist in the English language, though perhaps it should.

Equally destructive to Civil War history is the innocent compromising of historiography by writers swept up in the prevailing current with otherwise no intent to prejudice or bias readers. They do this by simply repeating what others have written believing it to be true. As authors Scott Bowden and Bill Ward put it in their study of Lee at Gettysburg, "As is often the case in military history, if a story is repeated frequently by a legion of writers, it becomes accepted as fact by many readers. These stories acquire a life of their own and become part of the popular culture; their factual foundation is no longer questioned, much less critically evaluated."[9]

Most authors are heavily influenced by earlier writers, especially when the tone and content of books and articles are similar. "One of the greatest

---

7 *The Battle of Franklin: Five Hours in the Valley of Death*, Wide Awake Films, Kansas City, MO, 2005.

8 American Historical Association, 400 A Street SE, Washington DC, 2006.

9 Scott Bowden and Bill Ward, *Last Chance for Victory: Robert E. Lee and the Gettysburg Campaign* (Cambridge, MA: Da Capo Press, 2001), 230.

difficulties in understanding how Civil War generals functioned," wrote late author and historian Thomas Buell, "is that much of the war's history is biased and distorted. Upon scholarly inquiry, truisms about popular historical events and personalities are often discovered to be wrong."[10] Writers hesitant to counter prevailing orthodoxy (or too lazy to perform their own firsthand research) often join an Amen chorus and repeat the same interpretation and imagery that exists in the broad Civil War culture. The result, if I may be so bold, is that much of what appears to be scholarship is in fact pop history decorated with sourcing notes.

Although some authors engage in intentional distortion and fact-filtering to establish and disseminate their own unique portrayal (behavior that could be termed "historiographic activism"), most writers do not intentionally repeat misinformation. Their mistake is their unquestioning confidence in the accuracy and completeness of earlier works, and faith that publishers scrupulously demand this before they will print a book or article. Awards and public recognition for books and authors, so often based on style, eloquence, and name-recognition rather than historical substance, exacerbate this problem. The most influential book on the 1864 Tennessee Campaign (and the most damaging to Hood's legacy) is Sword's *Embrace an Angry Wind: The Confederacy's Last Hurrah*, which was honored with the New York Civil War Round Table's prestigious Fletcher-Pratt award for the "best non-fiction book on the Civil War published during the course of the calendar year." As readers of *John Bell Hood* are about to learn, however, this title is riddled with questionable conclusions, factual errors, citation problems, and incomplete disclosure of vital historical evidence, none of which was likely known to the judges who bestowed the honor. Awards imply validity, and so make any book an attractive source for subsequent writers. The eloquence of the pen compounds these problems. I was often mesmerized by the gifted writing style of some of the authors mentioned in this book, only to later discover the beautifully expressed assertions incomplete or even spun from whole cloth.

It is not my intent to exploit honest mistakes by ethical writers. Nobody is perfect, and everyone makes errors. Some careful readers may well find mistakes in my own work. A careless keystroke, for example, can change the meaning of a sentence or provide an incorrect citation. Paraphrasing an

---

10 Thomas Buell, *The Warrior Generals: Combat Leadership in the Civil War* (New York: Crown Publishing, 1997), xxviii.

eyewitness quote can unintentionally mischaracterize the original writer's true intent. Authors can only be expected to "know what they know," and might be unaware of existing primary evidence, and new archival records are routinely discovered after a book's publication. The issues I raise in this book deal only with errors that in my opinion appear to be part of a consistent pattern, or when a specific mistake or mischaracterization—intentional or otherwise—alters the correct understanding of an important event or issue.

Many authors employ qualifying language such as "perhaps," "might," "may," or "could." These conditional words are of course necessary in all books—including this one—to qualify legitimate theories or opinions and to provide what are assumed to be facts when undeniable proof can't be found. However, these words also offer a shield of sorts that allow authors to present personal opinions and interpretations under the guise of fact, cleverly inducing readers to draw an incorrect inference that supports the writer's premise. According to *Weasel Words: The Dictionary of American Doublespeak*, Teddy Roosevelt (at the time a U.S. Army colonel) coined the term "weasel words" for those that undermine or contradict the meaning of the word, phrase, or clause it accompanies. According to Herbert M. Lloyd in a letter to the *New York Times* on June 3, 1916, Roosevelt said, "Weasel words are words that suck all the life out of the words next to them, just as a weasel sucks an egg and leaves the shell. If you heft the egg afterward it's as light as a feather, and not very filling when you're hungry, but a basketful of them would make quite a show, and would bamboozle the unwary."[11]

A classic illustration of the application of Roosevelt's pet peeve is found in Sword's *The Confederacy's Last Hurrah* when alleging that Hood attempted to save face after the disastrous Tennessee Campaign (italics added): "Already when en route to South Carolina, he had passed though Augusta and *probably* met with a distant relative, Gustavus Woodson Smith, the crusty old army engineer who was Hood's good friend. Hood *apparently* poured out his bitterness to Smith, who then *may* have published the long, rambling article that appeared in the Augusta, Georgia, *Daily Constitutionalist* on February 5, 1865." Read that again. Those two sentences tell us precisely . . . nothing. There is no proof that Hood met with Smith, no proof Hood "poured out his bitterness," and no proof that

---

11 Paul Wasserman and Don Hausrath, *Weasel Words: The Dictionary of American Doublespeak* (Herndon, VA: Capital Books, 2006).

Smith wrote the published article. Sword's source for these claims is two modern authors who also had no proof.[12]

Gary Ecelbarger's otherwise excellent *The Day That Dixie Died: The Battle of Atlanta* offers a similar example. While in Richmond in November 1863, wrote Ecelbarger, John Bell Hood "perhaps" aroused by the "teasing" of his flirtatious girlfriend Buck Preston, "found an outlet to his needs by frequently visiting a young prostitute." Ecelbarger's source is Thomas Lowry's book *The Stories the Soldiers Wouldn't Tell: Sex in the Civil War.* Lowry's source, in turn, is purportedly a quote from the diary of a Richmond prostitute who wrote about her encounter with a wounded general. Lowry suggested that the officer *might* have been Hood simply because a Richmond newspaper reported he was in the city at that time. Richmond was one of the South's primary locations for generals wounded or otherwise, and so it is fair to conclude there was more than one wounded general in the Southern capital at the time. Accusing Hood of using Richmond prostitutes as "an outlet for his needs" without reliable historical proof adds nothing to a book on the 1864 battle of Atlanta other than titillation and sensationalism. Lowry's speculation induced Ecelbarger, an otherwise careful researcher and writer, to make the leap from supposition to absolute fact, cloaked within one of Teddy Roosevelt's least favorite words: "perhaps."[13]

Sometimes authors define and employ their "literary license" rather elastically, stretching it in ways that lead readers to connect subjects and issues that are unrelated. Colorful and expressive writing makes for good reading, but when artistry morphs into hyperbole, when eloquent embellishment funnels readers in the direction of false or inaccurate inferences, the bounds of literary license cross into unethical writing. For example, Hood's fiancée Sally "Buck" Preston receives little or no ink in the pre-1975 books penned by Thomas Hay, Stanley Horn, and Thomas Connelly. In Sword's 1993 *The Confederacy's Last*

---

12 Sword, *The Confederacy's Last Hurrah*, 435. Whoever authored the 1865 newspaper article apparently wanted to remain anonymous, but signed it "GWS." If the well-known General Gustavus W. Smith, commander of the Georgia militia, wrote the article for a Georgia newspaper and wanted to remain anonymous, however, would he have used his own initials?

13 Gary Ecelbarger, *The Day Dixie Died: The Battle of Atlanta* (New York: St. Martin's Press, 2010), 23. Ecelbarger cites Thomas P. Lowry, *The Story Soldiers Wouldn't Tell: Sex in the Civil War* (Mechanicsburg, PA: Stackpole Books, 1994), 157. Lowry, the author of several books, called into question his own credibility when he admitted in 2011 to deliberately altering the date on a Lincoln pardon in the National Archives. He has been permanently banned from all of its facilities and research rooms.

Hurrah, however, she has more page listings in the index than do four of the six generals who were killed at the battle of Franklin *combined*. And yet, Preston had nothing at all to do with the Tennessee Campaign in general, or Franklin in particular. Were Hay, Horn, and Connelly negligent or was Sword's use of "artistic license" to weave in a love story and somehow try to tie it to Hood's battlefield decision-making excessive?

It is simply a fact that many casual readers skip past source notes, and those who flip to the back of a book to check a citation often do not have a cited book or a primary record used by the author. Even if a reader wants to examine a primary source document, most are located in private hands, in the National Archives or Library of Congress in Washington, DC, or reside in the library of a distant university or museum. Few readers (or amateur historians, for that matter) have the motivation, time, or resources to research and confirm what other authors assert as true.

The old adage that "The facts don't always equal the truth" is more valid in history than in any other literary genre. A letter from 1864 may prove that Johnny Reb wrote home one day to tell his wife that he and his comrades had "just whipped the Yankees" (and maybe in his limited field of vision that was was happened), but it may not be true that in the Yankees "got whipped." Healthy skepticism is important to a conscientious historian, who has a duty to reasonably examine available historical records to corroborate (or disclaim) Johnny's account. Unfortunately, as you will find in the pages ahead, too many modern authors do not research for themselves the primary sources cited by writers who have come before them. And thus, regrettably, John Bell Hood's reputation has, for the past few decades, marinated in erroneous, inaccurate, and often malicious portrayals of his words and deeds. For the sake of the accuracy of the historical record it is important that some of us find the motivation, make the time, and do the research to confirm what has been written and seared into the public's mind as historical truth.

"I came to the study of Hood's life by an indirect route," wrote historian Richard McMurry, who continued:

> At Virginia Military Institute in 1960 and 1961 in Tyson Wilson's course in Military History and John Barrett's in the Civil War and Reconstruction, I first began serious inquiry into the Atlanta Campaign. This study continued in graduate school at Emory University. At first I shared the belief that Hood was totally incompetent as a general and that his critics were correct in what they believed about the war in general and about Hood in particular. Years of study, however, led to the conviction that Hood's

career had never been fairly evaluated and that his place in Confederate history was misunderstood. He was a victim of historians who assumed that he could do nothing right and that his chief critic could do no wrong. It seemed time to try to restore the balance.[14]

☙   ❧

What is my motivation? As my name implies, I am a relative of John Bell Hood. Although I descend directly from his grandfather Lucas Hood, my line descends from Lucas's son Andrew, the brother of Hood's father, John. If this explanation is too headache-inducing, let's just say that I am a second cousin to the general. Although I have the honor of sharing his surname, there are many people alive today who share more of the general's DNA than I do.

My journey began innocently enough in July 2000 when I attended a "Staff Ride" tour of the battles of Spring Hill, Franklin, and Nashville. The high-powered staff and faculty included the legendary Edwin C. Bearss, A. P. Stewart biographer Sam Davis Elliott, Hood biographer Richard McMurry, and author Wiley Sword, whose *The Confederacy's Last Hurrah* was, at that time, the most influential book on Hood and the Tennessee Campaign. Sword's beautifully written award-winning study has almost single-handedly defined Hood's modern historical reputation, and the Civil War culture in general has embraced his charismatic portrayal of the campaign and battles as the definitive interpretation and presentation of the war in Middle Tennessee in the autumn of 1864. The tour included visits to, among other places, the Rippavilla plantation in Spring Hill, the Carter House and Carnton Plantation in Franklin, and Traveller's Rest in Nashville. The portrayal of Hood at most or all of these sites was universally derogatory. At one historic site, the only image of Hood to be found was on the inside of the men's restroom door. After a complaint the picture was moved from inside the restroom door to the outside. Soon thereafter, however, the restroom photo was removed and images of Hood (and Union General John M. Schofield, whose photo was also absent at this site) were respectfully presented in the facility, alongside other commanders and prominent historical figures.

Throughout the Staff Ride program, attendees were subjected to stories about an enraged and incompetent Hood taking out his frustrations on his army. These stories were further spiced with allegations of Hood's desire to

---

14 McMurry, *John Bell Hood*, ix.

impress Southern belle Buck Preston, Hood's reluctant fiancée. Nearly every Confederate military action conducted by the Army of Tennessee at Spring Hill, Franklin, and Nashville was said to have been influenced somehow by Hood's anger, his incompetence, or by his desire to impress his girlfriend. To be fair, not all of the faculty on the tour engaged in this baseless hyperbole, but the intense anti-Hood theme was present at most of the visited sites and facilities.

As the saying goes, "If it sounds too good to be true, it probably is." Conversely, if something sounds too bad to be true, it often isn't. My fellow attendees and I frequently spoke among ourselves about the conflicting logic with regard to John Bell Hood. On one hand he was portrayed as naïve, lacking in intellect, and socially unrefined. On the other hand, he is said to have successfully manipulated and bamboozled the Confederate president, his cabinet, and the Confederate war department into consistently attaining higher commands. During the Tennessee Campaign, Hood—who the Staff Ride faculty frequently painted as being devoid of any tactical or strategic ability—nonetheless conceived and executed what the faculty universally described as a "brilliant flank movement" at Spring Hill that nearly trapped and destroyed Schofield's army. Even at Franklin, where the staff claimed an incoherent Hood launched a hopeless suicidal attack, we attendees were told that his assault broke Schofield's main lines and that only the presence of a regiment under Col. Emerson Opdycke—which was in its position because of Opdycke's insubordination—saved the Union army from destruction. So was John Bell Hood smart and capable or was he dumb and vindictive? Was the Tennessee Campaign a bold strategic gambit or a fool's errand? Was the attack at Franklin a decisive assault that came close to destroying Schofield's Army of Ohio, or was it the insane act of a deranged, lovelorn, drug-crazed lunatic bent on punishing his subordinates for their failure at Spring Hill the previous evening?

Back in 2000 I had not yet thoroughly studied my famous cousin. I had read biographies by Richard O'Connor and John Dyer, as well as Hay's *Hood's Tennessee Campaign*, but that was about it. When I returned from the tour I immediately read Sword's book. Hood's face dominates the cover. The titles of the chapters foretold the author's premise: "A Cupid on Crutches," "The President's Watchdog," "Too Much Lion, Not Enough Fox," "Courage Versus Common Sense," and "One Whose Temper Is Less Fortunately Governed." On virtually every page where Hood is mentioned, the author's assertions and characterizations were inconsistent with those written by Hay, O'Connor, and Dyer. Many of his conclusions seemed illogical to me. Thus began my odyssey.

And here, I hope, it ends.

Acknowledgments

This book would not have happened without the assistance of many people, all of whom either directly assisted me with research or, perhaps more importantly, encouraged me and provided motivation when mine was waning.

I wish to thank my distant cousin, close friend, and confidant Oliver C. "OC" Hood of Franklin, North Carolina. The earliest of my fellow crusaders, nobody provided me more assistance or encouragement over a longer period of time than OC, who in many ways could be considered a co-author of this book.

I am also grateful to David Fraley, former interim executive director of the Carter House in Franklin, Tennessee, one of God's truly gentle people. David patiently endured my worst behavior and set an example of dignity and compassion that I will always try to emulate. Long-time Carter House executive director Thomas Cartwright also patiently indulged my annoying complaints, befriended me when I least deserved it, and helped guide me to valuable research materials. I cannot express sufficient gratitude to Eric Jacobson, current chief operations officer and historian of the Battle of Franklin Trust. Eric is the author of *For Cause & for Country: A Study of the Affair at Spring Hill & the Battle of Franklin*, the latest most balanced and objective book on the Spring Hill Affair and Franklin. Not only did he share primary source material with me, but my respect for him is immeasurable, as he publicly challenged many of the inaccurate and incomplete charges against John Bell Hood in the very eye of the storm: Franklin, Tennessee. I also wish to thank novelist Robert Hicks of Franklin, not only for his encouragement, but for his steadfast dedication to recovering and preserving the hallowed Franklin battlefield.

Thanks as well to Greg Wade, president of the Franklin Civil War Round Table for his open-mindedness and encouragement. My friend Daniel Mallock of Nashville also joined me in battle and supported my efforts and the encouragement of my "second mom" Betty Callis of Hendersonville, Tennessee, was always a breath of much-needed fresh air.

The first suggestion that I take up the cause of General Hood came from Jerry and Vicki Spier of Tucson, Arizona, who have supported and encouraged me for more than ten years. Infinite inspiration and endorsement for my efforts was provided by Ms. Rose Cox of Ohio, the great-granddaughter of General John Adams (who was killed at Franklin), whom Rose felt would undoubtedly have been disappointed by the historical treatment his commanding general has thus far received.

I must also thank Carlo DiVincenti of Metairie, Louisiana, General Hood's "Guardian Angel," and Dale "Fish" Fishel of Washington state, whose great-grandfather Warren Fishel fought at Franklin as a member of the immortal 125th Ohio Infantry ("Opdycke's Tigers"). My respect and appreciation for Fish's assistance and moral support cannot be overstated. Also standing beside me during the entire project were Bob Hufford of Hopewell, Virginia, Thomas Panter of Atlanta, Georgia, Ruth Hood Maddix of New Boston, Ohio, Steve Cagle of Hueytown, Alabama, and Dan Paterson of Centreville, Virginia, great-grandson of General James Longstreet.

Thanks as well to Herb Sayas of New Orleans, Jenseen Petersen of Honesdale, Pennsylvania, and Kentucky belle Elizabeth Whipkey for their research assistance, as well as Jack Dickinson, bibliographer of the Rosanna Blake Confederate Collection at the Marshall University library in Huntington, West Virginia. Acclaimed author Winston Groom of Point Clear, Alabama, patiently mentored me on matters of writing and publishing and introduced me to outstanding copyeditor Don Kennison.

Another eminently patient mentor was the managing director of Savas Beatie, Theodore P. Savas, who was expertly assisted by marketing director Sarah Keeney and copy editor Alexandra Maria Savas. Another mentor and encourager extraordinaire is the incomparable Dr. Stephen Davis of Atlanta, perhaps my most enthusiastic supporter.

I must also thank Dr. Keith Bohannon of the University of West Georgia for patiently and professionally indulging me and guiding me to important primary sources. My friend Dr. Brandon H. Beck, emeritus professor of history at Shenandoah University, has been a steadfast supporter and has assisted me with every aspect of the book. Academia is truly blessed to have these two outstanding and dedicated scholars among their ranks.

Members of General Hood's family have provided invaluable assistance in the extensive research required for this book. Special thanks to Susan Graves Tebbs of Lexington, Kentucky, Mary Hood Pearlman of Asheville, North Carolina, Holly Hennen Hood of New York City, and Jim Bagg of Galveston, Texas, a professional editor who generously shared his substantial talents by assisting me with final editing of the manuscript. Thanks as well to William and Joan Thomas for their generosity, assistance, and hospitality.

My late friend Thomas Brown of Spreckels, California, great-grand nephew of General George Thomas, the "Rock of Chickamauga," provided valuable assistance and inspiration far beyond words, demonstrating the very essence of scholastic integrity as well as personal courage, strength, and dedication. I am fortunate that his Foreword graces my book.

This book might never have been completed without the kind assistance of my wife of 35 years, Martha, who assisted me with photocopying, fact-checking, proofreading, and countless hours entertaining our English Bulldog, "Rebel" while I worked on the book.

Although the aforementioned people provided invaluable moral support and material assistance, I am solely responsible for the entire content—including the inevitable errors.

My study is critical of the historiography of many historians and other authors, living and dead. All assumptions, conclusions, and opinions expressed herein are mine and mine alone.

I must offer both thanks and apologies to Len Riedel, founder and executive director of the Blue Gray Education Society of Chatham, Virginia, whose advice—had I followed it explicitly—would doubtless have resulted in a book that would have served Civil War scholarship more completely. Being fully immersed in Civil War history, Len is deeply concerned with the deterioration of the historiography of Civil War scholarship in recent decades. He urged me to write a book that would communicate the need for disciplined and honest historiography as a basis for scholarly work, using John Bell Hood as a case study. As Len astutely observes, during the war Hood was among the senior Confederate military commanders forced to negotiate the convoluted web of petty personality conflicts and political alliances between and among disparate Richmond government officials; after the war, he became one of the pawns in the often ruthless work of prominent Southerners who wished to define the morality of the failed revolution, and to explain the defeat. A careful study of John Bell Hood from 1861 until now strongly suggests that his modern reputation is an extension of scapegoating that began in 1865—and an illustration of the power and influence of the Lost Cause architects. Unfortunately, I have neither the ability nor the energy to perform the necessary research for such a monumental project, which I leave to a more able and motivated future scholar.

Several chapters of this book include sections that relied heavily on articles and essays written by others. I wish to make a special acknowledgment and further thank the following gentlemen for their works, which in varying degrees provided not only factual material, but a template for my chapters and sections on specific subjects. Although they are appropriately cited in my endnotes, their contributions make them, in my mind, contributors rather than mere sources.

John Goddard, M.D., of Shreveport, Louisiana, wrote an article titled "Baptism of Fire" on the Battle of Eltham's Landing for the John Bell Hood Historical Society newsletter, as did Jim Bagg of Galveston, Texas, who wrote "Hood's Dilemma," on the subject of Hood's decision to leave the U.S. army for Confederate service. Oliver C. Hood of Franklin, North Carolina, published an article called "Hood's Epic," on Lieutenant John Bell Hood's 1857 battle with Comanches on the Texas frontier, which was a valuable resource. Stephen Davis's renowned forensic studies of the myth of Hood's laudanum use, published as an article in the October 1998 issue of *Blue and Gray* magazine ("John Bell Hood's 'Addictions' in Civil War Literature") and in essay form in *Confederate Generals in the Western Theater, vol. III, Essays on America's Civil War* (University of Tennessee Press, 2011) were important resources and served as a template for my section on Hood and laudanum. Mr. Timothy F. Weiss of Roswell, Georgia, whose essay on the Cassville controversy, published in the winter 2007 issue of the *Georgia Historical Quarterly*, was a guide to my section on that important event. Noel Carpenter's excellent micro-history, *A Slight Demonstration: Decatur, October 1864, A Clumsy Beginning of General John Bell Hood's Tennessee Campaign*, published posthumously in 2007 by his daughter Ms. Carol Powell of Austin, Texas, was a treasure trove of information on Hood's post-Atlanta campaign. These talented and generous writers have my greatest respect and gratitude.

Author's Note

I quote many authors in an effort to be scrupulously fair and for the purpose of objective scholarly criticism. I have endeavored to use only enough material from their books and/or articles for readers to make their own unbiased judgment. I encourage readers to purchase and read these books and articles, should they desire to do so, and in the end reach their own conclusions on this debate about historical accuracy.

Because my book is not chronologically presented, I have decided to introduce both Union and Confederate general officers as simply "General." Otherwise, the repeated use of Brig. Gen., Maj. Gen., etc., sometimes for the same officer, would not only slow the pace of the text but perhaps confuse the reader.

General John Bell Hood

Alfred Waud, Library of Congress

Chapter 1

"History to be above evasion must stand on
documents, not on opinion."

— Lord Acton

John Bell Hood: The Son
and the Soldier

Regardless of the subject, it is difficult to find unanimity of opinion among Civil War historians. But when considering the enigmatic career of Confederate General John Bell Hood, both pro- and anti-Hood historians would probably agree that the life and career of the native Kentuckian was extraordinary.

Hood's meteoric rise and precipitous fall paralleled that of the Confederacy. His remarkable successes at the head of the Texas brigade in Robert E. Lee's Army of Northern Virginia in 1862 made him a star of Richmond society, a genuine public hero, and a favorite of the government and high command. Arguably, Hood and the Confederacy reached their apex in 1863 just before Lee's invading army was defeated at Gettysburg, where Hood suffered his first serious wound while leading a division of infantry in an assault against General Dan Sickles's III Corps on the afternoon of July 2.

Although he is associated with Texas troops, Hood was not a native Texan. The dashing charismatic leader was born in Owingsville, Bath County,

Kentucky, on June 29, 1831, and reared in the rural Montgomery County community of Reid Village near Mount Sterling. The son of a scholarly rural doctor, John was heavily influenced by his grandfathers—one a crusty veteran of the French and Indian War and the other a Revolutionary War veteran. Hood's grandfathers were his primary male influences during the early 1830s while his father, John W. Hood, was absent on frequent trips to Pennsylvania studying medicine at the Philadelphia Medical Institute under a prominent physician believed to have been John Bell Hood's namesake, Dr. John Bell.[1]

Philadelphia's Dr. Bell, a native of Ireland, had studied medicine in Europe and in 1821 had attended the commencement ceremonies at Transylvania College in Lexington, Kentucky, near the Winchester, Kentucky, home of the aspiring young doctor John Hood. Since John Hood's two older brothers were also physicians, it is likely that the future doctor John W. Hood met Dr. John Bell in Kentucky in 1821.[2]

The adventurous life of a soldier appealed to the younger Hood, who gained an appointment to the United States Military Academy at West Point in 1849. It was there he received his nickname "Sam." Although no written explanation for the source of the nickname has been found, many of his modern descendants believe his classmates tagged him with the moniker after the famous British war hero, Admiral Samuel Hood (1724-1816), viscount of Whitley, whose naval exploits in the late 18th century were studied by West Point students in the mid-19th century. Academically Hood struggled at the academy. He graduated in 1853 near the bottom of his class (44 out of 52), though he was nearly removed from West Point in his last year when he bumped up against the demerit limit.[3]

Hood's first assignment in the U.S. Army was in the rugged and untamed environs of northern California, where the young second lieutenant of cavalry

1   John Dyer, *The Gallant Hood* (New York: Konecky and Konecky, 1950), 17-26.

2   Bell Family Papers, 1796-1927, compiled by Harriet C. Owsly, August 4, 1964, Tennessee State Library and Archives, IV-H-1, Microfilm 1289.

3   Special thanks to Ms. Colleen Mattson of Ripon, Wisconsin, a native Canadian and student of British and Canadian military history, for the theory on the origin of General Hood's nickname "Sam." West Point cadets studied military commanders in world history, among them famous British war admiral of the late 1700s Samuel Hood. Admiral Hood, one of the British navy's most celebrated commanders, was the namesake of Mount Hood, Oregon, so named on October 29,1792, by Lieutenant William Broughton, a member of Captain George Vancouver's discovery expedition of the northwest coast of North America.

served at Fort Jones. Described by Hood's comrade Lt. George Crook (later a Federal general in the Civil War) as "a few log huts built on the two pieces of a passage plan," the fort was established in October 1852 to protect miners and pioneer farmers from Indians.[4]

Hood's duties consisted primarily of commanding cavalry escorts for surveying parties into the rugged mountainous regions near the California-Oregon border. His final escort mission was in the summer of 1855, when he accompanied a party led by Lt. R. S. Williamson of the U.S. Army Corps of Topographical Engineers to explore and survey a railroad route from the Sacramento River Valley to the Columbia River. On August 4, Lt. Philip Sheridan (who would later become a prominent Federal cavalry commander) overtook the Williamson surveying expedition with orders to relieve Hood, who was instructed to return to northern California's Fort Reading and then proceed east for a new assignment in Texas. "Lt. Hood started this morning with a small escort, on his return to Fort Reading," Williamson wrote in his journal on August 5, "much to the regret of the whole party."[5]

ào ·%

"The duty of repressing hostilities among the Indian tribes, and of protecting frontier settlements from their depredations," wrote Secretary of War Jefferson Davis in September of 1853, "is the most difficult one which the Army has now to perform; and nowhere has it been found more difficult than on the Western frontier of Texas." After nearly two more years of little progress, Davis authorized in 1855 the formation and equipping of two new regiments of cavalry, whose mission was to suppress hostile Indian activity on the Texas frontier. One of these was the U.S. Second Cavalry Regiment.

The vast majority of U.S. Army officers (either veterans of the war with Mexico or recent graduates of West Point) were bored and despondent over the dull routine of an inactive or fading military career. For them, the news of the formation of new cavalry regiments—an active assignment, coupled with the

---

4   George Crook, *General George Crook: His Autobiography* (Norman: University of Oklahoma Press, 1986), 14.

5   R. S. Williamson, *Official Report, Explorations and Surveys for a Railroad Route from the Mississippi River to the Pacific Ocean. Explorations for a Railroad Route from the Sacramento Valley to the Columbia River*, U.S. War Department, 1855.

possibility of long-overdue promotions—was greeted with genuine enthusiasm. Among the fortunate few assigned to the new cavalry regiments were future Civil War notables Colonel Albert Sidney Johnston, Lieutenant Colonel Robert E. Lee, Major William J. Hardee, Major George H. Thomas, Captain Earl Van Dorn, and Second Lieutenant John Bell Hood.

A year passed, during which Hood traveled east from his northern California duty station, spent time in Kentucky, and then made his way at last to Jefferson Barracks in St. Louis, where the Second Cavalry Regiment was organized and outfitted. After reporting for duty to Lieutenant Colonel Lee in Texas in January of 1857, Hood soon transferred to serve under Major Thomas at Fort Mason, a stronghold built in 1851 on Post Oak Hill near Comanche and Centennial creeks in what would later be Mason County.

On July 5, Hood led a 24-man cavalry expedition south from the relative safety of the fort, embarking on what would become an extremely long and hazardous search for a renegade Indian war party reported to be in the remote and desolate area of the appropriately named Devil's River. On July 20, the patrol encountered 40 to 50 heavily armed mounted Comanche warriors and a hand-to-hand battle ensued. Hood, who was still mounted, suffered his first combat wound when an arrow pierced his left hand, pinning it to his saddle. Hood broke the arrow, freed his injured limb, discharged his shotgun, and then drew his Colt Navy revolvers, emptying the 12 rounds pointblank at his attackers. The Comanches killed two troopers and wounded several more during the initial round of fighting.

Unable to reload under such pressing conditions, Hood ordered a retreat. The troopers fell back and regrouped in the rear, where they prepared for another assault from the warriors. Much to the relief of Hood and his men, the Comanches ceased their attack and withdrew overnight, taking their dead with them. Hood praised his soldiers, writing in his official report, "It is due my non-commissioned officers and men, one and all . . . during the action they did all men could do, accomplishing more than could be expected from their number and the odds against which they had to contend."[6]

❧   ☙

---

6 Oliver C. Hood, "Hood's Epic: The Devil's River Fight," *John Bell Hood Historical Society Newsletter*, June 2005, from James R. Arnold, *Jeff Davis's Own: Cavalry, Comanches, and the Battle for the Texas Frontier* (New York: James Wiley and Sons, 2000), 130-164.

Hood resigned his U.S. Army commission on April 16, 1861, shortly after the bombardment of Fort Sumter and the outbreak of the Civil War, and enlisted in the Confederate Army. For a second time since their days at West Point he was reunited with Robert E. Lee, his former superintendent at the Academy. The young soldier reported to Lee in the Confederate capital at Richmond in the summer of 1861 and was assigned to the Virginia peninsula, where Confederate infantry and cavalry units were being organized and trained. Rapid promotions followed. Hood's first command was as colonel of the 4th Texas Infantry Regiment. He was promoted to brigadier general on March 6, 1862, and appointed commander of the Texas brigade, a mixed outfit of Texans, Georgians, and South Carolinians.[7]

Hood's decision to wear the blue or the gray had not been an easy one. On September 27, 1860, he declined a coveted assignment as an instructor of cavalry at West Point because he feared that civil war would soon break out, and he "preferred to be in a situation to act with entire freedom." Instead of accepting the prestigious West Point offer, he took an extended furlough from the Second Cavalry and spent the fall and winter of 1860 in his native Kentucky, waiting to see how the sectional crisis would evolve. He was still on furlough when he returned to Camp Wood, Texas, in January 1861. "I see that dissolution is now regarded as a fixed fact. And that Kentucky will have an important part to perform in this great movement," Hood wrote on January 15 to Beriah Magoffin, the governor of Kentucky. "I thereby have the honor to offer my sword & services to my native state. And shall hold myself in readiness to obey any call the Governor of said state may choose to make upon me."

On April 15, three days after the attack on Fort Sumter, President Abraham Lincoln called upon Governor Magoffin to provide four regiments to assist in suppressing the rebellion. Magoffin flatly refused and Lincoln dared not insist, for fear that he would drive Kentucky into the Confederacy. By April 16 Hood had lost his patience: "I have the honor to tender the resignation of my Commission as 1st Lieutenant 2nd Cavalry U.S. Army—To take effect on this date." His resignation was approved by the Secretary of War on the 25th and announced on the 27th. By then, Hood was already a first lieutenant of cavalry in the Confederate Army, and on his way back to Kentucky to recruit.[8]

7 Dyer, *The Gallant Hood*, 48-69. Lee served as superintendent at West Point from 1852-1855.

8 James E. Bagg Jr., "Hood's Dilemma." *John Bell Hood Historical Society Newsletter*, September 2005.

એ ઍ

By the end of April 1862, the focus of Confederate and Union military operations had moved from the environs of northern Virginia to the peninsula between the York and James rivers. Federal General George B. McClellan had transferred the bulk of his Army of the Potomac by water to Fort Monroe and was endeavoring to move up the peninsula to capture the Confederate capital at Richmond from the east. The strong fortifications at Yorktown and heavy rains, however, convinced McClellan to commence siege operations. Just hours before his artillery barrage was to begin, General Joseph Johnston withdrew his Confederate army from the Yorktown entrenchments and retreated west toward Richmond, followed by a brisk rearguard action at Williamsburg on May 5. Correctly assuming that McClellan would use the York River as a means of flanking his line of retreat, on the same day Williamsburg was raging Johnston ordered General Gustavus W. Smith's division, including the Texas brigade, to march hastily toward Richmond via Barhamsville, a small town a few miles inland from the headwaters of the York River.

By the morning of May 7, Johnston had most of his Confederate army positioned around Barhamsville. Smith's division, situated northeast of town, protected the army's main line of retreat toward Richmond. Johnston's fears of a Federal flanking maneuver by water were soon realized when Generals William B. Franklin and John Sedgwick landed with their divisions at Eltham's Landing near the head of the York River. The enemy column was only two miles from the road that was crowded with Johnston's retreating supply trains. To ensure that no Federals were moving to threaten the Confederate line of retreat, Johnston sent a portion of Smith's division under General William H. C. Whiting toward the enemy position. Whiting's orders were simple: drive the enemy back far enough so they could not threaten the Confederate withdrawal.

When orders arrived from Whiting, Hood marched his brigade forward at 7:00 a.m. In a bid to avoid accidental discharges that might reveal his position and also incur friendly fire losses, Hood's men moved through the heavy woods with unloaded muskets. After an uneventful march of about one mile, with Hood riding at the head of the column, the troops entered an open field that rose to a small hill upon which stood a small cabin. Hood ordered Company A of the 4th Texas to form in line at the base of the hill, followed by the rest of the regiment, and spurred his own horse up the slope with a staff member and courier to reconnoiter. The small party was approaching the crest when a squad of Federals appeared from the other side of the cabin. The men belonged to the

16th New York, and had climbed the height's steep counter-face while Hood and his aides ascended the gentler slope on the other side. Stunned by the sudden appearance of their opponents and just paces apart, everyone involved froze. After a short pause Hood and his companions instinctively turned their horses to provide cover, quickly dismounted, and sprinted back to the nearby Confederate line as the New Yorkers opened fire.

The unexpected appearance of the enemy, combined with their unloaded weapons, threw the Texans into confusion. Many scurried for any cover they could find. Hood was rallying his men when a Federal corporal named George Love raised his weapon and took aim at the Rebel general. Before he could pull the trigger, however, a Texan kneeling behind a stump fired first. The round whizzed past Hood and killed Love instantly. Hood's savior was John Deal, a private in the 4th Texas whose unsuccessful hunting expedition the night before had left him with the only loaded gun in the regiment.

Hood's brigade, along with the balance of Whiting's division, forced the Federals back to the York River landing and the protection of their gunboats. Whiting shelled the enemy position without much effect. The battle of Eltham's Landing was a well-fought heavy skirmish that secured the Confederate retreat route to Richmond at the cost of fewer than 50 Southern killed and wounded (Union losses were about 200). It was also the first Southern victory on the Peninsula. G. W. Smith praised Hood's brigade for having earned "the largest share of the honors of the day at Eltham," while Whiting wrote of Hood's "conspicuous gallantry." The Texas brigade was once again designated as the rearguard of the army as it continued withdrawing toward Richmond. Eltham's Landing established the brigade's early reputation as a hard-fighting unit, and Hood demonstrated capable and aggressive leadership in the fight.[9]

It is fair to say that the battle of Seven Pines (Fair Oaks) on May 31 and June 1, 1862, changed the course of the war in the Eastern Theater and with it, Hood's career. When Joseph E. Johnston fell severely wounded near the end of the first day of his botched offensive, President Jefferson Davis appointed Gen. Robert E. Lee to command the Virginia army, which would become famous under Lee as the Army of Northern Virginia.

In the Seven Days' Battles (fought the last week of June and the first day of July), Lee attacked McClellan north of the Chickahominy River and drove the

---

9   John Goddard, M. D., "Baptism of Fire: John Bell Hood and the Texas Brigade at Eltham's Landing," *John Bell Hood Historical Society Newsletter*, January 2007.

Union army southward toward the James River. The Texas brigade played an important role in the Confederate victory at Gaines's Mill when Hood led his troops in a stunning breakthrough of a strong fortified Union line that initiated the collapse of the entire position. Later that summer at Second Manassas, Hood (now in temporary command of the division) participated in Longstreet's massive counter-attack that swept John Pope's Army of Virginia from the field. Less than a month later on September 17 at Sharpsburg, Hood led his division in a vicious counter-assault against overwhelming numbers that helped stabilize the Confederate left flank and save Lee's army from disaster. His gallant performances and personal leadership abilities impressed Lieutenant General Thomas J. "Stonewall" Jackson, who recommended his promotion to major general and a permanent assignment to command a division.[10]

Hood's division did not see action at Fredericksburg in December of 1862, and missed Chancellorsville in May of 1863 because of his participation in a large-scale foraging operation known as the Suffolk Campaign. He and his division were back with the army when it moved out in June and headed north toward Pennsylvania. Late in the afternoon of July 2 at Gettysburg, Hood's division (part of Longstreet's corps) was deployed to attack the extreme Federal left, with another division under Lafayette McLaws aligned to attack on Hood's left. The Union line was anchored in heavy hilly terrain covered with rocks and boulders, trees, brush, and other obstacles. General Evander Law, the division's senior brigade commander, formally protested Longstreet's order to Hood, who agreed and in turn protested to Longstreet. According to John Dyer, Law noted,

> The strength of the enemy's position rendered the result of a direct assault extremely
> uncertain; that even if successful the victory would be at too great a sacrifice of life; that
> a frontal assault was unnecessary and a movement around the enemy's left flank was
> not only possible but comparatively easy; and that such a movement would compel the
> Federals to abandon their position on the ridge and thus reverse the situation, forcing
> the displaced Federals to attack the Confederates in position.[11]

10 Hood was promoted to major general on October 10, 1862, and given an infantry division in James Longstreet's First Corps. Richard McMurry, "John Bell Hood," in William C. Davis, ed., *The Confederate General*, 6 vols. (Harrisonburg, 1991), vol. 3, 121.

11 Dyer, *The Gallant Hood*, 192.

Hood's own account recalled sending staff officers to Longstreet on two occasions to appeal for the flanking movement. When Longstreet denied the requests, Hood sent his own adjutant, Colonel Harry Sellers, who was also unable to persuade Longstreet to change tactics. Hood was ordering the attack as planned when Longstreet arrived in person. Hood took the opportunity to once more request the abandonment of the frontal assault, and for the fourth time Longstreet insisted that Lee's original instructions be followed.[12]

Within minutes of ordering his division into action an artillery shell exploded and shredded Hood's left arm with iron fragments. He was carried from the field, his career with the Army of Northern Virginia at an end. Although his own division and that of McLaws achieved some initial success, Meade poured thousands of reinforcements into the fighting and by the close of the day the Federals held the important position of Little Round Top.

That September, Hood's division (as part of Longstreet's corps) was sent west to reinforce Braxton Bragg's Army of Tennessee. On September 20, the second day of the battle at Chickamauga, Hood was wounded in the upper right leg by a minie ball while leading his division as part of a large-scale attack that broke through the Union line and swept most of the Army of the Cumberland from the battlefield. The ball that struck Hood broke his femur and required the amputation of his leg. For his gallantry and conspicuous role in the Southern victory, the 32-year-old Hood was promoted to the rank of lieutenant general.[13]

As 1864 dawned, both the Confederacy and John Bell Hood were crippled. War had cost Hood half of his limbs, and the Confederacy had lost much of its territory and many of its senior commanders. With Southern resources and manpower on the wane, and Northern elections later that fall, President Lincoln and General Ulysses S. Grant, who was promoted to command all Union forces, planned a series of simultaneous major operations against Rebel forces in Louisiana, Virginia, and Georgia in the spring of 1864. They hoped this strategy would prevent the South from using its interior lines to shuttle reinforcements to threatened points, and that steady combat against enemy armies would weaken the South and bring the war to a decisive conclusion.

---

12 Hood, *Advance and Retreat*, 58-59.

13 The promotion was decided upon in October of 1863 but not formally made until February 11, 1864. It was backdated to rank from September 20, 1863, the day Hood was wounded at Chickamauga. McMurry, "John Bell Hood," 121.

Hood, who spent the winter of 1863-64 in Richmond recovering from his leg amputation, developed a close relationship with President Jefferson Davis. By all accounts the two men grew close; both were natives of Kentucky, and both advocated aggressive military tactics. With the rank of lieutenant general, Hood was assigned to command an infantry corps in Joseph Johnston's newly reinforced Army of Tennessee in northern Georgia.[14]

With three armies and a powerful cavalry arm under his direct control, Federal General William T. Sherman commenced his Atlanta Campaign in early May of 1864. Johnston fell back almost immediately. By the middle of July Sherman had advanced about 100 miles into Georgia and Johnston's army was within five miles of Atlanta. Desperate to save the important city, Davis on July 17 relieved Johnston of command of the Army of Tennessee and replaced him with the aggressive and enthusiastic Hood, who was promoted to the rank of full general. Although for political reasons Hood's promotion was temporary, at age 33 he became the youngest full general in the Civil War, Federal or Confederate. He remains the youngest full general in American military history.

Hood's later failures as an army commander in 1864 would be as notorious as his successes were notable in the war's early years. At a rank equivalent to that of Robert E. Lee (who was more than 20 years older), Hood conducted a spirited defense of Atlanta but failed to break the Federal siege. The important city fell to Sherman's forces on the second day of September. With the blessing of Davis and his immediate superior, General P. G. T. Beauregard, Hood led the Army of Tennessee on a desperate invasion of Tennessee, where he suffered decisive defeats at Franklin on November 30 and at Nashville on December 16. After leading the survivors of his army on its retreat to Tupelo, Mississippi, in early January, Hood resigned his command and returned to Richmond.

When the maimed young officer learned that General E. Kirby Smith had surrendered the Confederate forces in the Trans-Mississippi, Hood surrendered to Federal authorities in Natchez, Mississippi, on May 30, 1865. The remarkable military career of John Bell Hood had come to an end. How he and his actions would come to be judged was now a matter for history.

---

14 Kentucky Historical Society, historical marker at the former home of Lexington, Kentucky, postmaster Joseph Ficklin.

Chapter 2

"Every historian must learn to live within
the limits which his own freely chosen
assumptions impose upon him."

— *David H. Fischer*

Robert E. Lee's Opinion
of John Bell Hood

Among the many myths of the Civil War is the commonly repeated assertion that Robert E. Lee advised Jefferson Davis against the appointment of John Bell Hood to command of the Army of Tennessee. This is patently untrue.

In the oft-cited *The Wartime Papers of Robert E. Lee*, editors Clifford Dowdey and Louis Manarin wrote that in the middle of July 1864, Jefferson Davis "decided to remove Joe Johnston from command. Lee wrote an extremely strong letter, for him, advising him against a change of commanders, but Davis placed Hood in command." Albert Castel, in his *Decision in the West: The Atlanta Campaign of 1864*, claimed that Lee counseled Davis that "if Johnston is removed, it would be better to replace him with Hardee than with Hood," and Thomas Hay proclaimed assertively in *Hood's Tennessee Campaign* that "General Lee favored General Hardee, over all others, as Johnston's successor." In *The Confederacy's Last Hurrah*, Wiley Sword declared that Hardee "seemed to have

Robert E. Lee's endorsement." These authors cited correspondence between Lee and Davis dated July 12, 1864.[1]

The facts, fully revealed, paint quite a different picture. On July 12, 1864, Davis sent a telegram to Lee, apprising him of the command situation with regard to the Army of Tennessee and asked his opinion of Hood. Lee sent two replies the same day: the first a short telegram, the second a longer letter written that same evening.[2]

The complete text of General Lee's responses to Davis's request for his opinion on the replacement of Joseph Johnston yields a much different tone and interpretation than what these and other authors often characterize. Lee's prompt and brief initial reply from his headquarters near Petersburg reads as follows:

> Telegram of today received. I regret the fact stated. It is a bad time to release the commander of an army situated as that of Tennessee. We may lose Atlanta and the army too. Hood is a bold fighter. I am doubtful as to other qualities necessary.[3]

At 9:30 p.m. on the same day, Lee sent a longer, more detailed letter to Davis. The first paragraph concerned results of actions involving Gens. Jubal Early and Fitzhugh Lee and the Federal general David Gregg, but the remainder of the letter addressed the replacement of Johnston as commander of the Army of Tennessee. Lee wrote:

> I am distressed at the intelligence conveyed in your telegram of today. It is a grievous thing to change commander of an army situated as is that of the Tennessee. Still if necessary it ought to be done. I know nothing of the necessity. I had hoped that Johnston was strong enough to deliver battle. We must risk much to save Alabama, Mobile and communication with the Trans Mississippi. It would be better to concentrate all the cavalry in Mississippi and Tennessee on Sherman's communications. If Johnston abandons Atlanta I suppose he will fall back on Augusta. This loses us Mississippi and communications with Trans Mississippi. We had better

---

1   Clifford Dowdey and Louis Manarin, *The Wartime Papers of Robert E. Lee* (New York: Da Capo Press, 1961), 800; Albert Castel, *Decision in the West: The Atlanta Campaign of 1864* (Lawrence: University Press of Kansas, 1992), 353; Hay, *Hood's Tennessee Campaign*, 24; Sword, *The Confederacy's Last Hurrah*, 32.

2   Dowdey and Manarin, *Wartime Papers of Robert E. Lee*, 821.

3   Ibid.

therefore hazard that communication to retain the country. Hood is a good fighter, very industrious on the battle field, careless off, and I have had no opportunity of judging his action, when the whole responsibility rested upon him. I have a high opinion of his gallantry, earnestness and zeal. General Hardee has more experience in managing an army. May God give you wisdom to decide in this momentous matter.[4]

In the morning, Lee had rejected not Hood, but rather the act of changing the Army of Tennessee's command. However, later the same day, after considering the broad geopolitical and military consequences of losing Atlanta, Lee agreed that a change in commanders was necessary. Lee, upon further thought, seemed to endorse Hood, making five positive comments and one negative about his former subordinate. Lee—referring to Hardee's temporary command of the Army of Tennessee for three inactive months during the winter of 1863-64—noted only Hardee's previous army management experience but had nothing else to say about him. (Hardee had been offered permanent command of the army after Bragg's resignation, but declined.)

Considering that Sherman had steadily advanced over 100 miles into the heart of the Confederacy, Johnston's tactics clearly were not working, and a change of commanders was, in Davis's mind, absolutely necessary. With the enemy at the gates of Atlanta, would Davis want a new commander (Hardee) who could draw only a comment from Lee about his management experience, or Hood, a commander whose battlefield abilities, gallantry, and zeal were praised by Lee?

Lee's cautious advice to Davis about one of his favorite former subordinates can hardly be taken as a rejection of the proposal to install Hood, although many authors and historians have stated that Lee advised against elevating Hood. The full text of Lee's longer reply to Davis, rarely provided by authors, speaks for itself.

ಌ   ೕ

Combining presumptuousness and poor historiography, Gerard Patterson perpetrated another mischaracterization of Lee's opinion of Hood in his 1987 book *Rebels from West Point*. A member of Lee's staff had visited the camps of Hood's division near Fredericksburg, Virginia, in December 1862 and was critical of the living conditions of a single (unidentified) Texas regiment.

4   Ibid., 821, 822.

Patterson wrote that the conditions "reflected 'inexcusable neglect' on the part of its officers" and after reading the report, "Lee concluded that 'Hood is a good fighter, very industrious on the battlefield, careless off.'" Without any evidence, Patterson named an inspector's report of Hood's division—citing neglect by unnamed officers in one of the division's 15 regiments, dated December 1862—as the inspiration for Lee's "careless off" comment to Jefferson Davis in July 1864.[5]

Due to Lee's lack of specificity, scholars have never been able to identify what he was alluding to when he stated that Hood was "careless off" the battlefield. Their personal relationship began at West Point in 1852 and continued on the Texas frontier as officers in the elite U.S. Second Cavalry Regiment in the mid-to-late 1850s. Hood served under Lee as a brigade and division commander in 1862 and 1863 at Gaines's Mill, Second Manassas, Antietam, and Gettysburg. For Patterson to conclusively state that a report of a single inspector in December 1862 (which did not even mention Hood) was the source of Lee's "careless" comment is baseless speculation. Patterson should have noted Pvt. Henry Morehead of the 11th Mississippi Infantry, Army of Northern Virginia: "Gen. Hood would feed his men if he had to have a fight with the commissary department," or Major James Ratchford, who wrote of Hood's care for the soldiers of the Texas brigade: "He was very careful of their comfort, looking after every detail very much as if caring for his family."[6]

⇢ ⇣

It is difficult to find a modern book or article on Hood that fails to mention the assertion that Lee called Hood "All lion, no fox," "Too much lion, not enough fox," or some variation. Nowhere in the vast archives of Civil War documents is there evidence of Lee ever saying that about Hood, one of his

---

5   Gerard Patterson, *Rebels from West Point* (New York: Doubleday, 1987), 66.

6   Mamie Yeary, *Reminiscences of the Boys in Gray, 1861–1865* (Dayton, OH: Morningside Press, 1986), 539; James W. Ratchford, *Some Reminiscences of Persons and Incidents of the Civil War* (Austin TX: Shoal Creek Publishers, 1971), 56. In recently found Hood papers (cited herein as John Bell Hood Personal Papers) is an April 2, 1863, letter from Robert E. Lee to Hood regarding the murder of two civilians around Suffolk, which a Richmond newspaper claimed was done by members of Hood's division during a robbery. Lee sternly lectured Hood and implored him to appeal to the soldiers of his division to identify and punish the guilty men. We will likely never know for certain, but perhaps Lee was recalling this incident in the spring of 1863 when characterizing Hood as "careless off" the battlefield.

favorite young subordinate commanders. The iconic Virginian had much to say about Hood, mostly positive, some negative, but the words lion and fox appear nowhere. Nevertheless, repeated countless times, the witty label and its alleged source have stuck to both Hood and Lee.

In fact, this reference to Hood, repeatedly attributed to Lee, comes from a verse in the poem "Army of Northern Virginia," by Stephen Vincent Benet. The verse is an excerpt from Benet's Pulitzer Prize-winning narrative poem "John Brown's Body" (1928). Far from being an insult to Hood, the poem honors Lee's army and its commanders, beginning with the line, "Army of Northern Virginia, army of legend. Who were your captains that you could trust them so surely?" In praising Lee's subordinates—among them Thomas "Stonewall" Jackson, James Ewell Brown (Jeb) Stuart, Richard Ewell, A. P. Hill, and James Longstreet—the verse honoring Hood reads as follows:

> Yellow-haired Hood with his wounds and his empty sleeve,
> Leading his Texans, a Viking shape of a man,
> With the thrust and lack of craft of a berserk sword,
> All lion, none of the fox.

> When he supersedes
> Joe Johnston, he is lost, and his army with him,
> But he could lead forlorn hopes with the ghost of Ney.
> His bigboned Texans follow him into the mist.
> Who follows them?[7]

Many authors not only carelessly place "All lion, none of the fox" into General Lee's mouth, but—even worse—also distort the context. Benet clearly sought to express the admiration and respect that Lee had for his young warrior Hood, not words of doubt or disrespect for the soldierly abilities of his young protégé.

Nevertheless, in acts that would surely distress both Lee and Benet, examples abound of writers misusing the eloquent description. Without providing a source, Eddy Davison and Daniel Foxx wrote in *Nathan Bedford Forrest: In Search of an Enigma*, "Lee had advised Jefferson Davis against placing

---

7   Stephen Vincent Benet, *John Brown's Body* (Lanham, MD: Ivan R. Dee Publisher, 1990), 186.

Hood in command because he was 'all lion and no fox.' Lee was absolutely right."[8]

Wiley Sword, in *The Confederacy's Last Hurrah*, not only included the quotation but also titled a chapter "Too Much Lion, Not Enough Fox." Although he did not assert that the words came from Lee, here is what Sword wrote:

> Said another of the suspicion that Hood might not prove to be the general for the job at hand, there was perhaps too much "lion" in the man, and not enough "fox." Indeed, wrote Georgia Colonel James C. Nisbet, Hood might have a "lion's heart," but there was also a deep suspicion he had a "wooden head."[9]

By placing quotation marks around "lion" and "fox," Sword implies that Colonel Nisbet wrote the words, but Nisbet's memoir mentioned nothing about Hood being too much lion and not enough fox. In effect, Sword provided no source for the lion and fox quotation, cloaking it within a sentence with a legitimate citation. The paragraph cited by Sword is part of a longer un-sourced commentary by Nisbet regarding the affection the army had for Joseph Johnston and the disappointment of many of the soldiers upon hearing of his removal. Nisbet wrote:

> But we also knew Hood. He was simply a brave, hard fighter. There were no better fighters than Hood's Division. There were few equals of Hood's Texas Brigade. There was no better Division commander than John B. Hood. But as the commander of an army in the field, he was a failure. The same may be said of Burnside, Fighting Joe Hooker, and others. It has been said of Hood, "He was a man with a Lion's Heart but a Wooden Head." He soon demonstrated his incapacity to take Joe Johnston's place. Jeff Davis unwittingly hit the Southern Confederacy a heavy blow that morning.[10]

In his recent book *War Like the Thunderbolt: The Battle and Burning of Atlanta*, Russell Bonds mentioned the lion and fox reference in a curious manner. In the very chapter where Bonds persuasively argued that Hood was not the

---

8   Eddy Davison and Daniel Foxx, *Nathan Bedford Forrest: In Search of an Enigma* (Gretna, LA: Pelican Publishing, 2007), 348.

9   Sword, *The Confederacy's Last Hurrah*, 32.

10 James Cooper Nisbet, *Four Years on the Firing Line*, ed. Bell I. Wiley (Wilmington, NC: Broadfoot Publishing, 1987), 206.

unintelligent man he is so often portrayed to be, and disproved the myth that Hood was nicknamed "Old Woodenhead" by some of his troops, the author wrote this: "He was, as the saying goes, all lion, none of the fox." By including the reference, Bonds at least implies that he considers the "saying" credible, but he doesn't provide a source.[11]

Dr. Jean Edward Smith wrote in his acclaimed biography *Grant*, "All lion and no fox, said Lee dismissively, when he learned of Hood's appointment." Smith's source for this statement was a pair of pages from Dowdey and Manarin's *The Wartime Papers of Robert E. Lee*, which contain only the previously mentioned July 12, 1864, telegram from Lee to Jefferson Davis regarding Lee's opinion of Hood, and Lee's longer, more detailed letter to Davis penned later that day on the same subject. As we now all know, this correspondence between Lee and Davis does not mention "lion" and "fox."[12]

Archer Jones and Herman Hattaway wrote in *How the North Won the Civil War*, "'All lion, none of the fox,' Robert E. Lee had said of Hood." Although Jones and Hattaway's book is heavily footnoted, they rather curiously offer no citation for this purported comment by Lee.[13]

In one of the most acclaimed Civil War books of modern times, the Pulitzer Prize-winning *Battle Cry of Freedom*, historian James M. McPherson wrote of Hood, "'All lion' Lee said of him, 'none of the fox.'" Disappointingly, the only citation Dr. McPherson provided pointed readers to Jones's and Hattaway's unsubstantiated quotation.[14]

It would be difficult indeed to track down every reference in Civil War literature of the claim that Lee called Hood "all lion, no fox." As an illustration, when I searched the words "lion fox Lee Hood" in Google Books, 1,240 results appeared. Of the first 25 books listed that included Lee's purported lion and fox reference to Hood, not a single one was published before Benet's poem appeared in 1928. If indeed Robert E. Lee had said in 1864 that General Hood

---

11 Bonds, *War Like the Thunderbolt*, 78.

12 Jean Edward Smith, *Grant* (New York: Simon and Schuster, 2001), 388; Dowdey and Manarin, *Wartime Papers of Robert E. Lee*, 821-822.

13 Herman Hattaway and Archer Jones, *How the North Won: A Military History of the Civil War* (Champaign: University of Illinois Press, 1991), 607.

14 James McPherson, *Battle Cry of Freedom: The Civil War Era* (New York: Oxford University Press, 1988), 753.

was all lion and no fox, it stands to reason that this quotation would have appeared in Civil War literature prior to 1928.

Chapter 3

"An army of lions commanded by a deer
will never be an army of lions."

— *Napoleon Bonaparte*

Jeff Davis, Joe Johnston,
and John Bell Hood

Many modern Civil War authors, citing John Bell Hood's correspondence with the authorities in Richmond, Virginia, accuse the general of secretly scheming to replace Gen. Joseph Johnston as the commander of the Army of Tennessee. Although it is possible that Hood did attempt to do so, there is no conclusive evidence to support the charge.

The earliest writers on this subject generally refrained from accusing Hood of ill intent in corresponding with Richmond. Thomas Hay (1929) made no comment whatsoever about any impropriety in what Hood wrote to Braxton Bragg and Jefferson Davis while serving under Johnston. Rather, Hay wrote of Hood's replacement of Johnston:

> It was a desperate remedy for a desperate military and political situation, and Hood, by the logic of his appointment to command of the army in place of J. E. Johnston, was the one called upon to lead in this forlorn hope. That he came so near to success is a

tribute to his indomitable faith and courage, and to the real ability displayed in a campaign that on several occasions put him within reach of victory.[1]

There is evidence that strongly suggests that when Hood was sent west to join the Army of Tennessee, he was instructed to keep the Confederate high command informed of the situation in Georgia. Hood began his first letter to Davis on March 7, 1864, "I have delayed writing to you so as to allow myself time to see the condition of the army." One month later, Hood began a letter to Texas Senator Louis T. Wigfall by saying, "Your letter of March 29 has just been received. And I hasten to answer your direct questions . . ." Unless Davis had explicitly instructed Hood to write, why would the general feel compelled to explain his delay? Similarly, should Hood have refused to respond to Senator Wigfall's "direct" questions?

It is also interesting to note that in the several substantive letters Hood sent to various Richmond officials, nobody advised him to copy his correspondence to Johnston or counseled the young general of the impropriety of such correspondence. However, the matter was treated in a different manner just a little more than one decade after Hay saw no reason to mention any indecorum in Hood's correspondence. "In thus communicating directly with Davis and Bragg about the proper strategy for the army," wrote Stanley Horn in his 1941 *The Army of Tennessee: A Military History*, "Hood seems to have behaved in a fashion that borders close on insubordination." Horn's conclusion ignores clear evidence that Hood was directed to keep the government informed of the situation in Georgia, and by implication suggests that Hood should have disobeyed orders or ignored direct requests for information from Confederate government officials.[2]

Historian Thomas Connelly made a persuasive argument that Hood had been instructed by Confederate authorities to keep them informed of Johnston's plans, yet went on to describe Hood's correspondence with Richmond authorities and Robert E. Lee as "improper." Connelly also challenged Hood's truthfulness, claiming that "the correspondence created

---

1 Hay, *Hood's Tennessee Campaign*, 21.

2 *The War of the Rebellion: A Compellation of the Official Records of the Union and Confederate Armies*, 128 vols. (Washington, DC, 1880-1901), Series 1, vol. 32, pt. 3, 606. Hereafter cited as *OR*. All references are to Series 1 unless otherwise noted; Hood letter to Louis T. Wigfall, April 5, 1864, in John Bell Hood Personal Papers; Stanley Horn, *The Army of Tennessee: A Military History* (Bobbs-Merrill Co., Indianapolis, 1941), 318.

false impressions in Richmond," and that "at best, Hood was a chronic liar." "He had misrepresented the condition of Johnston's force," Connelly wrote, and "lied about Johnston's unwillingness to fight." While unabashedly calling Hood a liar, Connelly ignored clear evidence of what is now widely accepted as Johnston's timidity, and offered no proof that Hood knowingly provided Richmond with false or incorrect information. With no evidence to support his allegation, Connelly went on to claim that Hood wanted command of the army. In sending a memo to Bragg in July, concluded Connelly, "Apparently Hood was making his last bid for army generalship."[3]

Modern authors picked up the theme that had been absent in books for the first several decades after the war. In his 1992 *Decision in the West*, Albert Castel, without substantiation, boldly proclaimed that Hood's memo to Bragg was "nothing more nor less than a bid for command of the Army of Tennessee." According to Castel, Hood and Bragg were "collaborating for the purpose of assuring Johnston's dismissal and Hood's assignment as his successor."[4]

Wiley Sword condemned Hood in *The Confederacy's Last Hurrah*, labeling him a disloyal subordinate who not only misled Johnston but who wrote "poison pen" letters to Richmond within a few weeks of arriving in Georgia. Sword argued that, throughout the campaign, "Hood continued to convey to Davis and Bragg much self-serving propaganda," and that "Hood's deception should have been obvious from the beginning." Sword renewed his criticisms of Hood in a subsequent book *Courage Under Fire*: "Like a highly placed watchdog, Hood surreptitiously kept up a correspondence with the Davis administration, repeatedly discrediting Joe Johnston in deceitful commentaries about decisions and maneuvers during the Atlanta Campaign."[5]

Webb Garrison, Jr. wrote in his 2001 book *Strange Battles of the Civil War* that Hood, audaciously taking advantage of his war wounds, "exploited his reputation and appearance to gain command of one of the great armies of the Confederacy—the Army of Tennessee." Garrison provided no primary source for these accusations that Hood engaged in such devious conduct.[6]

---

3 Thomas Connelly, *Autumn of Glory: The Army of Tennessee 1862-1865* (Baton Rouge: Louisiana State University Press, 1971), 322-323, 430, 417.

4 Castel, *Decision in the West*, 356.

5 Sword, *The Confederacy's Last Hurrah*, 26, 29; Wiley Sword, *Courage Under Fire: Profiles in Bravery from the Battlefields of the Civil War* (New York: St. Martin's Press, 2007), 196.

6 Webb Garrison Jr., *Strange Battles of the Civil War* (New York: Bristol Park Books, 2009), 269.

In his 2002 book *Look Away*, respected historian William C. "Jack" Davis declared that Hood had "shamelessly politicked" to gain command of the Army of Tennessee. In the introduction to his 2005 book on the battles of Spring Hill and Franklin, Eric Jacobson cited only the "effective" arguments of other writers to assert that letters penned by Hood "further damned Johnston," and that "Hood had been positioning for the job" of commander of the Army of Tennessee.[7]

In each of these cases, these and other authors failed to provide the full verbatim text of Hood's letters they deemed so damning and despicable. For example, Connelly described Hood's April 13, 1864, letter to Bragg as "by far the most damaging letter during the spring," yet the full text reveals rather unremarkable tone and wording. Furthermore, this letter refers to other correspondence between Johnston's senior corps commander William Hardee and Bragg, and Robert E. Lee and Hood—neither of which drew criticism from Connelly. Hood's "most damaging" letter to Bragg reads as follows (italics added):

My dear General,

I received your letters and am sorry to inform you that I have done all in my power to induce Genl. Johnston to accept the proposition you made to move forward. He will not consent as he desires troops to be sent here and it left to him as to what use should be made of them. I regret this exceedingly as my heart was fixed upon our going to the front and regaining Tenn. and Ky. I have also had a long talk with Genl. Hardee and whilst he finds many difficulties in the way of our advancing he is at the same time ready and willing to do anything that is thought best for our general good. He has written a long letter to the President which will explain his views.

When we are to be in a better condition to drive the enemy from our Country I am not able to comprehend. To regain Tenn. would be of more value to us than a half dozen victories in Virginia. I received a letter from Genl. R. E. Lee on yesterday and he says "you can assist me by giving me some troops or driving the enemy in your front to the Ohio River. If the latter is to be done it should be executed at once." I still hope we shall yet go forward. 'Tis for the President and yourself to decide. I well know you have to grapple with many difficulties as the President has done since the beginning of this

---

7   William C. Davis, *Look Away!: A History of the Confederate States of America* (New York: The Free Press, 2003), 319; Eric. A. Jacobson, *For Cause and For Country: A Study of the Affair at Spring Hill and the Battle of Franklin* (Franklin, TN: O'More Publishing, 2006), 19, 21.

war. He has directed us thus far and in him I have unbounded confidence. Should we from the many impediments in the way fail to move forward from this position we must not allow ourselves to be deceived as to where the enemy will make his main effort. So soon as that is discovered we should concentrate and beat them decidedly. Since McPherson's Corps has moved up from the lower Mississippi to join the Army of the Potomac or that of the Cumberland would it not be well for Genl. Polk's troops to unite with this army? As we should then be in a condition to reinforce Genl. Lee in case it should be necessary.

Please present my kindest regards to the President.

Yours truly,

J.B. Hood[8]

Hood mentioned both correspondence between Hardee and Davis, and a letter from Robert E. Lee. If correspondence between disparate senior military commanders was as inappropriate (or rare) as some observers have asserted, then Lee would be among a plethora of offenders. And yet, no Army of Tennessee historian has ever condemned Lee for corresponding directly with Hood—Johnston's junior corps commander—regarding major army movements and troop deployment issues.

Another way of judging Hood's correspondence with Confederate government officials is to consider whether such conduct was considered inappropriate by 19th century standards. Civil War records are full of correspondence between and among officers who communicated directly with their commanders' superiors. Of the aforementioned authors, only Thomas Connelly elaborated on the fact that other Johnston subordinates also corresponded with Johnston's superiors.[9] Although Hood did indeed criticize Johnston's persistent retreating during the Dalton-to-Atlanta campaign, he was hardly alone. In addition to the correspondence between Hardee and Davis mentioned in Hood's April 13, 1864, letter to Bragg, on June 22, 1864, Hardee wrote to Davis: "If the present system continues we may find ourselves at Atlanta before a serious battle is fought." Another of Johnston's subordinates,

---

8 Connelly, *Autumn of Glory*, 323; Braxton Bragg Papers, Western Reserve Historical Society, Cleveland, OH.

9 Connelly, *Autumn of Glory*, 407-414.

division commander (and later corps commander) Gen. Alexander P. (A. P.) Stewart wrote to Bragg on March 19, 1864: "Are we to hold still, remaining on the defensive in this position until . . . [Sherman] comes down with his combined armies to drive us out?" Johnston's senior cavalry commander, Gen. Joseph Wheeler, wrote to Bragg on July 1, 1864: "I have begged General Johnston to allow me to go to the enemy's rear every day for the last three months," but Johnston consistently refused. "Here I am with one third rations of corn for horses, with my men building and defending rifle pits." Wheeler added to Richmond's growing anxiety by informing Bragg, "I think it very possible this army may fall back a short distance further. The cavalry leader had also written to Bragg on February 14, March 3, March 7, April 16, June 4, and June 5.[10]

Civil War records are replete with examples of commanders who corresponded with superiors outside of the chain of command. Although too numerous to chronicle, these examples include Hood's own subordinates. Their letters—critical and otherwise—are not judged as improper, nor are these officers labeled (nor necessarily should they be) disloyal to their commander. On September 14, Gen. Samuel French, one of Hood's division commanders, sent a letter to Davis (purportedly on behalf of several disgruntled generals) implicitly seeking Hood's removal as army commander:

Mr. President: Several officers have asked me to write you in regard to a feeling of depression more or less apparent in parts of this army, and I have declined doing so, but for your own satisfaction it might be well that you send one or two intelligent officers here to visit the different divisions and brigades to ascertain of that spirit of confidence so necessary for success has or has not been impaired within the past month or two. They might further inquire into the cause if they find in this army any

---

10 Ibid., 407; McMurry, *John Bell Hood and the War for Southern Independence*, 98; Joseph Wheeler Papers, Harvard University, Cambridge, MA; Braxton Bragg Papers, Western Reserve Historical Society, Cleveland, OH; Stephen Davis, *Atlanta Will Fall: Sherman, Joe Johnston and the Yankee Heavy Battalions* (Wilmington, DE: Scholarly Resources, 2001), 105; Jefferson Davis Papers, Emory University, Atlanta, GA. Although it cannot be conclusively stated that Lt. Gen. Leonidas Polk complained directly to Richmond, he was certainly perturbed by Johnston's refusal to attack Sherman. In a letter to his wife on May 21, 1864, the general wrote, "We have been falling back from point to point to find ground" where Johnston was willing to fight. Polk stated that the army was "strong enough to do all that ought to be asked of us," and added, "When General Johnston will offer battle I do not know." Letter, Polk to his Wife, May 21, 1864, in Leonidas Polk Papers, University of the South, Sewanee, TN.

want of enthusiasm. I am sure you will pardon my writing to you thus when I tell you it is dictated by the purest of motives and in the spirit of friendship.[11]

After the Tennessee Campaign ended in December 1864, Hood's corps commander Stephen D. Lee wrote to Hood's immediate superior, Gen. P. G. T. Beauregard to discuss "recent events in Tennessee." On January 2, 1865, Hood's cavalry commander during the Tennessee Campaign, Nathan Bedford Forrest, wrote to his department commander, Gen. Richard Taylor, seeking intervention by the Confederate high command. Historian Wiley Sword and others mentioned both of these letters, but neither Lee nor Forrest are criticized for their correspondence.[12]

Letters of complaint and criticism between subordinate commanders and Richmond authorities were not uncommon during the war. Unfortunately, John Bell Hood seems to be among the very few subalterns ever accused of deceitfully undermining his superior by communicating with others.

Civil War historian Len Riedel once described the political infighting of the Army of Tennessee as a "viper's pit." He was surely correct. When Hood took command of the army on July 17, 1864, squabbling, jealousy, and inexperience permeated the officer corps. W. W. Mackall, Joseph Johnston's close friend and the Army of Tennessee's chief of staff, departed soon after Johnston's removal —and took with him many of the army's important records. Johnston's former chief of artillery, Francis Shoup, replaced Mackall, with Col. Robert Beckham ascending to Shoup's position as the army's chief artillerist.[13] The only experienced high level senior commander in the army was Willliam Hardee, who so resented the younger Hood's appointment to army command that he requested a transfer (which Davis initially denied, but would later grant after the fall of Atlanta).

Another of Hood's three corps commanders, A. P. Stewart, had served in the position only three weeks prior to Hood's promotion to army command.

11 *OR* 39, pt. 2, 836.

12 Ibid., 42, pt. 2, 731; ibid., 65, pt. 2, 756; Sword, *The Confederacy's Last Hurrah*, 427.

13 Steven Woodworth, *The Chickamauga Campaign* (Carbondale, IL: Southern Illinois University, 2010), 84.

Stewart, who was brought in from outside the Army of Tennessee, commanded Leonidas Polk's former corps, and his promotion was not without controversy. General William W. Loring commanded Polk's corps for three weeks after Polk's death that June, and was "deeply chagrined" when he was passed over for permanent command in favor of the younger Stewart. In fact, 34 of Stewart's officers, including nine generals, had petitioned for Loring's permanent promotion to corps command.

Many other officers joined Hood, Shoup, and Beckham as neophytes with regard to their new responsibilities. Carter Stevenson was the senior division commander in Hood's former corps, but he was passed over for promotion to temporary corps command in favor of Frank Cheatham, whose own feelings for Hood were likely influenced by his friendship with Hardee and admiration for Johnston. Permanent command of Hood's former corps was assigned to Stephen D. Lee, who was then serving in Mississippi. Lee, whose wartime experience had been primarily as an artillery and cavalry commander, came to the Army of Tennessee as the youngest lieutenant general in the Confederate army.

Outnumbered by Sherman almost two-to-one, Hood—new to army command himself—had orders to defend Atlanta with three corps of infantry commanded at various times by generals (Stewart, Cheatham, and Lee) new to their positions, and another officer (Hardee) openly resentful of Hood. In addition to Hood's new chief of staff and new chief of artillery, many division and brigade commanders were strangers to their new responsibilities, including division commands for Gens. John C. Brown, Edward Walthall, Henry Clayton, George Maney, and James Patton Anderson (the latter of whom was transferred to Georgia from Florida).

In a letter to Hood after the war, Major B. W. Frobel wrote that "the world will never know the full extent of the difficulties" Hood endured during the campaigns in Georgia and Tennessee, "with a skeleton of an army, dispirited and broken down, filled with politicians in military garb, who were striving solely for their own advancement." Another of Hood's former subordinates, Leopold Perot of French's division, wrote to Hood after the war, attributing the lack of his success to "the disobedience and jealousy of many of your subalterns."[14]

---

14 B. W. Frobel letter to John Bell Hood, July 24, 1867, and Leopold Perot letter to John Bell Hood, February 8, 1876, John Bell Hood Personal Papers.

"It seems likely, therefore," concluded historian Richard McMurry, "that the entire army was pockmarked by pools of resentment" after John Bell Hood took command, and that throughout the long war the Army of Tennessee's generals "had shown themselves unable—often unwilling—to follow instructions."[15]

ॐ ॐ

One of the most persistent Civil War falsehoods is the purported wholesale approval within the Army of Tennessee of Joseph E. Johnston's handling of the campaign from Dalton in north Georgia down to the outskirts of Atlanta. Scholars who had advocated this were undoubtedly influenced by Hood's eventual failure to save Atlanta, coupled with his later crushing defeat in Tennessee. Although Johnston seems to have been universally liked as a person, a close examination of letters and diaries written during his Dalton-to-Atlanta tenure reveal varying opinions of his military strategy. In fact, large numbers of officers and soldiers did not approve of his habitual retreating. After reviewing hundreds of journals, diaries, and letters of soldiers who served in the Army of Tennessee, historian Larry Daniel concluded, "those who claim that Johnston's retreats did not affect morale do so in the face of significant evidence to the contrary."[16]

A good barometer of the morale in any army is its rate of desertion. According to a 1970 study conducted by Richard McMurry, Federal records revealed that during the months of May and June of 1864—during the course of Johnston's command tenure of the Army of Tennessee—an average of 142.5 deserters per week made their way into Federal lines. In July, General Sherman received a slightly higher number of deserters, but it is impossible to know how many left before and after Hood replaced Johnston as commander on July 17. However, that August, the only full month of Hood's command at Atlanta, desertions averaged 141 per week—essentially the same as when Johnston commanded the army. It should be remembered that this was after the bloody battles of Peachtree Creek, Atlanta, and Ezra Church. Desertion, McMurry

---

15 McMurry, *Atlanta 1864*, 144-145.

16 Larry Daniel, *Soldiering in the Army of Tennessee: A Portrait of Life in the Confederate Army* (Chapel Hill: University of North Carolina Press, 1991), 142.

concluded, "seems to have been about equally serious under both commanders."[17]

Yankee diarists seemed to view Rebel desertions as quite common while Johnston was in command. In mid-June, an Ohio officer recorded the desertion of an entire Southern company; on July 12, an Indiana officer wrote, "I never saw the like of deserters come in they came in squads they say there is lots of their Army would desert if they had a good Chance." According to a Federal general's writing from early July, many deserters were being taken after each Rebel withdrawal. Contrary to common belief, argued McMurry, "Federal comments concerning desertion during Hood's command . . . seem to be less frequent than their remarks about enemy desertion under Johnston."[18]

Johnston's persistent withdrawals clearly disappointed many Confederates. Private William Adams of the 30th Georgia wrote to his sister, "Well, it looks like we are gone up the spout. . . . I am worse out of hart than ever." Private Robert Patrick of the 4th Louisiana, who had earlier written that Johnston was a better general than even Robert E. Lee, recorded in his diary on July 3: "Another fall back. I must acknowledge that it begins to look a little squally for our side." Two days later, on July 5, Private Adams offered this damning assessment of what was transpiring in North Georgia: "It has been nothing but a run from Dalton down and there must be a stop somewhere, or we had just as well not have an army in front of Sherman." Adams's chagrin continued the next day. "It's a devilish gloomy looking time for us for certain, and I feel despondent," he complained. "One more retreat and the fate of Atlanta is irrevocably pronounced. 'It is now or never.'" On July 10, the Louisianan expressed his utter frustration with Johnston, writing, "We can't run much further, or we will soon be down to the Gulf of Mexico."[19]

Private Celathiel Helms of the 63rd Georgia agreed with these assessments. "The men is all out of heart and say that Georgia will soon have to go under and they are going to the Yankees by the tens and twenties and hundreds almost every night," Helms wrote to his wife in early July. "Johnston's army is very

---

17 Richard McMurry, "Confederate Morale in the Atlanta Campaign of 1864," *Georgia Historical Quarterly*, vol. 54, No. 2 (Summer 1970), 229, 232. Obviously only a fraction of Confederate deserters actually crossed into enemy lines. Many or most simply went home. Still, the number of deserters processed by the Federals outside Atlanta is illustrative of the general point of this argument.

18 Ibid., 230.

19 Bonds, *War Like the Thunderbolt*, 48.

much demoralized as much as an army ever gets to be for all the newspapers say that Johnston's army is in fine spirits but the papers has told nothing but lies since the war commenced. I see that the Officers is down in the mouth and their faces looks very long and some of them say that they are fearful that all their men will go to the Yankees." Private Sam Watkins of the 1st Tennessee, who wrote one of the finest memoirs of the war, asserted of Johnston: "He could fall back in the face of the foe as quietly and orderly as if on dress parade."[20]

Atlanta resident Lieutenant Andrew Neal of the Marion Light Artillery was also despondent about the steady retreats under Johnston's tenure. "I do pray we may never march with our face turned southward again," he wrote to his family on July 17. "There was not an officer or man in this Army who ever dreamed of Johnston falling back this far or ever doubted he would attack when the time came. But I think he has been woefully outgeneraled and though he has inflicted loss on the enemy only precedented by Grant's losses in Virginia he has made a losing bargain."[21]

On May 21, Johnston's chief of staff Mackall wrote in his journal that a recent withdrawal had "impaired confidence" in the army, and that there was "great alarm in [the] country around." The town of Marietta, Mackall recorded, was "full of stragglers," over 1,000 men were barefoot, and "some dissatisfaction" was noticed among the troops.[22]

After the war in 1874, W. J. Byrne, surgeon of the 9th Kentucky Infantry (part of the famous Kentucky "Orphan Brigade") wrote to Hood about the effects Johnston's policy had on the army:

> The campaign from Dalton to Atlanta was a terrible one in the shape of losses by desertions, and I [well] remember the disappointment of the army generally in not undertaking a movement in the rear of Genl. Sherman after he had entered what was known to us as Rocky Face Gap, at which time Genl Johnston moved off through Dalton south. In fact before we crossed the Chatahoochie river, it was estimated, from despondency and our retrograde movement, the army had lost between 17,000 and 20,000 men by desertion, the most of us regarding the movement as inexplicable from the fact that if we were not able to meet the Federal forces in a broken mountainous

---

20 Ibid., 49; Sam Watkins, *Company Aytch or, A Side Show of the Big Show and Other Sketches*, Thomas Inge, ed. (New York: Plume, 1999), 104.

21 Bonds, *War Like the Thunderbolt*, 49.

22 *OR* 38, pt. 3, 985.

country where we had the advantage of position, how could we properly be benefitted by a move to a level [campaign] country, where a superior force could more easily pass around us, with much less danger and more ease to themselves.[23]

Disapproval of Johnston's repeated withdrawals was also recorded by those outside the Army of Tennessee. Josiah Gorgas, the Confederate chief of ordnance stationed in Richmond, wrote in his diary in late May that "Johnston verifies all our predictions of him . . . he is falling back as fast as his legs can carry him . . . Where he will stop heaven only knows."[24]

S. J. Fleherty, a Federal soldier from the 102nd Illinois Infantry, ridiculed Johnston's strategy: "It is said that after Gen. Johnston had followed his re-treating policy several weeks, the rebels declared that their army was commanded by 'Old Billy Sherman,' that they invariably moved when Sherman gave the command and Johnston only superintended the details of the movement."[25]

Sherman's soldiers also remarked about the fighting spirit of Southerners, which seemed to diminish during Johnston's persistent retreating. After the battle of Resaca in mid-May, a Northerner wrote that, for the first time, he had seen Rebels who could have escaped allow themselves to be captured. "They were all thoroughly discouraged," he concluded. Another Yankee wrote on June 6 that "nearly all" captured Confederates declared their discouragement and intention to "shirk rather than fight" if sent back into their ranks. Later that month, another Federal observed Rebel defenders who not only failed to fire their guns, but also allowed themselves to be taken prisoner. Some Federals also noted decreased fighting spirit among some Confederates after Hood took command, but it was no more common than under Johnston. According to Army of Tennessee historian McMurry, "There is not sufficient evidence to conclude that the Confederates fought any better under one commander than the other."[26]

Hood replaced Johnston on July 17—an event often described as causing universal outrage among the soldiers of the Army of Tennessee. A study of

---

23 W. J. Byrne letter to John Bell Hood, June 26, 1874, John Bell Hood Personal Papers.

24 Bonds, *War Like the Thunderbolt*, 59.

25 S. F. Fleherty, *Our Regiment: A History of the 102nd Illinois Volunteer Infantry* (Chicago: Brewster and Hanscom, 1865), 86.

26 McMurry, "Confederate Morale," 232-233.

contemporary records, however, reveals that the army did not unanimously disapprove of the change. General William Bate, a division commander under Johnston and then Hood, wrote to Braxton Bragg on August 13, 1864:

> I think our Army is now convinced of the ill effects of our long "backslide" and that it might have been avoided by delivering battle north of the Etowah. With few exceptions, Gen. Hood has grown in favor with his command. As I told you, I had some apprehensions to the effect of the removal of Gen. Johnston for he was popular with his troops but the opinion is gradually gaining lodgment in the popular mind of the army and country that in all such matters the President knows what is best and is generally correct.[27]

Some who did not populate the senior command structure also approved of Hood's appointment. "Since Hood assumed command of this army," explained an officer from Mississippi, "its policy has been changed from a defensive to an offensive attitude. I hope and believe that there will be no more retreats, but that we will move upon the enemy's line at any and all times when practical." One Arkansan concluded in late July, "This army seems cheerful and confident of victory." "The change of Commanders no doubt caused the death or capture of those near and dear to us," wrote Sgt. Joel Murphree in late August, "but I do believe it was the best for the success of our cause." Colonel Irvine Walker of the 10th South Carolina Infantry wrote on July 26 that General Hood "intends fighting for Atlanta." The Palmetto State officer continued, "I have no doubt Johnston would have allowed himself flanked out of it before he risked a general engagement."[28]

After sifting through these sources and countless others, Richard McMurry reached this conclusion:

> Many, perhaps most, Southerners maintained their confidence in Johnston right up to the time he was relieved. A large number undoubtedly were demoralized by Hood's appointment to command and by the tactics that he used against Sherman. However, as one reads more and more letters of the men who were in the campaign, it becomes

---

27 Bragg Papers.

28 McMurry, "Confederate Morale," 236-237; Cornelius Irving Walker, *Great Things Are Expected of Us: The Letters of Colonel C. Irvine Walker, 10th South Carolina Infantry, CSA*, William L. White and Charles D. Runion, eds. (Knoxville: University of Tennessee Press, 2009), 134.

obvious that the evidence is so mixed that no simplified explanation of Confederate morale is possible. Feelings were nowhere near unanimous one way or the other.[29]

ॐ ॐ

By mid-July 1864, most of Atlanta's civilian population had evacuated and much of its industrial machinery had been transferred to other Southern cities. Although still a transportation hub, Atlanta was, as one historian explained it, "a city that had been reduced to a symbol, not a place that was itself any longer of value." Symbolic as it might be, Atlanta retained its critical importance to the political fortunes of the Confederacy as Jefferson Davis fought to deny Abraham Lincoln any significant and definitive military successes before the November 1864 national election. Lincoln's opponent was the widely popular, if not militarily successful, Gen. George McClellan, whose Democratic Party advocated peace negotiations with the Confederacy. Davis hoped that war weariness in the North would, as historian Larry E. Nelson wrote, "result in the election of a presidential candidate amenable to Confederate independence." The capitulation of Atlanta was a military victory Davis had to deny Lincoln.[30]

In an attempt to bring the war to a swift conclusion, Gen. Ulysses S. Grant launched five nearly simultaneous campaigns in the spring of 1864: Franz Sigel and David Hunter in the Shenandoah Valley, Nathaniel Banks along the Red River in Louisiana, Benjamin Butler on the Virginia peninsula, Sherman in Georgia, and his own offensive against Robert E. Lee in northern Virginia. Throughout these engagements, Lincoln anxiously awaited the major victories he knew he needed to win reelection. However, to the Northern president's dismay, vigorous Confederate efforts rebuffed the campaigns guided by Sigel, Hunter, Banks, and Butler. Grant, meanwhile, fought a bloody overland slog from the Rapidan River south to the James, and then beyond to Petersburg and Richmond, where a stalemate ensued with Lee's embattled Army of Northern Virginia. Sherman had spent most of April and all of June pressing Johnston closer to Atlanta. During this time frame, Northern casualties skyrocketed to their highest rate of the entire war. Sherman's steady progress against

---

29 McMurry, "Confederate Morale," 238.

30 McMurry, *Atlanta 1864*, 142; Larry Nelson, *Bullets, Ballots, and Rhetoric: Confederate Policy for the U.S. Presidential Contest of 1864* (Tuscaloosa: University of Alabama Press, 2004), 83.

Johnston's Army of Tennessee offered the only positive news available to the increasingly impatient and discouraged Northern populace.

In a letter to Illinois congressman Elihu Washburne on August 16, 1864, Grant, the commanding general of all the Union armies, expressed the need for the North to remain resolute: "I have no doubt that the enemy are exceedingly anxious to hold out until the presidential election," explained Grant. "They have many hopes from its effects." When he learned that Hood had replaced Johnston, Grant asserted that the Kentuckian might be overly aggressive, but that he was "not destitute of ability." Just eight days after Grant penned his letter, Henry Clayton, one of Hood's division commanders, wrote to his wife on August 24, "I really feel encouraged that the war is soon to terminate. The Northern press is getting very decidedly for Peace." Referring to Grant's campaign against Richmond, Clayton added, "Grant has failed—Oh if we can only succeed in driving Sherman from Georgia!"[31]

For his part, Jefferson Davis knew well that war weariness was a double-edged sword that could lead to Lincoln's defeat—but also weaken Confederate resolve. A letter to Davis from a friend in Mississippi written after Lincoln won reelection illustrated the problems Southern civilians encountered as the war dragged on, and the general despair that prevailed. "Many soldiers are writing home from Hood's army that if Lincoln is reelected, they will fight no longer, but will return home, and that such is the general sentiment and resolve of the army," explained Robert Hudson, who went on to add, "they will not fight four years longer," and that the soldiers "meet with favor at home in these propositions." Sherman's successes in Georgia strengthened Lincoln's hand while weakening Davis's ability to keep his armies in the field.[32]

31 U. S. Grant, *General Grant's Letters to a Friend, 1861-1880,* James Grant Wilson, ed. (New York: Crowell and Company, 1897 [1973]), 39; U. S. Grant, *Personal Memoirs of U. S. Grant,* 2 vols. (New York: Charles Webster and Company, 1886), vol. 1, 345; Henry Clayton Papers, University of Alabama, Tuscaloosa.

32 *OR* 45, pt. 1, 1,247. Robert Hudson's letter is dated November 25, 1864—after Lincoln was reelected. A transcriptionist may have misdated the letter for inclusion in the *OR,* but it is more likely the date is correct and that Hudson was simply making the point that war weariness was destroying the Southern will to fight on for much longer.

Davis's distrust of Johnston's ability to successfully lead an army in the field stretched back to the earliest months of the war. In Virginia, the general consistently refused to engage the Federals in battle on the peninsula. Instead, Johnston retreated up the neck of land to the outskirts of Richmond, where he finally launched an offensive. The bungled attack at Seven Pines/Fair Oaks failed and Johnston fell seriously wounded at the end of the first day. His penchant for persistently refusing to communicate his plans to Davis, his commander-in-chief, strained their relationship to the breaking point. The unreliability of what information Johnston was willing to share only further exacerbated the situation. When it came to military matters in general, as far as Davis was concerned, Joe Johnston was not to be trusted.

In his postwar memoirs, Johnston claimed that he had incurred only 9,972 losses in Georgia from Dalton to the outskirts of Atlanta, while inflicting some 60,000 casualties on Sherman's three armies. "From the observation of our most experienced officers, daily statements of prisoners, and publications we read in the newspapers of Louisville, Cincinnati and Chicago," Johnston wrote, "the Federal loss in killed and wounded must have been six times as great as ours." In an attempt to corroborate this astounding contention, Johnston wrote that Sherman's losses in the battles of Kennesaw Mountain and Pickett's Mill alone "exceeded ours by more than ten to one."[33]

On June 28, Georgia's troublesome governor Joseph Brown wrote to President Davis, "[Atlanta] is to the Confederacy almost as important as the heart is to the human body. We must hold it." Unwilling to surrender the important city, Davis relieved Johnston of command on July 17. Considering the president's long and contentious relationship with Johnston, it is clear that the general was relieved solely because of his consistent failures in previous commands and his unwillingness to cooperate with the Confederate War Department.[34]

On February 18, 1865, Davis wrote a detailed 4,000-word letter intended for the Confederate Congress. In it, Davis explained why he could not accede to political and public demands to restore Johnston to command of the Army of Tennessee in the late winter of 1865. (The president ultimately acquiesced to Robert E. Lee's request that he reappoint Johnston.) His letter (see Appendix 3)

---

33 Johnston, *Narrative of Military Operations*, 356-357.

34 OR 52, pt. 2, 680.

was never formally submitted to Congress, but he did send a copy to his friend, Mississippi Senator James Phelan, on March 1, 1865.[35]

Davis began his letter by expressing his early admiration for Johnston, voicing respect for the Virginian's personal gallantry and professional abilities while both men had served in "the former Government." The president went on to explain that he had assigned Johnston to three important army commands during the war, and that in all three instances he had failed, revealing "defects which unfit him" for further commands.[36]

During Johnston's first service as commander of the Army of the Valley of Virginia, Davis recalled that he had promptly retreated from Harpers Ferry at the first appearance of the enemy, abandoning "a large quantity of materials and machinery for the manufacture of small-arms of the greatest value to the Confederacy." The threat, according to Davis, had not been sufficient to withdraw the army, a fact that was later confirmed by the safe removal of the equipment by lightly armed Southern work parties.[37] Davis also cited Johnston's timidity and hesitation in moving his forces to Manassas to aid P. G. T. Beauregard's imperiled army. Johnston "made serious objections" to the movement, explained Davis, "and only after repeated and urgent instructions did he move to make the proposed junction." Johnston's subsequent tardy arrival resulted in the absence and inability of a portion of his force to assist Gen. E. Kirby Smith who, acting without orders, "succeeded in reaching the battlefield in time to avert disaster." Davis commented that Johnston (who after the Southern victory at First Manassas commanded his and Beauregard's combined forces) "constantly declared his inability to assume offensive operations unless furnished with re-enforcements, which, as he was several times informed, the Government was unable to supply." Moving his army to Centerville, Virginia, in the winter of 1861-62, Johnston "declared that his position was so insecure that it must be abandoned before the enemy could advance, but indicated no other line of defense as the proper one." When summoned to Richmond in February 1862 and asked of his plans, Johnston replied that "his lines there were untenable, but when asked what new position he proposed to occupy, declared himself ignorant of the topography of the

35 Ibid., 47, pt. 2, 1,303.

36 Ibid., 1,304.

37 Ibid., 1,304, 1,305.

country in his rear." Davis expressed shock at the native Virginian's ignorance of the country he was charged to defend. Johnston, he declared, "had neglected the primary duty of a commander." After he was provided engineers by the war department, Johnston announced that although his position was indeed favorable, he could not take the offensive unless he was again reinforced. Davis continued his letter intended for Congress:

> The Government was soon afterward surprised by learning that General Johnston had commenced a hasty retreat without giving notice of an intention to do so, though he had just been apprised of the improved prospect of re-enforcing him, and of the hope entertained by me that he would thus be enabled to assume the offensive. The retreat was with-out molestation or even demonstration from the enemy, but was conducted with such precipitation as to involve a heavy loss of supplies. Some valuable artillery was abandoned, a large depot of provisions was burned, blankets, shoes, and saddles were committed to flames, and this great sacrifice of property was so wanting in apparent justification as to produce a painful impression on the public mind, and to lead to an inquiry by a committee from Congress, which began an investigation into the subject, but did not report before Congress adjourned.[38]

The Federal army gave up its brief pursuit, changed its base to Fortress Monroe, and Johnston's army was eventually transferred to Yorktown near the tip of the Virginia peninsula to defend against an anticipated Federal move from that sector upon Richmond. Although Gen. John Magruder had been constructing defensive fortifications for several months, the persistently apprehensive Johnston "soon pronounced the position untenable, and made another hasty retreat, with another heavy loss of munitions and armament." He commenced his retreat before advising Richmond, which in turn led to the sudden loss of Norfolk, "and with it was lost large supplies of all kinds, including machinery which could not be replaced in the Confederacy." Johnston pulled his army back to the Chickahominy River where, according to Davis, he "suddenly crossed that stream without notice to the Government and retreated upon Richmond."[39]

Davis went on to complain that even though Johnston had remained idle in front of Richmond, he neglected to erect effective fortifications and had once

38 Ibid., 1,305.

39 Ibid., 1,306.

again failed to conduct adequate reconnaissance; therefore, he remained ignorant of the topography of the countryside and was unable to ascertain enemy movements. Davis also detailed Johnston's mistakes that led to the Confederate defeat at Seven Pines, where the commander was seriously wounded. Although he acknowledged Johnston's personal courage, the president concluded, "His wound rendered him unfit for further service in the field for some months, and terminated his first important command, which he had administered in a manner as to impair my confidence in his fitness to conduct a campaign."[40]

After recovering and returning to duty in November 1862, Johnston was given another important command by Davis, who admitted, "Though my confidence in him had been much shaken, it had not yet been destroyed." Having failed in the immediate command of an army in the field, the senior commander was assigned by Davis "to a different class of duties"—a departmental command of an area encompassing several armies, each with its own commander. The department included the forces commanded by Braxton Bragg in Tennessee, Franklin Gardner at Port Hudson, Louisiana, John Pemberton at Vicksburg, and John Forney in Alabama. Davis noted that proof of his confidence in Johnston was illustrated by the fact that this new command would "embrace within its limits my own home and those of my nearest relatives and friends." Indeed, "few were exposed to a more total loss of property than myself in the event of his disastrous failure in this new command."[41]

Johnston proved as ineffective during his second command tenure as he had during his first in northern Virginia. Johnston failed to promptly perceive General Grant's movement on Vicksburg, and he did not personally move to "that vital point" until he was ordered to do so by the Confederate War Department. When he arrived too late to join Pemberton's trapped army in Vicksburg, Johnston established his headquarters in Jackson and Canton, where he remained essentially inactive despite Richmond's pleas that he attack Grant. According to Davis, Johnston "was thereupon pressed to attack the forces of Banks at Port Hudson and rescue the army of General Gardner, but declined on the ground that he feared Grant would seize the occasion to

---

40 Ibid., 1,306, 1,307.

41 Ibid., 1,307.

advance upon Jackson, which place he considered too important to be exposed."[42]

A thoroughly exasperated Davis wrote that Grant seized both Vicksburg and Port Hudson "without one blow on his (Johnston's) part to relieve either," and then moved on Jackson, where Johnston "remained within his lines and permitted Grant again to concentrate a large force." Then, according to Davis, "No sooner had the enemy commenced investing Jackson than General Johnston pronounced it untenable." Despite commanding an army of some 25,000, Johnston evacuated Jackson and withdrew to eastern Mississippi. As a result, the Confederacy suffered "one of the most serious and irreparable sacrifices of property that has occurred during the war." Davis recalled that Johnston's actions had cost the South "a very large number of locomotives, said to be about ninety, and several hundred cars," and that the Confederate cause "never recovered from the injury to the transportation service occasioned by this failure on his part."[43]

"My confidence in General Johnston's fitness for separate command was now destroyed," confessed the Confederate president, who went on to add in no uncertain terms that one of his top generals was "deficient in enterprise, tardy in movement, defective in preparation, and singularly neglectful" of his duties.[44]

In a preview of what would become a major issue in the Atlanta Campaign of 1864, President Davis also took note of Johnston's tight-lipped demeanor. "Neither in this nor in his previous command had it been possible for me to obtain from General Johnston any communications of his plans or purposes beyond vague statements of an intention to counteract the enemy as their plans might be developed," complained the Southern president. "I came to the conclusion that it would be imprudent to entrust General Johnston with another independent command for active operations in the field."[45]

Several months later, with few viable options remaining, Davis "yielded my convictions, and gave him a third trial." Unfortunately, Johnston's performance

---

42 Ibid., 1,308.

43 Ibid.

44 Ibid.

45 Ibid., 1,309.

in north Georgia in 1864 proved to be identical in substance, style, and result to his first two commands.[46]

Davis recalled that after General Bragg's resignation following the disastrous battle of Missionary Ridge, the Army of Tennessee's senior subordinate, Gen. William J. Hardee "distrusting his own ability, earnestly requested the selection of another commander for the army." Of the three Confederate field generals holding sufficient rank, only Johnston was available because neither Robert E. Lee (commanding the Army of Northern Virginia) nor Pierre G. T. Beauregard (commanding Charleston and the coastal defenses in South Carolina, Georgia, and Florida) "could properly be withdrawn from the position occupied by them." (The Confederate Congress had not yet adopted the law authorizing the appointment of general officers to temporary rank.) President Davis went on to lament that although "there seemed to be scarcely a choice left," some members of his cabinet and other advisors "represented that it might well be the case that his assignment with the disasters apprehended from it would be less calamitous than the injury arising from an apparent indifference to the wishes and opinions of the officers of the State governments, of many members of Congress, and of other prominent citizens." Davis forever regretted the decision he finally made and clearly admitted as much. "I committed the error of yielding to these suggestions against my own deliberate convictions," he later explained, "and General Johnston entered upon his third important command, that of the army designed to recover the State of Tennessee from the enemy."[47]

Johnston assumed command of the Army of Tennessee in February of 1864 with instructions to advance into Tennessee as soon as reinforcements of both men and materials arrived. Davis explained that the winter was dry and mild, and that Hardee reported the army to be sufficiently rested and supplied after the defeat at Missionary Ridge three months earlier. "The government spared nothing of men and materials" in reinforcing Johnston, including "batteries made for General Lee's army" diverted to Johnston, Polk's Army of Mississippi "placed at his disposal," and cavalry "returned from East Tennessee to assist him."[48]

46 Ibid.

47 Ibid.

48 Ibid., 1,309, 1,318.

Johnston's indecisive tendencies, consistently demonstrated during the first three years of the war, persisted. "General Johnston made no attempt to advance," pointed out Davis. "As soon as he assumed command he suggested deficiencies and difficulties to be encountered in an offensive movement, which he declared himself unable to overcome. The enemy commenced advancing in May, and General Johnston began retreating." Abandoning vast regions of northern Georgia "abounding in supplies" and whose mountains and rivers provided "admirable facilities for defense," Johnston, according to Davis, "so disheartened and demoralized the army that he himself announced by telegram large losses from straggling and desertion," until the army "was finally brought to the suburbs of Atlanta."[49]

Johnston's persistent secretiveness also continued. "No information was sent to me," Davis recounted, "that tended to dispel the apprehension then generally expressed that Atlanta also was to be abandoned when seriously threatened." According to the Southern president, by this time public sentiment about Johnson had changed. Davis revealed that "some of those who had most earnestly urged General Johnston's assignment to the command of the army when it was at Dalton now with equal earnestness pressed his prompt removal."[50]

Davis continued his desperate and relentless attempts to learn of Johnston's intentions, writing that he "preferred, by direct inquiry of General Johnston, to obtain that which had been too long withheld, his plan for future operations." The commander's reply suggested "that he intended leaving the entrenchments of Atlanta under the guard of the Georgia militia, and moving out with his army into the field." This was confirmed by Georgia militia commander G. W. Smith, who wrote to Hood in 1879, "I wonder if Old Joe did intend to leave my little band in charge of Atlanta whilst the three corps and the cavalry were hunting for Sherman's right of left flank . . . Wouldn't that have been a kettle of fish?" According to Davis, "This was regarded as conclusive that Atlanta was also to be given up without a battle, and I could perceive no ground for hoping that General Johnston, who had failed to check the enemy's march from Dalton to Atlanta, through a country abounding in strong positions for defense, would be able to prevent the further advance through a level country to Macon." Davis concluded, "He was therefore relieved. If I had been

49 Ibid., 1,310.

50 Ibid.

slow to consent to his assignment to that command, I was at least equally slow to agree to his removal."[51]

In further justifying his action, Davis cited that although Sherman's army outnumbered Johnston's, the disparity was relatively small, and that during the entire war no other Confederate army in any department "has been so nearly equal in numbers with the enemy as in this last campaign of General Johnston." Davis also noted that, according to Johnston's own reports to Richmond, nearly 25,000 casualties had been incurred in the loss of most of north Georgia, which imperiled the South's second most important city.[52]

"It was not the want of men or means which caused the disastrous failure of his campaign," concluded Davis. "My opinion of General Johnston's unfitness for command has ripened slowly and against my inclinations into a conviction so settled that it would be impossible for me again to feel confidence in him as the commander of an army in the field."[53]

There was little doubt that Johnston was going to abandon Atlanta. Prior to the fall of the city, Capt. Samuel Foster of Hiram Granbury's brigade recorded in his diary that holding Atlanta was a futile task that "Joe Johnston said could not be done." An infantry captain was aware of Johnston's intentions (or believed he knew them) to surrender the city, yet Richmond was kept in the dark.[54] Johnston's dismissal from command of the Army of Tennessee was the fault of Joseph Johnston, not of John Bell Hood, nor of any other individual.

It is commonly believed that virtually all of the soldiers of the Army of Tennessee criticized the appointment of Hood to army command. Of Hood's ascension to command of the Army of Tennessee, historian Thomas Connelly concluded that "Hood's appointment . . . wreaked bitterness among the private soldiers of the army." It is certain that some soldiers did not like Hood, but

51 Ibid; G. W. Smith letter to John Bell Hood, January 23, 1879, John Bell Hood Personal Papers.

52 *OR* 47, pt. 2, 1,311.

53 Ibid.

54 Samuel T. Foster, *One of Cleburne's Command: The Civil War Reminiscences and Diary of Capt. Samuel T. Foster, Granbury's Texas Brigade, CSA*, Norman D. Brown, ed. (Austin: University of Texas Press, 1980), 129.

records suggest it was the removal of Johnston that most disappointed the disgruntled soldiers of the Army of Tennessee, not the appointment of Hood.[55]

Many authors cite Pvt. Sam Watkins of the 1st Tennessee Infantry in support of their assertions that the soldiers disliked Hood. At one point in his memoir *Company Aytch*, Watkins wrote the following: "The most terrible and disastrous blow the South ever received was when Hon. Jefferson Davis placed General Hood in command of the Army of Tennessee." Although Watkins's oft recited quote seems straightforward, it is rather enigmatic and contradicts several other comments he made in praise of Hood. Elsewhere in his book, for example, Watkins wrote of his and his comrades' affection and respect for him: "[Hood] was a noble, brave and good man, and we loved him for his many virtues and goodness of heart," and "General John B. Hood did all that he could. The die had been cast. Our cause had been lost before he took command. . . . [He] fought with the ferociousness of the wounded tiger and the everlasting grip of the bulldog." So was Hood's assignment to command the army the terrible and disastrous blow, or was it Johnston's removal?[56]

According to many soldiers, the army wanted nobody besides Joe Johnston. "The removal of General Johnston, and the appointment of Hood to succeed him in command of the Army of Tennessee," wrote S. A. Cunningham of the 41st Tennessee, "was an astounding event. So devoted to Johnston were his men that the presence and immediate command of General [Robert E.] Lee would not have been accepted without complaint." Dr. Samuel Thompson, also of the 41st Tennessee, echoed these sentiments when he wrote, "Having been under Johnston's command, it would be hard for any other commander to have pleased us." Captain F. H. Wigfall wrote of Johnston's removal, "A universal gloom seemed cast over the army, for they were entirely devoted to him. Gen. Hood, however, has all the qualities to attach men to him, and it was not a comparison between the two, but love for and confidence in Gen. Johnston" that disappointed the army.[57]

---

55 Connelly, *Autumn of Glory*, 423. Examples of this are provided later in this chapter.

56 Watkins, *Company Aytch*, 105, 206, 210, 225.

57 S. A. Cunningham, "The Battle of Franklin: The Carnage as Seen from the Center of the Conflict," in *Confederate Veteran*, 40 vols. (April 1893), vol. 1, 101-102; S. A. Cunningham, *Reminiscences of the 41st Tennessee: The Civil War in the West*, John A. Simpson, ed. (Shippensburg, PA: White Mane Books, 2001), 117; Louise Wigfall Wright, *A Southern Girl in '61: The War-Time Memories of a Confederate Senator's Daughter*, Mrs. D. Giraud Wright, ed. (New York: Doubleday, Page & Company, 1905), 182.

Judge Frank Smith echoed the army's general sentiments when he wrote in his *History of the Twenty-Fourth Tennessee* that the removal of Johnston "was one of the most unpopular acts of President Davis's whole administration, especially with the rank and file of the western army." But Smith did not claim that the soldiers disliked Hood, adding, "The soldiers had the greatest respect for Hood's fighting qualities, which had never been doubted, and for his personal gallantry in action."[58]

Captain Samuel Foster commented extensively on Hood's replacement of Johnston. After learning of Johnston's removal, Foster recorded in his diary, "Johnston has so endeared himself to his soldiers, that no man can take his place." The Texan continued, "All over camp (not only among Texas troops) can be seen this demoralization—and at all hours in the afternoon can be heard Hurrah for Joe Johnston and God D - - n Jeff Davis. For the first time, we hear men openly talk about going home, by tens and by fifties. They refuse to stand guard, or do any other camp duty, and talk open rebellion against all Military authority. The noise and confusion was kept up all night." The outraged Foster added, "If Jeff Davis had made his appearance in this army during the excitement he would not have lived an hour." Foster mentioned nothing of anyone's disdain for Hood; it was Davis's removal of Johnston that had upset the soldiers.[59]

Colonel Virgil S. Murphey of the 17th Alabama viewed Hood's replacement of Johnston differently than did Foster. "Our government had placed Hood in command," wrote the colonel, "and as such I yielded to him my confidence and cordial cooperation." Colonel J. N. Wyatt of the 12th Tennessee, who called Johnston "the idol of the army," wrote that "When the order relieving him of command was read, the spectacle was touching to see; men who have borne the heat and burden of this war shed tears. But they are determined to do their duty by their country, no matter who commands."[60]

Federal General James H. Wilson, who would later command Gen. George Thomas's cavalry against Hood in the Tennessee Campaign, supposed that the attitude of many in the Army of Tennessee might have had an impact on

---

58 Judge Frank. H. Smith, "History of the 24th Tennessee," Columbia, TN, March 1904.

59 Foster, *One of Cleburne's Command*, 105, 107.

60 Virgil Murphey diary, Southern Historical Collection, University of North Carolina, Chapel Hill; J. N. Wyatt, "Dalton-Atlanta Campaign," *Confederate Veteran*, vol. 5 (October 1897), 521.

Hood's results as an army commander. After the war Wilson wrote the following:

> It will be recalled that Hood succeeded Joseph E. Johnston in command of that army by the orders of Jefferson Davis, as a result of Johnston's failure to stay Sherman's progress toward Atlanta, and that Hood up to that time held an inferior command. Although a soldier of great personal courage and prowess, there is no doubt that he was looked upon by his contemporaries as possessing but limited ability and lacking the necessary experience for the great responsibilities thus imposed upon him. It was customary in both the Confederate and Federal armies after his advancement to decry his abilities, and this may account in some degree for the failure of his bold undertakings, but it has always seemed to me that they were ably planned and needed nothing but heavier battalions, greater resources, and better subordinates to make them successful.[61]

ক্ষ   ক্ষ

Hood's career is commonly described as an example of the so-called Peter Principle, and that he became "increasingly ineffective as he was promoted to lead larger, independent commands late in the war." Although such descriptions of Hood are often neither disrespectful nor technically inaccurate, they are not necessarily fair or instructive. Hood was spectacularly successful as a brigade and division commander in 1862 and 1863. He experienced only nominal success as a corps commander during Johnston's retreats in 1864, and as an army commander that summer failed to hold Atlanta before being soundly defeated in Tennessee. Aside from Confederate victories in 1864 in secondary theaters like Louisiana (the Red River Campaign), Shenandoah Valley, and below Richmond in the fighting in the Bermuda Hundred affair, how many Confederate army commanders could boast of major battlefield success during the final nine months of the war, when Southern resolve waned and resources became scarce? Did Robert E. Lee enjoy any decisive victories after his defeat at Gettysburg in the summer of 1863? Did Braxton Bragg win a battle after Chickamauga in September 1863? Could Joseph Johnston claim any major victories in Georgia or North Carolina in the war's final eighteen months that

---

61 James H. Wilson, *Under the Old Flag: Recollections of Military Operations in the War for the Union, The Spanish War, The Boxer Rebellion,* 2 vols. (New York: D. Appleton and Company, 1912), vol. 2, 44-45.

turned around the flow of Sherman's efforts? Did Richard Taylor or William Hardee succeed in defending their departments in late 1864 and 1865?[62]

Stephen D. Lee summed it up best when he wrote to Hood after the war, "I do not believe any other general could have done more with your army, when our cause had virtually already been lost before you took command."[63]

Like all other senior Confederate commanders, Hood enjoyed most of his successes in the first half of the war, and suffered consistent stalemates or defeats in 1864 and 1865.

---

62 Craig Symonds, *A Battlefield Atlas of the Civil War* (Mount Pleasant, SC: Nautical and Aviation Publishing Company of America, 1983), 79.

63 S. D. Lee letter to John Bell Hood, August 25, 1875, John Bell Hood Personal Papers.

Chapter 4

"The past actually happened but history is only what someone wrote down."

— *A. Whitney Brown*

The Cassville Controversy

One of the most hotly debated incidents of the Atlanta Campaign prior to Joseph Johnston's dismissal as commander of the Army of Tennessee occurred at Cassville, Georgia, on May 19, 1864. After the May 13-15 battle of Resaca, Johnston retreated across the Oostanaula River and marched about 15 miles south to Adairsville, pausing briefly at Calhoun. Neither position satisfied the cautious Johnston, but the Confederate commander saw an opportunity to isolate and attack a portion of Sherman's larger force.

Hoping to catch and engage Johnston before his army could withdraw south across the Etowah River, Sherman split his army into four columns to facilitate a more rapid pursuit. The Federals spread farther apart as they approached Adairsville, which provided Johnston with a tactical advantage and the opportunity to strike. Poor roads south of Adairsville ensured that Sherman would have to keep his forces divided. One of these roads ran south from Adairsville via Kingston, about 16 miles, and another ran generally southeast for about 10 miles directly to Cassville. Johnston correctly anticipated that

Sherman would send one column, comprising Gen. Joe Hooker's XX Corps and Gen. John Schofield's XXIII Corps (the Army of the Ohio) on the Cassville road. Rugged terrain in the area made cross-country travel difficult, which in turn impeded Sherman's ability to support the Cassville-bound portion of the Federal army.[1]

"The probability that the Federal army would divide . . . ," Johnston later wrote, "gave me a hope of engaging and defeating one of them before it could receive aid from the other." His plan involved the conspicuous march of William Hardee's corps and most of the army's wagons and cavalry on the road from Adairsville to Kingston to ensure Sherman's pursuit, while Hood's and Leonidas Polk's corps proceeded directly to Cassville. Rather than continuing south, however, Hardee would turn and march rapidly toward Cassville to unite with the rest of the army, giving the Confederates overwhelming numerical superiority over the isolated Federal column. Hood was tasked with initiating the Rebel attack against the Federal left flank as it approached Polk's command to the front.[2]

Johnston's plan took shape when, on May 18, Hooker's and Schofield's Federals advanced down the Adairsville-Cassville road toward Polk, whose corps had deployed for battle. Hood took up a position on Polk's right, while Hardee, who had completed his longer diversionary march, aligned on Polk's left west of Cassville. Hardee's position controlled the road from Kingston, over which any reinforcing troops from Sherman would have to travel to support Hooker and Schofield. On the morning of May 19, the long-retreating Army of Tennessee was poised to strike a potentially serious blow. Spirits were high, and Johnston exhorted his men with an eloquent, blood-stirring order.

Just as Hood's forward movement began, however, an enemy force of unknown size appeared unexpectedly on his exposed right flank. Hood, who did not have cavalry to protect his flank, exercised appropriate caution by halting his advance and repositioning his divisions to face the new threat. Hood's decision delayed the entire Confederate attack. When Johnston learned of the threat beyond Hood's right flank, he abandoned his attack plan

---

1   Timothy F. Weiss, "I Lead You to Battle: Jospeh E. Johnston and the Controversy at Cassville," *Georgia Historical Quarterly*, XCI (Winter 2007). The author wishes to thank Mr. Weiss of Roswell, Georgia, whose excellent essay was a valuable source of information and guide for the writing of the Cassville Controversy chapter.

2   Johnston, *Narrative of Military Operations*, 320.

altogether and renewed his retreat by crossing the nearby Etowah River, one of the few remaining natural obstacles between Sherman and Atlanta.

In exchange for minimal casualties, Sherman had driven some 35 miles in just four days and was now within 50 miles of Atlanta. Federal morale soared. On the Confederate side, hearts sank when the positions were abandoned and another demoralizing retreat resumed. "The sword of the army had been drawn," explained Johnston's biographer Craig Symonds, "but it did not strike."[3]

After the campaign, a debate raged between Hood and Johnston over the affair at Cassville that ended only with Hood's death in 1879. According to Johnston, Hood ruined one of the campaign's best opportunities to cripple Sherman by reacting to erroneous reports of enemy forces on his right flank "without informing me of this strange departure of instructions." Referring to Hood's movement as "erratic" and "based upon a wild report," Johnston accused Hood of "extraordinary disobedience." "The Federal army had been under our unceasing observation for thirteen days," Johnston wrote, "so the report on which General Hood acted was manifestly untrue."[4]

Hood, however, insisted that he had prudently shifted his command to face a wholly unexpected threat, and that to have done otherwise would have been careless and irresponsible. In his own memoirs, Hood stated that if Johnston was correct, his corps had been attacked by "an imaginary enemy" that killed and wounded several members of Gen. Thomas Hindman's division. Hood wrote that he acted appropriately. He informed Johnston's chief of staff Mackall of the situation, halted his advance, and repositioned his corps to "force the enemy to develop his strength and object." Hood added, "Five thousand witnesses, moreover, could be produced to testify to the truth of my assertion."[5]

The controversy continues in various forms up to the present day. In the late 1990s, however, Richard McMurry confirmed that Hood was correct. Federal troops from Dan Butterfield's brigade, part of the Hooker-Schofield column, "stumbled onto a country road leading into Cassville . . . and in following that route blundered into Hood's column." McMurry concluded,

---

3 Craig Symonds, *Joseph E. Johnston: A Civil War Biography* (New York: W.W. Norton and Company, 1994), 293.

4 Johnston, *Narrative of Military Operations*, 321-322; Stephen Davis, *Atlanta Will Fall*, 56.

5 Hood, *Advance and Retreat*, 100-103.

"For Hood to have launched an attack to the west with a Federal force of unknown strength to his rear would have been foolish in the extreme. His men could have been caught between fire from two hostile forces."[6]

Of the many controversies regarding Hood's tenure as a corps commander under Johnston, the interpretation and portrayal of the Cassville affair in Civil War scholarship is the most perplexing. Given the evidence, it is difficult to imagine how anyone could blame Hood for his actions. Still, many Civil War writers and scholars have come down on Johnston's side of the argument.

In the early 1940s, Stanley Horn seemed to have understood the imperilment of Hood's corps at Cassville when he wrote in his *The Army of Tennessee* that "Johnston just could not believe that enemy troops were there; even as late as 1874." The author acknowledged Hood had indeed been "briskly engaged" by a fragment of Hooker's column that had become lost and "blundered into the right wing of the whole Confederate army."[7]

Three decades later Thomas Connelly, unmoved by Horn's assessment as well as other historical evidence, was highly critical of Hood's actions at Cassville. "Hood told a curious story that does not coincide with other accounts," argued Connelly, who went on to make harsh assertions about Hood's forthrightness, relying exclusively on the widely discredited journal of committed Johnston devotee W. W. Mackall. According to Connelly, "Hood argued that the reason he fell back was not because a force appeared on his rear." In fact, Hood explained his withdrawal and repositioning for precisely that reason. Continuing his curious assertions, Connelly misinformed his readers that Hood "maintained that he knew all along what was later found to be true"—that the enemy encountered at Cassville "was only a cavalry reconnaissance." This is untrue. Hood never deviated from his contention that his right flank was attacked by a force that included not just cavalry, but artillery and infantry as well. Connelly also censured Hood for not ordering a reconnaissance of the enemy force. It must be remembered that Hood did not have cavalry to send out, so he ordered Hindman to advance infantry skirmishers to ascertain the identity and strength of the Federals. Connelly further criticized Hood for repositioning his corps without awaiting permission from Johnston. Surely Connelly did not expect Hood to maintain his command

---

6 McMurry, *1864*, 81.

7 Stanley Horn, *The Army of Tennessee* (Norman, OK: The University of Oklahoma Press, 1952), 328.

in an exposed position, and leave Hindman's division aligned to receive enfilading fire from Federal artillery while awaiting permission from Johnston to react and respond?[8]

Twenty years after Connelly wrote his study of the Confederate army, Albert Castel penned *Decision in the West*, which remains the most detailed analysis of the Atlanta Campaign to date. Hood, declared Castel, was blameless at Cassville. The historian presented a detailed analysis of the threat to Hood's exposed right flank, and provided primary source evidence to support his opinion. Curiously, Castel went out of his way to excuse Connelly's earlier analysis and condemnation of Hood at Cassville. In an endnote, Castel speculated that Connelly might not have known of the existence of the letter of a member of Hood's staff, Col. Taylor Beattie, who was an eyewitness to the events at Cassville. However, this is a difficult argument to make: Beattie's acount appeared in a March 29, 1874, letter reprinted in Hood's *Advance and Retreat*, which is cited extensively in Connelly's book.[9]

In his letter, Beattie recalled that during the commencement of the attack at Cassville, "a dark line" of troops appeared on the right of Hood's corps. Hood halted his corps, recalled the staff officers, and ordered Hindman to send out skirmishers to identify the unknown body of men. "In a few minutes a sharp skirmish was in progress," Beattie wrote, "and several of our men were wounded and killed." Beattie continued, "I recollect very distinctly that five men were hit at one time by the fragments of a shell, which exploded not more than twenty-five yards" from where Hood was sitting on horseback. According to Beattie, Hood turned his corps to face the enemy, who remained there throughout the day "erecting batteries in front and in flank of us, enfilading our line." Connelly cites Hood's memoirs numerous times throughout his *Army of Tennessee*, and Beattie's Cassville testimony appears in Hood's memoirs.[10]

Hood's memoirs also contain a May 26, 1874, letter from Maj. J. E. Austin, commander of the 14th Battalion Louisiana Sharpshooters. Austin's men were positioned on Hood's extreme right at Cassville. According to Austin, there was a "short and severe engagement" with enemy troops that had unexpectedly appeared "in force in my front, with artillery and infantry." After the initial

---

8   Connelly, *Autumn of Glory*, 347-348.

9   Castel, *Decision in the West*, 196-206, note 101 p. 589.

10 Hood, *Advance and Retreat*, 102-103.

repulse of the Federals, Austin stated that the enemy gathered reinforcements and moved around his unit "until I was completely isolated and cut off" from Hood's corps. "From my observations," Austin concluded, "I am forced to believe that General Johnston makes an error in his book in discrediting the presence of the enemy."[11]

Federal sources also record the fighting on Hood's flank. Federal Captain (later brevet general) Paul A. Oliver wrote to Daniel Butterfield on March 3, 1877, and described the attack on Johnston's (Hood's) right flank at Cassville. "Smith's battery first arrived together with yours," Oliver wrote, "and opened spiritedly and the arrival of Ward's brigade, just at the right moment, forming line of battle on your left, gave a display of force, which induced the enemy to halt and retire." Oliver, who realized that he had "imprudently attacked" a larger Rebel force, was "relieved from the unpleasant solitude" by the arrival of Hooker's main force late in the afternoon. After riding into Cassville later, Oliver continued, "I found that had I pushed Ward's brigade forward on the road they were on, they would have got right in the rear of Johnston's line of earthworks." "It is evident now that the enemy did not care to initiate an attack," because of the move "made on the right and rear of his right flank."[12]

Among those historians who have written recently on the Atlanta Campaign, authors McMurry and Stephen Davis recognize Hood's perilous position at Cassville and endorse the actions he took to protect his troops. As McMurry wrote, ignoring the threat "would have been foolish in the extreme."[13]

Despite the overwhelming evidence that Federals did indeed appear on his flank, harsh criticisms of Hood's actions at Cassville persist. The most acerbic written assault appeared in David J. Eicher's *The Civil War in Books*. The author

---

11 Ibid., 101-102.

12 Paul A. Oliver letter to Daniel Butterfield, March 3, 1877, John Bell Hood Personal Papers. It is not known how a copy of the letter from Oliver to Butterfield found its way into John Bell Hood's papers. If Hood had received a copy of the letter prior to 1879 he surely would have included Oliver's recollections in *Advance and Retreat*. After the war Butterfield lived in New York City, which was also the home of Hood's daughters Lillian and Ida; his daughters not only maintained his personal papers, but on some occasions in the 1900s also added to the collection. Wigfall's daughter returned wartime letters from Hood to L. T. Wigfall to Lillian in the early 1900s, and other letters dated in the late 1800s and early 1900s are in the collection of Hood's papers. It is possible that after Hood's death, a copy of the Oliver to Butterfield letter was sent to Lillian or Ida, who placed it with their father's papers.

13 McMurry, *Atlanta 1864*, 81.

of several books on Civil War history, Eicher berated Hood's memoirs and, without providing specific examples or sources, claimed that during Hood's tenure as a corps commander under Johnston, "Hood repeatedly ducked responsibility for unfolding actions, and occasionally placed others in command during times of risk." Eicher reserved his most outrageous charge for Hood's actions at Cassville, writing, At times, Hood "may have intentionally neglected his own duties to make his superior, Johnston, look bad," such as at the battle of Cassville.[14]

Eicher's accusations of gross insubordination (and perhaps criminal, treasonous conduct) by Hood transcend reason and is without evidence—credible or otherwise.

---

14 David John Eicher, *The Civil War in Books: An Analytical Bibliography* (Champaign: University of Illinois Press, 1997), 83. The author wrote several times to Mr. Eicher, a chemistry teacher who also writes on astronomical matters, to inquire which of Hood's statements in his memoirs were untruthful, and which responsibilities Hood had repeatedly avoided. He also asked Eicher to elaborate on his charge that Hood engaged in treasonous conduct at Cassville. No response was received.

Chapter 5

"The voice of history is often little more than
the organ of hatred or flattery."

— *Edward Gibbon*

The Battles for Atlanta:
Hood Fights

With Sherman's three armies now on the outskirts of Atlanta, Jefferson Davis removed Joseph Johnston on July 17, 1864, and replaced him with John Bell Hood. Modern scholar Steven Woodworth observed that "The fate of Atlanta, from the Confederate standpoint, was all but decided by Johnston," and that "Hood was given a hopeless assignment . . . so he had to attack." With orders from Richmond to hold Atlanta, retreat was out of the question. Historian Albert Castel agreed, citing the "virtually impossible situation" Hood inherited.[1]

The *Atlanta Appeal* newspaper declared that retreating had to cease and that attacks were required to restore the situation. "There is a limit to prudence," explained an editorial published immediately after Hood's appointment to command the Army of Tennessee. "When excessive, our enemies denominate

---

1 Steven Woodworth, *Civil War Gazette* interview, December 27, 2006; Albert Castel, *Decision in the West: The Atlanta Campaign of 1864* (Lawrence, KS: University Press of Kansas, 1992), 562.

it cowardice. This war must end and the final battle be fought. Why not here, and even now?" On July 20, the *Augusta Constitutionalist* editorialized on the meaning of Hood's elevation to replace Johnston: "If it means anything it must mean this: *Atlanta will not be given up without a fight* [emphasis in original]."[2]

A few hours before the new commander struck Sherman at Peachtree Creek on July 20, Hood told *Mobile Advertiser and Register* reporter Felix De Fontaine, "At once I attack the enemy. He has pressed our lines until he is within a short distance of Atlanta and I must fight or evacuate. I am going to fight. The odds are against us," Hood added, "but I leave the issue with the Gods of battle."[3]

One day earlier, Hood received intelligence that the Federals force, which was maneuvering around the perimeter of Atlanta, had split, with several miles now dividing George Thomas's Army of the Cumberland from Gen. James McPherson's Army of the Tennessee and Gen. John Schofield's Army of the Ohio. A rare opportunity beckoned Confederates to attack with at least equal numbers (Thomas's command totaled about 21,655 troops to Hardee's and Stewart's two corps of Hood's army of 20,250). More importantly, Thomas was just beginning to cross Peachtree Creek.[4]

Hood quickly devised a plan to assault Thomas after much of his command had crossed the waterway but before the Federals could construct fortifications and reorganize themselves. Hood's plan was to attack Thomas's left flank *en echelon* by division and drive the enemy westward down Peachtree Creek to its confluence with the Chattahoochee River. The intended offensive was designed to force Thomas away from the rest of Sherman's army, trapping the Federals without an escape route and without the support of McPherson's and Schofield's commands several miles away.

The key to Hood's plan rested with William Hardee, whose corps on the right side of the line was tasked with striking the enemy's left front and flank. If all went according to plan, Hardee would enjoy an almost three-to-one numerical advantage. The remaining Confederate corps on the left under A. P.

---

2 Stephen Davis, *Atlanta Will Fall: Sherman, Joe Johnston, and the Yankee Heavy Battalions* (Wilmington, DE: Scholarly Resources, 2001), 131.

3 Felix G. De Fontaine, "Severe Fighting Around Atlanta," *Mobile Advertiser and Register*, July 31, 1864.

4 Thomas Livermore, *Numbers and Losses in the Civil War in America, 1861-1865* (Houghton, Mifflin and Company: Boston and New York, 1900), 122; McMurry, *Atlanta 1864*, 153.

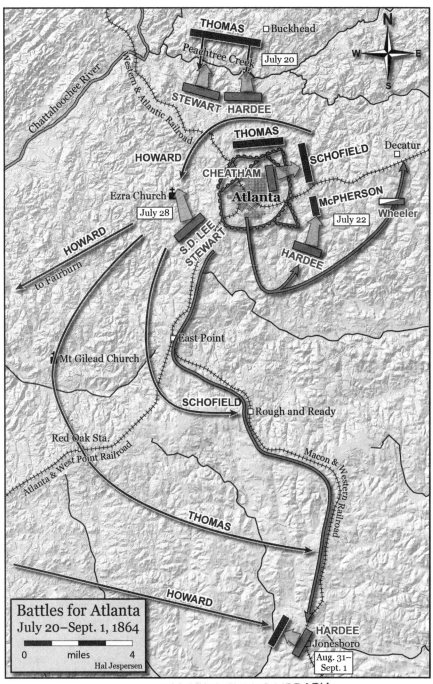

Battles for Atlanta
July 20–Sept. 1, 1864

0   miles   4

Hal Jespersen

Stewart was numerically inferior to Thomas. Stewart's role was to pressure the Federal front while Hardee rolled up the enemy line. As Hood intended, his attack initially caught Thomas in a vulnerable position. Hardee's thrust, however, was hours late, uncoordinated, and he committed only about one-third of his available command. The Confederate attack ultimately failed, and Hardee withdrew into his breastworks.

In *Decision in the West*, Castel blamed the Confederate failure at Peachtree Creek on Hardee's poor coordination and the "half hearted" performance of several of his regiments. Stewart's troops performed their role well, but lacked adequate numbers to make up for Hardee's weak effort. "In brief," wrote Castel, "where the Confederates had the advantage in strength, they did not fight well; and where they fought well, they were too weak. And because they did not fight well enough where they were strong enough, they lost. This in essence is the story of Peachtree Creek." Woodworth agreed and concluded the Confederate defeat was due, in part, to "Hardee's apparent lack of cordial cooperation."[5]

Both Hood's and Sherman's losses were about 10 percent of the forces engaged. Federal casualties totaled approximately 1,900 in killed, wounded, and captured, and Confederate losses were about 2,700—far fewer than the 4,800 casualties claimed by Sherman and repeated by many authors.[6]

Only two days after the failed attempt to destroy Thomas at Peachtree Creek, McPherson's Army of the Tennessee moved onto Bald Hill only two miles east of Atlanta and launched a howitzer bombardment of the city. McPherson was also within striking distance of the Macon and Western Railroad, the only remaining rail supply line into Atlanta. Cavalry reports informed Hood that McPherson's extreme left (southeast) flank was exposed, and that a large number of Federal supply wagons were situated in the Federal rear near Decatur. To Hood, this intelligence offered an opportunity to save the Macon and Western, end the bombardment of the civilians in Atlanta, and destroy or capture McPherson's wagon train of supplies. In addition, McPherson's command, although in proximity to Schofield's corps, was still separated from Thomas, who was several miles farther west (north of Atlanta). Hood decided to take the offensive a second time.

---

5   Castel, *Decision in the West*, 383; Woodworth, *Civil War Gazette*.

6   See Chapter 11 for a detailed discussion of Hood's losses at Peachtree Creek.

Hood's plan was to commit virtually all of his 30,000 available troops in a bold attack, the success of which depended upon a lengthy night march by Hardee's corps to reach McPherson's rear. If all went according to plan, Hardee would be in position to launch a surprise attack at sunrise on July 22. Unfortunately for the Army of Tennessee, the attack failed in large part because of the exhaustion of Hardee's troops, who did not succeed in reaching the Federal rear before daylight despite marching all night. Straggling also reduced Hardee's numbers so that when they did attack, only about two-thirds of their original strength was available to participate. In his book *Atlanta 1864*, Richard McMurry described Hardee's initial assaults by W. H. T. Walker's and William Bate's divisions as "delivered piecemeal by brigades" and "poorly led."[7]

Federal losses in the battle of Atlanta totaled 3,700 killed, wounded, and captured, including McPherson. Although Sherman's inflated estimate of 8,000 Southern losses is often repeated, Hood's casualties were in fact about 5,600. Hood's attack failed to destroy McPherson's army and repel Sherman, but the critical Macon and Western Railroad continued in operation and Atlanta remained in Confederate hands.[8]

Hood was again compelled to act less than a week later. During the early morning hours of July 28, he learned that Federal forces had withdrawn from their positions to the southeast, which seemed to indicate that the threat to the Macon and Western had subsided. The Federal Army of the Tennessee, however, which was now under the command of Gen. Oliver O. Howard, was observed maneuvering to the west of Atlanta. Hood promptly decided to attack the Federals before they could entrench in their new positions. Stephen D. Lee, who had arrived from Mississippi only one day earlier to assume command of Hood's former corps, was ordered to move two divisions into position along Lick Skillet Road to block Howard's advance. A. P. Stewart was also directed to move two of his three divisions out of the fortifications on Atlanta's northeast side and march down Lick Skillet behind Lee's divisions to a point beyond the Federal right flank. There, he would be in a position to attack Howard's right flank and rear. Hood's flanking plan was an attempt to do what the army was unable to achieve at the battles of Peachtree Creek and Atlanta. This time, however, Hood assigned the heavy fighting to Stewart's troops, who had

---

7   Richard McMurry, *Atlanta 1864: Last Chance for the Confederacy* (Lincoln, NE: University of Nebraska Press, 2000), 154.

8   See Chapter 11 for a detailed discussion of Hood's casualties in the July 22 battle of Atlanta.

performed admirably on July 20. Unlike the logistic difficulties encountered on July 22, ample time (a full 24 hours) was allowed for Lee and Stewart to assume their positions. Hardee's corps, which had been heavily engaged in the two previous battles, would remain in the Atlanta entrenchments to protect the city.

Lee moved his command into position and engaged the Federals about one-half mile north of Lick Skillet Road. Stewart's troops were moving along the road behind Lee to get into position when a message arrived from Lee informing Stewart that Hood had changed the plan. The new orders were for Stewart's divisions to immediately attack on Lee's left. Hood, however, had not changed the plan. Instead of continuing for another mile before deploying to sweep into the exposed Federal flank and rear, Stewart deployed his divisions on Lee's left and directly assaulted the entrenched Federal line.

The Federals easily repulsed the attack, suffering only 600 losses while inflicting some 2,900 casualties. "Lee disregarded his instructions and threw his men into a series of small-scale uncoordinated assaults," explained McMurry, and Stewart "concluded that he had no choice but to join the attacks." Castel agreed. "Historians will blame Hood for this slaughter," he explained in *Decision in the West*. "The true culprit is Stephen Lee. Disregarding his instructions and ignoring subsequent orders, he attempted to crush Sherman's supposedly vulnerable right flank with impromptu and disjointed attacks by his own and Stewart's troops long after the failure of the first one demonstrated that they had no chance of success—the exact duplicate of his conduct two weeks earlier in Tupelo, from which experience he obviously learned nothing. What he should have done," argued Castel, "is what Hood had directed him to do—simply keep open the Lick Skillet Road for the passage of Stewart's forces."[9]

Steven Woodworth described the Ezra Church battle as "an unmitigated flop—a complete fiasco from a Confederate point of view. It is attributable to a gross blunder by Stephen D. Lee." Woodworth speculated that the results might have been different had Hood himself been present. Hood, however, suspected that the Federal movement west of the city might be a diversion, and so remained in the Atlanta fortifications with Hardee's corps and the Georgia militia, sending instead Lee and Stewart to Ezra Church to deal with Howard. Hood could not have been in two places at once.[10]

---

9   McMurry, *Atlanta 1864*, 157; Castel, *Decision in the West*, 435.

10   Woodworth, *Civil War Gazette*.

Hood intended for Lee and Stewart to block, flank, and destroy a detached and outnumbered enemy force before they could entrench. His subordinates changed the plan.

Many modern authors stress the unpopularity of Hood's appointment and provide quotes and excerpts of critics to make their point. However, Hood had plenty of supporters, not only within the army but in the Southern press as well. Known as a fighter, the young general possessed optimism and enthusiasm that offered hope and inspired resolve among the war-weary Southern populace. "Amid the confusion and the destruction, the loneliness and the weariness, there rises one inspiring figure," opined the *Augusta Constitutionalist*. "Early or late, or by the branding campfire or the sun's first ray, may be seen a tall spare form, with a single arm and a single leg, a youthful face and a beaming eye in the line of the front. It is Hood."[11]

Although many officers of the Army of Tennessee opposed Hood's replacement of Johnston, some gained confidence as a result of Hood's efforts. "We still hold Atlanta," wrote division commander William Bate to Braxton Bragg on August 23, "& I think under the present regime will continue to do so. The movements & fights of the 20th & 22d and the intended sequel to that of the 28 of July were well conceived & exhibited a high order of military ability on the part of Genl. Hood." General Henry Clayton wrote to his wife the next day, August 24, "Our army which was very much depressed after the Battles of the 22d & 28th has very much improved in the past ten days. . . . I really feel encouraged that the war is soon to terminate."[12]

Cavalry commander Gen. Matthew C. Butler, who served in both the Army of Northern Virginia and, late in the war, under Johnston in North Carolina, wrote to Hood in 1874:

I have always said that I did not believe that Genl. Johnston would ever have fought Sherman, and I have been reckless enough to assert that under the circumstances of his army at Atlanta, the only thing left to be done was to make the movements which you did, as I suppose by Mr. Davis's directions, and I believe that the military critics of the

---

11 *Augusta Constitutionalist*, August 10, 1864.

12 Henry Clayton Papers, University of Alabama, Tuscaloosa; Braxton Bragg Papers, Western Reserve Historical Society, Cleveland, OH.

operations of that army—I believe the dispassionate and disinterested ones—will justify its wisdom.[13]

Although most modern students of the Civil War consider the July 1864 battles for Atlanta to be decisive defeats for Hood, many Southern soldiers viewed the engagements in a different light that summer. In his 1970 essay "Confederate Morale in the Atlanta Campaign of 1864," McMurry observed that letters from late July and August show "a surprisingly large number of Hood's men writing that they are confident of their ability to defeat Sherman," and that the three battles were "Southern victories" that halted Sherman's attempts to flank Atlanta.[14]

Johnston frustrated the Confederate high command with his unwillingness to communicate his plans and intentions, not only during the campaign in north Georgia but throughout his previous commands as well.[15] Unlike Johnston, Hood kept Richmond constantly acquainted with his plans. He wired Bragg on August 4, "I beg to assure you that I have no intention of abandoning this place, and that if no other recourse be left, I shall certainly give the enemy battle before I leave it."[16]

Davis had placed Hood in command to fight for and hold Atlanta, but after the three bloody July battles the Confederate president grew concerned about the increasing Confederate casualties and urged a measure of caution. "The loss consequent upon attacking him in his entrenchments," Davis told Hood, "requires you to avoid that if practicable." This admonishment of Hood's tactics was unfair and undeserved. All three assaults against portions of Sherman's command had been carefully calculated as flank attacks while the Federals were moving and before they could fully fortify. Unfortunately for the Confederates, unforeseen and unavoidable delays, among other factors, at the battles of Peachtree Creek and Atlanta gave the enemy time to entrench; at Ezra

13 M. C. Butler letter to John Bell Hood, July 18, 1874, John Bell Hood Personal Papers.

14 McMurry, "Confederate Morale in the Atlanta Campaign of 1864," 235.

15 *OR* 47, pt. 2, 1,303-1,311.

16 Gilder Lehrman Collection, New York City.

Church, S. D. Lee disregarded Hood's explicit instructions by launching a series of uncoordinated frontal attacks against fortified Federal positions.[17]

Hood achieved some success following the sharp setback at Ezra Church. In addition to maintaining control of Atlanta, Southern forces managed to land some heavy blows against Sherman's cavalry. A large contingent of Federal horsemen under Gens. Edward McCook and George Stoneman was sent on a raid to cut Hood's remaining railroad lifeline south of the city, and then possibly move farther south to Andersonville to release the thousands of Federal prisoners being held there. On July 31 and August 1, Joseph Wheeler's Confederate cavalry met and routed McCook's troopers south of Atlanta at Brown's Mill, and Stoneman and most of his cavalry were captured at Sunshine Church by Confederate forces under Alfred Iverson. With these defeats, Sherman lost about two-thirds of his entire mounted command. A few days later on August 5 and 6, a Federal infantry assault was repulsed west of Atlanta at Utoy Creek.[18]

Sherman, however, remained undeterred. During the last week of August, he shifted six of his seven infantry corps west of the city to cut the vital Macon and Western Railroad below Atlanta between Rough and Ready and Jonesboro. Marching on the Federal right, Howard's Army of the Tennessee reached Jonesboro about 15 miles south of the city. Unfortunately for Hood, Wheeler's cavalry was raiding Sherman's supply lines in north Georgia and thus was not available for reconnaissance purposes. Unsure whether this latest move by Sherman was a diversion, Hood remained in Atlanta with A. P. Stewart's corps and the Georgia militia and ordered his remaining two infantry corps under Hardee and Lee to move south to Jonesboro, with Hardee in charge of both corps. Hardee intended to attack the advancing Federals before they could construct fortifications, with the blow designed to fall upon the right flank of Gen. John Logan's corps. Hood was confident that Hardee had enough men to drive the Federals away and alleviate the threat to the railroad, not realizing that the bulk of Sherman's entire army was involved in the movement. However, just as had occurred in the Confederate attacks at Peachtree Creek and Atlanta, Hardee's and Lee's troops arrived late. Patrick Cleburne's division took almost

---

17 Hiram H. Hardesty, *The Military History of Ohio: Its Border Annals, Its Part in the Indian Wars, in the War of 1812, in the Mexican War, and in the War of the Rebellion* (New York, NY: H. H. Hardesty, 1889), 229.

18 Davis, *Atlanta Will Fall*, 155.

12 hours to move as many miles. According to Albert Castel, Lee's exhausted troops had little sleep. Scores of men dropped out, "unable or unwilling to go on."[19]

Hardee ended up frontally attacking two Union corps on August 31 and was easily repulsed with the loss of approximately 2,000 men. The fate of the city of Atlanta was effectively sealed when Howard's artillery unlimbered only 600 yards from the Jonesboro railroad depot, cutting the only remaining rail line into Atlanta.[20]

ॐ ॐ

It is commonly asserted, not always in a disrespectful or critical way, that Hood's physical condition kept him from overseeing important details—most notably in the fighting around Atlanta, where historian Steven Woodworth noted that Hood's physical incapacitation impeded him from "exercising fully effective command of a Confederate field army," and later that November at Spring Hill, Tennessee. The battles of Ezra Church and Jonesboro are often cited as examples of defeats attributable, at least in part, to Hood's absence. Although Hood wrote nothing of his specific reasoning, it seems clear that his motivation for not accompanying part of his army in the two battles mentioned was not due to his physical limitations but his desire to remain in the place of greatest potential peril—the fortifications of Atlanta. During those times, the city was held by only a single infantry corps and a small militia contingent, which would be heavily outnumbered if Sherman decided to launch a direct assault. No general could be in two places simultaneously.[21]

Before both Ezra Church and Jonesboro, Hood received intelligence that large Federal forces were moving to the west of Atlanta. In late August at Jonesboro, with most of Wheeler's cavalry in north Georgia and Tennessee ineffectively harassing Sherman's supply lines, Hood's ability to gather accurate and reliable intelligence was limited. According to historian Stephen Newton,

---

19 Castel, *Decision in the West*, 391.

20 After the loss of Atlanta, Hardee requested a transfer and was sent to command the Department of South Carolina, Georgia, and Florida. Hardee—who had been defeated in the battles of Peachtree Creek, Atlanta, and Jonesboro, and who would go on to lose the coastal cities of Savannah and Charleston—has retained a relatively good reputation in Civil War history.

21 Woodworth, *Civil War Gazette*.

Wheeler was conducting "a foolhardy raid that left John B. Hood's outnumbered army blind when Sherman started to maneuver south of Atlanta." Had he known that Sherman's maneuvers were not diversions, Hood—always a hands-on combat field commander throughout his career—undoubtedly would have accompanied his forces to Ezra Church and Jonesboro.[22]

By way of comparison, Robert E. Lee's reputation has not suffered because of the mistakes made that triggered the battle at Gettysburg on July 1, 1863. Rather, most of the blame has been placed upon his cavalry commander Jeb Stuart, whose tardiness deprived Lee of precious intelligence that would have helped his commander determine the location of the various segments of the Federal Army of the Potomac. Historians have gone out of their way to exonerate Lee for sending Stuart away from the army at the beginning of the campaign. Yet, very little has been written about how Hood faced the same situation during the Atlanta Campaign, and how adequate intelligence (Wheeler's presence) might have enabled him to adopt different tactics. It is reasonable to conclude that if Hood's cavalry had provided him with accurate and timely information about Sherman's movements to Ezra Church and Jonesboro, Hood would not have remained in the city while others fought those battles.

Hood evacuated Atlanta during the evening of September 1 and early morning of September 2. His tenacious but failed defensive effort to save the city incurred about 12,000 casualties, or roughly one-quarter of his army. Stanley Horn, not known for his generous compliments of Hood, wrote that "although Sherman and his generals have shown an inclination to belittle Hood as a mere headlong, impetuous fighter of no particular skill, his rapid hammer blows had served to slow down their aggressiveness." Horn continued, "In one of his dispatches Sherman grumbled that he could not get his men to move a hundred yards without entrenching—proof enough of wholesome respect for their bellicose antagonist."[23]

---

22 Stephen Newton, "Overrated Generals," *North and South* (December 2009), 15.

23 As detailed in Chapter 11 of this book, Confederate casualties for the battles of Peachtree Creek, Atlanta (Decatur), and Ezra Church were 9,800, plus 2,200 casualties for Jonesboro. Davis, *Atlanta Will Fall*, 185. The total casualties for Hood's four attacks around Atlanta were approximately 24 percent of the total troop strength of the Army of Tennessee of 50,414 on July 10, 1864, one week before Hood took command. See also, Horn, *The Army of Tennessee*, 368.

Offensive efforts to break sieges are always bloody affairs. Hood's attacks against Sherman around Atlanta are often portrayed as a foolish waste of life in an attempt to achieve the impossible. In a comparable situation in front of Richmond and Petersburg, however, Robert E. Lee's offensive on March 25, 1865, against Fort Stedman is rarely judged in a similar manner. Francis Miller and Robert Lanier described the circumstances surrounding the Fort Stedman effort:

> In an interview with General Gordon, Lee laid before him his reports, which showed how completely he understood the situation. Of his own 50,000 men but 35,000 were fit for duty. Lee's estimate of the forces of Grant was between 140,000 and 150,000. Coming up from Knoxville was Schofield with as estimated force of 30,000 superb troops. From the valley Grant was bringing up nearly 20,000 more, against whom, as Lee expressed it, he "could oppose scarcely a vidette." Sherman was approaching from North Carolina, and his force when united with Schofield's would reach 80,000. It was impossible, and yet it was after this, that Gordon made his charge.[24]

The all-but forlorn attack failed miserably and cost Lee an estimated 2,700 casualties—a sizeable portion of what was left of his depleted Army of Northern Virginia. Yet, Lee evades historical censure for continuing to fight when the fate of Richmond, Petersburg, and even the Confederacy itself appeared to be already decided. Hood's attacks at Atlanta and his later actions at Franklin and Nashville, however, are often considered a useless squandering of Southern lives. Men leading armies under the best of circumstances are tasked with making extremely difficult decisions under unimaginable duress. Commanders in desperate situations, such as Lee at Fort Stedman and Joe Johnston at Bentonville, had little choice but to attempt what later appear to have been hopeless attacks.

For his part, the man who appointed Hood to command the Army of Tennessee did not view his offensive efforts as useless or meaningless. "No one was more anxious than myself to prevent the fall of Atlanta," wrote Jefferson Davis to Georgia Senator Herschel V. Johnson. "I was not among those who deemed that result inevitable as soon as the enemy had crossed the

---

24 John S. Salmon, *Virginia Civil War Battlefield Guide* (Mechanicsville, PA: Stackpole Books 2001), 450; Francis T. Miller, *The Photographic History of the Civil War: The Decisive Battles* (Springfield, MA: Patriot Publishing, 1911), 287.

Chattahoochie, and I was not willing that it should be yielded before manly blows should be struck for its preservation."[25]

Although Hood is frequently condemned for blaming his subordinates for the Army of Tennessee's defeats, he was not alone. One of the Western armies' most talented brigadiers, Francis M. Cockrell, agreed: "Many attribute the fall [of Atlanta] to the failure of Lee's Corps to fight as was expected of them." James H. Wilson, a prominent Federal cavalry general, seemed of like mind when he wrote in his memoirs that Hood's campaigns were "ably planned," but needed more resources and "better subordinates" to succeed.

Another Federal commander, Gen. Francis Blair, largely excused Hood for the defeats at Atlanta. The attack on Sherman's exposed left flank outside Atlanta on July 22, predicted Blair, "would be rated, among military men, as probably the most brilliant of the war, and that the escape of the Union army from ruin was owing more to supineness in some Southern officers than from any skill in the Federal generals." The problem confronting Johnston and Hood, continued Blair, was that "they had not men enough to contend with Sherman's army. It was natural enough, after the failure of General Johnston to check our advance, other tactics should be employed, and no man could have been found who could have executed this policy with greater skill, ability and vigor than General Hood." Montgomery Blair, a member of Lincoln's cabinet and Francis Blair's brother, agreed: "If half the enterprise exhibited by Hood had been shown by his subordinates, the ranks of the Federals, weakened by the men sent to oppose the victorious onset of the Confederate-in-chief would have been broken through and Sherman put to flight, or collapsed into surrender." Colonel Irving Buck, Patrick Cleburne's adjutant, wrote of the battle of Atlanta, "General Hood had conceived a move worthy of Stonewall Jackson, in attempting to strike and crush Sherman's left wing in a flanking movement."[26]

---

25 Hudson Strode, *Jefferson Davis: American Patriot, 1808-1861* (New York: Harcourt, Brace, 1955), 89.

26 Francis M. Cockrell letter, Letters Sent and Received by the Confederate Secretary of War/Letters Sent and Received by the Confederate Adjutant and Inspector General, National Archives, 1727-H-1864; Wilson, *Under the Old Flag*, 44-45; *New Orleans Times Picayune,*

The poor scholarship endemic of Hood's role with the Army of Tennessee is on full display at the Atlanta Cyclorama and Civil War Museum. The very impressive cyclorama—perhaps the largest painting in the world at 42 feet tall and 358 feet long—offers a sweeping 360-degree, three-dimensional panoramic portrayal of the July 22 Atlanta battle. Some 80,000 people visit the cyclorama each year. The wall of the main gallery includes portraits of the commanding generals of the Federal and Confederate armies. Curiously, Joe Johnston appears as the commander of the Army of Tennessee, with his portrait opposite Federal army commander William T. Sherman. The only problem is that Johnston was not there during the fighting on July 22. In fact, he was in Macon, Georgia, because he had been removed from command and replaced by Hood five days prior to the battle depicted on the cyclorama. Johnston had nothing to do with either the conception or execution of the July 22 engagement.[27]

ॐ ॐ

In his 1993 book *The Campaign for Atlanta*, local historian William Scaife provided his version of an often-repeated and widely known incident following the Confederate defeat west of Atlanta at Ezra Church on November 28, 1864. His source is a memoir penned by Federal officer Gen. Jacob Cox. "General Jacob D. Cox later related a frequently repeated story which seemed to reflect the futility of Hood's impetuous tactics," explained Scaife. "After the fighting ceased, one of Logan's pickets called out across the lines at twilight: 'Well, Johnny, how many of you are left?' A despondent Confederate replied, still maintaining a semblance of the sense of humor so essential to a soldier: 'Oh, about enough for another killing.'" General Cox places the story in late July without providing any more specific information. As it turns out, Cox was wrong.[28]

September 8, 1879; Mrs. C. M. Winkler, *Life and Character of General John B. Hood* (Austin, TX: Draughon and Lambert, 1885), 37. Blair quote from *New Orleans Times Picayune*, September 8, 1879; Irving A. Buck, *Cleburne and His Command* (Jackson, TN: McCowat-Mercer Press, 1959), 234.

27 Joseph E. Johnston, *Narrative of Military Operations Directed During the Civil War* (New York, NY: Da Capo, 1990), 369.

28 William R. Scaife, *The Campaign for Atlanta* (Atlanta: W. R. Scaife, 1993), 108; Jacob D. Cox, *Atlanta* (New York: Charles Scribner's Sons, 1882), 186.

The original source for the story is John W. Clemson, who told the tale in an article entitled "Surprised the Johnnies" in the September 1897 issue of the *National Tribune*. According to Clemson, the 46th Ohio Infantry was entrenched before the Confederate lines and came up with a trick: "a fake charge" with bugles blowing and soldiers yelling. When the startled Rebels raised their heads above their parapet, they would be shot in "a galling fire from well-aimed Spencer rifles." Afterward, a taunting Yankee called out, "Say, Johnny, how many of you are there over there?" A Confederate replied, "Well I guess there's enough for another killin." The incident, routinely presented by authors to illustrate the discouragement of the Army of Tennessee and their disdain for their new commander's tactics, didn't have anything to do with Ezra Church in late July, as Cox wrote, or even any of the fighting around Atlanta. In fact, it happened at Dallas, Georgia, on May 30 during Joseph Johnston's tenure—a full six weeks before Hood even took command.[29]

Other versions of the same story permeate Civil War literature. Even iconic writer Shelby Foote and the National Park Service got it wrong. Writing of the battle of Ezra Church in his acclaimed three-volume narrative *The Civil War*, Foote included the incident this way: "'Say Johnny,' one of Logan's soldiers called across the breastworks, into the outer darkness. 'How many of you are there left?' 'Oh about enough for another killin,' a butternut replied." The National Park Service's e-library conveys its own version of the story (without a source) as set at Ezra Church two months after the actual event transpired.[30]

Such is the state of Civil War literature, where too many authors simply repeat earlier writers or, in the case of primary sources, often neglect to confirm their accuracy or credibility. Jacob Cox, the primary source authors use to convey this Ezra Church fable, penned his memoirs 24 years after the war and almost certainly confused the Dallas incident with a similarly worded—though quite different—occurrence at Ezra Church. In a letter to his wife on July 29, Federal officer Maj. Thomas T. Taylor wrote about a Rebel officer captured at Ezra Church being asked how many troops Hood had with him. According to Taylor, the captive officer replied, "Enough to make two more killings," which is often interpreted as meaning the despondent prisoner was grimly telling his

29 John W. Clemson, "Surprised the Johnnies," *National Tribune*, September 30, 1897, 150.

30 Shelby Foote, *The Civil War: A Narrative*, 3 vols. (New York: Random House, 1974), vol. 3: *Red River to Appomattox*, 490; See also http://www.nps.gov/history/online_books/civil_war_series/7/ sec10.htm.

captors that after two more defeats Hood would be out of men. In fact, a careful reading suggests just the opposite meaning. The Rebel officer's choice of words—"enough to make two more killings"—suggests instead that in this particular instance, the Southern officer was defiantly warning his captors that Hood's army was ready, willing, and able to inflict more killings upon them.

Taylor wrote another letter to his wife the following week that supports this interpretation. Although by all accounts a loyal and dedicated Federal officer, Taylor had grown disenchanted with the war and was a harsh critic of Abraham Lincoln. On August 10, he wrote:

> Now however I can say to a certainty that I am a "conscript," held to service against my will. How long I shall be so held I know not, but can assure you that I shall retire from the service as quickly as it is possible to do so. Our government is [illegible]—our rulers are despots—the administration the most despotic of any in the world, at the present age is reckless and corrupt. As an executive officer Lincoln has proved a miserable failure. His vacillating policy besides prolonging this war and [illegible] it from its original course and design has cost the nation thousands of lives and millions of treasure. His hypocritical treatment and unwarranted course of action has alienated thousands and hundreds of the best population of the Union from the support of the Government. If Lincoln were the Government, the embodiment of American freedom, I would curse it, damn the whole institution and shaking the dirt from my feet emigrate to Brazil or some other empire where an intelligent and just man governs.[31]

Although the Confederate defeat at Ezra Church was certainly demoralizing to many in Hood's army, scholars should refrain from illustrating the discouragement with the common "oh, about enough for another killin'" quote from Jacob Cox's memoirs. Perhaps a more suitable summation is McMurry's conclusion, as noted earlier, about the "surprisingly large number of Hood's men writing that they are confident of their ability to defeat Sherman," and who looked upon the three major battles as "Southern victories" that kept Sherman out of Atlanta.

---

31 Thomas T. Taylor Letters, Ohio Historical Society, Columbus, OH.

Chapter 6

"Perhaps nobody has changed the course of
history as much as historians."

— *Franklin P. Jones*

Desperate Times,
Desperate Measures:
The Tennessee Campaign

a notable characteristic of the often slanted interpretation and one-sided portrayal of John Bell Hood's military career is the highly critical account of the conception and planning of the failed 1864 Tennessee Campaign. The incomplete and often biased presentation of Hood's final campaign has, unfortunately, largely defined his otherwise remarkable military career.

It had long been the desire of the Confederate government that a major offensive movement be undertaken into Tennessee. In fact, Joseph Johnston was been placed in command of a heavily reinforced Army of Tennessee in early 1864 with the expectation that he would launch just such an offensive. After the fall of Atlanta, the need for an invasion of Tennessee became even more critical. Despite postwar denials, Jefferson Davis publicly announced Hood's planned move into Tennessee (although the details were left to Hood and to P. G. T. Beauregard).

Hood's memoirs recorded for posterity his personal and unambiguous account of how the Tennessee Campaign was conceived and molded into a workable plan. Far from being solely dependent on one man's judgment, the details of the campaign, so crucial to the war effort in late 1864, was the product of consultation, advice, and approval at the highest levels of the Confederate government and War Department. Hood's long account (reproduced below) is important reading for the purposes of our discussion:

> No better proof can be adduced of the wisdom of this campaign than the foregoing dispatches, together with our success in drawing Sherman back, within ten days, to Snake Creek Gap, the identical position he occupied in May, 1864. Had the Army been in the fighting condition in which it was at Dalton, or at Franklin, I feel confident of our ability to have at least so crippled the enemy in pitched battle as to have retained possession of the mountains of Georgia. When I consider also the effect of this movement upon the Federal commanders, I cannot but become impressed with the facility with which the Confederate Army would have taken possession of the country as far north as the Ohio [River], if it had marched in the early Spring of '64, to the rear of the Federals (who were at Chattanooga assembling their forces); and when, in addition to the troops at Dalton, Polk's Army, Longstreet's Corps, and ten thousand men from Beauregard, were proffered for that purpose.

> After halting two days at Cross Roads, I decided to make provision for twenty days' supply of rations in the haversacks and wagons; to order a heavy reserve of artillery to accompany the Army, in order to overcome any serious opposition by the Federal gunboats; to cross the Tennessee at or near Guntersville, and destroy Sherman's communications, at Stevenson and Bridgeport; to move upon Thomas and Schofield, and attempt to route and capture their Army before it could reach Nashville. I intended then to march upon that city where I would supply the Army and reinforce it, if possible, by the accessions from Tennessee. I was imbued with the belief that I could accomplish this feat, afterward march northeast, pass the Cumberland River at some crossing where the gunboats, if too formidable at other points, were unable to interfere; then move into Kentucky, and take position with our left at or near Richmond, and our right extending toward Hazelgreen, with Pound and Stoney Gaps, in the Cumberland Mountains, at our rear.

> In this position I could threaten Cincinnati, and recruit the Army from Kentucky and Tennessee; the former State was reported, at this juncture, to be more aroused and embittered against the Federals than at any period of the war. While Sherman was debating between the alternative of following our Army or marching through Georgia, I hoped, by rapid movements, to achieve these results.

If Sherman cut loose and moved south—as I then believed he would do after I left his front without previously worsting him in battle—I would occupy at Richmond, Kentucky, a position of superior advantage, as Sherman, upon his arrival at the sea coast, would be forced to go on board ship, and, after a long detour by water and land, repair to the defense of Kentucky and Ohio or march direct to the support of Grant. If he returned to confront my forces, or followed me directly from Georgia into Tennessee and Kentucky, I hoped then to be in position to offer battle; and, if blessed with victory, to send reinforcements to General Lee, in Virginia, or to march through the gaps in the Cumberland Mountains, and attack Grant in rear. This latter course I would pursue in the event of defeat or of inability to offer battle to Sherman. If on the other hand he marched to join Grant, I could pass through the Cumberland gaps to Petersburg, and attack Grant in rear, at least two weeks before he, Sherman, could render him assistance. This move, I believed, would defeat Grant, and allow General Lee, in command of our entire Armies, to march upon Washington or turn and annihilate Sherman.

Such is the plan which during the 15th and 16th, as we lay in bivouac near Lafayette, I maturely considered, and determined to endeavor to carry out. In accordance therewith, I decided to move to Gadsden, where, if I met General Beauregard, I intended to submit to him, the foregoing plan of operations, expressing at the same time my conviction that therein lay the only hope to bring victory to the Confederate arms. . . .

Shortly after my arrival at Gadsden, General Beauregard reached the same point: I at once unfolded to him my plan, and requested that he confer apart with the corps commanders, Lieutenant-Generals Lee and Stewart and Major-General Cheatham. If after calm deliberation he deemed it expedient we should remain upon the Alabama line and attack Sherman, or take position, entrench, and finally follow on his rear when he moved south, I would of course acquiesce, albeit with reluctance. If, contrariwise, he should agree to my proposed plan to cross into Tennessee, I would move immediately to Guntersville, thence to Stevenson, Bridgeport, and Nashville.

This important question at issue was discussed during the greater part of one night, with maps before us. General Beauregard at length took the ground that if I engaged in the projected campaign, it would be necessary to leave in Georgia all the cavalry at present with the Army, in order to watch and harass Sherman in case he moved south, and to instruct Forrest to join me as soon as I crossed the Tennessee river. To this proposition I acceded. After he had held a separate conference with the corps commanders, we again debated several hours over the course of action to be pursued; and, during the interview, I discovered that he had gone to work in earnest to ascertain, in person, the true condition of the Army; that he had sought information not only from the corps commanders, but from a number of officers and had reached the same conclusion I had formed at Lafayette: we were not competent to offer pitched battle to Sherman, nor could we follow him south without causing our retrograde movement to be construed by the troops into a recurrence of retreat, which would entail desertions and render the army of little or no use in its opposition to the enemy's march through Georgia. After two days deliberation General Beauregard authorized me, on the evening of the 21st of October, to proceed to the execution of my plan of operations into Tennessee. At this point, it may be considered, closed the campaign to the Alabama line.[1]

In spite of Hood's explanation, modern authors have taken an opposing view of his rationale as well as his competence to accomplish the mission. In his biography of the general, historian Richard McMurry—by comparison with most other historians a generally sympathetic and very careful Hood scholar— labeled the Tennessee Campaign an "unrealistic dream," and in a later publication described it as "probably the most poorly planned and executed major campaign of the war." In their treatment of Hood's Tennessee Campaign entitled *Five Tragic Hours: The Battle of Franklin*, Thomas Connelly and James McDonough seemed to concur with McMurry, alluding to the abundance of "outright errors" in Hood's plan. They concluded with a suggestion that the failed campaign should be utilized for military study: "the difficulties and outright errors in such a plan were so profuse that the scheme would have made a textbook study at West Point." Likewise, James McPherson depicted Hood's late 1864 plan to press into Tennessee as one that "seemed to have been scripted in never-never land."[2]

Eric Jacobson, one of Hood's most supportive modern authors, described Hood's 1864 strategy as "grandiose," and criticized Hood for wanting to go north: "Furthermore, as he readied for the offensive, the old and dated dream of the Ohio River and what lay beyond came alive." There is no record of Hood desiring to take his army beyond the Ohio River.[3]

1   Hood, *Advance and Retreat*, 266-269.

2   McMurry, *John Bell Hood and the War for Southern Independence*, 167; Richard McMurry, *Two Great Rebel Armies: An Essay in Confederate Military History* (Chapel Hill: University of North Carolina Press, 1989), 130-131; James L. McDonough and Thomas Connelly, *Five Tragic Hours: The Battle of Franklin* (Knoxville: The University of Tennessee Press, 1991), 15; McPherson, *Battle Cry of Freedom*, 811.

3   Jacobson, *For Cause and For Country*, 45, 49.

In retrospect, it is easy to judge the late-war Confederate invasion of Tennessee as unrealistic, unnecessary, and futile. In late 1864, however, Southern politicians urged the military to act. In a speech to the Confederate Congress on November 29, 1864—delivered during Hood's flank march to Spring Hill, as fate would have it—Tennessee's Senator Gustavus Henry appealed to the Confederate War Department with flamboyant eloquence:

> The Jews when they were carried away into captivity in Babylon, never looked more anxiously for deliverance than they are looking even now for the Confederate army to enter (Tennessee), and strike from their limbs their galling chains. They are now, sir, standing on tiptoe, straining their eyes to catch the first glimpse of the Confederate flag as it floats out upon the wild winds free on yonder hill, and long for its coming as the hunted heart pants for the water brook. I confidently predict, if our army enters (Tennessee) and maintains its position there for three months, that its numbers will be doubled.
>
> I further predict, Mr. President, if our army goes into Kentucky and stays there three months, and gives to that people any assurance that we will hold it and stand by them and not, by coming speedily away, hand them over to the ravenous wolves who will thirst for their blood, thousands will join our army, and re-enact the scenes of the "dark and bloody ground," and add new lustre to this, the most memorable struggle in the annals of time, in which Kentucky has not as yet, as a State, participated. I do not overestimate it when I predict that fifty thousand as gallant men as ever shouldered a musket or hung a sabre to the thigh, will be added as fresh recruits to our army from Kentucky and Tennessee. Sir, they constitute the best recruiting grounds now in America. The people of both States are now ripe for action, and will come to the rescue of our gallant army with alacrity.[4]

It is quite revealing that a copy of Henry's speech was found in one of the recently discovered collections of Hood's personal papers. Among the artifacts held by a private collector in Fort Worth, Texas, are Hood family photographs, news articles, memorabilia, and miscellaneous ephemera. Hood, who died in New Orleans in 1879, kept a typescript of the Tennessee senator's speech in his collection of important papers, which strongly suggests that Senator Henry's

---

4 Tennessee Senator Gustavus A. Henry speech before the Confederate senate, November 29, 1864. A typescript of Henry's speech was retained by John Bell Hood and is among a small collection of Hood's personal papers and other artifacts owned by Wesley Clark, hereafter cited as The Gen. John B. Hood Collection of Wes Clark, Dallas, Texas.

view on the contemporary public mindset and importance of the Tennessee invasion may have been a primary influence on Hood's decision-making in the winter of 1864.[5]

~p ‍

In *Autumn of Glory*, Thomas Connelly ominously titled his chapter on the Tennessee Campaign "Dreams of Glory," a clear foretelling of the cynical interpretation and portrayal that followed. Writing of Hood's postwar explanation, Connelly called him a liar: "Hood was blatantly dishonest. He asserted in his memoirs that from the outset he had planned to defeat forces accumulating in Tennessee under the command of Generals George Thomas and John Schofield. Yet Hood did not even know such forces were accumulating." (Surely Connelly did not believe that Hood and his superiors assumed Tennessee would be surrendered by Lincoln and Grant without a fight?)[6]

Continuing his allegations, Connelly strongly opined in eloquent detail for several paragraphs (supported by no primary sources) that Hood's invasion was little short of lunacy. Moreover, Connelly belittled Hood's long-range plan of moving to Tennessee, Kentucky, and Virginia, asserting that he had no short-term plan for contending with Schofield and Thomas: "Hood's objectives in the march were clouded. Apparently the general himself was not certain where he was going. . . . Later he claimed that he knew that Thomas was at Nashville, separated from Schofield. . . . Thus, he and others created the impression of a race for Columbia that probably was more fiction than reality."[7]

The historical record conclusively proves Connelly was wrong. General Henry Clayton wrote to his wife on September 21 from Palmetto, Georgia, that "The troops are delighted at the idea of an advance move and in most excellent spirits." Clayton wrote to her again on October 15 from Lafayette, Georgia: "The spirit of our men is improving daily. The Tennesseans are perfectly jubilant at the prospect of going again into their state." On November 8, Clayton confirmed the movement to Nashville, writing: "The impression is that we move in the direction of Nashville." A regimental surgeon, Dr. Urban

---

5   Ibid.

6   Connelly, *Autumn of Glory*, 483, 490-493.

7   Ibid., 490.

Owen, wrote to his wife on November 19, 1864, from Florence, Alabama, confirming that Hood knew Federal forces commanded by Schofield had been detached from Nashville: "Our Gen'ls all say that our route is to get between Thomas's army and Nashville." (At that time "Thomas's army" consisted solely of Schofield's single corps, camped in Pulaski, Tennessee.)[8]

Many scholars have innocently misinterpreted Hood's long-range plans and intentions for the campaign, among them bestselling novelist and military author Winston Groom. After evacuating Atlanta, Groom wrote, Hood decided to "march his army up to capture Chicago, an expedition that ended in tragedy with the battles in and around Nashville, Tenn." In fact, Hood said nothing about Chicago; rather, it was Ulysses S. Grant who wrote, "If I had been in Hood's place I would have gone to Louisville and on north until I came to Chicago. . . . We would have had to raise new levies. I was never so anxious during the war as at that time." The popular concept of Chicago being a possible goal of Hood originated from Grant's pen, not Hood's.[9]

After the fall of Atlanta, Hood and others were convinced of the urgent need for the Army of Tennessee to take the offensive. Beginning with the defeat at Missionary Ridge in late 1863, the army had retreated steadily from the mountains of north Georgia in the spring of 1864 to the gates of Atlanta in mid-July. After the change of commanders, the Confederate army fought a series of large-scale battles in July and August, but Atlanta fell in early September. Although still a potent force numbering some 40,000 battle-hardened veterans and support personnel, the Army of Tennessee, like all Confederate armies at this point in the war, was plagued by desertions during the tenures of both Johnston and Hood.

Hood believed that taking the offensive was absolutely necessary in order to restore the morale of the army, and he was not alone in this estimation. In his official report dated January 30, 1865, corps commander Stephen D. Lee commented on the disposition of the army after the Atlanta Campaign but before the movement north into Tennessee: "It was my opinion that the Army should take up the offensive, with the hope that favorable opportunities would

8 Henry Clayton Papers, University of Alabama, Tuscaloosa; Jacobson, *For Cause and For Country*, 84.

9 Winston Groom review of Russell Bonds's *War Like the Thunderbolt*, in the *Wall Street Journal*, August 28, 2009; John Russell Young, *Around the World with General Grant*, 2 vols. (New York: The American News Company, New York, 1879), vol. 2, 294.

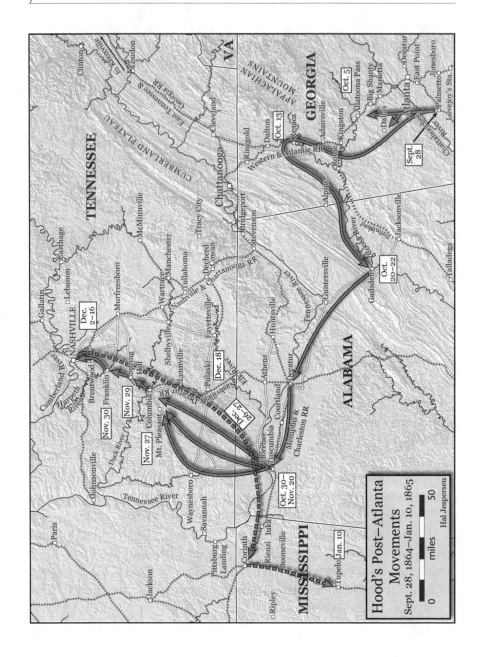

Hood's Post–Atlanta
Movements
Sept. 28, 1864–Jan. 10, 1865

be offered for striking the enemy successfully, thus ensuring the efficiency of the army for future operations." Another of Hood's corps commanders, A. P. Stewart, concurred that the Army of Tennessee's low morale after losing Atlanta made an offensive movement of paramount importance: "I deem it proper to say that after the fall of Atlanta, the condition of the army and other considerations rendered it necessary, in my judgment, that an offensive campaign should be made in the enemy's rear and on his line of communications."[10]

A Canadian journalist who interviewed Hood in mid-November 1865 recalled the general's explanation for the invasion of Tennessee: "It was necessary for him to go on, he said, for the men were losing spirit by failure, and only some bold effort could reanimate them."[11] As Hood explained in an 1867 letter to postbellum Southern author Sarah A. Dorsey, "My experience as a soldier taught me at an early day during the Revolution that an army could not retreat in the face of an enemy without great loss in spirit and numbers." Noting that the Army of Tennessee was depleted when he took command in the summer of 1864, having lost more than 20,000 men during Johnston's "unfortunate" retreat, Hood was promoted to lead the Western army "although I did not desire the command." "The holding of my position around Atlanta for forty-three days improved the morale of the soldiers," Hood claimed, "but finally being forced to abandon this untenable city, again causing the recommence of retreat, my army was very much discouraged." Thereafter, according to Hood,

All the corps commanders expressed the opinion that to stand still was certain ruin, and recommended that the offensive be taken as the only hope of improving & increasing the army. Mississippi, Alabama, Georgia & the Carolinas had no men at the ready that could be sent to my aid, I decided to push forward into Tennessee, attempt the capture of Nashville, move into Kentucky and open communications with Genl. Lee.

This accomplished I thought would compel Genl. Sherman to abandon the swamps of Georgia and accept battle between the waters of the Cumberland & Ohio.

10 *OR* 39, pt. 1, 810; Bromfield L. Ridley, *Battles and Sketches of the Army of Tennessee* (Mexico, MO: Missouri Publishing, 1906), 443.

11 "Hood's Version of His Tennessee Campaign," *Louisville Daily Journal*, November 19, 1865. Typescript provided to the author by Jamie Gillum, Franklin, TN.

The capture of Nashville and regaining so much lost territory, I was quite certain would give new life to our people, recruit our thinned ranks, and give that tone to the army I had been so long accustomed in Virginia, [and] would ensure victory to our arms, and finally secure our freedom.

"Accidents, however, perhaps beyond human control," concluded Hood, "caused the campaign to fail at a time the fruits of victory were seemingly within our grasp."[12]

In an address to Confederate veterans delivered in 1872, Hood explained the importance of aggressiveness when he said that "twenty-five thousand soldiers, made veterans by offensive war, were equal to fifty thousand kept constantly on the defensive." Robert E. Lee and Stonewall Jackson, Hood explained, "appreciated the supreme necessity of maintaining splendent and spotless the morale of an army. They knew that to remain in trenches, even for a short time, was to dampen the ardor of the bravest. Lee and Jackson," he added, "knew not how to retreat day after day in the face of the enemy, losing more in stragglers than in killed and wounded, nor how to demoralize their armies by throwing up breastworks by day, to be given up in the stillness of night, and thus unfit their men for battle save within well-fortified lines."[13]

Contrary to popular belief, the movement into Tennessee had a positive impact on the army. "The army is a unit," Col. E. J. Harvie informed the Confederate War Department in Richmond, "and buoyant with hope." Dr. Charles Quintard agreed. A chaplain in the Army of Tennessee, Quintard recorded in his diary on October 17, 1864, that "The spirit of the Army has been greatly improved by this forward movement." Dr. Urban Owen wrote on November 19, 1864, just before the invasion, "Our whole army is eager to move onward. . . . Our army is very confident and in fine health." General Henry Clayton was also in good spirits and wrote about it on November 8: "We have the brightest anticipations—our march so far has been entirely satisfactory. Our troops are perfectly jubilant. They are well clad and in all respects we are ready to move forward, or do whatever else our General may order." Clayton continued: "I had a review of my Division today & it looked

---

12 J. B. Hood letter to Sarah A. Dorsey, March 30, 1867, John Bell Hood Personal Papers.

13 John Bell Hood, Oration, delivered before the *Annual Meeting of the Survivors' Association of the State of South Carolina, December 12, 1872* (Charleston, SC: Walker, Evans and Cogswell, Printers, 1873), Rosanna Blake Library of Confederate History, Marshall University, Huntington, WV.

finely. Whatever our people at home may do or say I do not believe our army can ever be conquered. We may suffer temporary defeat, but will rally and fight on." Private Sam Watkins of the 1st Tennessee Infantry later recalled how "every pulse did beat and leap, and how every heart did throb with emotions of joy" as the invasion commenced and the army approached Tennessee.[14]

In contrast to the cynical and often belittling portrayal of Hood's Tennessee Campaign set forth by most modern authors, the tone of earlier historians toward both Hood and the concept of the offensive move north was much different. Typical of the more composed and reasoned tone of early 20th century commentators was David S. Muzzey's 1922 assessment of Hood's movement:

> General Hood, who had replaced Johnston when Sherman was approaching Atlanta, left Georgia to take care of itself as best it could and struck across the Tennessee River to crush Thomas. If he succeeded it would mean the undoing of Chattanooga, the reoccupation of Tennessee, and the opportunity for Hood with his victorious army to move eastward and cooperate with either the Confederate troops in the Carolinas or Lee's hard-pressed army near Richmond. The anxiety of the men in high position, from Lincoln down through Stanton, Grant and Halleck, was great. Grant repeatedly urged Thomas to attack and even went so far as to designate General Logan to supersede him. But Thomas knew his ground and coolly waited until he was ready. On December 13 [sic] he completely shattered Hood's force before Nashville. The Southern army, which had numbered 53,000 when Johnston had faced Sherman, melted away and Hood was relieved from the service at his own request.[15]

Impartial and objective observer Lord Garnet Joseph Wolseley, adjutant general of the British army, described Hood's Tennessee Campaign not as a reckless, vain attempt by an incompetent general, but as a legitimate military campaign he labeled "dashing in the extreme." Another early commentator, George Henderson, wrote in *The Science of War* in 1908 that "Hood's scheme offered some chances of success if he moved fast enough, and executed his plan

---

14 OR 39, pt. 3, 871; Sam Davis Elliott, *Doctor Quintard, Chaplain C.S.A. and Second Bishop of Tennessee: The Memoir and Civil War Diary of Charles Todd Quintard* (Baton Rouge: Louisiana State University Press, 2003), 161; Rick Warwick, *Williamson County: The Civil War Years Revealed Through Letters, Diaries and Memoirs* (Nashville, TN: The Panacea Press, 2006), 181; Henry Clayton Papers, University of Alabama; Watkins, *Company Aytch*, 214.

15 *The United States of America*, vol. I, "Through the Civil War," by David S. Muzzey, Ph. D. (Barnard College, Ginn & Company, 1922), 589.

effectively. The Federal forces in Tennessee were not united . . . and vulnerable to defeat in detail."[16]

Thomas Hay published the earliest major study of the Tennessee Campaign in 1929. Like so many authors of the era, Hay informed his readers with a mature, factually complete explanation of the political and military circumstances confronting the Confederate government in the fall of 1864; he did so without conjecture, hyperbole, and melodramatic commentary. "Even by the fall of 1864 the Southern people and their leaders were not prepared to admit that their task consisted in prolonging what had patently become nearly a hopeless defense," explained Hay, who continued as follows:

> There was still the hope that a bold and aggressive campaign would splendidly retrieve the situation in the west and relieve the pressure on Lee's embattled front. It was a desperate remedy for a desperate military and political situation, and Hood, by the logic of his appointment to command of the army in place of J. E. Johnston, was the one called upon to lead in this forlorn hope. That he came so near to success is a tribute to his indomitable faith and courage, and to the real ability played in a campaign that on several occasions put him within reach of victory. . . .

> And yet a silent factor of no little importance, which undoubtedly influenced Davis in connection with his agitation for a movement into Tennessee, was the approaching Northern election. Lincoln was standing for reelection and for a vindication of his policies and conduct of the war, while McClellan and the Democrats, accused of being allied with the Southern sympathizing Copperheads, had declared the war to be a failure and sought to replace Lincoln and his party in the Northern leadership. A bold stroke by Hood, even if uncompleted by the election time, Davis probably felt would strengthen the opposition to the Lincoln government and might even force it from office and thus, it was hoped, lead to the opening of peace negotiations or of foreign recognition. Considering the uncertain state of Northern opinion, at the time, as evidenced in the daily press, there is much to be said in favor of such an attitude on the part of Davis. A move by Hood into Tennessee would be positive rather than negative. The Confederacy had everything to gain and no more to lose than was actually lost. The existing political situation, in its foreign and domestic aspects, and the military situation both made such a move seem worth a trial.[17]

16 Garnet Joseph Wolseley, "An English View of the Civil War," in *North American Review* (December 1889), 713-727; George Henderson, *The Science of War: A Collection of Essays and Lectures* (London: Longmans, Green and Co., 1908), 643.

17 Hay, *Hood's Tennessee Campaign*, 21, 69.

Endorsing Hood's ascension to command of the Army of Tennessee, Hay quoted Field Marshal Ferdinand Foch's description of the necessary qualities of a successful military commander: "No victory is possible without a vigorous commander, ready for responsibility, eager for daring enterprises, himself possessing, and inspiring in others, the determination and energy that will go through to the end. Nothing will be won without his personal action, based on will, judgment, and freedom of mind in the midst of danger. These are the natural qualities of the gifted man, the born general."[18]

Stanley Horn, a Middle Tennessee native and grandson of a Southern soldier, wrote of Hood's campaign in his influential 1941 book *The Army of Tennessee*: "It was an entrancing dream—and it was by no means impossible." Three years later Horn penned the following in *The Decisive Battle of Nashville*:

> Some military experts, with the priceless advantage of hindsight, have therefore felt free to describe (Hood's) plan as "fantastic." It cannot be emphasized too strongly, however, that nobody seemed to think it fantastic at the time. Grant's almost hysterical telegrams to General George H. Thomas, as Hood's threat developed, revealed a very genuine fear that this "fantastic" plan of campaign would be successful—an apprehension that was shared by Chief of Staff Henry W. Halleck, Secretary of War Edwin Stanton, and President Lincoln.[19]

Nonetheless, later authors remained unimpressed with both the concept of an offensive thrust north into Tennessee by the Confederacy's Western army, and the ability of its young commander to conduct such a difficult campaign. Eric Jacobson, the most judicious of modern Tennessee Campaign authors, suggested that the invasion was irrational and referred to a postwar statement made by Jefferson Davis that Hood's movement was "ill-advised" as proof. Unfortunately, the usually inquisitive Jacobson did not challenge the credibility of Davis's disingenuous comment.[20]

In both his contemporary and postwar writings, Davis expressed the desire of the Confederate government to recover Tennessee in early 1864. Referring to instructions he gave to Joseph Johnston in February 1864, Davis confirmed

---

18 Ibid., viii-ix.

19 Horn, *The Army of Tennessee*, 379; Stanley Horn, *The Decisive Battle of Nashville* (Knoxville: The University of Tennessee Press, 1978), viii-ix.

20 Jacobson, *For Cause and For Country*, 50.

that Johnston "was informed of the policy of the Government for his army. It was proposed to reinforce him largely, and that he should advance at once and assume the recovery of at least a part of the State of Tennessee." Later, immediately after the fall of Atlanta, Davis made public pronouncements alluding to an impending invasion of Tennessee, and during the invasion exchanged correspondence with Beauregard regarding the progress of Hood's campaign. When he visited the Army of Tennessee in Palmetto, Georgia, on September 26, 1864, the president encouraged the troops with the following words: "Be of good cheer, for within a short while your faces will be turned homeward and your feet will press Tennessee soil." The following week in Augusta, Georgia, Davis alluded to the Army of Tennessee "treading Tennessee soil" and "pushing on to the Ohio." Davis's public proclamations about a movement into Tennessee at Palmetto and earlier in Macon were noted by Union spies in the audiences, who promptly informed Sherman. "He [Davis] made no concealment of [his] vainglorious boasts," Sherman wrote in his memoirs, "and thus gave us the full key to his future designs."[21]

The most convincing and detailed primary evidence explaining the rationale behind the Tennessee Campaign, rarely provided by authors to their readers, is Beauregard's December 6, 1864, letter to President Davis. The lengthy excerpt is powerful proof that Hood's superiors, both military and political, knew of and gave their blessings to his northward movement, and that other alternatives were simply unviable:

> I did not countermand the campaign in Tennessee to pursue Sherman with Hood's army for the following reasons:
>
> 1st. The Roads and creeks from the Tennessee to the Coosa River across Sand and Lookout Mountains had been, by the prevailing heavy rains, rendered almost impassable to artillery and the wagon trains.
>
> 2nd. General Sherman, with an army better appointed, had already the start of about two hundred seventy five miles on comparatively good roads. The transfer of Hood's army into Georgia could not have been more expeditious by railway than by marching

21 *OR* 47, pt. 2, 1,309; Watkins, *Company Aytch*, 186; *Augusta Constitutionalist*, October 4, 1864; William T. Sherman, *Memoirs of William T. Sherman, by Himself*, 2 vols. (Bloomington: University of Indiana Press, 1957), vol. 2, 141; Hood letter to L. T. Wigfall, April 5, 1864, John Bell Hood Personal Papers.

through the country, on account of the delays unavoidably resulting from the condition of the railroads.

3rd. To pursue Sherman, the passage of the Army of Tennessee would, necessarily, have been over roads with all the bridges destroyed, and through a devastated country, affording no subsistence or forage; and, moreover, it was feared that a retrograde movement on our part would seriously deplete the army by desertions.

4th. To have sent off the most or the whole of the Army of Tennessee in pursuit of Sherman, would have opened to Thomas's force the richest portion of the State of Alabama, and would have made nearly certain the capture of Montgomery, Selma, and Mobile, without insuring the defeat of Sherman. . . .

Under these circumstances, after consultation with General Hood, I concluded to allow him to prosecute with vigor his campaign into Tennessee and Kentucky, hoping that by defeating Thomas's army and such other forces as might hastily be sent against him, he would compel Sherman, should he reach the coast of Georgia or South Carolina, to repair at once to the defense of Kentucky and, perhaps, Ohio, and thus prevent him from reinforcing Grant. Meanwhile, supplies might be sent to Virginia from Middle and East Tennessee, thus relieving Georgia from the present constant drain upon its limited resources.[22]

Two weeks earlier on November 24, Beauregard had written to Davis from Macon, Georgia: "Have ordered Gen. Hood to take active offensive in Middle Tennessee to relieve Gen. Lee." In reply, Davis urged Hood onward, "Until Hood reaches the country proper of the enemy, he can scarcely change the plans of Sherman's or Grant's campaigns." (The "country proper" was doubtless a reference to Kentucky.)[23]

Authors routinely ridicule Hood for thinking he could invade Tennessee, secure a major victory, and then determine a proper course of action based upon contemporary circumstances. The historical record, however, proves that Hood was not only in favor of the idea, but was also ordered by the Confederate government to do exactly what he did. Historians consider Hood's stated goal to reach Kentucky, and in a long-shot, perhaps Virginia, quixotic, grandiose,

---

22 Alfred Roman, *The Military Operations of General Beauregard in the War Between the States 1861-1865*, 2 vols. (New York: Franklin Square Harper and Brothers, 1884), vol. 2, 305-306.

23 Ibid., 303; *OR* 45, pt. 1, 1,242; ibid, 44, pt. 1, 910.

and delusional—even though his immediate superior Beauregard and the Confederacy's president both approved the plan and encouraged the movement.

Many of the Civil War's most respected scholars completely ignore the goals of Hood's Tennessee invasion, despite their explicit documentation by Davis and Beauregard. Stanley Horn proposed several options after Hood's failure to destroy Schofield at Franklin, including the admission of defeat and retreat back into Alabama. It is doubtful that any Confederate commander (except perhaps Joseph Johnston) would have abandoned a critical campaign after having lost none of his artillery or assets and with 80 percent of his original troop strength in hand. Horn also suggested that "a more artful strategist" might have overpowered the garrison at Murfreesboro, "entrenched himself there, and restored the *status quo* of late 1862 [emphasis in original]." Davis's and Beauregard's stated campaign goals were to help relieve Robert E. Lee and force a retrograde movement by Sherman. A restoration of the 1862 status quo in Middle Tennessee would have had little if any influence on Sherman's determined march to the Atlantic coast.[24]

Wiley Sword's 500-page anti-Hood polemic on the Tennessee Campaign included voluminous tales of romances, myths, legends, political intrigue, Southern belles and beaus, and melodramatic Richmond society gossip—but mentioned little of Davis's and Beauregard's involvement in the conception and planning of the campaign. According to Sword, "P. G. T. Beauregard was thoroughly shocked [that] Hood had unilaterally decided on a new plan to force Sherman to pursue his army into mid-Tennessee." Sword spared no ink on details of melodrama and romance, yet kept readers in the dark by failing to discuss the political and strategic rationale of the Tennessee invasion as detailed by Beauregard and Davis in numerous readily available sources.[25]

Stanley Horn provided some balance to the Confederate dilemma as it stood in late 1864 by presenting a quote from Hood's adversary: "General Thomas, writing in later years after mature deliberation, said of Hood's plan of campaign, 'Though a failure in the end, who will say that it was not the best plan that could have been adopted by the enemy?'" Indeed, Thomas's conclusion justifies Beauregard's decision-making, as set forth in his December 6, 1864, letter to President Davis (earlier quoted). To summarize Beauregard, what other

24 Horn, *The Decisive Battle of Nashville*, ix.

25 Sword, *The Confederacy's Last Hurrah*, 63.

alternatives offered a better chance for success? Horn also revealed that General Grant, the supreme commander of the Federal armies, viewed the Confederate invasion as a very serious threat. "Grant was keenly aware of the dire consequences to the Federal cause if Nashville should fall, thereby freeing Hood's Army of Tennessee to operate offensively through Kentucky to the north and east," wrote Horn. "He not only did not consider Hood's plan impracticable or foredoomed to failure, but in discussing the matter after the war he attributed its failure to Hood's lack of enterprise." Horn's assessment was correct. Writing about Hood's army at Nashville, Grant observed: "The country was alarmed, the administration was alarmed, and I was alarmed lest the very thing would take place which I have just described—that is, Hood would get north."[26]

General James H. Wilson, the Federal commander of the Cavalry Corps of the Military Division of the Mississippi, figured prominently in opposing Hood's Tennessee invasion. Wilson's recollections counter the popular critical slant on the entire Tennessee Campaign. "Fortunately for us, Hood lost a whole month at Gadsden, waiting for ammunition, supplies and recruits, while Forrest was making a senseless raid toward the Cumberland River," explained the accomplished Union cavalryman. "It was this delay and this raid . . . that gave Thomas time to assemble all his forces for a sturdy defense. . . . Had Hood advanced at once with his three corps of infantry and his cavalry in better condition . . . he must have overthrown Thomas and overrun both Tennessee and Kentucky."[27]

Grant, Thomas, and Wilson were not alone in their apprehension of Hood's army marching north. From the Federal perspective in the fall of 1864, the situation was potentially perilous. Hood was threatening an invasion and there was precious little on hand to stop him. One of Schofield's corps commanders, Gen. David Stanley, was deeply concerned with the task of defending Tennessee against Hood. "Thomas was expected to beat Hood with one corps and two divisions," wrote Stanley. "Sherman had failed to do this with six additional corps during an entire summer." Indeed, in the early fall when Hood was plotting his strategy, all that stood in the way of a Confederate advance was the meager Union garrison at Nashville—a single corps and two

26 Horn, *Decisive Battle of Nashville*, ix; Grant, *Personal Memoirs of U. S. Grant*, vol. 2, 503.

27 Wilson, *Under the Old Flag*, 28, 30.

divisions. Stanley concluded, "If Hood succeeded, Nashville, Louisville, Cincinnati, and possibly Chicago were doomed."[28]

John N. Beach, a surgeon with the 40th Ohio Infantry, fully agreed with these Federal assessments. "Even after the Battle of Franklin, in which Hood lost one-fifth of his army, the anxiety in the North was hardly lessened, and his presence in front of Nashville was a menace that was looked upon with solicitude," confirmed the surgeon. "The campaign was disastrous to Hood's army to a degree not paralleled by any other of the war, hence it has been criticized as ill planned and badly managed, but it was so nearly a success that we should credit him [Hood] with judgment in its planning as well as audacity in its execution."[29]

Colonel Arthur MacArthur of the 24th Wisconsin Infantry, a veteran of the battle of Franklin and Medal of Honor winner (and the father of World War II hero General Douglas MacArthur), wrote the following about Hood's campaign:

General Sherman was in Georgia, rapidly approaching Savannah, but still without a base; General Grant had no troops to spare from the front of Petersburg and Richmond; in New Orleans and other places in the far South and West we had only a few thousand men. Hood's success at Franklin, therefore, meant Confederate supremacy over Tennessee and Kentucky, with the numerical strength of his army raised probably to at least 100,000 men. With such a force it was possible for him to sweep up to the Ohio River, and thereby oblige General Grant to detach largely from his army for the protection of the West, thus exposing General Sherman in Georgia to a concentrated attack by Lee before he could reach his new base. In a word, had Hood entered Nashville sword in hand at the head of a victorious army, which would have resulted from defeat of the Union army at Franklin, the civil war in all its subsequent scenes might have been essentially varied.[30]

Whether Hood could have ever fielded an army of 100,000 is doubtful, and it is also irrelevant. His thrust was dangerous, and it was taken very seriously by

---

28 David S. Stanley, *Personal Memoirs of Major-General D.S. Stanley, U.S.A.* (Cambridge, MA: Harvard University Press, 1917), 189, 198.

29 John N. Beach, *History of the Fortieth Ohio Volunteer Infantry* (London, OH: Shepard & Craig Printers, 1884) 93.

30 Charles T. Clark, *Opdycke's Tigers: 125th Ohio* (Columbus, OH: Sparr & Glenn, 1895), 446-447.

the Federal high command. If the Federal authorities in 1864 treated Hood's invasion with apprehension, sobriety, and a genuine threat with devastating ramifications, why do modern historians and writers deride Hood's objectives as rash and impractical? Horn, who as noted earlier judged Hood's campaign "by no means impossible" wrote, "If Hood had been able to move with just a little more celerity, if on just one or two occasions Fortune's balance had tilted in his favor instead of against him, his daringly conceived plan might well have succeeded. And then perhaps the little village of Appomattox Court House might have slept on forever in its dusty obscurity."[31]

Hood's planning for the Tennessee invasion extended well beyond his own army. Unlike the careless commander of customary portrayals, Hood left a force behind under Gen. Philip D. Roddey, cavalry commander of the District of Northern Alabama, to repair bridges and maintain a retreat route in case the army suffered a severe defeat in Tennessee and was forced to withdraw.[32]

In celebration of the Civil War centennial, the editors of the *Nashville Banner* published a special 36-page insert on Sunday, February 22, 1964, entitled "The Civil War in Middle Tennessee, Commemorating the Centennial." Even though the highly critical books by Thomas Connelly, James McDonough, and Wiley Sword had yet to appear, the publication seemed to anticipate the deterioration of Hood's public image. The only major studies of the invasion available were Thomas Hay's *Hood's Tennessee Campaign* (1929) and Stanley Horn's *Hood's Tennessee Campaign* (1941) and *The Decisive Battle of Nashville* (1956). The authors of the special newspaper centennial supplement primarily relied upon Horn's studies. Near the end of the feature, the authors referred to Horn's description of Hood's campaign as "fantastic," due to its difficulty and ambition. Sympathetic toward Hood's courageous attempt to liberate Tennessee from Federal occupation, the 10,000-word treatise concluded with a poem:

Fantastic, Middle Tennessee?
No! I saw you lift your weary head
To the windrows of my dead;
To Hood, the headlong, dead-wrong man—
How mad could I be?

31 Horn, *The Decisive Battle of Nashville*, 6-7.

32 *OR* 45, pt. 1, 655.

Well before you hiss
When you think of me,
Remember this—
I was trying to set you free.

Fantastic, Nashville?
No, not then!
When I saw you captive, trembling,
At the end of Johnson's rope.
For I, Hood, the one-legged man,
I and my ragged, shoeless men—
I was your only hope.[33]

The *Nashville Banner* poem seems to mirror the view of James H. McNeilly, a Confederate chaplain in Gen. William A. Quarles's brigade, who wrote of the Tennessee Campaign, "Thus ended a campaign inspired by a sense of our need, entered upon in hope, carried forward with dauntless courage against overwhelming forces, and exhibiting the most heroic devotion to a righteous cause. Our compensation for failure is that it is better to have deserved success than to have won it unjustly."[34]

33 *Nashville Banner*, "The Civil War in Middle Tennessee, Commemorating the Centennial, Part III, 1864," February 22, 1964. The newspaper that published the centennial insert is now the *Nashville Tennessean*.

34 James H. McNeilly, "With Hood Before Nashville," *Confederate Veteran* (June 1918), vol. 26, 254.

Chapter 7

"To look back upon history is
inevitably to distort it."

— *Norman Pearson*

John Bell Hood:
Feeding and Supplying His Army

When he was promoted on July 17, 1864, six weeks after his 33rd birthday, John Bell Hood became the youngest full general in American military history and the youngest officer to command an army. Because he had served as a corps commander for only five months, his inexperience at logistics is frequently emphasized. The supply problems suffered by the Army of Tennessee are usually attributed solely to his alleged inattention to detail and lack of appreciation for logistics. Some recent books toss in the allegation of an acrimonious relationship between Hood and his immediate superior, Gen. P. G. T. Beauregard during the planning stages of the Tennessee Campaign. As is typical of most portrayals of Hood, the depth and degree of the criticism has increased over time.

Hood's predecessor Joseph Johnston is unanimously praised for his successful supplying of the Army of Tennessee during his tenure as commander during the first seven months of 1864. The circumstances facing Johnston, however, were much different from those of his successors, Hood and Richard Taylor. Except for brief interruptions, Johnston's Army of Tennessee was served by the Western and Atlantic Railroad every day of his command tenure. Each of his persistent withdrawals shortened the distance to his supply base in Atlanta, which was itself served by the Georgia Railroad from the east, the Macon and Western Railroad from the southeast, and the Atlanta and West Point Railroad from the southwest. Because of these many advantages, it is unfair to compare Johnston's logistical performance to virtually any other commander, Federal or Confederate, during any major campaign of the war.

Even Robert E. Lee fighting throughout the war in proximity to the Confederate capital, struggled mightily to keep his army supplied. On August 31, 1862, Col. J. B. Robertson of the 5th Texas wrote that the supply of clothing was insufficient for "cleanliness necessary for health. Many of the men are barefooted." "Starvation, literal starvation, was doing its deadly work," wrote Gen. George B. Gordon about the dire situation outside Petersburg by March of 1865. "So depleted and poisoned was the blood of many of Lee's men from insufficient and unsound food that a slight wound, which would probably not have been reported at the beginning of the war, would often cause blood-poison, gangrene and death."[1]

Criticism of Hood's army management does not begin with the Tennessee Campaign. Before the evacuation of Atlanta, Hood was forced to destroy a trainload of ammunition and supplies. The blast, so vividly portrayed in the motion picture *Gone with the Wind*, resulted in a giant firestorm. Some historians have described the event as the greatest explosion of the American Civil War. Flames illuminated the sky and damaged or destroyed numerous buildings (which had survived Sherman's relentless bombardment) within a quarter-mile radius of the train. Historian Thomas Connelly blamed the debacle on Hood, who "simply waited too late to get many of his stores out of Atlanta [due to] a confusion of orders." Wiley Sword echoed Connelly by writing that "Hood had waited too long" to remove the army's enormous stockpile of supplies.

As Connelly and Sword aptly demonstrate, the destruction of Hood's ordnance train is often presented as a dramatic illustration of his incompetence and inattention to detail. However, the facts suggest something different. The Confederate defeat at Jonesboro on September 1 severed the last open rail line feeding Atlanta. Before it was cut, Hood's quartermaster, Col. M. B. McMicken, had failed to evacuate a trainload of supplies and ordnance that included

---

1 Harold Simpson, *Hood's Texas Brigade: Lee's Grenadier Guard* (Fort Worth, TX: Landmark Publishing, 1999), 158; Patterson, *Rebels From West Point*, 135.

cannon, caissons, howitzers, 14,000 artillery rounds, and 5,000 Enfield muskets, as well as numerous small arms, ammunition, tools, and other equipment.[2] Hood, via his chief of staff Gen. Francis Shoup, had issued "repeated instructions" to remove the valuable train before the fall of the city. "Owing to the wanton neglect of the chief quartermaster of this army a large amount of ammunition and railroad stock had to be destroyed at Atlanta," Hood explained to Braxton Bragg from Lovejoy's Station on September 4. "He had more than ample time to remove the whole and had repeated instructions. I am reliably informed that he is too much addicted to drink of late to attend to his duties. Am greatly in want of an officer to take his place. Can you not send one?" The quartermaster general in Richmond granted Hood's request and appointed a replacement for McMicken on September 23.[3]

Even under the difficult circumstances at Atlanta, Hood not only kept the Army of Tennessee reasonably well supplied, but provided assistance to needy civilians. Hood, wrote the *Augusta Constitutionalist*, "had been supplying up to 1,500 rations per day to the city's poor during the month of August."[4]

Thomas Hay, the earliest book-length chronicler of the Tennessee Campaign, made no mention of negligence or disregard of supply and logistics by Hood in his 1929 study *Hood's Tennessee Campaign*. The same was true of Stanley Horn's *The Army of Tennessee*, which mentioned nothing about Hood's inattention to supply and logistics. Even Connelly, one of the earliest of Hood's critics, made no mention of any laxity or ineptitude in logistics by Hood in his influential 1971 *Autumn of Glory*. The first major author to slam Hood's lack of logistical ability was Wiley Sword, whose influential 1993 *The Confederacy's Last Hurrah* claimed the general displayed both ineptitude and negligence.[5]

Extraordinary circumstances made planning the Tennessee Campaign and supplying Hood's army especially difficult. Soon after the fall of Atlanta, the Confederate government in Richmond established a new administrative entity, the Military Division of the West, and appointed P. G. T. Beauregard its first commander effective October 17, 1864. The new theater command

---

2   Connelly, *Autumn of Glory*, 467; Sword, *The Confederacy's Last Hurrah*, 35.

3   Castel, *Decision in the West*, 523; OR 38, pt. 5, 1,018; OR 39, pt. 2, 865.

4   *Augusta Daily Constitutionalist*, August 13, 1864.

5   Sword, *The Confederacy's Last Hurrah*, 64-74. This was originally published one year earlier as *Embrace an Angry Wind: The Confederacy's Last Hurrah: Spring Hill, Franklin, and Nashville* (Harper Collins, 1992).

encompassed Richard Taylor's Department of Alabama, Mississippi, and East Louisiana, and Hood's department, which included Tennessee and northwest Georgia. Departmental politics further complicated matters because Hood was expected to draw supplies for the campaign from Taylor's department, even though he would be operating outside Taylor's purview when in Tennessee. While Beauregard's new Western theater command was being organized, the earliest logistical preparations for the campaign had to be communicated by Hood directly to Jefferson Davis's chief military advisor Braxton Bragg, and to the Confederate Secretary of War James Seddon. Instead of demonstrating ineptitude or sloth, Hood repeatedly displayed a keen appreciation for logistical matters and the importance of launching the invasion as soon as possible.[6]

On September 23, two weeks before Beauregard was available and the new theater command established, Hood asked that an ordnance reserve be accumulated at Selma, Alabama, or Columbus, Mississippi. That same day, after acknowledging the need for footwear—the absence of which would torture many of Hood's men throughout the ensuing fall and winter campaign—Hood requested an order of shoes from Columbus, Georgia. This was his second request for shoes, the first having been made to Richmond more than two weeks earlier on September 6.[7]

On October 8, Hood wired Bragg from Cedartown, Georgia, the first of his many requests to have key railroads repaired: "Please have the Memphis and Charleston Railroad repaired at once to Decatur [Alabama], if possible." The anticipated river crossing at Decatur was later changed because neither Richmond nor Taylor's department made any effort to repair the railroad.[8]

Beauregard and Hood first met on October 9 at Cave Springs, Georgia, "and conferred in regard to Hood's future movements." Beauregard departed the next day and rejoined the army at Gadsden, Alabama, on October 21 for two days of meetings with Hood.[9]

Hood's plans constantly evolved because of changing circumstances. These included the presence of the enemy, a lack of adequate supplies, the absence of sufficient cavalry, inaccurate and incomplete intelligence,

---

6   Roman, *The Military Operations of General Beauregard*, 278.

7   *OR* 39, pt. 2, 865; *OR* 38, pt. 5, 1,023.

8   Ibid., 39, pt. 3, 805.

9   *OR* 45, pt. 1, 647.

convoluted and inefficient administrative entities, and ineffective and often nonexistent communications. The original plan for the Tennessee invasion was for the Army of Tennessee to cross the Tennessee River at Guntersville. Hood, however, was informed by cavalryman P. D. Roddey on October 18 that Guntersville was heavily guarded by Federal infantry, while Decatur was but lightly defended. This important intelligence, coupled with the absence of Nathan Bedford Forrest's veteran cavalry, convinced Hood to change his plans and move the army west toward Decatur. Wiley Sword disparaged this wise and necessary decision when he wrote that, while en route to Guntersville, Hood "impulsively changed the army's destination to Decatur."[10]

During the Gadsden meeting on October 22 and 23, Beauregard instructed General Taylor to cooperate with Hood and provide him with supplies for the campaign from his own department, with Tuscumbia as the designated supply base. Repairs to the Mobile and Ohio Railroad were also ordered. Taylor informed Hood that supply trains were en route to Tuscumbia from Corinth, Mississippi, but failed to tell him that a 15-mile stretch of track from Cherokee, Alabama, to Tuscumbia was unusable. It is not known whether Taylor was unaware of the severed state of the railroad, or whether he simply neglected to tell Hood. William T. Sherman knew of its dilapidated condition, however, and told George Thomas on October 29, "I don't see how Beauregard can support his army." Sherman also wired Henry Halleck in Washington on November 3, "The country round about Florence has been again and again devastated during the past three years, and Beauregard must be dependent on the Mobile and Ohio Railroad, which also has been broken and patched up in its whole extent."[11]

It was after departing Gadsden and during the march toward Guntersville that Hood learned about the strong Federal defenses there and changed his planned river crossing to Decatur. Once at Decatur, however, Hood learned that Roddey's information was incorrect. Rather than a small garrison, the town was in fact heavily fortified and defended by 3,000 entrenched Federals supported by gunboats. Beauregard, who had remained in Gadsden, caught up with the army at Decatur. With the soldiers hungry and supplies scarce, Hood and Beauregard flooded available telegraph wires and courier lines asking for

---

10 Roman, *The Military Operations of General Beauregard*, 285; OR 39, pt.3, 913-914; Sword, *The Confederacy's Last Hurrah*, 64.

11 *OR* 39, pt. 3, 845; *OR* 39, pt. 3, 499; *OR* 39, pt. 3, 613.

rations. On October 28, Hood wired Taylor to request that 20 days of food for 50,000 men be sent "as rapidly as possible."[12]

Hood's army remained outside Decatur for three days awaiting supplies and information regarding the whereabouts of Forrest's cavalry. A river crossing at Decatur required the defeat of the well-entrenched Federal garrison. Hood believed that a forced crossing at Decatur would result in a "great and unnecessary sacrifice of life," and he had still not heard from Forrest. Hood marched the army westward to Lamb's Ferry, Bainbridge, and arrived at Tuscumbia on October 30. During the seven-day period since departing Gadsden, Hood was obliged to change plans because of the continued absence of Forrest's cavalry, the proximity of Federal forces at various crossing points, and communications impeded by enemy control of important telegraph lines.[13]

After the Army of Tennessee arrived at Tuscumbia, Hood immediately wired Taylor, "I am here, and need at once twenty days supply of breadstuffs and salt." Because Taylor had not repaired the railroad from Cherokee to Tuscumbia, Hood was forced to send empty wagons 15 miles to Cherokee, transfer the supplies from train cars to wagons, and haul the supplies back to Tuscumbia over poor roads. The 30-mile roundtrip also forced Hood to ask Taylor for forage for supply-train animals.[14]

With Thomas gathering Federal forces in central Tennessee around Nashville and Sherman marching across Georgia, Hood—anxious to launch the invasion—continued to press Confederate authorities for supplies. Hood attempted to clear up a railroad bottleneck that was contributing to delays in shipments. Because supplies were transported by multiple railroad companies, offloading and transferring was required in Corinth, Mississippi, before the final shipment of supplies reached the rail terminus in Cherokee. In an effort to get results as fast as possible, Hood bypassed the nominally effective Taylor by appealing directly to L. J. Fleming, the general superintendent of the Mobile and Ohio Railroad. "I must have 20 days supply of rations for this army at Cherokee with the least possible delay," he pleaded on October 31. Hood also asked that Fleming allow his trains to run directly to Cherokee to avoid transfer at Corinth

---

12 Noel Carpenter, *A Slight Demonstration: Decatur October 1864, A Clumsy Beginning of Gen. John B. Hood's Tennessee Campaign* (Austin, TX: Carol Powell, publisher, 2007), 137; *OR* 52, pt. 2, 769; *OR* 39, pt. 3, 868, 871.

13 *OR* 45, pt.1, 648.

14 Ibid., 39, pt. 3, 868.

before closing with "time is of the utmost importance." That same day, Hood wired the quartermaster in Meridian, Mississippi, "Give me all the aid you can in transporting twenty days supply of rations for this army to Cherokee station at once. Time is all important."[15]

Disputes among the civilian-owned railroads were out of Hood's control, but they seriously affected the delivery of supplies. While in Tuscumbia, Beauregard wired Taylor on November 1, "The Mobile and Ohio Railroad refuse to send rolling stock enough to supply the wants of the service on the road from Corinth here. It is most important that this be attended to at once." Beauregard added, "You will take measures promptly to get the Mobile and Ohio and the Memphis and Charleston Railroads to work together and secure enough cars and motive power." Earlier, Beauregard had requested that Taylor come to Tuscumbia, but, noting the delivery problems, withdrew his request and instructed instead that Taylor remain in Selma and solve the problems with the railroads. Like Hood, Beauregard sometimes found it necessary to bypass Taylor and communicate directly with civilian authorities. On November 2, Beauregard implored railroad superintendent Fleming to "Use every effort to forward stores arriving at Corinth to Cherokee without transshipment. Delays embarrass us and impede our movement."[16]

The myriad problems in supply and logistics encountered by Hood—among the most complex in all the years of the Civil War—do not impress his critics. According to Wiley Sword, diary entries penned by Hood's men during the movements in northern Alabama reveal "plummeting" morale as a result of insufficient supplies. Sword provided two quotes of complaint, one from an individual identified as "a disgruntled captain," and the other identified simply as "a soldier." A careful check of the sources cited by Sword, however, reveals that the "disgruntled captain" and the "soldier" were one and the same: Capt. Samuel Foster of Granbury's brigade, a Joseph Johnston devotee who despised Hood. Foster, who later condemned Hood's aggressiveness at Franklin, complained when Hood wisely decided to avoid unnecessary bloodshed and bypass Decatur. "We left Decatur last evening, without making an effort to take it," wrote Foster, who noted that the Yankees left their flag "flying in full view" of the Confederate army. Sword, who quotes liberally from the words of

15 Ibid., 871; 52, pt. 2, 772.

16 Ibid.

Hood's detractors such as Foster, routinely disregards the records of men who concurred with Hood's decision. A. L. Orr of Cleburne's division wrote to his sister in Ellis County, Texas, "We could of taken it [Decatur] but would of lost a grate many men."[17]

Notwithstanding Hood's repeated and conscientious efforts, adequate supplies had still not reached the army in Tuscumbia as late as November 17. Beauregard, meanwhile, pressed him to launch the invasion. "I have now seven days rations on hand, and need thirteen days additional," replied Hood in defense of his actions. "Please use every effort to have these supplies pressed forward." Beauregard's biographer Alfred Roman, however, mischaracterized Hood's reasonable and wise desire to feed his men before moving north: "Realizing the fact that nothing could be gained—while much might be lost—by further procrastination, and wishing to spur on General Hood to definitive action, General Beauregard, on the same day, sent him the following letter." Claiming that "nothing could be gained" by a commander awaiting adequate supplies for his men before launching an invasion of Tennessee, and that waiting for these provisions was "procrastination," are manifestly unfair characterizations of Hood's actions. Beauregard replied the same day, directing Hood to "take the offensive at the earliest practical moment."[18]

During the early days of the Tennessee invasion, in spite of the difficulties incurred by Taylor's inability to adequately supply the army, Hood issued General Order Number 37 from outside Columbia, Tennessee, on November 28, ordering his troops not to plunder the property of civilians, either Confederate or Unionist.[19]

The indifference and ineptitude demonstrated by senior Confederate authorities following the evacuation of Atlanta resulted in the suffering and deprivations of the soldiers at the front. Their distress persisted well into December, by which time Hood's army was in front of Nashville. As late as December 6, Hood asked Beauregard, "Please have the railroad to Decatur

---

17 Sword, *The Confederacy's Last Hurrah*, 65; Foster, *One of Cleburne's Command*, 142; Carpenter, *A Slight Demonstration*, 131.

18 Roman, *The Military Operations of General Beauregard*, 301. Alfred Roman was Beauregard's friend, and the former general is widely considered to be an unacknowledged co-author of his own biography.

19 *OR* 45, pt. 1, 1,255. (According to Judge Frank H. Smith's *History of the 24th Tennessee*, troops from Carter Stevenson's division were reported to have looted civilian homes and stores in Columbia, prompting Hood to issue the general order.)

repaired at once." When a week passed without result, Hood wrote again on December 13, complaining that the "quarter master charged with rebuilding the railroad from Cherokee toward Decatur, still complains of not being able to obtain the necessary labor and material." Because it was imperative to bypass Taylor, Hood added, "Please give [the quartermaster] authority to impress at once all that is necessary." Beauregard's own difficult position of administrative responsibility without operational control required constant haggling with other commanders and Confederate politicians. He asked Governor Joe Brown of Georgia on December 2 to repair railroads from west Georgia to Augusta to facilitate the transportation of supplies for Hood's army. On the same day, Beauregard appealed directly to the Confederate adjutant general Samuel Cooper in Richmond, stating that Hood's army was "sadly in need of every disposition of military supplies—horses and mules for artillery and other transportation," as well as blankets and clothing. The exasperated Beauregard fumed to Cooper that nobody in the central government "whose powers should be ample, and whose instructions should be full and clear," seemed willing to take charge of problems that directly affected acquisition of supplies.[20]

On the same day (December 13) that he complained about the lack of materials to fix the railroad from Cherokee toward Decatur, Hood wired Beauregard from his headquarters outside Nashville about the severe weather and the suffering of his men: "Major Ayer, chief quartermaster, informs me that Major Bridewell at Augusta [Georgia] has fifty bales of blankets belonging to this army. Please have them sent forward at once." Because the Confederate government and his superiors were unable to provide for his army and the winter weather was battering his men, Hood had little choice but to take matters into his own hands when the opportunity arose. In a letter to Beauregard on December 14, Taylor complained that Hood was issuing orders and taking actions in his department. "Citizens residing in the northern counties of Mississippi and Alabama represent that officers, acting under the orders of Gen. Hood, are seizing their good mules . . . and replacing them with broken down and worthless animals," complained Taylor, who added that "camps of dismounted men belonging to the Army of Tennessee have been established in this department by Gen. Hood without consultation or notification of me."

20 OR 45, pt. 2, 637, 640, 653, 685, 689.

Rather than being uninterested in logistics, Hood was, if anything, overzealous.[21]

"Though fairly well supplied with food," wrote Thomas Hay regarding the army's supply situation while outside Nashville, "it was in need of shoes and clothing." Six pages later, however, Hay stated that the army was "poorly fed." These conflicting statements make it impossible to know what Hay really believed about the situation, but Confederate Gen. Henry Clayton knew it firsthand and wrote his wife about it on December 11: "The great thing which reconciles us to this uncertain condition of things is that we are getting enough to eat, man and beast." Even after the army was soundly defeated at Nashville in the middle of the month and forced to retreat, W. G. Davenport of the 10th Texas Cavalry noted that "food could generally be had." General William Bate confirmed Hood's pre-invasion opinion that the army could find provisions in Tennessee when he wrote in his official report that the army enjoyed "a superabundance of rations" from the countryside.[22]

Once the Tennessee Campaign ended, Beauregard penned his January 9, 1865, report to the Confederate War Department. In it, he discussed the delays encountered by Hood in launching the invasion. His explanation, although technically correct, omitted many important details that made it at best misleading. The plan of campaign into Middle Tennessee as originally conceived and designed might have compelled Sherman to abandon his raid across Georgia to the coast and pursue Hood into Middle Tennessee. "But instead of crossing the Tennessee River at Gunter's Landing as General Hood intended at Gadsden," wrote Beauregard, "he suddenly changed his line of march . . . and repaired to Tuscumbia and Florence." The poor condition of the railroads forced Hood to await supplies, added Beauregard, which "delayed his advance for nearly three weeks.[23]

Historian Thomas Hay was unmoved by Hood's efforts to supply his army and prepare for the movement into Tennessee. "The paralysis of Hood's decision," concluded Hay, "cost him many lives, the campaign, and finally his

21 Ibid., 636, 689.

22 Hay, *Hood's Tennessee Campaign*, 140, 146; Henry Clayton Papers, University of Alabama, Tuscaloosa; W. G. Davenport, *Incidents in the Life of WG Davenport Which Occurred During the Time of His Service in the Civil War*, Tularosa, New Mexico, January 16, 1915 (Salt Lake City: LDS Church Archives), Microfiche No. 6082730; *OR* 45, pt. 1, 747.

23 *OR* 45, pt. 1, 651.

command." Wiley Sword also shrugged off Hood's difficulties and used a metaphor that belittled the physical condition of the crippled, one-legged general. Hood, observed Sword, was "tripping over his foot" as he tried to commence the invasion.[24]

Problems supplying the Army of Tennessee persisted even after Hood's resignation. When the army was under the temporary command of Richard Taylor, Confederate authorities were no more successful supplying it than when Hood was in command—even though the army was operating in Taylor's own department. In a February 9, 1865, letter to Jefferson Davis, the Reverend John Talley from Hancock County (Culverton), Georgia, described the behavior and condition of the army as it passed through the area en route to Augusta. Officers and men frequently visited his home, Talley wrote, adding, "There can be no doubt but the disasters were the result of want of discipline and subordination," and that "the quartermaster's department was badly managed [in Tennessee] and the men were neglected and are now suffering from that neglect." Talley conveyed to Davis that during the retreat from Nashville, many men were "without a shoe and nearly naked, because the quartermaster did not do his duty." The soldiers, who had been passing Talley's home for 10 days, were described as "not half clothed" and "without blankets." Many Georgia troops, added the reverend, "have left the army to go home to obtain supplies of necessary articles."[25]

Although the historical record demonstrates that circumstances beyond Hood's control contributed mightily to the Confederacy's inability to adequately supply the Army of Tennessee during the fall and winter of 1864, Hood is held solely culpable and routinely characterized as indifferent and inept at army logistics.[26]

---

24 Hay, *Hood's Tennessee Campaign*, 66; Sword, *The Confederacy's Last Hurrah*, 74.

25 *OR* 49, pt. 1, 966-967.

26 Shortages of supplies were not exclusive to the Army of Tennessee under Hood. While serving in the Army of Northern Virginia in 1862 and 1863 his own Texas brigade was not always adequately supplied. Diarist Mary Chesnut described the Texans as they passed through Richmond: "Such rags and tags . . . Nothing was like anything else. Most garments and arms were such as had been taken from the enemy. Such shoes as they had on . . . They did not seem to mind their shabby condition. They laughed, shouted and cheered as they marched by." Mary Chesnut, *A Diary from Dixie*, Isabella Martin and Myrta Avary, eds. (Avenel, NJ: Gramercy Books, 1997), 231.

In addition to logistical difficulties, the absence of sufficient cavalry further complicated matters for Hood. The bulk of the Army of Tennessee's mounted arm under Gen. Joseph Wheeler was ordered by Beauregard on October 21 to return to Georgia to resist Sherman.[27] Wheeler's command was replaced by veteran troopers under Nathan Bedford Forrest, who were based in and operated out of Gen. Richard Taylor's Department of Alabama, Mississippi, and East Louisiana.

Even if the railroads had been repaired and adequate supplies obtained, Hood's move into northern Alabama later in October was largely without the protection of adequate cavalry. Informed on October 20 that Forrest was departing Clifton, Tennessee, for an eventual rendezvous with the army, Beauregard and Hood spent the next 15 days laboring under the impression that Forrest was moving into Middle Tennessee, which fit into the overall Confederate strategy. Although his exact whereabouts temporarily remained unknown, Forrest would be moving in a general direction that would intersect with Hood's army as it moved north from Alabama. Unfortunately, Taylor neglected to share details of Hood's plan with the cavalryman, who rode to Jackson, Tennessee, in preparation for a raid into northern Tennessee near the Kentucky border.[28]

The miscommunication between Beauregard, Taylor, and Forrest began on October 22, when Beauregard instructed Taylor to order Forrest to join Hood. Taylor complied the next day when Beauregard repeated the order, but his message to Forrest on October 23 expressed no sense of urgency. Instead, Taylor directed the cavalry commander to join Hood "as soon as you have accomplished the objects of your present movement."[29]

Hood learned on the morning of October 23 that Forrest was not operating in the area and that if the army crossed the Tennessee River, it would be escorted by only a single division of cavalry under the command of Gen. William H. "Red" Jackson. Demonstrating appropriate caution, Hood decided to stay on the south side of the river and move farther west toward his supply base at Tuscumbia. As noted earlier, intelligence provided by Roddey convinced Hood that Decatur was less heavily defended than Guntersville.

27 Carpenter, *A Slight Demonstration*, 25.

28 Ibid., 24; *OR* 39, pt. 3, 837.

29 Ibid., 853.

Although Hood did not know Forrest's exact whereabouts, Decatur was farther west and thus closer to Forrest.[30]

On October 28, having heard nothing from Nathan Bedford Forrest, Hood (with General Beauregard present) sent a message directly to the cavalry commander. The communication, which bypassed General Taylor (whom Hood notified the next day) directed Forrest to at once meet the main army near Bainbridge, Alabama. Hood sent the message via General Roddey's cavalry, since other channels of communication had failed to reach Forrest. Although Hood's critics may portray Hood's action as insubordinate and disrespectful, he understood the urgency of the situation and took the appropriate action.[31]

In response to Hood's entreaties, Taylor once again instructed Forrest on October 29 to report to Hood. Like his initial message, however, the tone was cool and casual: "As soon as you have accomplished the objects of your present movement your course will be directed toward middle Tennessee, where you will put yourself in communications with General Hood." Forrest, who inferred no sense of urgency from Taylor's communication, did not reply for several days. With Sherman advancing steadily eastward through Georgia toward Savannah and Thomas organizing his growing Federal army around Nashville, Hood was forced to await Forrest's arrival. Unbeknownst to Hood, however, the cavalryman was conducting a raid in northern Tennessee near the Kentucky border.[32]

On November 2, nearly two full weeks after the original request that Forrest join Hood, and still having heard nothing from the cavalryman, both Beauregard and Hood once again bypassed General Taylor by sending more messages directly to Forrest. Beauregard directed the cavalryman "to report at once to General Hood." Hood's own message inquired with some deserved angst, "When can I expect you here or when can I hear from you? I am waiting for you." Beauregard's adjutant went so far as to try and contact Forrest via another route. He sent a telegram to his counterpart Maj. J. P. Strange, assistant adjutant general in Jackson, Tennessee, asking, "Where is General Forrest?"[33]

---

30 Carpenter, *A Slight Demonstration*, 33.

31 *OR* 39, pt. 3, 863.

32 Ibid., 853.

33 Ibid., 52, pt. 2, 770; 39, pt. 3, 879; 52, pt. 2, 773.

Forrest finally acknowledged receipt of Hood's and Beauregard's messages by replying to Taylor in a rather reluctant manner, stating that he would "obey the order unless it was countermanded." Although Sherman was ravaging Georgia and Thomas was consolidating his army in Middle Tennessee, Forrest claimed that his activities blocking the river would be more detrimental to the enemy. The cavalryman agreed to comply and join Hood, but only after he had gathered his command and attended to his horses.[34]

Although Hood is commonly held completely responsible for the delay in commencing the Tennessee Campaign, Nathan Bedford Forrest's entire command did not join Hood's army in Tuscumbia, Alabama, until the 14th of November—23 days after Beauregard sent instructions to Taylor calling for Forrest to join the army and participate in the movement.

෬ ෯

In recent decades, the historiography on Hood's efforts to obtain supplies and launch the Tennessee Campaign includes the charge that bitterness and rank rivalry came between Gens. Beauregard and Hood. It is time to review the literature and determine from where this idea originated, and whether it has any merit.

Thomas Hay, who made only brief and constrained comments on Beauregard's possible frustration at not being adequately consulted during the planning phase of the campaign, dedicated only a single paragraph of his book to any possible impropriety regarding Hood's treatment of Beauregard. Stanley Horn raised the issue of the difficulties incurred by Beauregard, and perhaps some annoyance, but failed to mention any conflict between the two generals. Thomas Connelly was the first author to assert that a rancorous relationship existed between the two men. In fact, Connelly implied that at times, Hood's conduct in October and November 1864 toed the line of mutiny. A reading of the correspondence between Hood and Beauregard in the *Official Records*, together with reminiscences by both commanders, demonstrates that Connelly's assertions are baseless. The tone and content of the correspondence cited by Connelly is no different from those of thousands of other exchanges between military commanders of the era, Federal and Confederate alike.

---

34 Ibid., 39, pt. 1, 869.

Connelly went out of his way to create a conflict between the two generals that never existed.[35]

In his portrayal of events, Connelly made the ludicrous accusation that Hood "totally disobeyed orders" after the fall of Atlanta by moving away from north Georgia and into northeastern Alabama in preparation for an invasion of Tennessee. Connelly ignored the fact that President Davis fully sanctioned the movement, and that Hood's march toward Tennessee and the eventual invasion of the state were so broadly known that even the Federal high command was aware of what was about to transpire. Sherman wrote in his memoirs that his spies informed him of Jefferson Davis's statements in a speech to Hood's army outside Atlanta that "Forrest was already on our roads in Middle Tennessee; and that Hood's army would soon be there.... He [Davis] promised Tennessee and Kentucky soldiers that their feet should soon tread their 'native soil' . . . and thus gave us the full key to his future designs." Connelly knew full well that if Hood had "totally disobeyed orders" by marching his 40,000-man army anywhere against Davis's wishes, the president would have relieved Hood of command and perhaps have called for his court-martial.[36]

Connelly also accused Hood of being "blatantly dishonest" in the explanation of his Tennessee Campaign strategy in his postwar memoirs. Connelly's justification for challenging Hood's integrity is difficult to explain. He cited Hood's postwar statements that in mid-October, he could defeat enemy forces gathering to defend Tennessee, to support his contention that Hood could not have known at the time that the Federals were actually gathering troops to defend Tennessee. Apparently Connelly believed that Hood should have assumed that the Lincoln administration would have surrendered Nashville and Middle Tennessee without a fight![37]

Wiley Sword surpassed Connelly in his depth of criticism, investing several pages to create a dramatic rivalry between Hood and Beauregard that is nearly all fiction sprinkled with bits of fact. Casting Hood as the villain and Beauregard as the victim, Sword wrote of Hood's performance in the days before the Tennessee invasion: "Beauregard . . . now began to fully perceive Hood's

---

35 Hay, *Hood's Tennessee Campaign*, 60; Horn, *The Army of Tennessee*, 379-383; Connelly, *Autumn of Glory*, 480-489.

36 Ibid., 483; Sherman, *Memoirs*, 508-509.

37 Connelly, *Autumn of Glory*, 483.

woeful indiscretion and careless planning in the management of his army." Sword went on to accuse Hood of being "rash and careless with operational details."[38]

Producers of the documentary film *The Battle of Franklin: Five Hours in the Valley of Death* used Sword's book as a primary resource for their script. The film criticizes Hood for constantly changing locations in northern Alabama during the days and weeks preceding the invasion of Tennessee. "It is becoming abundantly clear that Hood hasn't adequately planned for the campaign," explained the narrator, who goes on to lecture viewers that Hood considered Beauregard "nothing more than a highly ranked supply clerk."[39]

Often overlooked by authors and historians is the complicated and convoluted command and logistics structure that Hood confronted. Beauregard had just been appointed commander of the newly created Military Division of the West and was Hood's immediate superior. Both the organizational structure and areas of authority of the new theater command were being developed concurrent with Hood's planning of the campaign. As late as early November, even the most fundamental structure and areas of authority remained yet unknown, which obliged Beauregard to ask Davis exactly what specific command authority he held when present with the armies in his region.[40]

Although portrayed by Sword as independent and indifferent, Hood attempted to keep in touch with his multiple and changing superiors as much as possible. The army was in nearly constant motion, dictated by circumstances often beyond Hood's control—including the absence of his cavalry, Sherman's nearby forces, flooded rivers, Federal gunboats, and unreliable and sometimes nonexistent telegraph service.

During the last week of October, communications between the Army of Tennessee and the various branches of the overall command structure of the Confederate armies of the West broke down. Hood's army was often out of touch with the authorities because telegraph offices in Courtland, Decatur, Athens, Mooresville, Huntsville, Bridgeport, and Stevenson, Alabama, had fallen into Federal hands. This compelled Beauregard to organize a courier

---

38 Sword, *The Confederacy's Last Hurrah*, 65.

39 *The Battle of Franklin: Five Hours in the Valley of Death*, Wide Awake Films, Kansas City, MO, 2005.

40 *OR* 39, pt. 3, 870.

network between Taylor's headquarters in Selma and Wheeler's cavalry headquarters in Gadsden, Alabama. Any dispatches Wheeler received from Taylor had to be forwarded to the rear of Hood's army. This arrangement of communicating via couriers proved complicated and ineffective, and by October 22, when Hood's army began marching west in preparation to cross the Tennessee River, couriers became totally useless. As a result, communication between Hood and Beauregard was difficult, and sometimes nearly impossible. In fact, Beauregard was so out of touch at this time that he instructed Gen. Howell Cobb to issue all necessary orders "when difficult to communicate with me."[41]

After Beauregard and Hood's initial conference on October 9, while Beauregard was en route to Jacksonville, Alabama, Hood kept Confederate authorities informed of his movements. "Headquarters will be to-morrow at Gadsden, where I hope not to be delayed more than forty-eight hours, when I shall move for the Tennessee River," Hood wired Bragg and Secretary of War James Seddon on October 19. The next day Hood wired Taylor: "I will move to-morrow for Guntersville on the Tennessee." To impede any Federal movements from the west, Hood asked Taylor to "please place all the garrison you can at Corinth, and have the railroad iron from there to Memphis taken up as close as possible to Memphis." Rather than avoid Beauregard, as Hood's critics assert, Hood added, "Have not yet seen General Beauregard. Give all the assistance you can to get my supplies to Tuscumbia." Beauregard's exact whereabouts were unknown, so Hood sent his request for supplies directly to Taylor. Although this act technically bypassed Beauregard in the command structure, Hood had little choice in the matter. Had he done otherwise, critics would have charged him with being irresponsible for ignoring his supply requirements to wait for Beauregard's appearance.[42]

Beauregard finally caught up with the army in Gadsden on October 21 and met with Hood for two days. The generals consulted closely on details of the upcoming campaign, which Beauregard as well as the Richmond authorities approved. Hood recalled the particulars in his memoirs:

> I proposed to move directly on to Guntersville, as indicated to General Taylor, and to take into Tennessee about one-half of Wheeler's cavalry (leaving the remainder to look

41 Carpenter, *A Slight Demonstration*, 32; OR 52, pt. 2, 767, 769.

42 Roman, *The Military Operations of General Beauregard*, 281; Hood, *Advance and Retreat*, 268.

after Sherman), and to have a depot of supplies at Tuscumbia, in the event that I met with defeat in Tennessee. Shortly after my arrival at Gadsden, General Beauregard reached the same point; I at once unfolded to him my plan, and requested that he confer apart with the corps commanders, Lieutenant-Generals Lee and Stewart and Major-General Cheatham. If after calm deliberation he deemed it expedient we should remain upon the Alabama line and attack Sherman, or take position, entrench, and finally follow on his rear when he should move south, I would of course acquiesce, albeit with reluctance. If, contrariwise, he should agree to my proposal into Tennessee, I would move immediately to Guntersville, thence to Stevenson, Bridgeport, and Nashville.[43]

Sword and subsequent writers claimed Beauregard had grown weary and impatient, even to the point of becoming angry with Hood for moving ahead without prior notification and for changing his plans as it suited him. There is little evidence that Beauregard was resentful of Hood's constant movements; but even if this were true, Hood's reasons for advancing quickly and, in Beauregard's absence, maintaining communication with Bragg, Seddon, and Taylor, were fully justified. Sword was at his most animated when asserting the existence of an acrimonious relationship between Hood and Beauregard, repeatedly accusing Hood of disrespect and discourtesy. Sword floods several pages of his book with dramatic and hyperbolic descriptions of Beauregard's disgust, not one of which is supported by any primary source materials if Sword's cited records are read objectively. Although Sword provides footnotes, comparison of the actual records with his paraphrasing often reveals gross inaccuracies and the frequent insertion of harsh and unwarranted personal interpretations.

In addition to inaccurately paraphrasing Beauregard's correspondence, Sword liberally cited Beauregard's biographer Alfred Roman. The descriptions offered of Beauregard's emotional reaction to these events were Roman's and not Beauregard's, but Sword uses those expressions extensively, relying on Roman's version even when contemporary primary source evidence does not support the portrayal.[44] The simple and obvious truth is that if General Beauregard was as miffed as Sword and Connelly asserted, he would have been much madder with Hood than the tenor of the words that appear in "Roman's"

---

43 OR 45, pt. 1, 647; Hood, *Advance and Retreat,* 268-269.

44 Roman, *The Military Operations of General Beauregard,* 288-302.

book indicate. Sword and Connelly took whatever slight irritation Roman hinted at and turned it into a Hatfield and McCoy feud.

The credibility of Sword's interpretations is further called into question by the close relationship the former generals maintained after the war. Both men later resided in New Orleans and by all accounts were firm friends. In fact, Beauregard arranged for the posthumous publication of Hood's memoirs and served as chairman of the Hood Relief Committee, which was established to care for Hood's ten surviving children who were orphaned when Hood and his wife died in August 1879.[45]

Regarding Hood's movements in northern Alabama, Sword boldly posited that on October 19, "Beauregard was thoroughly shocked" at Hood's conduct, and that the "exasperated Beauregard" resented Hood's disrespectful behavior, and was "very much disturbed." To support this claim Sword cited a telegram from Beauregard to Jefferson Davis, a page in Beauregard's biography by Roman, and Beauregard's official report of his tenure as commander of the Military Division of the West. None of these sources say anything of the sort.[46]

In an extraordinary distortion, Sword informs his readers that Beauregard, "fuming about the callous treatment by Hood," sent a message to President Davis "seeking to determine if he might actually run the forthcoming campaign." The source cited by Sword for this is an innocuous and unemotional inquiry Beauregard sent to Davis seeking clarification on his specific authority as the first commander of the newly created Military Division on the West. In fact, Beauregard questioned Davis about the limits of his authority when physically present with *any* Confederate force in the Western Theater—not just Hood's Army of Tennessee. Here is what Beauregard actually wrote the president:

> To prevent confusion, please inform me whether my presence with any army in the field imposes on me the necessity of assuming command, and whether in that case it relieves from duty the immediate commander. Should not my orders pass merely through that officer, without destroying the existing system of the organization?[47]

45 Dyer, *The Gallant Hood*, 319.

46 Sword, *The Confederacy's Last Hurrah*, 63, 65.

47 Ibid., 66; 39, pt. 3, 870.

Not only was Beauregard's correspondence devoid of animosity, but Sword also ignored or disregarded his later official report, which was equally unremarkable in tone and content. Of Hood's movements in northern Alabama, Beauregard wrote that after "conferring with him in regard to his future movements," he learned on two occasions that Hood had moved ahead, heading west "without advising me." Beauregard simply stated that he had not received notification of Hood's route changes and revealed the difficulty in communications, explaining that as of October 9, Richard Taylor had not yet even provided him (Beauregard) with a staff or horses. According to Beauregard, he was en route to meet with Taylor in Jacksonville, Alabama, when he learned of Hood's change in plans, at which time he simply turned around and met Hood at Gadsden. Beauregard did not censure Hood for the change in plans, nor did he express any personal offense at Hood's actions. As discussed earlier, when Hood learned of the presence of enemy forces at his proposed crossing point, he justifiably and reasonably changed his plans but was unable to immediately communicate this to Beauregard, whose own whereabouts were unknown to Hood because he was on the way to Jacksonville to meet with Taylor. Nonetheless, Sword characterizes this activity as "callous treatment" by Hood that angered Beauregard.[48]

Here is what Beauregard wrote of the Gadsden meeting:

> In an interview with General Hood he informed me that he was then en route to Middle Tennessee, via Gunter's Landing, on the Tennessee River. At Gadsden I had conversations during two days with him in relation to the future operations of the army, in the course of which he stated that his general plan had been submitted to and approved by General Bragg, then commanding the Armies of the Confederate States. In view of existing condition of affairs the movement then in progress met my approval.

Sword used these three sentences to support a description of a "thoroughly shocked" Beauregard who was "exasperated" at the October 22-23 Gadsden meeting. Characterizing Hood as "rash and careless," and speaking "with insistence" to Beauregard, Sword asserted that Hood "felt contempt for Beauregard's nitpicking." For these bold and harsh assertions, Sword cited a

---

48 OR 45, pt. 1, 647.

single page in the *Official Records*, which offers nothing to support any of Sword's claims.[49]

Even Thomas Connelly, hardly a firm Hood supporter, admitted that Beauregard's correspondence to the Confederate capital regarding the Gadsden meeting with Hood was not contentious. According to Connelly, Beauregard's tone with the government in Richmond explaining his decision to send Hood into Tennessee "seemed almost enthusiastic."[50]

In yet another attempt to portray Hood as disrespectful and insubordinate, Sword wrote that Beauregard, via his aide, sent a "curt note" to Hood asking for a summary of the army's past actions and a statement of future plans. The note, which Sword did not reproduce verbatim, reads as follows:

> General Beauregard desires that you will forward him for the information of the War Department a brief summary of the operations of your army from the date of its departure from Jonesborough, Georgia, to the present time; also a concise statement of your plans for future operations, intended for the same office.[51]

Sword continued slamming the Army of Tennessee's commander when he alleged that "Hood remained silent, ignoring this request for three days." Sword failed to inform his readers that Hood did reply via a message sent by his inspector general to Richmond the following day, in which he clearly explained the reasons why reports and routine administrative functions were being delayed:

> I beg leave respectfully to report that it is impracticable to render any inspection reports for the army of Tennessee for the month of October, 1864. Since the 29th of September this army has been marching from fifteen to twenty miles a day. The campaign is still going on. General Hood unites with me in saying that these reports cannot be rendered, and hopes that this statement of facts will satisfy you that it is impracticable to do so. When you hear from me next, I hope that it will be in the heart of Tennessee, after Sherman has been whipped and the state reclaimed. The army is a unit, buoyant with hope.[52]

---

49 Ibid.; Sword, *The Confederacy's Last Hurrah*, 64; *OR* 45, pt. 1, 647.

50 Connelly, *Autumn of Glory*, 484.

51 *OR* 39, pt. 3, 867.

52 Sword, *The Confederacy's Last Hurrah*, 66; *OR* 39, pt. 3, 871.

Notwithstanding Sword's dramatic portrayal, Beauregard's request to Hood clearly was not "curt," and Hood did not defiantly ignore the request.

Bypassing Decatur, Hood moved the army on to Tuscumbia to await Forrest and his cavalry and receive much-needed supplies. Sword continued to create the illusion of a conflict between Hood and Beauregard: "Within ten days Hood was back to his routine of ignoring Beauregard," who again was forced to endure "callous treatment by Hood with smoldering resentment until finally another heated confrontation occurred." Sword, who did not provide a primary source for these claims, explained the absence of historical evidence by claiming that both Beauregard and Hood hid their conflict from Richmond, "muted by a mutually advantageous" agreement, and as cover Beauregard sent a "syrupy note" to Jefferson Davis regarding the state of affairs at Tuscumbia.[53]

Another mischaracterization by Sword involves an event in Tuscumbia on November 11, when Hood suggested changing his supply base to Purdy, Tennessee. In response, Beauregard (according to Sword) not only rejected the idea but was "determined to retaliate." The retaliation, continued Sword, was a review of A. P. Stewart's corps arranged by Beauregard without informing Hood, who "responded to the perceived challenge like a petulant child," sending an "acid-laced note to Beauregard." It is unknown how Sword could interpret Beauregard's request to review one of Hood's corps as revenge for suggesting a change of supply bases. In any event, none of the language in the note from Hood to Beauregard described by Sword as "acid-laced" is out of the ordinary.[54]

Beauregard's reply to Hood was equally benign. In it, the department commander explained to the army commander that he and General Stewart had mutually agreed to an informal troop review, and by an innocent oversight Hood had not been informed. (According to Beauregard, he thought Stewart would naturally inform Hood, but had failed to do so.) Sword injected even more melodrama into this non-event, writing, "Beauregard had Hood's dander up, and he pushed even further . . . as soon as circumstances permitted, Beauregard said, he would separately review the corps of Cheatham and Lee." In fact, Beauregard closed his reply by politely expressing his desire to also review Cheatham's and Lee's corps, adding courteously, "As soon as

53 Sword, *The Confederacy's Last Hurrah*, 66.

54 Ibid., 70.

circumstances permit . . . provided it will not interfere with the movements of the army."[55]

Sword's version of these events continued. He informed readers that "to rub salt in Hood's wounds," Beauregard sent a note to Hood "about alleged mistreatment of [black] prisoners" being used as laborers on the railroad and fortifications around Corinth. Although Beauregard's adjutant had indeed sent Hood a note inquiring about the medical treatment of the black laborers, on the same day Beauregard also sent Hood a request for the repair of some nearby bridges. Sword's conclusion that correspondence over routine administrative matters was vengeful retaliation by Beauregard is baseless and inconsistent with Beauregard's own words.[56]

According to Sword, a "livid" Beauregard would ultimately "fully perceive Hood's woeful indiscretion and careless planning in the maintenance of his army." Considering Sword's allegation that a "frustrated" and "exasperated" Beauregard was wary of Hood's ineptitude and disregard for operations, observers might reasonably wonder why the senior general would depart on November 16 and leave the Confederacy's Western army under Hood's exclusive care for two full months. Beauregard would spend the next eight weeks personally overseeing affairs in Richard Taylor's and William Hardee's departments—and not visit the Army of Tennessee again until January 13, 1865.[57]

55 Ibid.; *OR* 39, pt. 3, 914.

56 Sword, *The Confederacy's Last Hurrah*, 70; Roman, *The Military Operations of General Beauregard*, 605-606; Sword, *The Confederacy's Last Hurrah*, 70; ibid., 913-914.

57 Ibid., 65, 74-75; Roman, *The Military Operations of General Beauregard*, 332.

Chapter 8

"It is striking how history, when resting on
the memory of men, always touches the
bounds of mythology."

— *Leopold von Ranke*

Frank Cheatham and the
Spring Hill Affair

Much has been written over the past 140 years of the
Confederate failure at Spring Hill, Tennessee. Exactly
what happened and who was responsible have never been conclusively
established. None of what has been written on the so-called Spring Hill Affair
identifies the specific reasons for the puzzling breakdown in Confederate
command that resulted in the successful withdrawal of John Schofield's army
from Columbia to Franklin—right past Hood's sleeping Army of Tennessee—
on the night of November 29, 1864.

Virtually any Southern force of size could have trapped Schofield that
night. An excellent brief summary of these events appeared in the early classic
Battles and Leaders of the Civil War:

> A single Rebel brigade like Adams's or Cockrell's or Maney's—veterans since Shiloh—
> planted squarely across the pike, either south or north of Spring Hill, would have
> effectually prevented Schofield's retreat, and daylight would have found his whole

force cut off from every avenue of escape by more than twice its numbers, to assault whom would have been madness, and to avoid whom would have been impossible.

Why Cleburne and Brown failed to drive away Stanley's one division before dark; why Bate failed to possess himself of the pike south of the town; why Stewart failed to lead his troops to the pike at the north; why Forrest, with his audacious temper and his enterprising cavalry, did not fully hold Thompson's Station or the crossing of the West Harpeth, half-way to Franklin; these are to this day disputed questions among . . . the Confederate commanders.[1]

Although virtually every aspect of the Spring Hill Affair seems to have been considered, two questions are rarely, if ever, raised regarding the roles played by Stephen D. Lee and Nathan Bedford Forrest. First, why did corps commander Lee not inform Hood that Schofield's entire force had completely evacuated Columbia? Although the Federal withdrawal lasted several hours and was completed about 3:00 a.m., it is inconceivable that none of Lee's pickets or scouts would have missed the movement of 800 wagons, dozens of artillery batteries, and 22,000 infantry. If Hood had been informed that the entire Federal army was withdrawing en masse earlier, it is reasonable to assume that he would have taken a different course of action. Among the Confederate commanders routinely criticized for the Spring Hill debacle, Lee escapes mention.

Second, why has Nathan Bedford Forrest evaded reproach for his role at Spring Hill? He is likewise held blameless for the Federal escape even though he was instructed to seize control of the road. He acknowledged his instructions, failed to do as instructed, and never informed Hood that the road remained open. Throughout the night of November 29-30, Hood received several visitors at his headquarters near Spring Hill. Although multiple orders were issued throughout the evening, none resulted in the road being blocked. Forrest was among the senior commanders known to have met with Hood that evening. The two generals held a long meeting that began around 9:30 p.m. Forrest had ridden to Hood's headquarters to inform him that Frank Cheatham's corps had failed to block the road. The meeting included Hood, Forrest, and A. P. Stewart, whose corps had arrived and was resting nearby. According to Governor Isham Harris of Tennessee, who was present at this

---

1   Henry Stone, "Repelling Hood's Invasion of Tennessee," *Battles and Leaders of the Civil War*, 4 vols. (New York: The Century Company, 1888), vol. 4, 446.

meeting, Hood said to Stewart, "It is of great importance that a brigade should be put on the road tonight. Can you send one?"

Stewart replied, "Well General my men have had nothing to eat all day, and are very tired and . . ."

Hood interrupted Stewart and turned to his cavalry commander, "General Forrest, can you put a brigade there?"

Forrest replied, "Yes, General, if I can get ammunition, though my men have been fighting all day with nothing to eat besides."

To accommodate rapid movement, Forrest had left his ordnance wagons at Columbia earlier that day, so Hood ordered Stewart to provide ammunition to Forrest and the two generals departed Hood's headquarters. According to Harris, "Hearing no more, [Hood] and his staff presently went to bed."[2]

As Forrest departed, Gen. William Bate arrived to inform Hood that the road was still open. Hood told Bate not to worry, because Forrest had just been ordered to seize the road north of Spring Hill. Confident in his intrepid cavalryman, Hood told Bate to rest well and that tomorrow the army would have "a surrender without a fight."[3]

In an effort to comply with Hood's orders, Forrest sent Gen. Lawrence Sullivan "Sul" Ross's Texas cavalry brigade north of Spring Hill to Thompson's Station, where the Texans briefly succeeded in holding the road before being repelled by Federal infantry. Ross withdrew to a nearby hilltop, from which point he later recalled watching the enemy march past his position throughout the night. What is not known is whether Ross reported back to Forrest that the Federals still controlled the road. Either he did not, or if he did and Forrest received the news, Forrest failed to report the failure to Hood. Hearing nothing from Forrest to the contrary, Hood reasonably assumed the reliable cavalryman had succeeded in gaining control of the road. In Civil War literature, neither Ross nor Forrest is criticized for failing to notify Hood that they were unable to hold the road.[4]

2   Brown-Ewell Papers, Tennessee State Library and Archives, Nashville.

3   Horn, *The Army of Tennessee*, 393.

4   Jacobson, *For Cause and For Country*, 173.

Civil War historians frequently censure Hood for neglecting to personally confirm that his important orders to block the road had been followed. A typical example is provided by A. P. Stewart's biographer Sam Elliott in *Soldier of Tennessee:* "Stewart remarked, as he consistently would in later years, that as Hood was present on the field, he should have made sure that his orders were obeyed." Considering the tragic consequences of the Confederate failure to seize the road—and that Hood was the army commander—this criticism of Hood is not completely unfair. However, Capt. A. C. Jones of the 3rd Arkansas Infantry, who served under Hood in the Army of Northern Virginia, disagreed with Stewart. "It seems a strange sort of military discipline that a commander in chief should issue his orders to his corps commanders and then go to the front to see those orders executed," explained Jones. "Was that the custom of General Johnston or any other great commander?. . . . How could General Hood know of the dereliction of any particular officer and be on the spot to correct it? His proper place was at some central point, where he could have been communicated with by his subordinates."5

If failing to ensure compliance of an important order is blameworthy, how does Forrest evade censure for his actions at Spring Hill? Forrest gave an order of the most critical importance to a subordinate (Ross), assumed it would be accomplished, and went to bed. Using A. P. Stewart's logic, Forrest should have ridden to Thompson's Station to personally make sure that Ross had blocked the road. Unlike Hood, Forrest's inaction is never deemed negligent, nor is he blamed for the Confederate failure at Spring Hill.6

In a postwar letter, Gen. Daniel Govan held Hood directly responsible for the Spring Hill failure. "I should say the blame must be his," Govan insisted. "[H]e should have mounted his horse, taken personal command and directed the advance himself." Govan then asked, "Would this not have been the course of Lee, Jackson, and Forrest?" Govan's belief that Forrest would have taken personal charge in such a situation is curious because Forrest had that opportunity at Spring Hill—and failed to do so.7

5   A. C. Jones, "Criticism of General Hood," *Confederate Veteran*, vol. 22 (November, 1914), 508.

6   Sam Davis Elliott, *Soldier of Tennessee: General Alexander P. Stewart and the Civil War in the West* (Baton Rouge: Louisiana State University Press, 1999), 234.

7   Daniel Govan letter to George Williams, June 1906.

ᔆ᠕   ᕽ᠕

In addition to the well-known laudanum myth, some authors have described Hood as being physically and intellectually impaired at Spring Hill. In *The Finishing Stroke: Texans in the 1864 Tennessee Campaign*, John Lundberg claimed that Hood was "confused and half asleep" when A. P. Stewart visited him at his headquarters on the evening of November 29. The author's footnote implies that the source for the observation comes from Stewart. Lundberg's source, however, is not Stewart but author Wiley Sword, who wrote (without proper sourcing) that Hood's mind was "clouded by fatigue and perhaps laudanum." Lundberg repeated elsewhere in his book, again without a reliable source, that Forrest visited Hood later in the evening and that Hood was "still half asleep."[8]

It is interesting to note that Hood met with generals Forrest, Stewart, Cheatham, and Bate during the night at Spring Hill, and interacted with several staff members including majors Cumming, Hamilton, Blanton, and Mason, as well as Governor Isham Harris (who served as a volunteer staff member for Hood), yet none of these men ever wrote a word about Hood being fatigued or in any way mentally infirmed.

Another florid and unfounded account of the Spring Hill Affair was crafted by Eddy Davison and Daniel Foxx in their biography of Forrest. In describing the breakfast meeting at Rippavilla on the morning of November 30, after it was discovered that Schofield had escaped during the night, they wrote the following: "Once everyone was present, Hood began throwing the blame at nearly each commander. As he dressed down this illustrious array of Confederate officers, Hood mainly accused Generals Cheatham and Cleburne. Hood blamed everyone but himself, and it was well known within the ranks of the Army of Tennessee that Hood had no great love for his new command." As a source for these astounding comments, Davison and Foxx cite a single page of Hood's memoirs and Confederate Gen. James Chalmers's official report of the Tennessee Campaign. Neither source mentions anything that remotely relates to these unfounded assertions.[9]

---

8   Lundberg, *The Finishing Stroke: Texans in the 1864 Tennessee Campaign*, 82-83; Sword, *The Confederacy's Last Hurrah*, 147. The laudanum issue is discussed extensively in Chapter 19.

9   Davison and Foxx, *Nathan Bedford Forrest*, 358.

No written records of the Rippavilla meeting have been located, and it is not known with certainty even who was in attendance. If Hood blamed any specific officer(s) at the meeting for some lapse in command judgment, their identities remain unknown. Davison's and Foxx's contention that the soldiers of the Army of Tennessee knew that Hood "had no great love for his new command" is as remarkable as it is unbelievable. If it was so well known, why did neither Hood nor any of the 20,000 soldiers and officers of the Army of Tennessee who survived the Tennessee Campaign ever write a word about it?

☞   ☜

Unable to identify those responsible for the failure at Spring Hill, modern authors routinely defer blame to Hood, who as senior commander can rightly be held ultimately responsible. Although Hood may be considered the culprit today, it was not so in late November 1864.

Of the failure at Spring Hill, Dr. Charles T. Quintard, chaplain of the Army of Tennessee, wrote, "Who was to blame of the subordinate commanders I cannot say exactly, but General Hood's orders were positive and specific, conveyed by two of his staff officers and lastly by Governor Harris to General Cheatham." According to S. A. Cunningham of the 41st Tennessee Infantry, the Federal escape at Spring Hill was "a failure for which it was understood General Hood was not to blame. There were grave mistakes made," he continued, "but the ability and the faithfulness of Confederate generals are a source of pride and gratitude to which we should cling for all time. Even at Spring Hill, where the greatest misfortunes occurred, I have no word of reproach."[10]

Captain Jones of the 3rd Arkansas Infantry wrote that many men in the Army of Tennessee, especially among the commanding officers, bitterly resented the removal of Joe Johnston, and that Hood "found himself in the embarrassing condition of having neither the confidence nor sympathy of his subordinates. The consequence of this feeling," continued Jones, "was that in the execution of this movement on Spring Hill a portion of his command at least seemed more afraid of being led into a trap than anxious to make a success

---

10 Elliott, *Doctor Quintard*, 220; Cunningham, "The Battle of Franklin"; S. A. Cunningham, "Events Leading to the Battle of Franklin on the 45th Anniversary of the Battle," *Confederate Veteran*, vol. 18 (January 1910).

of what was, in fact, up to a certain point one of the most brilliant achievements of the war."[11]

Colonel W. D. Gale, a member of A. P. Stewart's staff, believed that Hood's flanking movement at Spring Hill was "in conception worthy of Stonewall Jackson, and in execution feeble and disgraceful." Blaming Hood's subordinates for not attacking the fleeing enemy, Gale wrote, "Not a blow was struck, though orders were sent by Gen. Hood several times to attack at once." Major James Ratchford of Hood's staff agreed, and wrote the following:

> General [Stonewall] Jackson, in all his campaigns, never planned a movement that gave greater promise of success than did the movement of General Hood at Spring Hill. General Hood said in his report that he gave General Cheatham positive orders in person, while in sight of the turnpike at Spring Hill, to attack the retreating enemy, and place his men across the pike. He said further that he sent staff officers to Cheatham several times after that, urging him to place troops across the pike to intercept the fleeing Federals. Major Blanton and Major Hamilton, both of Hood's staff, each told me personally that [they] had carried the orders to General Cheatham. That grand old hero [General Hood] died without ever defending himself, allowing the world to believe that he was responsible for the failure.[12]

Schofield's cavalry commander, James Wilson, was impressed with Hood's actions. "His [Hood's] plan was brilliant," wrote Wilson about Spring Hill, "and so obviously proper that Schofield should have divined it from the start." Wilson later supposed that the failures of Hood's "bold undertakings," such as the flank march from Columbia to Spring Hill, was due in part to the indifference of Hood's subordinate officers.[13]

Private J. P. Young of the 7th Tennessee Cavalry, later a judge in Memphis, Tennessee, wrote a lengthy article in *Confederate Veteran* magazine entitled "Hood's Failure at Spring Hill." Young, who described Hood as "able but unfortunate," realized, as did everyone else, how important Spring Hill was to the campaign: "Hood, successful here [Spring Hill], would have taken his place as one of the great captains of the war." Commenting on the debate that had

---

11 Jones, "Criticism of General Hood," 507.

12 W. D. Gale, "Hood's Campaign in Tennessee," *Confederate Veteran*, vol. 2 (January 1894), 4; James Ratchford, *Memoirs of a Confederate Staff Officer: From Bethel to Bentonville*, Evelyn Sieburg, ed. (Shippensburg, PA: White Mane Books, 1998), 61.

13 Wilson, *Under the Old Flag*, 42, 45.

raged in the decades after the war, Young wrote, "There are not lacking writers who have striven to demonstrate that General Schofield in the operations of the 29th was engaged in a game of profound strategy with General Hood, that he had known Hood at the Military Academy and known him to be a rash blunderer without mathematical capacity or power of combination, and that he [Schofield] had reasoned that Hood would helplessly dally before Spring Hill without power to attack or decide what next to be done. . . . It is scarcely necessary to point out the weakness of such an argument." Young went on to point out that Schofield, in his correspondence with Gen. George Thomas during the desperate retreat from Pulaski to Franklin, made no claim of Hood's lack of prowess or potency, and mentioned nothing of any ineptitude by Hood in his later reports. To the contrary, Schofield openly declared his perilous position to Thomas and that a mistake by him or his subordinates would have been disastrous.

Judge Young went on to offer the following observation:

> It must be patent to the most casual observer . . . but for the failure of Hood's subordinates to act promptly at Spring Hill, Stanley would have been crushed before nightfall, the wagon train and reserve artillery of the army captured, Schofield entrapped as he approached in the darkness with Ruger's Division, and the remaining divisions . . . left at the mercy of Hood at daylight next morning. . . .

> Success here and the destruction of his antagonist would have placed Hood in the most exalted position among his people and his name high among the great masters of strategy in the war. The move was faultless; the success of it up to 4 p.m. startling. Triumph was within his grasp, but failure came, whatever the cause, where least to be expected among those splendid officers and men. General Schofield has been honored by the nation with the highest military office in the gift of the people. Hood, failing through no fault of his own, unless it was his failure to personally see that his orders were obeyed, is reckoned by the average reader of history as mediocre and inefficient.[14]

Colonel Virgil Murphey of the 17th Alabama Infantry was captured during the fighting at Franklin on November 30 and taken to Schofield's headquarters for interrogation. Murphey later recalled Schofield's acknowledgment of his army's "perilous position" at Spring Hill, and his chastisement of Hood for

---

14 J. P. Young, "Hood's Failure at Spring Hill," *Confederate Veteran*, vol. 16 (January 1908), 40-41.

allowing the escape. According to Murphey, he responded in Hood's defense that "a grave responsibility rested upon the general who failed to make the attack as we knew our advantage and Hood had ordered the attack." While imprisoned at Johnson's Island in Ohio, Murphey wrote of Hood's assault at Franklin: "The same blow delivered with equal power at Spring Hill or Thompson's Station would have yielded us dominion over Tennessee. A failure to obey [Hood's] order lost us a noble commonwealth."[15]

John Copley of the 49th Tennessee Infantry described Forrest on the morning of November 30. When he learned that the Federals had slipped away during the night, an enraged Forrest "cursed out some of the commanding officers, and censured them for allowing the Federal army to escape." It is important to note that Copley recalled Forrest's blaming multiple officers—and not specifically Hood, or Hood alone.[16]

Even a Yankee officer, Lieutenant Chesley Mosman of the 59th Illinois Infantry, felt compelled to comment on the matter. Having heard that Frank Cheatham was responsible for the Federal escape, according to the lieutenant, the Confederate corps commander "deferred seriously engaging for fear he would be flanked, thus refusing to obey General Hood's positive orders. Had Hood's order been obeyed, the entire face of the campaign would have been changed."[17]

However, none of these or other eyewitness accounts impressed author Barbara G. Ellis, who wrote in her 2003 book *The Moving Appeal* that Hood "ignored his generals' frantic pleas" to attack Schofield's retreating columns. As should be more than readily apparent, no pleas by Hood's subordinates—frantic or otherwise—appear in the Ellis's sources.[18]

---

15 Virgil Murphey Diary.

16 John Copley, "A Sketch of the Battle of Franklin, with Reminiscences of Camp Douglass," Southern Historical Collection, University of North Carolina-Chapel Hill, 1893, 34-35.

17 Arnold Gates, ed., *The Rough Side of War: The Civil War Journal of Chesley A. Mosman, 1st Lieutenant, Company D, 59th Illinois Volunteer Infantry Regiment*, (Othello, WA: Basin Publishing Company, 1987), 312.

18 Barbara G. Ellis, *The Moving Appeal: Mr. McClanahan, Mrs. Dill and the Civil War's Great Newspaper Run* (Macon, GA: Mercer University Press, 2003), 334. In an email exchange with the author on December 13, 2011, Dr. Ellis also asserted that General Hood, "permitted the Yankee army to march unchallenged up the road between the Confederate army as his subordinates wrung their hands at his 'indisposition' and refusal to turn over the command to one of them." Dr. Ellis was asked to provide a source for the claim, but did not respond.

∾   ∽

General Benjamin F. Cheatham, who led one of Hood's three infantry corps during the Tennessee Campaign, played a major role in the Spring Hill Affair. Hood claimed in his memoir, published posthumously in 1880, that he sent repeated orders to Cheatham on November 29 to attack the Federals and seize the road to block the passage of Schofield's army. In order to fully understand this issue, Hood's discussion is quoted below at length:

> I thought it probable that Cheatham had taken possession of Spring Hill without encountering material opposition, or had formed line across the pike, north of town, and entrenched without coming in serious contact with the enemy, which would account for the little musketry heard in his direction. However, to ascertain the truth, I sent an officer to ask Cheatham if he held the pike, and to inform him of the arrival of Stewart, whose corps I intended to throw on his left, in order to assail the Federals in flank that evening or the next morning, as they formed to attack Cheatham. At this juncture, the last messenger returned with the report that the road had not been taken possession of. General Stewart was then ordered to proceed to the right of Cheatham and place his Corps across the pike, north of Spring Hill.

> By this hour, however, twilight was upon us, when General Cheatham rode up in person. I at once directed Stewart to halt, and, turning to Cheatham, I exclaimed with deep emotion, as I felt the golden opportunity fast slipping from me, "General, why in the name of God have you not attacked the enemy, and taken possession of the pike?" He replied that the line looked a little too long for him, and that Stewart should first form on his right. I could hardly believe it possible that this brave soldier, who had given proof of such courage and ability upon so many hard-fought fields, would even make such a report. After leading him within full view of the enemy, and pointing out to him the Federals, retreating in great haste and confusion, along the pike, and then giving explicit orders to attack, I would have soon expected the midday to turn into darkness as for him to have disobeyed my orders. I then asked General Cheatham whether or not Stewart's Corps, if formed on the right, would extend across the pike. He answered in the affirmative.[19]

---

19   Hood, *Advance & Retreat*, 285-286.

After reading this account, Cheatham denied Hood's charge in a speech in Louisville in late 1881. The former corps commander accused Hood (who was now dead) of lying. Here is the bulk of Cheatham's reply:

> When I had returned from my left, where I had been to get Bate in position, and was on the way to the right of my line, it was dark; but I intended to move forward with Cleburne and Brown and make the attack, knowing that Bate would be in position to support them. Stewart's column had already passed by on the way toward the turnpike, and I presumed he would be in position on my right.
>
> On reaching the road where General Hood's field headquarters had been established, I found a courier with a message from General Hood, requesting me to come to him at Captain Thompson's house, about one and a fourth miles back on the road to Rutherford's creek. I found General Stewart with General Hood. The Commanding General there informed me that he had concluded to postpone the attack till daylight. The road was still open—orders to remain quiet until morning—and nothing to prevent the enemy from marching toward Franklin.

"The dramatic scene with which [Hood] embellishes his narrative of the day's operations," Cheatham added, "only occurred in the imagination of General Hood."[20]

Unfortunately for Hood and the various Confederate commanders who have been accused over the decades of full or partial blame for the failure at Spring Hill, the person most responsible survived the campaign and the war, lived 21 years after the conflict ended, and repeatedly denied responsibility while accusing Hood of dishonesty. According to multiple witnesses, the person responsible for the Spring Hill debacle was Frank Cheatham.

Among the many witnesses who made various claims and denials after the war pertaining to events at Spring Hill was Maj. Joseph B. Cumming, one of Hood's staff officers. Cumming left a detailed account of what he saw and heard on the evening of November 29:

> General Hood sent me forward with an order to General Cheatham to attack at once. I delivered the order, and as I had ridden hard to deliver it I returned to Gen. Hood's headquarters at a slow pace expecting every minute to hear the sound of the attack on the pike. It was now getting dark. It was the 29th of November, chilly and drizzling.

20 Benjamin F. Cheatham, *Southern Historical Society Papers*, vol. 9, 526, 530.

When I reached Gen. Hood's headquarters, to my astonishment I found Gen. Cheatham there, he having out-ridden me by a different route. He was remonstrating with Gen. Hood against a night attack.[21]

As a member of Hood's staff, Cumming's credibility has always been questioned, for he would have had a natural tendency to support his commander. However, among recently discovered documents are two postwar letters to Hood that corroborate Cumming's account, one from Stephen D. Lee and another from William W. Old.

Lee wrote the following in a letter dated August 25, 1875: "I met A. P. Stewart at Columbus about 6 weeks ago and profounded, why was no battle delivered at Spring Hill? He replied in substance that *Cheatham & Cleburne determined it was not best to bring on an engagement at night* [emphasis added]." Lee clarified that Stewart had not personally heard the two senior officers' conversation firsthand, but "believed such was the case and had heard so." In this same letter, Lee urged Hood to set the record straight on Spring Hill, and continued to do so up until his last correspondence a few months before Hood's death four years later. Referring to Hood's "natural modesty," Lee wrote, "I think now you can write with more propriety than at any time to this date and possibly it is now your duty." In reference to both Atlanta and Spring Hill, Lee added, "I believe now a correct statement as to your movements would do good. I will aid you all in my power as I sympathize with you in your feelings to vindicate yourself."[22]

Because Lee conveyed to Hood that Stewart did not personally hear Cheatham or Cleburne express displeasure with launching a night attack, "but believed such was the case and had heard so," Hood apparently sought additional validation to support Cumming's and Lee's revealing information. Further corroboration arrived two years later.

On September 10, 1877, William W. Old, a former Confederate major, met with another former major named E. L. Martin. Both men had been members of Gen. Edward Johnson's staff during the Tennessee Campaign. The

---

21 Joseph B. Cumming, Recollections, Southern Historical Collection, University of North Carolina-Chapel Hill, 72. Cumming was a major in the 5th Georgia, served on the Florida coast in 1861 and thereafter spent most of the war in the Western Theater. He joined W. H. T. Walker's brigade and, after Walker was killed in the battle of Atlanta on July 22, 1864, became a member of John B. Hood's staff.

22 S. D. Lee letter to John Bell Hood, August 25, 1875, John Bell Hood Personal Papers.

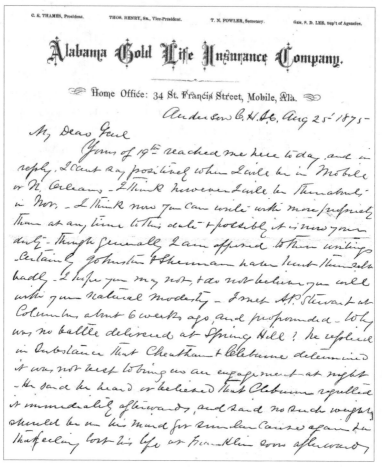

Stephen D. Lee letter to John Bell Hood, August 25, 1877.

John Bell Hood Personal Papers

discussion that ensued so stunned Old that he sent a letter (see page 126) to Hood the same day. "In regard to the attack at Spring Hill," wrote Old, "Mr. Martin says that Genl. Johnson did go to Gen. Cheatham and <u>beg</u> him to let him attack with his division, stating that he did not even require any support, but that Genl. Cheatham refused, stating <u>finally</u> he was opposed to night attacks. Mr. Martin says he was present [*emphasis in the original letter*]."[23]

23 William W. Old letter to John Bell Hood, September 10, 1877, John Bell Hood Personal Papers. In the letter, Old invited Hood to write Martin, and provided Martin's mailing address

Major James Ratchford, a member of General Lee's staff, offered support for Major Martin's claim and Old's letter to Hood when he also recalled Cheatham's refusal to allow Johnson to attack. "I heard General Ed Johnson say that during the night he could have routed the entire Federal army with only his division," Ratchford wrote in 1909, "but was not permitted to attack them."[24]

In 1879, Hood was working feverishly on his memoirs and corresponding regularly with Lee, who implored Hood to rectify the narrative of Spring Hill.

in New York City. It is not known at this time if Hood indeed wrote to Martin, or if Martin replied.

24 Ratchford, *Some Reminiscences of Persons and Incidents of the Civil War*, 61-62.

WM. W. OLD,
ATTORNEY AT LAW,
OFFICE, 146 MAIN STREET,
(FRONT ROOM, UP STAIRS.)

Norfolk, Va., September 10ᵗʰ 1877.

Genl. Jno. B. Hood,

    Alleghany Springs:

      My dear Sir: I met, this morning, Mr. E. L. Martin, who was an aide-de-Camp of Genl. Edward Johnson at Nashville, and had a conversation with him in regard to the cause of the general's capture. He says the General had left his horse with a Courier, and not with a staff officer, and that the Courier took fright and left with the General's horse. I was under the impression he had left the horse with a staff officer, and I wish to correct the impression I made on your mind. In regard to the attack at Spring Hill, Mr. Martin says that Genl. Johnson did go to Genl. Cheatham and beg him to let him attack with his Division, stating he did not even require any support, but that Genl. Cheatham refused, stating finally he was opposed to night attacks. Mr. Martin says he was present. If you wish to correspond with him, his address is 104 East 22ᵈ Street, New York. My recollection of that occurrence as detailed to me by Genl. Johnson was entirely correct.

      Yours very truly, Wm. W. Old.

William W. Old letter to John Bell Hood, September 10, 1877.
John Bell Hood Personal Papers

Lee wrote on April 25 of that year, "I do hope your book will make clear the Spring Hill matter, for it is time for that mystery to be cleared up." Lee's feelings on the matter were so strong that he, in effect, threatened Hood that he would do it himself if the former army commander refused: "If you do not," Lee bluntly wrote, "I will feel it my duty to do so after your book comes out."[25]

---

25 Stephen. D. Lee letter to John Bell Hood, April 25, 1879, John Bell Hood Personal Papers.

Hood complied with Lee's suggestion (which was more of an ultimatum) by revealing in his memoirs that Cheatham had disobeyed orders to block the road at Spring Hill. Unfortunately, he failed to provide enough details to withstand Cheatham's persistent denials. Because Hood died before the publication of his memoir, the more convincing details were consigned to Hood's work papers, whose existence and whereabouts remained unknown until only recently. Hood's premature death allowed Cheatham to deny Hood's charges with impunity for the seven years he outlived his former commander. Hood's lost letters contained testimony from others that were both explicitly and implicitly confidential, and Hood honored that confidentiality by not revealing evidence that would have otherwise strengthened his account. With those letters seemingly lost and Hood in his grave, Tennessee native Frank Cheatham's repeated and eloquent denials convinced historians that Hood was the real culprit, unfairly blaming others for the Spring Hill fiasco.

In *Hood's Tennessee Campaign*, Thomas Hay held Hood culpable for failing to ensure that his orders were "promptly obeyed and correctly executed." Hay believed Cheatham's false denials. "General Cheatham" the historian boldly asserted, "was not to blame" for the failure at Spring Hill.[26]

Stanley Horn wrote in *The Army of Tennessee*, "From reading Hood's account and Cheatham's account of the same events, it is clear that both cannot be right. Either one of them misrepresents the facts, or one or both had a hazy recollection. And though it is a serious matter to challenge a commanding general's veracity, the weight of evidence favors Cheatham." Horn added that "Cheatham says even more positively and convincingly that Hood's recital of his alleged responsibility is 'a statement for which there was not the slightest foundation.'"[27]

Wiley Sword picked up the cudgel to once again bludgeon Hood. "It was Hood's mismanagement and his assorted careless errors that led to such disastrous consequences," he wrote about Spring Hill in *The Confederacy's Last Hurrah*. "Indeed, despite the failure of others the primary fault was Hood's. His careless attitude can perhaps be explained only in terms of the fatigue and possibly the opium derivative which clouded his mind. The responsibility for the conduct of operations was Hood's, and yet he had acted with gross

26 Hay, *Hood's Tennessee Campaign*, 101.

27 Horn, *The Army of Tennessee*, 387.

carelessness. By failing to adequately communicate with his chief subordinates, he had created a fatal leadership malaise."[28]

Thomas Connelly was less critical than Sword in *Autumn of Glory*. Hood's corps commanders "had not served him well," explained Connelly, but "Hood was partially responsible." Several years later, Connelly and co-author James McDonough sharpened their pen when they described Hood's reaction to the Spring Hill failure in their book *Five Tragic Hours*: "Hood furiously lashed out at his subordinates, placing the blame on them rather than on himself."[29]

With the recent discovery of Hood's personal papers, at least four separate witnesses are now known to have testified that Cheatham, despite his repeated denials, disobeyed orders to attack at Spring Hill. S. D. Lee wrote to Hood, "The blunder was at Spring Hill. Had that not occurred all would have been well. There the responsibility of failure in the campaign rests. As noble and gallant an effort was made at Franklin by commander and army knowing the blunder, as was ever made and it was the last chance to strike with success. With what results we both know."[30]

According to Lee, "Franklin was a result of blunders made at Spring Hill." The ensuing bloodbath on November 30 was among the most tragic in American military history, and has been consistently portrayed as John Bell Hood's fault. Unless four independent witnesses are not to be believed, Cheatham's insubordination resulted in the Federal escape at Spring Hill, precipitating the tragedy that followed hours later at Franklin. It will be interesting to see what changes, if any, are made to Civil War scholarship's future portrayals of John Bell Hood and Benjamin Franklin Cheatham at Spring Hill, and by extension, the battle of Franklin.[31]

ஒ   ஒ

As previously noted, Frank Cheatham outlived Hood for seven years, and during that time took full advantage of the opportunity to promote his version of the disputed events of November 29, 1864. Scholars and writers found one

---

28 Sword, *The Confederacy's Last Hurrah*, 154-155.

29 Connelly, *Autumn of Glory*, 500-501; Connelly and McDonough, *Five Tragic Hours*, 55.

30 S. D. Lee letter to John Bell Hood, April 16, 1879, John Bell Hood Personal Papers.

31 S. D. Lee letters to John Bell Hood, April 16 and 25, 1879, John Bell Hood Personal Papers.

of his stories in particular to be persuasive. During the march from Columbia to Spring Hill, Hood recalled pointing out the retreating Federals to Cheatham. Hood wrote in his memoirs, "I led the main body of the army to within about two miles and in full view of the pike from Columbia to Spring Hill and Franklin. I here halted at about 3 p.m., and requested General Cheatham, commanding the leading corps, and Major General Cleburne to advance to the spot where, sitting upon my horse, I had in sight the enemy's wagons and men passing at double-quick along the pike." According to Hood, he ordered Cheatham to go "at once" with Cleburne's division and take possession of the pike at or near Spring Hill.[32]

Cheatham later admitted that Hood did personally give him orders to seize the pike, but placed the location of the brief meeting at the Rutherford Creek crossing, roughly two and one-half miles south of Spring Hill. However, Cheatham vehemently denied that Hood ever pointed out the retreating Federal trains on the road, and added that the Columbia to Spring Hill pike "was never in view" at any point along the adjacent roads over which the Confederate army marched. With Hood in his grave, Cheatham wrote, "Only a mirage would have made possible the vision which this remarkable statement [by Hood] professes to record."[33]

Since Cheatham and Hood both agreed that Cheatham had been given orders to move rapidly to Spring Hill and seize control of the pike, the dispute is solely over the location of the meeting between the two commanders, and whether or not the retreating enemy could be seen. Remarkably, historians have become captivated by this seemingly minor quarrel, perhaps because its resolution would shed light on which commander was more truthful in his account of Spring Hill. For whatever reason, the disagreement over where Hood and Cheatham precisely met has taken on a prominent life of its own. In this otherwise insignificant feud of facts, historians have unanimously sided with Cheatham.

The point where present-day Mahlon Moore Road crosses Rutherford Creek is in fact approximately two miles south of Spring Hill, and from that point it is physically impossible to see the pike. However, that spot at Rutherford Creek is where Cheatham, not Hood, placed the location of their

32 Hood, *Advance & Retreat*, 284-285.

33 Benjamin F. Cheatham, "The Lost Opportunity at Spring Hill, Tenn.—General Cheatham's Reply to General Hood," 524-525, 529.

brief meeting. According to Hood, the location of his encounter with Cheatham was not two miles from Spring Hill; it was about two miles from the road to Spring Hill over which Schofield's army was retreating. Those who have written on the subject failed to mention this not insignificant detail.

Approximately one mile farther south of the Rutherford Creek crossing are four hills directly adjacent to the country road over which Hood's two corps made their flanking march. From atop the highest knoll, the Columbia to Spring Hill pike is clearly visible in the distance at multiple places—even without the aid of field glasses. Cheatham attempted to buttress his contention by stating that the road on which the Federals were retreating was never in view from any point along the route taken by the Confederates, a statement that is undeniably and demonstratively untrue.[34]

The Rutherford Creek crossing is a popular stop for Tennessee Campaign and battle of Spring Hill historical tours, and guides routinely take attendees to the top of a nearby knoll to prove beyond all doubt that Frank Cheatham was telling the truth and that John Bell Hood was lying about their meeting. In fact, the view from that knoll proves nothing: a visit to the highest knoll adjacent to present day Cliff Amos Road and John Sharp Road one mile south, where modern Route 31 (the former Columbia Pike) can be clearly seen, conclusively proves that Frank Cheatham was wrong.[35]

34 On September 28, 2012, the author and local historian Eric Jacobson identified and personally visited one of the hilltops from which the Columbia Pike can be seen. It is not conclusively known whether Hood's army at this point marched on the modern day Cliff Amos Road or John Sharp Road, but both are near to one another and to the four hills where the Columbia to Spring Hill pike can be seen. See also Cheatham, "The Lost Opportunity at Spring Hill," 529.

35 The author has personally attended multiple field tours that include the Columbia to Spring Hill movements of Hood's and Schofield's forces and the battle of Spring Hill. Every tour has included a stop at the Mahlon Moore Road bridge over Rutherford Creek, where attendees are taken to the top of a nearby hill, shown that the Columbia Pike cannot be seen, and told that Hood was wrong and Cheatham correct. Tour operators and guides assert, without proof, that this is the place of Hood's alleged meeting with Cheatham.

"Some write a narrative of wars and feats,
Of heroes little known, and call the rant
a history."

— *William Cowper*

Chapter 9

John Bell Hood and the Battle of Franklin

The battle of Franklin on November 30, 1864, was one of the most tragic events of the Civil War. In terms of the number of casualties suffered over a compact area during such a short time, it ranks among the bloodiest battles of the war, rivaling those of Cold Harbor, Antietam, Malvern Hill, and the more famous Pickett's Charge at Gettysburg.

To the well-traveled Civil War enthusiast, Franklin is also notable for the extent to which the battlefield was built over and thus obliterated in the decades after the war. Franklin was once considered the consummate example of hallowed ground lost to apathy. By the late 1990s, only two locations where heavy combat occurred had been preserved: the Collins Farm on the eastern flank, and the Carter House at the epicenter of the battle. Fortunately, a near-miraculous reclamation of core battlefield land was recently accomplished. Hundreds of acres of land have been acquired on the battle's eastern flank, and several acres of hallowed ground around the Carter House and Carter cotton gin have now been preserved.

The Franklin community's passive attitude toward the battle during the mid-to-late 20th century may have been due, in part, to the common interpretation of the battle that had taken hold of the public's imagination. This portrayal reduced the desperate high-stakes struggle between Schofield's Federals and Hood's Army of Tennessee to little more than a suicidal charge ordered by an inept and unstable Confederate commander, with Federal defenders casually decimating the attacking enemy from behind a line of entrenchments. The battlefield was considered by many to be a site of mass murder, rather than a pivotal Civil War battle with major strategic and political ramifications. Given this perception, it is little wonder that houses, restaurants, and other commercial buildings were built on this hallowed land. It has been a long time coming, but the community (both local and the Civil War community across the country) has finally come to better understand that the outcome at Franklin would have significantly influenced the course of the war.

Franklin, Tennessee, on November 30, 1864, was much more than a crime scene.

ᗌ   ᗌ

Any analysis of the decisions made during a historical event should be as comprehensive, accurate, and unbiased as possible, with a goal of revealing the credible historical evidence. Hood's critics and detractors have been heard; his supporters deserve a voice as well.

John Bell Hood made the decision to attack and should be held accountable for the results. Many contemporaries, both Federal and Confederate, disagreed with and even condemned his decision to launch an assault. There were many, however, who supported his decision. Unfortunately, the voices of most diarists and memoirists who sympathized with Hood (or understood and concurred with his decisions) have been largely ignored or suppressed. Most modern historians simply repeat or paraphrase earlier writers, thus perpetuating and even intensifying the incomplete history of Hood the commander.

The decision made by the Confederate high command (President Jefferson Davis, Lt. Gen. John B. Hood, Gen. P. G. T. Beauregard, and others) to launch a post-Atlanta invasion of Tennessee was, like all military campaigns, a death warrant for soldiers in both armies—the number dependent upon circumstances then unknown. The performance of thousands of participants from privates up to generals, Federal and Confederate, would influence the outcome and decide the fate of many. The invasion was an effort to force

Sherman's marauding army to withdraw in pursuit rather than pursue its course of slicing across Georgia to the coast. Sherman's ultimate objective was to join Grant and crush Robert E. Lee's beleaguered defenders of the Confederate capital and Petersburg.[1]

The only viable way to stop Sherman's onslaught was to defeat Gen. George Thomas's small but growing force defending Nashville—the key to Tennessee and the gateway to Kentucky and beyond. Once Hood's Army of Tennessee moved north into its namesake state, several thousand lives—both Confederate and Federal—were doomed to be maimed or lost. How many casualties both sides would incur could not be known, and circumstances had yet to dictate where the blood would be spilled.

After Schofield's army had escaped the Confederate trap at Spring Hill on the evening of November 29, a battle was all but ensured thereafter. Logic dictated that the combat would unfold either around Nashville or, as fate would soon dictate, the small town of Franklin 15 miles south of the capital city, where Schofield's desperate Federal retreat was halted by the raging Harpeth River, which had destroyed the bridges. By the time his pursuing army arrived at Franklin at midday on November 30, Hood faced few remaining options. His first was a flanking maneuver to the east and north to cut the road leading to Nashville—a movement similar to what had failed the day before at Spring Hill, when a river crossing was unopposed and more hours of daylight remained. A second option was to simply allow Schofield to withdraw to Nashville across hastily repaired bridges. Hood's third alternative was to launch an immediate assault against Schofield's 25,000 exhausted troops, most of whom were pinned against a swollen river. That afternoon, Hood had available a force roughly equal to Schofield's, with Stephen D. Lee's three additional Confederate divisions (about 8,500 infantry) and more than 100 artillery pieces due in later that day from Columbia. After careful consideration, Hood rode to Lee, who had arrived at Winstead Hill ahead of his corps, greeted him cordially, and announced, "General, we shall make the fight."[2]

During the mid-20th century, several authors, each of whom embellished statements written by the previous writer, created an impression in mainstream Civil War scholarship that Hood attacked at Franklin without legitimate reason

---

1 Sherman, *Memoirs*, 152.

2 *News Herald* (Hillsboro, OH), December 23, 1909.

and with a sinister intent. The most outrageous statement appears on a historical marker at the city of Franklin's own Winstead Hill Park, which, notwithstanding the absence of any supporting evidence, states that General Hood "gained his revenge" for the lost opportunity at Spring Hill, and "sacrificed" his troops in a "fit of rage."[3]

There is little doubt that Hood was upset when he learned that Schofield's command had escaped at Spring Hill—and he had every right to be. After the fall of Atlanta, Hood acknowledged that his resources were limited. Sherman, explained Hood, "is weaker now than he will be in future, and I as strong as I can expect to be." Hood's actions also demonstrated that he appreciated the importance of husbanding his strength and risking the lives of his men wisely. For example, when he opened his post-Atlanta campaign, Hood bypassed Resaca because of its heavy defenses and dispatched only a single division to attack the Federal garrison at Allatoona, Georgia. When he began moving west into northern Alabama in preparation for the Tennessee invasion, Hood bypassed Decatur because he realized an assault against that stronghold would not be worth the casualties it would cost. Hood even declined to give Schofield battle at Columbia, in favor of a flanking operation to Spring Hill to block the withdrawal of Schofield's Federals. Hood outmaneuvered Schofield at Columbia in an effort to reduce the bloodletting and score a major, and perhaps largely bloodless surrender by trapping the Federals. As recorded in a previous chapter, Hood ordered the road blocked at Spring Hill and an attack against Schofield; neither ensued. Schofield's escape understandably disturbed the experienced and aggressive combat commander who learned his craft in the Army of Northern Virginia under Robert E. Lee. Once Schofield escaped, Hood knew that defeating the Federal army would be much more costly. It is unreasonable and unrealistic to expect any commander to react with indifference upon learning that a skillfully trapped enemy had escaped.[4]

Hood's decision to attack Schofield's exhausted trapped Federals at Franklin is rarely fully explained. Instead, most authors simply state that Hood was angered over the failure to trap the enemy at Spring Hill and ordered the attack at Franklin the next day to punish his army. For decades, authors have promoted the myth of an incoherently enraged Hood rejecting the pleas of his

---

3 Repeated inquiries by the author to identify who was responsible for the text on the city's historical sign were unsuccessful.

4 *OR* 39, pt. 2, 862.

subordinates and throwing his troops against the enemy regardless of the consequences. Some authors, without any evidence at all, have even falsely asserted that Hood intentionally positioned specific divisions and brigades to incur the heaviest casualties.

Like the rest of his army, Hood awoke early on the morning of November 30 thinking that Schofield's army had been trapped in the open country between Columbia and Spring Hill, caught between two of S. D. Lee's divisions with 100 cannon at Columbia, and seven infantry divisions plus Forrest's cavalry at Spring Hill with no viable chance of reinforcements. If such was the case (as Hood had carefully planned), the Federal position would have been untenable and all feasible routes of escape to Nashville cut off. If Hood was indeed angry or upset that morning, he had every right to be. His bold flank march, later described as "brilliant" and "equal to Stonewall Jackson" by Federal cavalry commander Gen. James Wilson, had not only earned his Confederate army a rare numerical superiority over a Federal opponent, but cornered the Federals in an indefensible position. After destroying or capturing Schofield's army, which at the time constituted most of the veteran infantry Thomas was working to consolidate around Tennessee, Hood would move farther north and attack Thomas with either a numerical advantage or at least near-even numbers.

Instead, Hood learned that morning of Schofield's unlikely escape. The hard-earned chance of capturing or destroying Schofield's army had vanished. The Confederate advantage had slipped through his fingers, and now Hood would have to meet and defeat Schofield and Thomas under much more difficult—and certainly bloodier—conditions.[5]

There are only two known historical records that described Hood as upset or angry at any time on the day of Franklin. Both accounts discuss his demeanor that morning. However, dozens of sources describe Hood acting within normal parameters. Let's examine these accounts in an effort to determine their reliability and relative merit.

The two sources that describe Hood as acting inappropriate or angry have come to epitomize the perception of his mood on the day of Franklin, and have been repeated so often that Hood's fury is considered an undisputed reality in today's Civil War culture. The first account that described Hood as irate occurred during the breakfast meeting at Rippavilla, the home of Nathaniel

---

5 Wilson, *Under the Old Flag*, 43.

Cheairs in Spring Hill. It is not known precisely who was in attendance; firsthand accounts identify only Hood, Cheatham, and Forrest, although others might have been present. No written records exist of the Cheairs house meeting nor its tone or content. The only account we have is the oral recollection of Mrs. Cheairs passed down through the decades. Although she wrote nothing of the event, Mrs. Cheairs purportedly said that the language used by the generals was inappropriate "for women's ears." In addition to its vagueness, the entire account is simply local lore. Neither Mrs. Cheairs, nor Hood, Forrest, Cheatham, or any staff officers wrote a word about it.

Corps commander Stephen D. Lee arrived from Columbia about the time Hood was departing Rippavilla. Lee wrote the following in a postwar letter to Hood: "I was careful and made careful notes as to events & time to impress permanently in my mind, and particularly on my arrival at Spring Hill the morning of the enemy's escape, when the blunder was apparent and your well planned movement had come to naught in the execution at the critical moment [emphasis in the original]." Lee recalled Hood's "chagrin and mortification" at what had occurred the previous night, but if Hood was angry to the point of rage or incoherence (as later writers who were not present would allege), Lee failed to note it. Instead, Hood announced, "They have eluded me," and went on to inform Lee, "I have put the troops in motion."[6]

The only written account that claimed Hood was angry at any point on November 30 entered the historical record more than four decades after the event as tertiary evidence. Although such provenance and the total absence of any corroboration would normally raise serious doubt as to its credibility, this is the sole written source historians routinely cite to make the claim that Hood was incoherently angry on the day of the battle of Franklin. It is difficult to find a book or article on Franklin that does not include the famous description of Hood as being "wrathy as a rattlesnake" on the morning of the battle. This quotation is attributed to Gen. John Brown, and although conveyed into the historical record via a lengthy and multi-source route, its accuracy has never been questioned.

The supposed Brown quote comes from a 1908 magazine article by Army of Tennessee veteran J. P. Young. In the article, Young recounts a conversation

---

6   Jacobson, *For Cause and For Country*, 203; S. D. Lee letter to John Bell Hood, April 16, 1879, John Bell Hood Personal Papers.

with Maj. Joseph Vaulx of Cheatham's staff during which Vaulx claimed that Brown told him the following:

> General Hood is mad about the enemy getting away last night, and he is going to charge the blame of it on somebody. He is wrathy as a rattlesnake this morning, striking at everybody. As he passed along to the front a while ago he rode up to me and said, "General Brown, in the movement today I wish you to bear in mind this military principle: that when a pursuing army comes up with the retreating enemy he must be immediately attacked. If you have a brigade in front as advance guard, order its commander to attack as soon as he comes up with him. If you have a regiment in advance and it comes up with the enemy, give the colonel orders to attack him; if there is but a company in advance, and if it overtakes the entire Yankee army, order the captain to attack it forthwith; and if anything blocks the road in front of you today, don't stop a minute, but turn out into the fields or woods and move up to the front."[7]

General Samuel French later recalled a brief and unremarkable conversation with Hood during the march from Spring Hill to Franklin, wherein Hood supposedly told him, "Well General French, we have missed the great opportunity of the war." French, who was not an admirer of Hood and would certainly have noted any aberrational behavior, made no mention of Hood's demeanor.[8]

John C. Brown was the younger brother of a former Tennessee governor and a lawyer from Giles County, Tennessee. He had no formal military training and no military experience prior to the outbreak of the Civil War. Brown enlisted as a private in early 1861 and quickly rose to the rank of brigadier general in only 18 months. A lecture on fundamental offensive warfare principles from the West Point-educated Hood—a combat command veteran of frontier Indian wars, Gaines's Mill, Second Manassas, Sharpsburg, Gettysburg, and Chickamauga—would not be unusual or inappropriate considering the debacle that had just unfolded the night before in front of Brown's position at Spring Hill. Other than in a limited tactical sense, it is doubtful that Brown, whether serving in the capacity of brigade or division commander in the Army of Tennessee, had ever commanded troops in pursuit of a retreating enemy. Regardless of his mood, it would be understandable for

---

7   J. P. Young, "Hood's Failure at Spring Hill," 36.

8   Samuel French, *Two Wars: An Autobiography of General Samuel G. French* (Nashville, TN: published by Confederate Veteran, 1901), 292.

Hood to want to deliver to Brown—neither a West Pointer nor a Mexican War veteran—a forceful lecture of basic military principles on the pursuit of a retreating foe. It is interesting to note that, just a few hours after his supposed lecture to Brown, Hood refused to order an assault against Schofield's rearguard positions on the southerly slope of Winstead Hill. When the initial contact was made with the Federal rearguard, Hood resorted once again to a flanking maneuver by sending A. P. Stewart's corps to the east. His decision forced the Federals to fall back from their positions with few, if any, Confederate casualties.[9]

Even if we assume that Hood's strong directive to Brown on the morning of November 30, recorded more than four decades after the event, is accurate, it is the sole piece of written evidence used by many authors to assert that Hood was enraged—not just in the morning but even as late as 4:00 p.m. when the final decision to attack at Franklin was made. We have established that Hood, like any reasonable commander, would have been justifiably upset that morning, but some authors have embellished Hood's brief morning anger (which also remains in doubt) by extending it into the late afternoon and even into the early morning hours of the next day, in the complete absence of any evidence to support the assertion.

On the day of the Franklin battle, Hood would have come in direct contact with dozens of officers and been observed by potentially thousands of soldiers. To date, no contemporary evidence has surfaced that describes Hood as acting unusual that day. Of the approximately 18,000 soldiers who fought at Franklin and survived the war, none other than Brown (as conveyed to Young by Vaulx) recorded that Hood was angry early that morning. Nevertheless, in his acclaimed biography of Patrick Cleburne *Stonewall of the West*, award-winning historian Craig Symonds wrote that Hood's anger on November 30 "was the talk of the army." Symonds made that statement without citing a single primary source. During the council of war meeting at the Harrison house, which is commonly portrayed as contentious, Hood dismissed the advice of his subordinates and decided upon an immediate assault. No one present left a written record of the event that portrayed Hood as enraged. In other words, there is no known contemporary evidence—the foundation of good historiography—sufficient to declare that Hood was enraged, or that his anger

---

9 Hood, *Advance and Retreat*, 293.

was "the talk of the army." All that can be professed with certainty is that he disagreed with the opinions of his subordinates.[10]

If Hood was indeed upset in the early morning of November 30, he was not alone. Chaplain James H. McNeilly of the 49th Tennessee Infantry described Nathan Bedford Forrest's intense anger during the march to Franklin, stating, "He seemed to be in a rage . . . his face was livid, his eyes blazed. . . . He seemed to me the most dangerous animal I ever saw." John Copley, also of the 49th Tennessee, described Forrest's reaction to news that the Federals had escaped in much more detail:

> When we discovered their successful escape on the morning of the 30th, our chagrin and disappointment can be better imagined than described. General Forrest was so enraged that his face turned almost to a chalky whiteness, and his lips quivered. He cursed out some of the commanding officers, and censured them for allowing the Federal army to escape. I looked at him, as he sat in his saddle pouring forth his volumes of wrath, and was almost thunderstruck to listen to him, and to see no one dare resent it.[11]

It is important to note that according to Copley, Forrest cursed and censured multiple Confederate commanders for the failure at Spring Hill. He did not mention General Hood at all.

Another Confederate, a Mississippi soldier named Rhett Thomas, also placed the blame on multiple commanders, though not specifically the commanding general: "I have never seen more intense rage and profound disgust" among the troops "when they discovered that their officers had allowed their prey to escape."[12]

Unfounded accusations and hyperbole regarding Hood's demeanor at the battle of Franklin abound in Civil War literature. "Probably he [Hood] intended the assault, in his own tormented way, as an exercise of discipline for the army," speculated historian Thomas Connelly. "He [Hood] later admitted that he utilized frontal assaults for such a purpose, and reveled in the shedding of blood

---

10 Craig L. Symonds, *Stonewall of the West: Patrick Cleburne and the Civil War* (Lawrence: University Press of Kansas, 1997), 254.

11 Quoted in Jamie Gillum, *Spring Hill: Twenty-Five Hours to Tragedy* (Franklin, TN: Jamie Gillum, 2004), 211; Copley, *A Sketch of the Battle of Franklin*, 34-35.

12 Jacobson, *For Cause and For Country*, 200.

as a booster of morale. For him, the Franklin attack would be a last great effort to mold the army into his image of the Virginia army as he had known it." Connelly relies upon several pages of Hood's own memoir for these eyebrow-raising statements, wherein Hood elaborated on the importance of offensive warfare. Nowhere did Hood accuse any soldier of cowardice, and he wrote nothing of penance, nothing of utilizing assaults—frontal or otherwise—to discipline troops, and absolutely nothing that even hinted that he "reveled in the shedding of blood." I encourage all readers to turn to the pages cited by Connelly (and reproduced in Appendix 1 of this book) and compare them to his interpretation.[13]

Authors John McKay, James Bradford, and Rebeccah Pawlowski described Hood at Franklin in their co-authored *The Big Book of Civil War Sites: From Fort Sumter to Appomattox*. According to McKay and company, "This is when Hood threw another one of his fits. He had habitually considered anyone who disagreed with him an enemy and was loathe to change any plan he had created, even in the face of overwhelming evidence that it was a poor one." They continued, claming that Hood ordered his troops to attack the enemy works "even at the cost of their own lives, almost as a punishment for daring to disagree with him." Not a single contemporary source is offered as proof for these claims.[14]

Historian Steven Woodworth, who is normally very careful with the facts and an outstanding researcher and crafter of prose, made similar claims. "His [Hood's] generals—Cheatham, Cleburne and the others—had let him down. They were incompetent and probably cowardly, too. The soldiers, cowardly and afraid to charge an entrenched enemy, had also failed him," wrote Woodworth. "And Hood had their penance ready: They would catch the Federals and smash them, regardless of casualties. No more fancy flanking maneuvers—from now on, his men were going to go right down the enemy's throat." Although Woodworth, without qualification, informed his readers of Hood's reasoning, the usually thorough academician failed to cite a single primary source. His support consisted of the subjective assessment written many years earlier by

---

13 Connelly, *Autumn of Glory*, 504. These pages from Hood's *Advance and Retreat* (161, 162, 181, 290, 292, 294, and 297) are reproduced in Appendix 1 for the convenience of the reader.

14 John McKay, James Bradford, Rebeccah Pawlowski, *The Big Book of Civil War Sites: From Fort Sumpter to Appomattox, a Visitors Guide to the History, Personalities, and Places of America's Battlefields* (Guilford, CT: Globe Piquot, 2011), 195.

Thomas Connelly, who also did not provide a primary source for his harsh condemnation of Hood.[15]

Thomas Hay, one of the earliest scholars to write about the Tennessee Campaign, wrote in *Hood's Tennessee Campaign* (without citing a source) that Hood was "piqued" over the affair at Spring Hill, and that the army's failure "perhaps temporarily unbalanced him and had so warped his judgment and distorted his conception of conditions that he could see no alternative course" than to attack at Franklin.[16]

The writers of the documentary film "The Battle of Franklin" went even further, attributing Hood's motivation to personal gratification. They alleged that Hood launched an assault at Franklin, "perhaps to restore his military glory." There was no mention of the obvious: Hood's desire to defeat his exhausted and trapped enemy before they could escape to the relative safety of Nashville and unite with Federal troops. The actual military situation Hood confronted at Franklin on November 30, 1864, and his viable options, are completely ignored by the producers (and most writers) in favor of a more sensational portrayal of events.[17]

John Lundberg joined the chorus of many other historians when he provided a detailed analysis of Hood's reasoning and his true intentions at Franklin without offering a shred of evidence. He wrote the following in his book *The Finishing Stroke*: "When the Army of Tennessee arrived in front of Franklin, Hood had already made up his mind . . . a direct, all-out frontal assault." Lundberg completely disregarded a written account by corps commander A. P. Stewart, who recalled that Hood considered a flank attempt as the army arrived south of Franklin. According to Stewart, Hood asked if he could get troops north of the flooded Harpeth River (which blocked Schofield's further hasty retreat). When Stewart answered in the affirmative, Hood directed him to "send some cavalry and infantry to drive the Federals out of a bend in the Harpeth to the south of the town, and to await further word." Although Hood ultimately decided against undertaking a flanking operation, he had

15 Steven Woodworth, *Jefferson Davis and His Generals: The Failure of Confederate Command in the West* (Lawrence: University Press of Kansas, 1990), 299.

16 Hay, *Hood's Tennessee Campaign*, 149.

17 Wide Awake Films.

clearly not made up his mind before or as he arrived at Franklin, as Lundberg contended.[18]

Of all the major books written on Spring Hill and Franklin, the one that most embellishes Hood's anger is Wiley Sword's influential *The Confederacy's Last Hurrah*. In it, Sword described Hood as "morose" and that, "Throughout the morning Hood continued to chafe at and bitterly denounce his generals." According to Sword, Hood was "still seething" in the afternoon and those subordinates who disagreed with his decision to attack at Franklin only accentuated his "smoldering resentment over the Spring Hill affair." The intensity of Sword's subjectivity is best illustrated by his repeated accusations of near-psychopathic behavior by the Southern commander. "Hood on November 30 was angry, overeager, frustrated and not reasoning well," claimed Sword, who added that "his disabled personality" and "vindictive disposition" made him "a fool with a license to kill his own men." In a later book entitled *Courage Under Fire*, Sword asserted first that Hood's decision to attack at Franklin was merely a "remedial lesson in courage" before asking, "Where had been the moral courage to act upon what was right rather than upon unreasoned emotion?" For none of these accusations does Sword offer any contemporary firsthand accounts other than what has been heretofore described.[19]

Sword made many inflammatory comments concerning Hood's supposed vengeance mission against his own troops, but this may be the most sensational: "Cheatham, Cleburne and Brown, in particular, became the focus of Hood's ire. If not outright punishment for their behavior on November 29, the assault at Franklin would be a severe corrective lesson in what he would demand in aggressive behavior." Sword cites but a single page of Hood's memoirs to support this astonishing claim. For the record, there is nothing on that page, or those before or after, where Hood says anything about using any commanders or troops anywhere for any reason.[20]

Thomas Connelly and James McDonough used perhaps the most outlandish language describing Hood's state of mind in their monograph *Five Tragic Hours: The Battle of Franklin*. Once again without offering a credible

18 Lundberg, *The Finishing Stroke*, 86; Elliott, *Soldier of Tennessee*, 237.

19 Sword, *The Confederacy's Last Hurrah*, 156, 157, 177, 179, 263; Sword, *Courage Under Fire*, 199.

20 Sword, *The Confederacy's Last Hurrah*, 179.

primary citation, these authors assert that after months of frustration, Hood was "Tired and distraught—perhaps sick is not too strong a term—he was too emotionally unhinged to command." For the purposes of discipline, they continued, Hood decided "what the army needed was a frontal assault." Similarly, the narrator of the film "The Battle of Franklin" recited in a dramatically ominous tone that Hood at Franklin "would sound a battle cry that many would call very peculiar behavior." Records that do exist describe Hood as confident and robust—physically, intellectually, and emotionally. For example, Dr. Charles T. Quintard, a chaplain and physician with the 1st Tennessee Infantry, recorded in his diary on November 25 (just days before Spring Hill and Franklin) that after visiting Hood, "The General is in the best of health and spirits." That was five days before Spring Hill. As one recent historian found out, evidence that Hood was "emotionally unhinged" immediately following that failure does not exist.[21]

Eric Jacobson, the chief historian of the Battle of Franklin Trust and the latest to write a detailed campaign study of Franklin, mentioned Hood's early morning anger in *For Cause and for Country: A Study of the Affair at Spring Hill and the Battle of Franklin*. Jacobson noted the absence of any eyewitness accounts. "There is no evidence that Hood was angry by the time he got to Franklin," Jacobson honestly observed. "Surely he had been upset earlier in the day. . . . But the claims that Hood was still boiling by the time he viewed the Federal works from Spring Hill obscures the probable reality." Jacobson routinely discusses during numerous public lectures and tours that, after personally reading thousands of pages of eyewitness accounts of the battle of Franklin, he has been unable to find any evidence of an angry or agitated Hood at any time after the early morning hours. A. P. Stewart's biographer Sam Davis Elliott apparently agreed with Jacobson in this regard when he wrote that Stewart disagreed with Hood's decision to attack at Franklin, "although he [Stewart] was willing to absolve Hood of the ill motive of taking the Spring Hill debacle out on the Army of Tennessee on Nov. 30, 1864."[22]

Of the many unfounded accusations made against Hood, the most notable is the claim that he intentionally positioned Cheatham's corps to incur the

21 McDonough and Connelly, *Five Tragic Hours*, 59; Wide Awake Films; Elliott, *Doctor Quintard*, 181.

22 Jacobson, *For Cause and For Country*, 254; personal interview with Jacobson, December 11, 2010; Elliott, *Soldier of Tennessee*, 257.

heaviest casualties in the Franklin assault. An example of this accusation is provided by John Lundberg, who claims the following without a single credible source: "Because Cleburne's and Brown's divisions had been principally to blame for the debacle at Spring Hill, Hood reasoned, they would occupy the center of the Confederate attack in order to 'eradicate this evil' of unwillingness to assault breastworks." There is absolutely no primary source evidence that Hood "reasoned," believed, or felt that Cleburne was to blame for Spring Hill, or that he intentionally positioned his and Brown's divisions to take the brunt of the Federal resistance. In fact, it was Gen. William W. Loring's division of A. P. Stewart's corps that faced the heaviest enemy fire and crossed the most difficult terrain at Franklin.[23]

Wiley Sword also weighed in on this non-issue when he wrote, "By specific design . . . Cheatham, Brown and Cleburne would be thrust in the very storm center of any fighting; Hood would purge their ranks of their apparent reluctance to fight except when behind breastworks." Once again Sword cited a page from Hood's *Advance and Retreat* that makes no mention whatsoever of troop positioning or situating specific units to intentionally purge their reluctance to fight except when behind fortifications. Sword continued: "It was no accident when he assigned Cheatham's Corps to make the frontal assault against the center of the enemy's formidable fortifications. Brown and Cleburne were posted to the front rank and told to attack along the Columbia Pike, where the Federal lines were the strongest and the ground entirely open." In reality, the ground was essentially entirely open in front of all six Confederate divisions attacking Schofield's army—not just Brown's and Cleburne's commands. The source for these charges is a paltry single page in the *Official Records* that says nothing about Hood's reasoning for specific troop positions, and a book by an author who described the configuration of the entire army—without any comment on the reasons for the alignment or any hint at anything out of the ordinary.[24]

Contrary to these wholly unfounded assertions, the strategy behind the army's alignment for the assault at Franklin was quite simple and devoid of any malevolent intent by Hood. As was customary, corps, divisions, and brigades

---

23 Lundberg, *The Finishing Stroke*, 86.

24 Sword, *The Confederacy's Last Hurrah*, 177, 179; OR 45, pt. 1, 731; Buck, *Cleburne and His Command*, 280. Those two sources simply say where each corps and division was in relation to one another, which is common in all such records dealing with any battle at any location.

alternated (rotated) their marching order each day. Stewart's corps had followed Cheatham's corps on the march from Columbia to Spring Hill on November 29, so it led the army column on the November 30 march to Franklin. As a result, it was the first to arrive at Franklin. Stewart's vanguard corps, with Cheatham trailing three or four miles behind, was the first to contact the Federal rearguard situated on the southerly slopes of Winstead and Breezy hills.

Rather than assault the defenders, Hood sent Stewart east to flank the enemy and force their withdrawal northward to the main lines at Franklin. After Stewart's flanking movement compelled the Federals to retreat, Cheatham's trailing corps continued up the road unmolested and assumed a position on the Confederate left (Stewart already held the right). Brown's division led Cheatham's column on the march from Spring Hill and so arrived at Franklin ahead of Cleburne's division, with William Bate's division bringing up the rear. On the previous day's march from Columbia to Spring Hill, Cleburne had been in the lead, Bate was second, and Brown third. The customary daily march rotation of the divisions placed Brown's division in the lead on November 30, followed by Cleburne and then Bate. With Stewart already positioned to the east, occupying the right half of the Confederate formation from the river to near the Columbia Pike, Cheatham's arriving corps necessarily constituted the left half of the Confederate front line, with its right flank connecting with the left of Stewart's corps.

In summary, the first of Hood's two corps (Stewart's) arrived and deployed to the right, and the second corps (Cheatham's) arrived next and deployed to the left. Cheatham's three divisions, like the army's two corps, simply deployed right to left in the order they arrived from Spring Hill. Hood's positioning of his corps and divisions at Franklin was consistent with usual and customary practices of his time. To assert otherwise without credible contemporary evidence is simply wrong.[25]

Basic research alone dictates why the army was aligned as it was, but critics need not have looked for any sources beyond Hood himself, who correctly recognized the Federal center (Gen. George D. Wagner's advanced positions) as the weakest point in the Federal line, and thus offered the key to victory. Hood would have wanted to spearhead the assault with his most accomplished and successful troops (Patrick Cleburne's division, which included Hiram Granbury's brigade of mostly Texans; Hood was familiar with soldiers from

---

25 Ibid.; *OR* 45, pt. 1, 742.

Texas from his service in Virginia). As luck would have it, Cleburne and his men took up a position directly opposite that weak section of the enemy line.

Comparing Franklin and Gaines's Mill (part of the 1862 Seven Days' battles) in his memoirs, Hood saw similarities between Schofield's position at Franklin and Gen. Fitz John Porter's reinforced lines at Gaines's Mill. At the latter location, Hood led his Texas brigade in a frontal assault against entrenched enemy lines. Robert E. Lee's prior attacks there had failed, in part because the men were shot down while stopping to reload. This time, Hood's men advanced with the bayonet and, enjoying some flank protection due to the topography, pierced the Union line and helped collapse the entire front. At Franklin, Hood instructed Cleburne to charge the forward Federal lines without firing, overrun the lines, and follow the retreating enemy into the works. Hood's tactics at Franklin were essentially identical to those he employed in the stunning victory at Gaines's Mill, and Cleburne followed Hood's directive explicitly.[26]

Before the attack, recalled W. A. Washburn of the 1st Arkansas Infantry, "Gen. Cleburne rode along the line, cautioning us to save ammunition and 'use the bayonet.'" However, unlike the enemy at Gaines's Mill, the Federals stood firm. "We had never seen the Federals fail to run before under like circumstances," Washburn admitted. Although the positioning of Cleburne's division was a result of their sequence of arrival at Franklin, Hood would have been satisfied that his best troops and commanders were occupying the position at Franklin identical to that which had been occupied at Gaines's Mill by Hood's Texas brigade, Lee's hardest-fighting and most accomplished troops.[27]

☙ ❧

Hood is frequently criticized for not allowing Nathan Bedford Forrest to attempt a flanking maneuver around Franklin to cut off Schofield's escape route to Nashville. Historians across the love-hate spectrum almost universally criticize Hood for rejecting the legendary cavalryman's proposal. Franklin historian Eric Jacobson, a generally objective and keen observer, believed that "Hood made woeful use" of Forrest by denying his flanking request and

26 Hood, *Advance and Retreat*, 26-27, 296.

27 W. A. Washburn, *Confederate Veteran*, vol. 13 (January 1905), 27.

splitting the cavalry during the assault. On the other end of the spectrum, Hood critic Wiley Sword strongly condemned Hood's rejection of the flank option.[28]

In *The Confederacy's Last Hurrah*, Sword claimed that Hollow Tree Gap—the point where the Federal escape to Nashville could be cut off—was as close to Hood's forces as to Schofield's. "Of specific use to Forrest was Hollow Tree Gap, a defile in the range of hills through which the Nashville Pike passed, only about four and a half miles distant from Hood's present position," explained Sword. "Here the Yankees might be cut off from Nashville, urged Forrest, since Hood's army was as close to this gap as was Schofield's at Franklin." In fact, Hollow Tree Gap ("Holly Tree Gap" on modern maps) is significantly farther from Hood's position than it was from Schofield's. On a direct route from Winstead Hill through the very center of the Federal lines between the Carter House and Carter cotton gin house, the distance to Hollow Tree Gap is about seven miles. From the extreme right of Hood's army's position, along the bank of the Harpeth River, the distance is slightly shorter as the crow flies, but this direct route passed through the Federal positions around Fort Granger. If infantry or cavalry from any point along the Confederate lines had attempted to march to Hollow Tree Gap, the route would have had to have been circuitous in a northeasterly direction, a distance of at least ten to twelve miles, in order to avoid Schofield's artillery at Fort Granger. To accomplish such a flanking movement, Forrest's cavalry and his requested 2,000 infantry would have had to ford the rushing rain-swollen Harpeth River, march cross-country 10 to 12 miles in clear view of the Federals, meet up with heavy resistance from 5,000 Yankee cavalrymen and at least one 4,500-man infantry division, all in a matter of three or four hours.

Sword (and other writers) disregarded the large enemy force available to resist Forrest by writing that Hood "easily could have outflanked Schofield from Franklin by crossing the Harpeth River at Hughes's Ford or various other sites." By this time, most of James Wilson's 5,000 cavalry had consolidated at Franklin and held a strong position on a high bluff overlooking McGavock Ford, the nearest possible crossing point on the Harpeth. Any unmolested crossing of the river by infantry would have been at Hughes Ford, more than a mile farther south of Franklin, which in turn would have added even more time to any attempted flanking movement. The functional distance to Hollow Tree

---

28 Jacobson, *For Cause and For Country*, 379; Horn, *The Army of Tennessee*, 398; Dyer, *The Gallant Hood*, 291; Hay, *Hood's Tennessee Campaign*, 120.

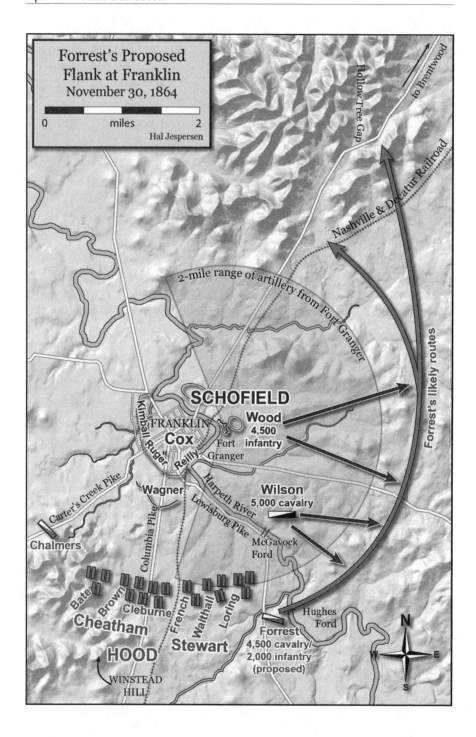

Forrest's Proposed
Flank at Franklin
November 30, 1864

0   miles   2

Hal Jespersen

to Brentwood

Hollow-Tree Gap

Nashville & Decatur Railroad

2-mile range of artillery from Fort Granger

Forrest's likely routes

SCHOFIELD

Wood
4,500
infantry

FRANKLIN
Cox
"Kimball Ruger"
Reilly
Fort Granger

Carter's Creek Pike

Wagner

Harpeth River
Lewisburg Pike

Wilson
5,000 cavalry

Chalmers

Columbia Pike

McGavock Ford

Bate
Brown
Cleburne
French
Walthall
Loring

Cheatham
Stewart

HOOD

WINSTEAD HILL

Hughes Ford

Forrest
4,500 cavalry/
2,000 infantry
(proposed)

N
W   E
S

Gap for Hood's forces was at least double, and most likely triple, the distance from Schofield's lines. Sword's unequivocal statement that the Confederates and the Federals were equidistant from the point where Schofield's retreat could be blocked is patently wrong. This misleading information makes Hood look ignorant, incompetent, or worse, by lending validity to Forrest's impracticable proposal. Additionally, Sword and many other historians overlooked the diminishing daylight and the treacherously high river that had trapped much of Schofield's army in Franklin. A simple question settles the matter: If the river was so easy to ford, why did Schofield stop and entrench at Franklin rather than continue to march his column north to Nashville?[29]

Some authors have made the bewildering case for flanking Schofield out of Franklin, as if gaining the town offered some strategic benefit to the Confederates. Hood had no interest in occupying the town; his goal was to destroy Schofield, who was trapped inside Franklin. According to Thomas Hay, "Hood should not have attacked at Franklin, but should have continued his flanking movements and forced Schofield out of that place by himself crossing the Harpeth River." Cleburne biographer Craig Symonds echoed Hay when he wrote that a flanking movement across the river would "force a Federal evacuation." These suggestions that Hood could have forced an evacuation are bewildering, since it is well known that the Federals were trapped with their back to a river, and that Hood was attempting to destroy Schofield's army, not seize and occupy the town of Franklin.[30]

The producers of "The Battle of Franklin" documentary also missed the point of Hood's attack when the narrator stated that Schofield's retreat from Franklin "would have happened without a Confederate attack." No contemporary record by any Confederate or Federal even suggested that the contending armies had an interest in occupying Franklin. Hood was attempting to destroy the Federal army, not seize and occupy a strategically insignificant spot on a Tennessee map. Stanley Horn, in *The Army of Tennessee*, went so far as to claim that Schofield was merely an obstacle to Hood's march toward Nashville, telling his readers that "if Hood could have restrained his headlong assault that evening, he would have found that the enemy was out of his way."[31]

---

29 Sword, *The Confederacy's Last Hurrah*, 262.

30 Hay, *Hood's Tennessee Campaign*, 133-134; Symonds, *Stonewall of the West*, 256.

31 Wide Awake Films; Horn, *The Army of Tennessee*, 398.

How quickly could Forrest have moved a division of infantry to Hollow Tree Gap? One of the fastest documented marches by an infantry division during the Civil War was conducted by Gen. A. P. Hill, who pushed his "Light Division" from Harpers Ferry to Sharpsburg on September 17, 1862, roughly 17 miles in seven hours. Hill's troops marched unmolested along a well-maintained road. Even if a flanking column at Franklin managed to match Hill's pace from Harpers Ferry, Forrest and his infantry would have reached Hollow Tree Gap long after nightfall.[32]

There is another aspect to this flanking operation that is also routinely overlooked: Hood's extensive knowledge of cavalry operations. He gained several years of experience in the saddle leading up to the Civil War, including combat as a cavalry commander with the elite U.S. Second Cavalry in Texas. Hood was also ordered to West Point to serve as chief instructor of cavalry in 1860 (which as earlier noted, he turned down). After enlisting in the Confederate army in 1861, Hood was assigned by Robert E. Lee to organize and train cavalry units on the Virginia peninsula. One Southern newspaper even reported (incorrectly) that Hood had been appointed to lead the Army of Northern Virginia's cavalry. Hood had led brigades and divisions and corps of infantry in campaigns and battles across several states. He also fully understood cavalry and its uses, capabilities, and limitations. Forrest could never have flanked Schofield before darkness, and Hood (unlike modern commentators) knew it.[33]

☙   ❧

Contrary to the common allegation that Hood sought to punish his army at Franklin for allowing the Federals to escape at Spring Hill, eyewitness accounts of Hood's demeanor immediately prior to the battle offer a starkly different portrait. S. A. Cunningham of the 41st Tennessee Infantry (later founder and editor of *Confederate Veteran*) was standing near Hood on Winstead Hill as the army commander contemplated the attack. In his memoirs, Cunningham

---

32 *OR* 19, pt. 1, 981.

33 Hood, *Advance and Retreat*, 15-18; *Richmond Daily Dispatch*, August 8, 1863: "The *Petersburg Express* states that Gen. Hood, of Texas, has been appointed Commander in Chief of all the cavalry in the army of Northern Virginia, and that Generals Stuart and Wade Hampton will rank as Major-Generals under him."

recalled a composed and pensive commander immediately before the final decision was made to assault Schofield:

> While making ready for the charge, General Hood rode up to our lines, having left his escort and staff in the rear. He remained at the front in plain view of the enemy for, perhaps, half an hour making a most careful survey of their lines. . . . Hood rode up to General S. D. Lee, and after shaking hands, he gave orders which we could not hear. But, from his gestures it was clear that the word was *forward* [emphasis in original].[34]

Cunningham wrote a slightly different version in a later article in *Confederate Veteran*:

> I happened, though in the line of battle (as I was "right guide" to my regiment), to be close to where Gen. Hood halted his staff and rode along to the top of the hill, and with his field glasses surveyed the situation. It was an extraordinary moment. Those of us who were near could see, as private soldiers rarely did, the position of both armies. Although Franklin was some two miles in the distance, the plain presented a scene of great commotion. But I was absorbed in the one man whose mind was deciding the fate of thousands. With an arm and a leg in the grave, and with the consciousness that he had not until within a couple of days won the confidence which his army had in his predecessor, he had now a very trying ordeal to pass through. It was all-important to act, if at all, at once. He rode to Stephen D. Lee, the nearest of his subordinate generals, and, shaking hands with him cordially, announced his decision to make an immediate charge.[35]

In another interview, Cunningham recalled, "I watched him closely while there, meditating upon his responsibility."[36]

Hood had witnessed his army's enthusiasm on the march from Columbia to Spring Hill, and may well have believed that the same fervor would be shown at Franklin. Of the troops' morale, Cunningham wrote:

> The march to Spring Hill, where the Federal retreat was so nearly cut off, a failure for which it was understood General Hood was not to blame, created an enthusiasm for him equal to that entertained for Stonewall Jackson after his extraordinary

---

34 Cunningham, *Reminiscences of the 41st Tennessee*, 96-97.

35 Cunningham, "The Battle of Franklin," *Confederate Veteran*, 101-102.

36 *Hillsboro News Herald* (Hillsboro, OH), December 23, 1909.

achievements. The soldiers were full of ardor, and confident of success. They had unbounded faith in General Hood, whom they believed would achieve a victory that would give us Nashville.[37]

Cunningham reported that although much of the rank and file of the Army of Tennessee was initially upset at the removal of Joseph Johnston, the men as a whole later embraced Hood. "So devoted to Johnston were his men that the presence and immediate command of Gen. [Robert E.] Lee would not have been accepted without complaint," explained Cunningham, who went on to add that the men "were not reconciled to the change until the day before the battle of Franklin."[38]

The Confederates saw evidence of the Federal desperation during the pursuit from Spring Hill to Franklin. "The next morning," Cunningham wrote, "as we marched in quick time toward Franklin, we were confirmed in our impressions of federal alarm. I counted on the way thirty four wagons that had been abandoned on the smooth turnpike. In some instances whole teams of mules had been killed to prevent their capture." Cunningham described the spirit of the army while forming for the charge. "The soldiers, as a general thing, seemed to have an unprecedented determination and, indeed, were confident of success," he confirmed, adding that "the highest eulogies were heaped upon General Hood. It was believed that he would achieve victories unprecedented in the past."[39]

Federal Col. Emerson Opdycke, who led a brigade of seven regiments at Franklin, similarly observed the degree of desperation that had gripped the retreating Federal army under Schofield. "I was informed that our situation was critical, and the greatest efforts would be needed," wrote Colonel Opdycke. As Federal stragglers began filling the road, Opdycke observed that most of the men were new recruits hauling "immense knapsacks" and that they seemed indifferent to the very real risk of being captured. Opdycke came up with the solution: "I ordered each of my three lines to bring along every man at the point of the bayonet, and to cut off the knapsacks. These orders were obeyed rigidly, and probably less than 20 of our men escaped our vigilance and were captured. I

37 Cunningham, "The Battle of Franklin," *Confederate Veteran*.

38 Ibid.

39 Ibid.

am sure we saved five hundred men from capture by these extreme measures."[40]

The debris observed by the pursuing Confederates spoke for itself. Sam Watkins of the 1st Tennessee Infantry recalled the Rebel army being cheered by locals along the roadside, who told the pursuing gray clad soldiers that the Yankees were just ahead. Like Cunningham, Watkins also observed abandoned wagons with teams of mules shot and bayoneted while still in their harnesses to avoid their capture. "All that we want to do now is catch the blue coated rascals," confessed Watkins, and "we all want to see them surrender." Captain W. O. Dodd of Chalmers' division recalled that "each man felt a pride in wiping out the stain" of the failure at Spring Hill.[41]

Another Confederate wrote that the spirits of the army "were animated by encouraging orders from General Hood who held out to them the prospect that at any moment he might call upon them to deal the enemy a decisive blow." Modern authors appropriately provided extensive quotes of soldiers who felt fear and despair prior to the attack at Franklin. These are understandable human emotions not uncommon among men about to assault a determined veteran enemy. However, these same authors rarely provided contemporary testimony that demonstrates the confidence and resolve many soldiers in the Army of Tennessee felt at the prospect of finally destroying their longtime antagonists. "Hood was not to be frightened," explained Cunningham, "and his men were never more in the spirit to conquer or die, to make Tennessee indeed 'a grave or a free home.'"[42]

From Winstead and Breezy hills, two miles south of the main Federal lines, the soldiers and their commanders could see the trapped chaos that was Schofield's army in Franklin. While some were deployed for battle, others were quickly crossing the Harpeth River on a hastily repaired bridge in their desperate attempt to reach Nashville farther north. There were only a few hours of daylight left, after which any chance for a successful assault, flanking, or delaying action would be lost. The moment of decision was at hand, and it was at this time that Hood decided to assault the enemy lines and crush Schofield against the swollen river. Hood called his key officers together and issued the

---

40 Clark, *Opdycke's Tigers*, 331.

41 Watkins, *Company Aytch*, 201; Dyer, *The Gallant Hood*, 289.

42 Ibid.; Cunningham, *Reminiscences*, 96.

appropriate orders. While Stewart's and Cheatham's corps were on hand and ready, Stephen D. Lee's entire corps, with 90 percent of the army's artillery, was still miles away. Two of Lee's three divisions and the bulk of the army's artillery would not arrive on the field until long after dark. Despite this fact, some historians condemned Hood for not waiting for Lee. Thomas Hay described Hood's decision to attack without awaiting artillery as unwise, stating that Hood "was unwilling to wait for his guns."[43]

As noted earlier, when the Confederates initially approached the two hills south of Franklin and Stewart flanked the initial enemy positions by moving east, Schofield's rearguard retreated. Hood concluded the Federal deployment was a delaying tactic, an appearance of holding ground at Franklin to buy time for a successful retreat across the Harpeth River to Nashville. When Stephen D. Lee had arrived in Spring Hill earlier that day, he recalled Hood telling him, "I have put the troops in motion but the enemy will not probably make another serious stand short of Nashville." Although Hood knew that fortifications had been constructed in Franklin two years earlier, he also knew that Schofield had little time to restore and strengthen them. Hood later explained his reasons for risking a frontal assault, stating plainly that he would rather fight the Federals at Franklin, where they had only eight hours to fortify, than at Nashville, where they had been building defenses for three years.[44]

Although certain portions of the Federal positions, such as Wagner's advanced line, could be clearly seen from Winstead Hill, other areas of the line, including the details of fortifications in some areas, were not so easily discernible; some were completely hidden from view. Exactly what Hood was able to see through the field glasses of the period is difficult to discern. Today, large trees populate residential neighborhoods constructed where Federal entrenchments once stood; structures from modern commercial development cover most of the plain south of Franklin, which is softly sculpted with gentle rises and shallow depressions. From atop Winstead Hill, it was (and remains) difficult to see detail in the area of the Carter House.

What was clearly visible to Hood and his generals was Wagner's advance line, which did not boast natural or significant improvised defenses. Cleburne reportedly rode to the top of Privet Knob, well in front of Winstead Hill, to

---

43 Hay, *Hood's Tennessee Campaign*, 134; Hattaway and Jones, *How the North Won*, 646.

44 S. D. Lee letter to John Bell Hood, April 16, 1879, John Bell Hood Personal Papers; Horn, *Army of Tennessee*, 398.

view the enemy's main fortifications, but it is not known if any other Confederate commanders did likewise. Nor is it known whether Cleburne conveyed specific information to Hood about what he saw. Forrest purportedly advised Hood against an attack, but it isn't known what specific intelligence Forrest was able to provide to Hood regarding the strength of the Federal fortifications.[45]

What Hood and other Confederate commanders saw depended upon where they were standing. Cleburne reportedly said that the Federal works were strong, yet many of the Federals described their own defenses as slight. "We had but fairly begun to throw a temporary work, with the very limited means at our disposal," confessed Lt. Col. Milton Barnes of the 97th Ohio. A letter penned by Maj. Henry Leaming of the 40th Indiana Infantry six weeks after the battle agreed with Barnes's observation: "Our works were very hastily put up, and not finished when the attack was commenced." In condemning Hood's assault at Franklin, Stanley Horn wrote in *The Army of Tennessee* that "Schofield had already made himself strong in his works." Schofield's own assessment, however, flatly contradicts Horn. The Federal army commander's memoir stated frankly that his Franklin fortifications were "of the slightest character," and that it was impossible to strengthen them adequately in the short time available to him before Hood attacked. Horn's direct contradiction of Schofield's own words is perplexing, especially since Horn utilized Schofield's account extensively elsewhere in his book. Federal Gen. Thomas Wood described just how close Hood's men came to carrying the hastily constructed fortifications early in the battle: "The enemy had come on with a terrific dash, had entered our entrenchment, and victory seemed almost within his grasp. Our line had been broken in the center, two 4-gun batteries had fallen into the hands of the enemy, and it seemed that it was only necessary for him to press the advantage he had gained to complete his success."[46]

---

45 Mauriel Joslyn, *A Meteor Shining Brightly: Essay on the Life and Career of Major General Patrick R. Cleburne* (Macon, GA: Mercer University Press, 2000), 174.

46 *OR* 45, pt. 1, 265; Catherine Merrill, *The Soldier of Indiana in the War for the Union,* 2 vols. (Merrill and Company, 1889), vol. 2, 764-766; Horn, *Army of Tennessee*, 398; John M. Schofield, *Forty-Six Years in the Army* (New York: The Century Company, 1897), 184; *OR* 45, pt. 1, 124.

What was Hood's mood and demeanor just prior to launching the large attack at Franklin? Contrary to the highly embellished and often fabricated portrayals of many later authors, eyewitness accounts of Hood's words and deportment in the critical moments immediately preceding the assault described a confident commander encouraging his officers and men. Hood rode along the lines as his army formed for the assault, stopping at several points to tell his soldiers, "These lines must be broken boys, they are weak and cannot stand you." Promising the men that if they carried the Federal position the campaign in Tennessee would be over, Hood is also recorded as having said, "No enemy will exist who will dare to oppose your march to the Ohio." A short time earlier, a witness recalled Hood giving Cleburne final instructions before concluding with, "Franklin is the key to Nashville, and Nashville is the key to independence." Another soldier recorded in his diary, "General Hood's last words to his generals were: 'Now, go down to the work to be done and go at it.'" Virtually every eyewitness testimonial, largely ignored by most historians, unambiguously describes Hood's demeanor as soldierly and rational on the afternoon of November 30. And yet, as we have seen, Hood's understandable and brief early-morning anger and frustration at Schofield's escape has been both exaggerated and extended without any evidence up to the time of the attack.[47]

Like other authors, Thomas Hay's own observations on Franklin often conflicted. On the one hand, Hay described the Franklin battle as "an unnecessary and bloody fight, waged in an effort to make up for the hesitation of the day before at Spring Hill, a battle in which men's lives were given up in the vain hope of retrieving errors of the high command that were committed, primarily, because of lack of personal supervision on the part of the one responsible for the execution of orders." Yet, here is what he wrote in the following paragraph:

> To a certain extent Hood was justified in his attack at Franklin. . . . He knew of Thomas's concentration at Nashville and that if he allowed Schofield to get away he would not again have so great an opportunity, on equal terms. Schofield was only a night's march from Thomas's advanced defenses in front of Nashville. A. J. Smith, just

---

47 *Augusta Constitutionalist*, December 16, 1864; Jacobson, *For Cause and For Country*, 257; article in the May 3, 1902 edition of the *Atlanta Journal* by Army of Tennessee veteran Dr. W. T. Burt, formerly of the 46th Georgia Infantry, quoted from his wartime diary of Hood's final orders at Franklin. Carter House files.

arrived in Nashville, could meet him and together they would move on Hood or take up an advanced defensive position, as circumstances dictated. Under these conditions Hood felt he must attack or lose his advantage. Schofield had a river, spanned by poor and inadequate bridges, at his back; the defenses at Franklin were of a hasty and slight character; and the opposing forces were about equal.[48]

How is one to make sense of these conflicting statements? What, then, in Thomas Hay's judgment should Hood have done that evening? He was damned for attacking, and it seems just as likely he would have been damned for not doing so.

Some authors rarely shared Hood's own words verbatim with their readers, preferring instead to act as a filter for their own analysis and interpretation. According to Wiley Sword, Hood's memoir "is merely a bitter, misleading, and highly distorted treatise" replete with "distortions, misrepresentations, and outright falsifications." As demonstrated several times earlier in this study, however, Sword's own statements and analysis evidenced a distinctly anti-Hood bias, were often misleading and incomplete, and consistently omitted or ignored important facts. In his memoir, Hood clearly explained his decision to attack at Franklin, a decision supported by many Confederates and Federals alike. "I thereupon decided, before the enemy would be able to reach his stronghold at Nashville," explained Hood matter-of-factly, "to make that same afternoon another and final effort to overtake and rout him, and drive him into the Big Harpeth river at Franklin, since I could no longer hope to get between him and Nashville, by reason of the short distance from Franklin to that city, and the advantage which the Federals enjoyed in the possession of the direct road."

Hood's official Tennessee Campaign report explained his decision this way:

> I learned from dispatches captured at Spring Hill, from Thomas to Schofield, that the latter was instructed to hold that place till the position at Franklin could be made secure, indicating the intention of Thomas to hold Franklin and his strong works at Murfreesboro. Thus I knew that it was all important to attack Schofield before he could make himself strong, and if he should escape at Franklin he would gain his works about Nashville. The nature of the position was such as to render it inexpedient to

48 Hay, *Hood's Tennessee Campaign*, 130-131.

attempt any further flank movement, and I therefore determined to attack him in front, and without delay.[49]

An officer serving on A. P. Stewart's staff that day concurred with Hood:

It has been charged that he [Hood] gave the order to attack at Franklin because of chagrin at his failure at Spring Hill. This supposition does Hood great injustice. A Federal courier had been captured bearing dispatches between Thomas and Schofield of the Federal army. The tenor of the dispatches led Hood to believe that Franklin was not in a defensible position, and that therefore, as he expressed it, he thought his "time to fight had come."[50]

Texas cavalryman James Wood Baldwin, who served as a scout for Hood, recalled an incident that occurred before the combat at Franklin commenced. It is not conclusively known whether or not the dispatches captured by Baldwin were those alluded to in Hood's campaign report. According to Baldwin:

On the 2nd day before the battle of Franklin [Nov. 28], while acting as a scout for Gen. Hood, I was directed by him to take twelve men and reconnoiter in the vicinity of Murfreesboro and as near Nashville as I could safely go, for the purpose of locating the enemy and finding out his plans. . . . I was instructed after making my tour to report to Gen. Cleburne the following morning who would be encamped at Caney Springs. About daylight of the morning before the battle of Franklin we rode into Caney Springs and as we approached it, we discovered that an army was encamped there. Naturally we thought it was Gen. Cleburne. However, we soon learned that it was a Yankee outfit. We reconnoitered and located the Marque or headquarters of Gen. Hatch and we decided to capture the general. We quietly and silently dismounted walked up to the headquarters, disarmed the sentinel, went into the tent and captured the adjutant and his body guard. We then took them out and mounted them on horses which were tied to a corral and carried them to Gen. Hood's headquarters. We also captured many papers which disclosed their plans and purposes. We met Gen. Hood about fifteen miles from Caney Springs on the road to Columbia.[51]

49 Sword, *The Confederacy's Last Hurrah*, 179, 438; Hood, *Advance and Retreat*, 291, 329-330.

50 B. L. Ridley, *Battles and Sketches of the Army of Tennessee* (Mexico, MO: Missouri Publishing, 1906), 416.

51 James Wood Baldwin, typescript provided by Jamie Gillum, author and historian of the battle of Spring Hill, Franklin, TN.

Tennessee Governor Isham Harris, who accompanied the army on the invasion into his state and served as a volunteer aide to Hood, wrote to Jefferson Davis after the campaign ended. "I have been with General Hood from the beginning of the campaign, and beg to say, disastrous as it has ended, I am not able to see anything that General Hood has done that he should not, or neglected anything that he should have done. . . . and regret to say that if all had performed their parts as well as he, the results would have been very different."[52]

In *The Confederacy's Last Hurrah*, Wiley Sword related a conversation that took place between Schofield and captured Col. Virgil S. Murphey of the 17th Alabama Infantry. Quoting from Murphey's diary, Sword revealed to his readers that Schofield called Hood a butcher. Murphey responded, "butchery always seemed to involve a considerable mixture of the Rebels' enemies." What Sword did not provide was the rest of what Murphey wrote, which in fact supported Hood's decision to attack: "Had Hood succeeded, Nashville would have opened her gates to the head of his victorious legions and the throat of Tennessee released from the grasp of remorseless despotism. It was worth the hazard. Its failure does not diminish the value of the prize." Sword also failed to include additional Murphey entries that prove the Alabama colonel informed Schofield that Hood's orders had been disobeyed at Spring Hill, which in turn enabled the Federal escape.[53]

Many of Colonel Murphey's opponents at Franklin also understood Hood's dilemma that late afternoon, but historians writing about the battle utilize precious few of these Federal accounts. "By the way, I was somewhat surprised, and may say pained, during my recent trip South, to note the disposition among soldiers of the late Confederate Army to criticize and disparage the merits of Gen. Hood," recalled Washington Gardner of the 65th Ohio Infantry, a veteran of Franklin who would survive the war and be elected a U.S. congressman from Michigan. Gardner continued:

> That he [Hood] made mistakes no unprejudiced student of the War Between the States will deny, but that he was possessed of some of the best qualities that belong to great military commanders is equally indisputable. As between the General and his critics

52 Jefferson Davis, *The Rise and Fall of the Confederate Government*, 2 vols. (New York: D. Appleton and Company, 1881), vol. 2, 491.

53 Sword, *The Confederacy's Last Hurrah*, 252; Virgil Murphey diary.

touching the Battle of Franklin, my sympathies are entirely with the former; while my admiration for the splendid valor exhibited by his heroic legions on that bloody field is not diminished by the fact that they were Americans all . . . Franklin, from the Confederate standpoint of view, must ever remain one of the saddest tragedies of the Civil War; on the other hand, there were in that battle possibilities to the Confederate cause, and that came near being realized, scarcely second to those of any other in the great conflict. Had Hood won—and he came within an ace of it—and reaped the legitimate fruits of his victory, the verdict of history would have been reversed, and William T. Sherman, who took the flower of his army and with it made an unobstructed march to the sea, leaving but a remnant to contend against a foe that had taxed his every resource from Chattanooga to Atlanta, would have been called at the close as at the beginning of the war, "Crazy Sherman." No individual, not even Hood himself, had so much at stake at Franklin as the hero of the "march to the sea."[54]

L. A. Simmons of the 84th Illinois Infantry agreed with Gardner's assessment, adding additional details that confirmed Hood's decision to attack heavily at Franklin:

In speaking of this battle, very many are inclined to wonder at the terrible pertinacity of the rebel General Hood, in dashing column after column with such tremendous force and energy upon our center—involving their decimation, almost their annihilation. Yet this we have considered a most brilliant design, and the brightest record of his generalship, that will be preserved in history. He was playing a stupendous game, for enormous stakes. Could he have succeeded in breaking the center, our whole army was at his mercy. In our rear was a deep and rapid river, swollen by recent rains—only fordable by infantry at one or two places—and to retreat across it an utter impossibility. To break the center was to defeat our army; and defeat inevitably involved a surrender. If this army surrendered to him, Nashville, with all its fortifications, all its vast accumulation of army stores, was at his mercy, and could be taken in a day. Hence, with heavy odds—a vastly superior force—in his hands, he made the impetuous attack upon our center, and lost in the momentous game. His army well understood that they were fighting for the possession of Nashville. Ours knew they were fighting to preserve that valuable city, and to avoid annihilation.

Simmons added that the Federals quickly withdrew northward to Nashville after the bloody battle because Franklin was "untenable." He also stated that

---

54 Washington Gardner, letter in *Confederate Veteran*, vol. I (December 1893), 375.

with Schofield's force absent from Nashville, the city was "scantily protected."[55]

Lieutenant Henry Shaw of the 125th Ohio Infantry also agreed with these assessments. "Hood saw his opportunity, and true to his combative proclivity availed himself thereof. From a high hill he could easily see our position, and saw our forces gradually withdrawing to the opposite bank of the Little Harpeth. Military men will not condemn Hood's generalship in launching heavy assaulting columns, as he did upon our line," concluded the Buckeye officer.[56]

Colonel Arthur MacArthur of the 24th Wisconsin described the battle as one of particular importance. Generals Grant's and Sherman's campaigns would have been drastically imperiled by a Hood victory at Franklin, explained MacArthur, who also wrote: "In a word, had Hood entered Nashville sword in hand at the head of a victorious army, which would have resulted from defeat of the Union army at Franklin, the Civil War in all its subsequent scenes might have been essentially varied." MacArthur added, "Franklin was essentially a battle that saved [the Union], and as such must be classified as second only to Gettysburg in importance during the entire war."[57]

Private J. K. Merrifield of the 88th Illinois Infantry, part of Col. Emerson Opdycke's brigade, understood the value of the Union victory at Franklin and why Hood fought there. "Opdycke's Brigade at the battle of Franklin, Tenn., saved the Army of the Cumberland from destruction; for had the break in the lines been successful, the two wings of our army would have been whipped in detail, and either driven into the river behind us or captured." Merrifield continued: "Then what was there to stop Hood from going to Louisville? A. J. Smith, with his troops, was all; and with a victorious army as Hood would have had, he would have swept Smith's troops aside, and Grant would have had to send troops from the East to intercept Hood."[58]

Hood's counterpart, John Schofield, had little confidence that he could hold his position at Franklin. Just one hour before Hood attacked, the Union army commander sent a message to George Thomas that included this line: "A

---

55 L. A. Simmons, *The History of the 84th Regiment Illinois Volunteers* (Macomb, IL: Hampton Brothers, 1866) 112.

56 "The Battle of Franklin," *The Herald* (Cleveland, OH), December 8, 1864.

57 Clark, *Opdycke Tigers*, 446-447.

58 J. K. Merrifield letter, *Confederate Veteran*, vol. 13 (December 1905), 564.

worse position than this for an inferior force could hardly be found." Schofield explained Hood's dilemma in a letter published in *Confederate Veteran* magazine in 1895: "Gen. Hood, on the other hand, designed to cut off or crush my command before I could unite with Gen. Thomas. This, in my judgment, fully justified his direct assault in front of Franklin, for which some have criticized him. He did not have time to turn that position before our concentration at Nashville would be effected. Hence, he had no alternative but the desperate one of a direct assault."[59]

Schofield elaborated in his memoir, dismissing Hood's critics with a backhanded flair for failing to understand the facts on the ground that day:

Hood's assault at Franklin has been severely criticized. Even so able a general as J. E. Johnston has characterized it as "A useless butchery." These criticisms are founded on a misapprehension of the facts, and are essentially erroneous. Hood must have been fully aware of our relative weakness of numbers at Franklin, and of the probable, if not certain, concentration of large reinforcements at Nashville. He could not hope to have at any future time anything like so great an advantage in that respect. The army at Franklin and the troops at Nashville were within one night's march of each other; Hood must therefore attack on November 30 or lose the advantage of greatly superior numbers. It was impossible, after the pursuit from Spring Hill, in a short day to turn our position or make any other attack but a direct one in front. Besides our position with the river on our rear, gave him the chance of vastly greater results, if his assault were successful, than could be hoped for by any attack he could make after we had crossed the Harpeth. Still more, there was no unusual obstacle to a successful assault at Franklin. The defenses were of the slightest character, and it was not possible to make them formidable during the short time our troops were in position, after the previous exhausting operations of both day and night, which had rendered some rest on the 30th absolutely necessary.

Schofield continued:

The Confederate cause had reached a condition closely verging on desperation, and Hood's commander-in-chief had called upon him to undertake operations which he thought appropriate to such an emergency. Franklin was the last opportunity he could expect to have to reap the results hoped for in his aggressive movement. He must

59 John M. Schofield letter, *Confederate Veteran*, vol. 3 (September 1895), 274.

strike there, as best he could, or give up his cause as lost. I believe, therefore, that there can be no room for doubt that Hood's assault was entirely justifiable.[60]

Hood's decision to attack at Franklin was based solely upon the unique circumstances presented to him and the desperate state of the war, as he perceived it. Contrary to the accepted portrayal of Hood's state of mind on November 30, anger, vengeance, or any other ulterior motive had nothing to do with his decision to attack Schofield's lines at Franklin.

The mind-set of military men of the 19th century is understood and well explained by the respected author and military historian Winston Groom, who wrote,

> Great infantry or cavalry charges are as often remembered for the ones that failed as for the ones that succeeded. On July 3, 1863, General Robert E. Lee sent 15,000 infantry under George Pickett charging into the Union lines at Gettysburg. The resulting failure presaged the decline of the Confederacy. A decade earlier, England's Lord Cardigan had dispatched his light brigade of cavalry to charge against a strong Russian position during the Crimean War, and nearly all were killed or wounded; this became the stuff that poems were made of. In World War I, millions of soldiers were killed in frontal infantry assaults; it was likewise with the Japanese in World War II, who died by the tens of thousands in pointless banzai charges.
>
> The psychology of the tactic was a leftover from the days of the rock, the club, the spear, and the sword, in which battles were won or lost in close combat with one side ultimately overwhelming and terrifying the other by dint of sheer audacity and ferocity. With the evolution of gunpowder and weapons of distance—rifles, cannons, and the like—personal physical prowess had become less and less important. Still, as military scholars continued to emphasize, most wars are fought based upon the strategies and tactics gleaned from the previous one, yet men commanding warriors of the nineteenth and even twentieth century were slow to understand this.[61]

Civil War history is replete with testimony of soldiers whose courage and ardor surpassed their instincts for self-protection and survival. Southern soldiers were especially motivated by their view that the Northerners were

---

60 OR 45, pt. 1, 1,171; Schofield, *Forty-Six Years in the Army*, 184.

61 Winston Groom, *Patriotic Fire: Andrew Jackson, Jean Laffite and the Battle of New Orleans* (New York: Knopf, 2006), 247.

invaders and occupiers. By November of 1864, the soldiers of the Army of Tennessee, defeated or stalemated in every major battle except Chickamauga in September of 1863, and constantly forced to yield territory because of the numerical superiority of the enemy, were in a do-or-die state of mind. They had finally cornered their enemy at Franklin against a swollen river and revenge was in their hearts.

According to the "The Battle of Franklin's" narrator, "In seventeen separate attacks, according to one Federal witness, John Bell Hood sacrificed his men." Hood issued or approved only two attack orders that afternoon. The first was the general assault by the army, and the second (technically ordered by Cheatham) was the night attack by Edward Johnson's division, which had arrived from Spring Hill after the main army assault. The "seventeen separate attacks" stated in the film script presumably came from a wounded Yankee soldier who later wrote that while he lay injured in the trench, he heard the shouts of attacking Rebels 17 times. If this number is correct, what the Union soldier heard was 17 separate attacks by various Confederate regiments—some or many of which were different regiments attacking various portions of the Federal lines multiple times. The wounded Federal, or course, was not physically situated to definitively state what took place. To claim that Hood personally ordered 17 attacks is not only unwarranted, but also misleading and unsupported by any known historical record. With Hood at his headquarters more than a mile away near Winstead Hill, and with much of the battle occurring after dark, he would have been in no position to order attacks by specific regiments or brigades.[62]

Simple human logic and survival instinct dictated that the soldiers withdraw after the first few attempts to storm Schofield's works failed, but their patriotism and courage, coupled with what they knew was at stake, forced them repeatedly forward and contributed to the horrible casualty toll. The intensity with which so many of the Confederates fought was perhaps best described by Capt. Daniel Turney of the 2nd Kentucky (Confederate) Infantry at the battle of Murfreesboro. "As well might you ask the winged lightnings to quit their celestial course or the planetary worlds to change their orbits as to bid the Southern patriot to withdraw from the slaughter of the destroyer of his peace, despoiler of his land and desecrator of his home," explained Turney, a member of the Kentucky Orphan Brigade, part of the Army of Tennessee. "No; revenge

---

62 Wide Awake Films.

was in his heart and vengeance was in his eye and he sped recklessly on regardless of his own safety's fate."[63]

Hood fully understood the valor and commitment to honor of the Confederate soldier. "The troops would, I believed, return better satisfied even after defeat if, in grasping at the last straw, they felt that a brave and vigorous effort had been made to save the country from disaster," explained Hood.

A Confederate veteran of the battle of Franklin agreed:

> It has been said that the battle of Franklin was bad generalship, and a mistake. It was neither the one nor the other. It was the inevitable. Had Hood failed to attack Thomas here, the Confederate soldier could never have been made to believe that he had not lost his supreme opportunity, and that a beaten, demoralized and routed foe had been let slip from his grasp. It was the crowning wave of Southern valor, endurance and vengeance sweeping northward, that dashed its crest into bloody foam on the breastworks at Franklin; and sixteen days later it was the undertow of defeat that drove it south again, beaten, vanquished and discomfited forever.[64]

The late-night reports that reached Hood were nothing but discouraging, and his reaction the next morning when he rode out to inspect the forward lines confirmed his shock and despair at the sheer magnitude of the casualties his army had sustained. "His sturdy visage assumed a melancholy appearance," recalled one soldier, "and for a considerable time he sat on his horse and wept like a child."[65]

Around midnight, after the fighting at Franklin had died down to fitful firing, senior Southern leaders met to discuss the day's events. During the meeting, Hood announced his intention to renew the attack the next morning. Thomas Connelly boldly asserted that the decision indicated a "deterioration of Hood's mental condition" and claimed that he was even "disappointed that he

63 Sam Flora in *The Lost Cause* (Winter 2005), a journal of the Kentucky Division SCV. (Flora edited the diary of Captain Dan Turney of the Second Kentucky Infantry, who wrote about the battle of Stone's River.)

64 Hood, *Advance and Retreat*, 300; Typescript of letter dated August 20, 1907, in Carter House files, provided to the author by David Fraley.

65 Miller, *John Bell Hood and the Fight for Civil War Memory*, 157.

could not renew the attack." Connelly's source for these astounding statements is two pages of Hood's own memoirs that only offer a composed, detailed, reasoned explanation of his limited options after Franklin, and his difficult decision to proceed on to Nashville. In their narrative *Five Tragic Hours*, Connelly and McDonough proclaimed, "Of course Hood intended to continue the fight," and was prepared "to renew an assault that would have proved as suicidal as the first attack, and gave orders to do so."

Wiley Sword described Hood at this time as "almost savage in his fury" at the lack of success of the battle, citing Henry Field's 1890 travelogue *Bright Skies and Dark Shadows* as his source. Field, a New England minister who first visited Franklin in 1889, was of course not present at this command meeting and provided no specific source in his own book. Generals Stephan D. Lee, Frank Cheatham, and A. P. Stewart, however, were all present at the meeting, and none of them mentioned anything about Hood's specific mood in any of their extensive postwar writings. Field's credibility nonetheless satisfied Sword, even though the clergyman claimed that the effectively one-armed Hood impossibly "raised his hands, clasping them together" in despair when hearing of the heavy casualties incurred by Cheatham's corps. As often happens with portrayals of Hood, credible primary sources are disregarded in favor of unlikely secondary sources, especially when they yield to melodrama.[66]

During the night, two of Lee's infantry divisions arrived from Columbia, as did all of the army's nearly 100 artillery pieces. Hood ordered an artillery barrage to commence at daybreak, followed by a renewed infantry attack. The artillery barrage took place, but because of Schofield's withdrawal that night across the river toward Nashville, no infantry or cavalry operations were initiated.[67]

Hood is widely criticized for intending to renew the assault at Franklin. It was impossible for him to know the magnitude of his casualties at the time he announced his intentions, however, and it cannot be assumed that he would have attacked Schofield with the same tactics after learning the extent of his losses when dawn arrived. Considering that Schofield abandoned Franklin during the night, it is nothing more than conjecture to state that Hood would have in fact carried out his plan to renew the attack had the Federals remained in

---

66 Connelly, *Autumn of Glory*, 506; Connelly and McDonough, *Five Tragic Hours*, 155-156; Sword, *The Confederacy's Last Hurrah*, 256; Henry Field, *Bright Skies and Dark Shadows* (Freeport, NY: Books for Libraries Press, 1970), 241.

67 Jacobson, *For Cause and For Country*, 422.

place, or, if an attack had been made, what tactics he would have ultimately employed.

Most of the Confederate casualties occurred immediately in front of the second of Schofield's two inner lines, and the Federals were still in possession of the works. It was therefore impossible for Confederate staff officers (or anyone wearing Southern gray) to view and calculate casualties in the dark of night within only short distance of the enemy guns. Although Cheatham and Stewart reported significant losses during the midnight meeting, they could not have known just how badly things had gone for their corps. It wasn't until morning, after the planned attack had been canceled, that Hood—and everyone else—realized the severity of the Confederate casualties. All Hood and his staff could have seen before darkness, smoke, and haze obscured their visibility was the rout of Wagner's two brigades and the second enemy line being broken near the Carter House. Most Federal casualties were incurred in Wagner's division— far behind the high water mark of the Confederate assault, so it is likely that Hood overestimated the magnitude of enemy casualties before nightfall. Schofield ultimately reported 2,300 casualties, including 1,100 missing, but only 189 were officially reported as killed. Modern research, however, has concluded that approximately 400-450 Federals were killed or mortally wounded in the battle. Most of these men were from Wagner's division and left on the field during Schofield's nighttime evacuation of Franklin. Most Federal losses were sustained before darkness and smoke obscured the view, while most of the Southern casualties occurred later and in close proximity to the Union lines— the farthest point from Hood's observation post, initially on the northerly slope of Winstead Hill some two miles away, and later to the Neely house on the Columbia Pike, approximately one mile north of the Carter House.[68]

The battle of Franklin ended in a typical Civil War bloodbath, with the attackers sustaining about three casualties to every one suffered by the defenders. What was atypical about Franklin was the concentration of the carnage in terms of time and space. In its intensity, Franklin rivaled any Civil War battle. Scholars have been debating Hood's assault for decades, and his dilemma that afternoon offers a target-rich environment for critics.

---

68 Conversation with Eric Jacobson, Chief Historian of the battle of Franklin Trust, January 2013. Jacobson has conducted exhaustive research of Federal records and for soldiers listed as missing at Franklin, and has concluded that the number of Schofield's troops killed or mortally wounded was between 400 and 450.

What is too often downplayed is the desperation of the overall Confederate cause and the short amount of time Hood had to make up his mind at Franklin. As S. A. Cunningham wrote of Hood's decision, "It was all important to act, if at all, at once."[69]

---

69 Cunningham, *Reminiscences*, 97.

Chapter 10

The Death of Cleburne:
Resentment or Remorse?

Another persistent allegation against John Bell Hood involves Gen. Patrick Cleburne. According to this legend, Hood blamed Cleburne for the failure at Spring Hill, and Cleburne learned of the accusation. Insulted by Hood's belief and the stain on his honor, Cleburne launched a reckless charge with his division against the enemy works at Franklin and was killed. Other than a single hearsay source recorded in the early 1880s, no contemporary evidence has been located suggesting that Hood blamed Cleburne for the failure at Spring Hill. However, among Hood's recently found papers is a letter from Gen. Stephen D. Lee that reveals what might have been weighing on Cleburne's mind on November 30, 1864. And it had nothing to do with John Bell Hood.

The lack of any real evidence that Hood blamed Cleburne for the failure at Spring Hill did not prevent earlier historians and others from promoting this baseless allegation into the mainstream of Civil War consciousness. Unfounded interpretations and conjecture against Hood have been the norm almost since the guns of the Civil War fell silent.

Hood wrote in his memoirs about his final meeting with Cleburne who, "expressing himself with an enthusiasm which he had never before betrayed in our intercourse, said, 'General, I am ready, and have more hope in the final success of our cause than I have had at any time since the first gun was fired.'" Hood went on to write a glowing tribute to the fallen general, recalling that after their final meeting, he sensed in Cleburne a "sudden revolution of feeling and his hopefulness." Hood attributed this to Cleburne's recognition on the morning of November 30 that Hood's offensive-minded military tactics were "dealing blows and making moves which had at least the promise of happy results," and that success should have been achieved at Atlanta and Spring Hill. It is important to note that Hood never claimed that Cleburne spoke those actual words; rather, this was Hood's impression of Cleburne's resolute demeanor.[1]

Hood's recollection of his final meeting with Cleburne, as well as his heartfelt tribute, has been consistently rejected by historians as disingenuous. Thomas Hay wrote unequivocally that Hood's remarks were "more a pathetic after-attempt at justification than a statement of actual fact," and suggested to his readers to reject Hood's recollections in favor of one of Cleburne's brigade commanders, Gen. Daniel C. Govan, who wrote that Cleburne "never seemed to be so despondent," and to whom Cleburne uttered his famous words, "Well Govan, if we are to die, let us die like men." Regarding Hood's recollection of his last meeting with Cleburne, Hay wrote: "That such a clear-headed, practical, and intelligent soldier as Cleburne could have made such a statement at such a time and under such circumstances is preposterous."[2]

Wiley Sword acknowledged that Hood blamed Frank Cheatham for the Federal escape at Spring Hill, but claimed that Cheatham, in turn, blamed Cleburne and John C. Brown. "While reliable reports of the gathering are lacking," wrote Sword about the meeting of Confederate commanders at the Rippavilla plantation on the morning after the Federal escape, "from circumstantial evidence it appears Cheatham excused his inaction by placing much of the blame for not attacking on Generals Brown and Cleburne, neither of whom were present at the breakfast." Later, however, Sword contradicted

---

1   Hood, *Advance and Retreat*, 294, 297.

2   Hay, *Hood's Tennessee Campaign*, 121.

himself when he stated that it was Hood, not Cheatham, who had blamed Cleburne: "Pat Cleburne evidently received word of Hood's displeasure with his conduct at Spring Hill from Cheatham, following the morning's breakfast." Ironically, Sword informed his readers that no contemporary evidence existed proving that Hood blamed Cleburne, and he even stated that circumstantial evidence pointed to Cheatham. Yet, Sword wrote that it was Hood who blamed Cleburne.[3]

If Cleburne was indeed upset with Hood that day, it is reasonable to conclude or at least suspect that someone falsely told him that Hood blamed him for the Spring Hill fiasco. Thomas Hay cited a postwar letter from Brown to Cheatham that Cleburne was insulted and angry with the army commander for holding him responsible for the Federal escape. Hay did not mention the possibility that Cleburne had received false information from Cheatham. Instead, the author blamed Hood: "On this fateful day, stung by the unjust censures of the commanding general, all were determined to conquer or die" as Cleburne led his troops headlong into the attack, "seemingly with a madness of despair."

After the war on October 24, 1881, Brown wrote this to Cheatham:

> On the march to Franklin General Cleburne, with whom I had long enjoyed very close personal relations, sent a message to the head of my column requesting an interview. Allowing my column to pass on, I awaited his arrival. When he came up we rode apart from the column through the fields, and he told me with much feeling that he had heard that the Commanding General was endeavoring to place upon him the responsibility of allowing the enemy to pass our position on the night previous. I replied to him that I had heard nothing on that subject; and that I hoped he was mistaken. He said: "No, I think not; my information comes from a very reliable channel," and said that he could not afford to rest under such an imputation, and that he should certainly have the matter investigated to the fullest extent, so soon as we were away from the immediate presence of the enemy. General Cleburne was quite angry, and evidently was deeply hurt, under the conviction that the Commander-in-Chief had censured him. I asked General Cleburne who was responsible for the escape of the enemy during the afternoon and night previous. In reply to that inquiry he indulged in some criticisms of a command occupying a position on the left, and concluded by saying that "of course the responsibility rests with the Commander-in-Chief, as he was upon the field during the afternoon and was fully

---

3 Sword, *The Confederacy's Last Hurrah*, 156, 157.

advised during the night of the movement of the enemy." The conversation at this point was abruptly terminated by the arrival of orders for both of us from yourself or the Commanding General. As he left he said: "We will resume this conversation at the earliest convenient moment," but in less than three hours after that time this gallant soldier was a corpse upon the bloody field of Franklin.[4]

Brown's detailed recitation rings plausible. If his recollection is in fact true, it proves only that someone told Cleburne that Hood blamed him for the failure at Spring Hill. Nowhere in the extant historical records is there any eyewitness who claimed to have heard Hood blame Cleburne for Spring Hill.

Another respected and influential historian who blamed Hood for Cleburne's despair did so in a rather confusing manner. In *Stonewall of the West*, Craig Symonds wrote this about Cleburne's final meeting with Hood: "But with Hood's yet unspoken accusations still sharp in his memory, he [Cleburne] could not bring himself to protest Hood's desperate orders." Symonds seemed to acknowledge that Hood had not accused Cleburne of anything ("unspoken accusations"), and yet made the bewildering claim that unspoken accusations by Hood were sharp in Cleburne's memory. The urge for some historians to blame Hood for insulting Cleburne is so irresistible that Hood is now criticized for "unspoken" words.[5]

Wiley Sword went further, claiming that Cleburne considered the assault at Franklin an "outrageous tactical blunder," and that he "well realized that the commanding general's orders were likely to be his own death warrant." Sword added, "Perhaps the South's most brilliant major general, the 'Stonewall Jackson of the West,' his ideas scorned by his president and his competence punished by his commanding general, had been required to lead a suicidal frontal charge like some captain of infantry. Was it God's decreed fate, or simply man's stupidity?" Such commentary is wholly without merit. There is absolutely no evidence that Hood "punished" Cleburne's competence. Cleburne was well known for daringly leading his men into battle and it was not unusual for any soldier—commander or private—to have feelings of impending doom before a battle. Yet, Sword characterized Cleburne's mood as an anomaly and the result of Hood's "blunder." Cleburne did not survive and

---

4 Hay, *Hood's Tennessee Campaign*, 123; *Southern Historical Society Papers*, 52 vols. (Richmond, VA), vol. 9, 538, 539.

5 Symonds, *Stonewall of the West*, 256.

therefore did not leave a record of this appraisal. Neither did anyone else. Statements like Hay's and Sword's are not history, but speculation. Although Cleburne was rational and direct by nature, he was also a loyal subordinate, and was never known to be disrespectful or belligerent to his superiors. Regardless of Cleburne's opinion of his commander's decision, he would not only obey it, but also do so respectfully and confidently. There is no evidence that Hood ordered Cleburne to personally lead a suicidal attack "like some captain of infantry." Going into the thick of the fighting at Franklin was Cleburne's decision, and he—like so many Civil War generals—always led by example. Fearless generals such as Cleburne—including Albert Sidney Johnston at Shiloh, A. P. Hill at Petersburg, Jeb Stuart at Yellow Tavern, Thomas "Stonewall" Jackson at Chancellorsville, and James McPherson at Bald Hill—exposed themselves to death with their men and were often killed or wounded for this bravery and leadership style. Cleburne's death at Franklin was no more Hood's fault than Jackson's death was Lee's fault, or McPherson's death was the fault of Sherman.[6]

Hay and Sword supported their contention of Hood's dishonesty by quoting Daniel Govan's observation of Cleburne's apparent melancholy soon after his final meeting with Hood. According to an eyewitness, however, the last conversation between Cleburne and Hood regarded the formation of Cleburne's division to minimize its exposure to enemy fire, and instructions from Hood to overrun the advanced Federal positions and follow them into their works. As previously mentioned, according to an eyewitness Hood concluded the discussion with Cleburne with a patriotic exhortation, "Franklin is the key to Nashville, and Nashville is the key to independence," to which Cleburne replied, "I will take the enemy's works or fall in the attempt." There is nothing out of the ordinary in these final words between the two commanders. Cleburne may indeed have heard the false assertion that Hood had censured him for the failure at Spring Hill or he may have disagreed with the decision to attack, but he would respond to his superior with obedience and respect. It is possible that both Hood and Govan accurately recorded their recollections, and the quantum leaps in speculation taken by critics like Hay and Sword are simply wrong.[7]

---

6   Sword, *The Confederacy's Last Hurrah*, 180, 224.

7   Buck, *Cleburne and His Command*, 290; Jacobson, *For Cause and For Country*, 257; French, *Two Wars*, 292.

As previously stated, a letter penned in 1875 by Stephen D. Lee was recently found in a large cache of Hood's personal papers. This document offers important evidence suggesting that Cleburne's anomalous demeanor at Franklin (if in fact it was so) was attributable to Cleburne's personal remorse, not anger at his commanding general. In his letter, Lee wrote of a meeting he had with fellow corps commander A. P. Stewart several weeks earlier in Columbus, Mississippi. During this 1875 meeting, Stewart told Lee that Cheatham and Cleburne had decided against launching a night attack at Spring Hill. According to Stewart, Cleburne "regretted it immediately afterwards" (doubtless alluding to the next morning, after learning of the enemy's escape), felt personally responsible, and "in that feeling lost his life at Franklin soon afterward." Lee noted that Stewart did not personally hear Cleburne's contrition, but he added that Stewart "believed such was the case and had heard so."[8]

When considering whether Cleburne might have counseled against a night attack, or concurred with Cheatham in not launching the night assault at Spring Hill, it is instructive to consider Cleburne's only experience with night assaults. A little more than one year earlier at the battle of Chickamauga in September of 1863, Cleburne's division commenced an assault after dark that was, according to Cleburne's official report, so confusing as to make distinguishing friend from foe impossible. Cleburne also wrote of "the difficulty of moving my artillery through the woods in the dark" that rendered a further advance "inexpedient." Of the infantry, Cleburne wrote, "Accurate shooting was impossible. Each party was aiming at the flashes of the other guns, and few of the shots from either side took effect." The assertion that the enemy fire was ineffective is curious, since Cleburne reported 445 killed and wounded in the night attack—which translates into very high casualties for such brief combat.[9]

General Govan's exact words in describing Cleburne before the attack were: "General Cleburne seemed to be more despondent than I ever saw him." Assuming that Govan's recollection was accurate, it is now logical to ask whether Cleburne's mood was attributable to resentment at being told that his commanding general blamed him for the failure at Spring Hill, or because of

---

8   S. D. Lee letter to John Bell Hood, August 25, 1875, John Bell Hood Personal Papers.

9   *OR* 30, pt. 2, 154, 158.

feelings of personal responsibility for the Federal escape at Spring Hill—and by extension, the ensuing assault that—victorious or otherwise—was sure to be bloody. According to A. P. Stewart, it was the latter.[10]

In any case, many authors ignored the eyewitness account penned by William Stanton (Granbury's brigade) about Hood learning of Cleburne's death. According to Stanton, Hood approached him on the morning after the battle and asked for the location of Cleburne's division. Stanton replied that the division was gathered around Cleburne's body, at which time Hood, according to Stanton, lowered his head and wept for half an hour. It seems unlikely that Hood would have cried at all, much less uncontrollably, upon learning of the death of any subordinate he believed was personally responsible for the surrounding carnage.[11]

Many historians cynically questioned the accuracy and sincerity of Hood's memoirs, unless his words can be interpreted in such a way as to soil his own image. The result is that Hood's words of respect and affection for Patrick Cleburne are all but absent from the major books on the Army of Tennessee and the Tennessee Campaign. For example, Hood wrote, "Major General Cleburne had been distinguished for his admirable conduct upon many fields, and his loss, at this moment, was irreparable." Calling Cleburne "a man of equally quick perception and strong character," Hood noted his "boldness and wisdom" in proposing the enlistment of slaves into the Confederate army, which in Hood's opinion, would have resulted in Southern independence.

Regardless of whether Cleburne's behavior at Franklin stemmed from the "madness of despair" of unjust accusations, or feelings of personal culpability for the escape of Schofield's army and the bloodbath that was about to ensue, his legacy is best described by Hood, who wrote, "The heroic career and death of this distinguished soldier must ever endear the memory of his last words to his commander, and should entitle his name to be inscribed in immortal characters in the annals of our history."[12]

---

10 Buck, *Cleburne and His Command*, 290; S. D. Lee letter to John Bell Hood, August 25, 1875, John Bell Hood Personal Papers.

11 William Stanton letter to Mary Moody, Barker Center Archives, University of Texas, Austin.

12 Hood, *Advance and Retreat*, 296.

Chapter 11

"The historian reports to us, not events
themselves, but the impressions
they have made on him."

— *Heinrich von Sybel*

John Bell Hood and the
Battle of Nashville

Another common criticism of John Bell Hood involves his move to Nashville after what Gen. P. G. T. Beauregard described as the "barren Confederate victory" at Franklin. This is a fair criticism, especially when considering the heavy casualties sustained there, and the decimation of its officer corps. After sustaining 6,300 casualties from all sources, Hood's army consisted of about 26,000 veteran infantry, artillerists, and cavalry. Two of Stephen D. Lee's infantry divisions had not fired a shot at Franklin, and none of the army's 100 or so cannon or other assets had been lost. Given the state of the war and his orders from Richmond, Hood refused to abandon the campaign. It should be noted that neither Beauregard nor the Confederate high command instructed him to withdraw from Tennessee.[1]

---

1 Roman, *The Military Operations of General Beauregard,* 303.

Middle Tennessee was a hotbed of Confederate sympathy, and Hood's spies kept him informed of Gen. George Thomas's desperate consolidation of forces around Nashville. On December 1, when Hood made his decision to continue north to Tennessee's capital city, Thomas's army was much smaller and less organized than the 60,000 men he would eventually field. Federal Col. Henry Stone described Thomas's command at this time as "an ill-assorted and heterogeneous mass, not yet welded into an army." Thomas Van Horne wrote in his *History of the Army of the Cumberland* that in early December, Thomas led "an improvised army . . . of raw infantry regiments" with cavalry "still largely dismounted," and black troops who would have their first opportunity to fight in organized units. Simply put, immediately after the battle of Franklin, Thomas's army at Nashville was not as formidable as it would become by December 15. Much of Hood's reasoning for continuing his forward movement was based upon this information.[2]

Some authors have asserted that Hood intentionally kept his superiors uninformed of the condition of the army after Franklin, and that this explains why neither Beauregard nor the Confederate War Department ordered Hood to withdraw. This is not true. On December 3, Hood wired Beauregard the results of Franklin, including, "We have to lament the loss of many gallant officers and brave men," and listed the names of the dozen generals wounded, killed, and captured. On December 11, Hood sent a longer dispatch to Confederate Secretary of War James Seddon informing him that the army had lost 4,500 men at Franklin. Although that figure is lower than the broadly accepted number of 6,300 casualties, many slightly wounded men returned to the ranks after the army entrenched at Nashville. In any event, Hood reported this information, including that he had lost some 15 percent of his army, to the Confederate War Department. This is indisputable proof that he was not trying to conceal anything.[3]

It is fair to ask what Confederate commander would have abandoned a crucial campaign with a fully equipped army of 26,000 veterans at such a desperate point in the war. Robert E. Lee faced a much more perilous state after the fall of Richmond and Petersburg. By that time there was no doubt that the

---

2   Stone, "Repelling Hood's Invasion of Tennessee," *Battles and Leaders of the Civil War*, 454; Hood, *Advance and Retreat*, 299-300; Thomas Van Horne, *History of the Army of the Cumberland*, 2 vols. (Cincinnati, OH: Robert Clarke and Company, 1875), vol. 2, 223.

3   Roman, *The Military Operations of General Beauregard*, 611-613.

war had been utterly lost (which was not as clear in early December 1864). However, rather than surrender the Army of Northern Virginia, he headed west. His intent was to continue fighting in an effort to unite his dwindling army with Joe Johnston in North Carolina. By this time Lee's army was not that much larger than was Hood's army before Nashville. By the time Lee reached Appomattox, the Army of Northern Virginia had been reduced to fewer than 7,800 effectives. Even Johnston attacked Sherman's larger army at Bentonville on March 19, 1865, in an effort to slow or halt the Federal drive through the Carolinas. Sherman's 60,000-man army was roughly the size of Thomas's at Nashville, while Johnston's motley command of some 20,000 was smaller than Hood's at Nashville.[4]

Like Lee in Maryland in 1862 and in Pennsylvania the following year, Hood did not abandon the Confederate offensive until his army had been depleted to the point where he deemed victory impossible. After losing about one-third of his army at Sharpsburg, Lee remained in place for one full day before abandoning his invasion and retreating from Maryland. The following year, Lee withdrew from Pennsylvania only after losing about 37 percent of his army at Gettysburg, a loss similar to what Hood sustained at Franklin and Nashville.[5]

Hood elaborated upon his reasons for the movement to Nashville in *Advance and Retreat.* After the failure of his plan to destroy Schofield's army before it reached the relative security of Nashville, Hood, with an effective force of approximately 26,000 infantry and cavalry, believed that a northerly movement bypassing Nashville was unwise without reinforcements. Admitting that he could not expect to attract recruits from Tennessee and Kentucky "in the absence of the prestige of complete victory" over Thomas, "the only remaining chance of success at this juncture was to take position, entrench around Nashville, and await Thomas's attack, which, if handsomely repulsed, might afford us an opportunity to follow up our advantage on the spot, and enter the city on the heels of the enemy." At the risk of destroying the morale that remained in the army, a southward movement was not an option. "In truth," explained Hood, "our army was then in that condition which rendered it more judicious the men should face a decisive issue rather than retreat—in other words, rather than renounce the honor of their cause, without having

---

4 Dowdey and Manarin, *The Wartime Papers of Robert E. Lee,* 938.

5 National Park Service, U.S. Department of the Interior, Civil War Sites Advisory Commission on Civil War Battlefields, Battle Summaries, 1997.

made a last and manful effort to lift up the sinking fortunes of the Confederacy." Hood wrote to an acquaintance after the war, "The capture of Nashville and regaining so much lost territory, I was quite certain would give new life to our people, recruit our thinned ranks, and give that tone to the army I had been so long accustomed in Virginia would ensure victory to our arms, and finally secure our freedom." Hood also knew that the possibility of receiving reinforcements, timely or otherwise, was essentially impossible: "Mississippi, Alabama, Georgia & the Carolinas having no men at the ready and that could be sent to my aid," required that he act on his own. He declared his unwillingness to abandon Tennessee "as long as I saw a shadow of probability of assistance from the Trans-Mississippi Department or of victory in battle."[6]

Why would Hood allude to a "shadow of probability" (an 18th century term for "possibility") of "assistance" from the Trans-Mississippi? Hood had been requesting reinforcements from any quarter since the fall of Atlanta— including the Trans-Mississippi—and had at some point (the record is unclear when) received indications that reinforcements might be able to cross the Mississippi River. When Hood learned that no crossing of any size was likely, he awaited Gen. E. Kirby Smith's decision regarding Richmond's request that Smith feign a threat against St. Louis, Missouri, to force Thomas to return Federal reinforcements that had left the Trans-Mississippi to help defend Nashville. Hood took note of the transfer away from St. Louis of 15,000 Union troops and believed that their movement created an opportunity that might allow the crossing of Confederate troops from the Trans-Mississippi. The record on all these points is instructive.

For example, less than a week after the fall of Atlanta, Hood asked Braxton Bragg in a dispatch dated September 7, "Is it not of the first importance . . . to get as soon as possible all the troops over from Kirby Smith?" Apparently having been informed that some Trans-Mississippi troops were en route, Hood wired Gen. Richard Taylor on September 8, "How many of your cavalry crossed the river as yet? If not, when will they be over?" The next day Taylor sent two replies. The first was a three-word message: "None—expect none." The second, via Bragg, read: "General Taylor informs me, in reply to my dispatch on the subject of troops crossing the river, that none have crossed, and believes no effort is being made to cross over." On September 11 Hood

---

6 John Bell Hood letter to Sarah Dorsey, March 30, 1867, John Bell Hood Personal Papers; Hood, *Advance and Retreat*, 300.

continued to press for reinforcements, telegramming Taylor, "Why is no effort being made to cross your troops?" Two days later Taylor responded, "I will have to refer you to Genl E. K. Smith for answer to your inquiry of 11th." Hood again wired Taylor on September 24, "How many troops crossed to this side of the Mississippi River? The newspaper so reports." Taylor answered, "Your telegram of yesterday received. None have crossed, & I believe no effort is being made to cross any at this time."[7]

When his battered Army of Tennessee began taking up a position just south of Nashville on December 2, Hood was fully aware of the heavy odds facing him. His knowledge that defeating Thomas would be difficult accounts for the contingency plans he made for retreat, not once but on two occasions. In a circular issued on December 10, Hood mentioned the high probability that a battle would be fought "before the close of the present year," but not necessarily at Nashville. However, "should it occur in front of Nashville," Hood stated, his corps commanders were to immediately "send all wagons . . . except artillery, ordnance and ambulances" 10 miles south to Brentwood, Tennessee. Early in the morning of December 16, during the second and final day of the battle of Nashville, Hood sent A. P. Stewart special instructions in case a serious reversal occurred. Taking note of Thomas's newly gained reinforcements and the hard results of the previous day's fighting, Hood told Stewart:

> Should any disaster happen to us today . . . you will retire by the Franklin Pike, and Lee is directed to hold it in front of his large ridge that you may pass to his rear. After passing Brentwood you should again form your corps in the best position you can find, and let the whole army pass through you. There are some narrow gorges beyond Brentwood toward Franklin. At all times the roads must be left open for artillery and wagons, [with] the men marching through the fields and woods.[8]

Although Franklin adversely affected the morale of the army, a solid fighting spirit persisted within many of the soldiers. Colonel Virgil S. Murphey, who had been captured at Franklin and was being held in Nashville, wrote in his diary that when his fellow prisoners learned that Hood's army was advancing on

---

7 Telegram book II and IIa, John Bell Hood Personal Papers.

8 OR 45, pt. 2, 672, 696.

Nashville, "About 300 Yankee bounty jumpers and prisoners in the yard yelled with delight and declared their readiness to rejoin Hood."[9]

Major G. W. Garrett of the 23rd Mississippi Infantry recorded an incident on the first day of the Nashville fighting that proved the morale of the Confederates had not completely evaporated, nor was all affection for Hood lost. While under a fierce Federal assault, the Mississippians were enveloped by enemy troops and ordered to surrender. A Confederate artillery barrage commenced while they were preparing to capitulate. According to Major Garrett, "One of my men raised up while the shells of Hood's guns were falling around us and yelled out: 'Hurrah for Hood! Give them h-ll; our shells won't hurt us!'" Reiterating his desire for the army to earn victory or honor, Hood felt the soldiers would "return better satisfied even after defeat if, in grasping at the last straw, they felt that a brave and vigorous effort had been made to save the country from disaster."[10]

Early authors struggled with Hood's movement to Nashville after Franklin. Thomas Hay wrote in *Hood's Tennessee Campaign*, "Hood's rashness in following after Schofield was characteristic and, in a sense, was made necessary by the desperate condition of the Confederacy. It imposed on the country, North and South, the appearance of confidence and success and tended to deceive his opponents as to his real strength and resources. Thomas was no doubt influenced . . . by this bold front. Another impelling motive for Hood was the hope, born of necessity, that the army might be recruited by the illusion of success. . . . Hood might have retired, but he elected to fight." Yet, concluded Hay, "Thus was a brilliant strategical conception marred, first by tactical failures and blunders and then precipitated into an unnecessary deluge of blood and suffering, which finally ended in complete defeat and rout." It seems as though Hay could not decide whether Nashville was an unnecessary bloodbath, or a final justified gamble made necessary by the military and political plight of the Confederacy.[11]

Hay offered additional contradictory observations in the same book. "After his defeat at Franklin," he continued, "Hood had small chance of accomplishing anything by pushing on to Nashville," and that the movement

---

9   Virgil Murphey Diary.

10 G. W. Garrett letter, *Confederate Veteran* (October 1910), vol. 18, 470; Hood, *Advance and Retreat*, 300.

11 Hay, *Hood's Tennessee Campaign*, 131-132, 136.

was simply a "vainglorious gesture." In further conflict with his own earlier words, Hay stated that Hood might have become mentally unhinged after Spring Hill, the subsequent events at Franklin and Nashville having occurred because he was "perhaps temporarily unbalanced," and that the Spring Hill fiasco "so warped his judgment and distorted his conception of conditions that he could see no alternative course."[12]

In addition to what has already been noted, Hood had good reason for continuing the campaign. A major consideration for launching an offensive was the declining morale of the Army of Tennessee. The decline had existed to some degree even before Hood assumed command back in July. Notwithstanding assertions by some authors that Johnston's army unanimously approved of his tactics in Georgia, many officers and men were displeased and disheartened by his constant retreating from north Georgia all the way to Atlanta's gate.[13] At West Point, Hood and his fellow cadets were taught Napoleon's military maxims. In 19th century warfare, these were considered to be the most fundamental of military tactics. Maxim VI reads as follows:

> At the commencement of a campaign, to advance or not to advance is a matter for grave consideration; but when once the offensive has been assumed, it must be sustained to the last extremity. However skillful the maneuvers in a retreat, it will always weaken the morale of an army, because in losing the chances of success these last are transferred to the enemy. Besides, retreats always cost more men and materiel than the most bloody engagements; with this difference, that in a battle the enemy's loss is nearly equal to your own—whereas in a retreat the loss is on your side only.[14]

Although many modern scholars considered Hood's invasion of Tennessee a fool's errand, Ulysses S. Grant felt otherwise. Writing of Hood's army at Nashville, he observed, "The country was alarmed, the administration was alarmed, and I was alarmed lest the very thing would take place which I have just described—that is, Hood would get north." In fact on December 6, 1864, Grant, besieging Lee in Richmond and Petersburg, was so disturbed by Hood's threat that he ordered Thomas to launch an immediate attack. Thomas had yet to comply with the order by December 11, so Grant sent the following

---

12 Ibid., 149.

13 Disapproval of Johnston's retreating tactics is detailed in Chapter 3 of this book.

14 *Napoleon's Maxims of War* (New York: C. A. Alvord, Printer, 1861), 19.

urgent message: "If you delay attacking longer, the mortifying spectacle will be witnessed of a rebel army moving for the Ohio." Worried and exasperated, Grant decided to relieve Thomas—who is universally recognized today as one of the finest Union generals of the entire Civil War—and take command himself. First, however, he sent Gen. John A. Logan to Nashville. "Knowing him as a prompt, gallant and efficient officer," Grant wrote of Logan, "I gave him an order to proceed to Nashville to relieve Thomas. . . . After Logan started, in thinking over the situation, I became restless, and concluded to go myself." When he learned of Thomas's attack on December 15, Grant recalled Logan. By that time Grant was en route to Nashville and had traveled as far as Washington, D.C. He returned to the Richmond-Petersburg front.

Grant, who had been locked in a bloody six-month stalemate with Robert E. Lee, considered Hood's threat at Nashville so great that he was willing to leave Lee to his subordinates so that he could personally deal with the Tennessee invasion. After the carnage at the Wilderness, Grant did not retreat and regroup as his predecessors had done. Instead, he slogged on mile after mile in his determined drive to defeat Lee's army. He eventually reached the outskirts of Richmond and Petersburg. Hood, after the heavy fighting and well-planned attacks around Atlanta, invaded Tennessee, nearly bagged Schofield's army at Spring Hill, suffered heavily at Franklin, and then continued moving north to Nashville. It is possible that Grant may well have recognized in Hood the same determined resolve he himself possessed.[15]

Author Thomas Hay utilized Beauregard's opinion to describe Hood's movement to Nashville. On January 9, 1865, Beauregard claimed in a letter that, after Franklin, Hood should not have invested Nashville. Instead, argued the general, he should have seized Murfreesboro and wintered there with the "prestige of success." Hay does not challenge Beauregard, who had written to Richmond only a few weeks earlier that the Tennessee Campaign was being conducted exclusively to force a retrograde movement by Sherman, and had exchanged letters with Jefferson Davis, each alluding to Hood acting boldly to relieve Lee in Virginia and the importance of Hood reaching "the country proper of the enemy." The loss of Murfreesboro would not have concerned Sherman, and certainly would not have compelled Grant to ease his noose around Richmond and Petersburg. How the "prestige" of occupying

15 Grant, *Personal Memoirs*, vol. 1, 503, and vol. 2, 380, 382, 384.

Murfreesboro would have strengthened the fragile morale of the Army of Tennessee is left unspoken.[16]

Misinformation on Hood's actions at Nashville is relatively common in Civil War literature. In fact, some historians have incorrectly asserted that Hood attacked Thomas at Nashville, when in fact it was Thomas who launched the assault against Hood's fortified troops on December 15. Even respected historian William C. "Jack" Davis wrote that at Nashville Hood "launched an attack" on Thomas and that after his defeat, "Hood could do nothing but pull his shattered divisions back into Georgia [sic]." Thomas Hay contrasted Thomas's methodical behavior with Hood's "rash and aggressive" actions at Nashville, when in fact Thomas was by far the more aggressive of the two generals at Nashville.[17]

The perception of Hood's movement to Nashville as sensational still exists at the highest levels of scholarship. Disregarding the 2,500 casualties inflicted on Thomas's attacking army, Tennessee state historian Walter T. Durham described Hood's investment of Nashville as "reckless" and "a suicidal move"—completely ignoring why Hood was there in the first place. Although driven from the field, Chaplain James McNeilly of Quarles's brigade wrote that the battle of Nashville "was very disastrous to us in the loss of guns and prisoners captured from us, but we lost comparatively few in killed and wounded."[18]

࿐ ࿐

Too many historians and students of the war have concluded that Hood moved his army to Nashville and simply waited to be attacked. A careful examination of the record suggests otherwise.

As part of his overall strategy, Hood dispatched Nathan Bedford Forrest on December 2 with two cavalry divisions and Gen. William Bate's infantry division to Murfreesboro, a move that historian Thomas Connelly called "ignorant." Connelly went on to inquire, "Why did [Hood] . . . detach Bate's

---

16 Hay, *Hood's Tennessee Campaign*, 140; Roman, *The Military Operations of General Beauregard*, 303.

17 Davis, *Look Away!*, 321; Hay, *Hood's Tennessee Campaign*, 142.

18 Walter T. Durham quoted in "Preserving Nashville's Past" by Nicole Young, *The Nashville Tennessean*, January 8, 2012; McNeilly, "With Hood Before Nashville," *Confederate Veteran* (June 1918), vol. 26, 253.

division, Forrest with two cavalry divisions . . . to seize the Federal garrison at Murfreesboro?" Author Stanley Horn also deemed the move worse than a wasted effort, labeling the detachment of Forrest and Bate a "suicidal" mistake and "a blunder of colossal proportions." Contemporary author Eric Jacobson also questioned Hood's decision, writing, "Hood once again played with his cavalry, leaving his right flank at Nashville completely unprotected."[19]

Why did Hood detach this substantial force of horsemen and foot soldiers? Did he really ignore his right flank? As will be seen, the facts are straightforward and the circumstances that convinced Hood to make the movement more than justified. In fact, it was prudent. Murfreesboro, just 25 miles to the east, was garrisoned by Gen. Lovell H. Rousseau's 8,000 Federals. Rousseau posed a very real threat not only to Hood's right flank at Nashville, but also to the Army of Tennessee's supply line and retreat route.

Initially, Hood believed the Murfreesboro garrison was smaller. He sent Forrest and Bate in early December to attack Rousseau in the hope that Thomas would send reinforcements to save the beleaguered garrison. Hood planned to attack the Federal relief troops en route from Nashville. When he learned the true strength of the Murfreesboro garrison, Hood changed his plan and replaced Bate's division with a single infantry brigade and recalled one of Forrest's two cavalry divisions, leaving Forrest in command of the smaller force to keep Rousseau in check. Hood changed his instructions to Forrest on December 8—six days after the initial detachment—by directing the cavalryman "not to construe the order as meant to attack the enemy's works." If the Federals moved out of their works, advised Hood, "you will endeavor to drive them back to Murfreesboro." In other words, Hood was endeavoring to protect his right flank and the army's logistical lifeline and route of retreat.[20]

If Hood needed a senior subordinate to place in independent command at Murfreesboro with full discretionary authority, who would have been a better appointee than Forrest? With fewer than 22,000 effective infantry at Nashville, Hood could not have spared any of his three corps commanders (Lee, Stewart, or Cheatham). Forrest's previous success in independent command made him the best available commander. Hood instructed Forrest to "continue to act upon your best judgment." He did, and he succeeded by keeping Rousseau

19 Connelly, *Autumn of Glory*, 507; Horn, *The Decisive Battle of Nashville*, 41; Jacobson, *For Cause and For Country*, 447.

20 OR 45, pt. 2, 666.

confined to Murfreesboro and Hood's army's supply line and retreat route open. Although Forrest was not at Nashville when Thomas attacked on December 15, Hood immediately recalled him on December 16 when the Confederate lines collapsed and the retreat began. At that point, Rousseau's threat was no longer a concern.[21]

Because Hood has been so deeply castigated for sending Forrest and an independent command to watch Rousseau, the natural line of inquiry is whether the absence of Forrest and one brigade from Bate's division fatally weakened Hood and led to the loss at Nashville. On December 16, Thomas's attack broke the left side of Hood's line on the second day of the battle. It was not Hood's under-strength cavalry that was turned and defeated. Rather, it was that portion of the line manned by Gen. Jesse J. Finley's Florida brigade, which belonged to Bate's division of Cheatham's corps. Had Forrest and his single cavalry division been at Nashville, the fatal break in the Confederate line would almost certainly still have occurred.[22]

Civil War writers and historians often ignored the persistent problems surrounding the performance and conduct of Bate's division during the campaign. Forrest was displeased with two of Bate's brigades and reported what he called "shameful" conduct by Finley's and Henry R. Jackson's brigades during an engagement on December 7 outside Murfreesboro. "I seized the colors of the retreating troops and endeavored to rally them," Forrest explained in his official report of the fighting, "but they could not be moved by any entreaty or appeal to their patriotism. Major-General Bate did the same thing, but was equally unsuccessful as myself." Finley's and Jackson's brigades were then recalled by Hood to Nashville (as noted earlier) and took up positions in the Confederate defensive line, where they played a prominent role in the result of the ensuing battle. On the second and final day of fighting at Nashville, a large Federal force, protected by the crest of a hill, stormed the position held by Bate's division, whose men had neglected to construct rifle pits at the locations specified by the army's chief engineer Colonel Stephen Presstman. The portion of the Southern line occupied by Finley's brigade was the first to break. Like a

---

21 Ibid.; Hood, *Advance and Retreat*, 300-303.

22 Ibid.

line of dominoes, their sudden retreat destabilized the entire line and led to the Confederate collapse.[23]

Problems with Bate and his troops were later reported to Richmond by the Reverend John Talley of Culverton, Georgia. Talley penned his letter to Jefferson Davis on February 9, 1865, as Bate's division passed near his home en route to North Carolina. Wholly unimpressed by what he saw, the reverend called the Army of Tennessee "not much better than an armed mob." He went on to say of Bate, "I am satisfied you must relieve General Bate; he has not the shadow of authority over his men for good. The unanimous voice of the men is he is unfit for the responsible position. He lacks influence and has no authority over his men." This was not an isolated instance.[24]

Although not directly related to Hood's command decisions during the Nashville Campaign and treatment by various writers, it is worthwhile to consider the general performance of William Bate's division to add context to the subject. As it turns out, the performance of this general and his brigades was an issue throughout the Tennessee Campaign (and thereafter, as evidenced by Talley's letter to President Davis), and yet Bate and his troops have largely evaded criticism by Civil War historians. In a postwar letter to Hood, Stephen D. Lee complained bitterly about the performance of Bate and his division at Franklin. Ed Johnson's division of Lee's corps (which had been assigned to Cheatham's corps during the flank march from Columbia to Spring Hill), was returned to Lee's command on the morning of November 30 and was the first of Lee's three divisions to reach Franklin. Johnson's men arrived at Winstead Hill around 5:00 p.m. (about dusk)—after the Confederate charge was well underway. Once on the field, Johnson's division was sent to Cheatham, who ordered the command to immediately attack that same portion of the Federal line being assaulted by Bate's division. After lamenting the heavy casualties Johnson's division suffered, Lee wrote: "When Johnson made his most gallant

---

23 OR 45, pt. 1, 755; Hood, *Advance and Retreat*, 302-303. The Army of Tennessee's chief engineer during the Tennessee Campaign was Col. Stephen W. Presstman (often misspelled "Pressman" and "Prestman"). A native of Maryland, Presstman enrolled at West Point in 1846 as a sixteen-year-old and did not graduate, although he achieved high academic scores. Presstman enlisted in the Confederate army in May 1861, and organized a company of infantry in Fairfax County, Virginia, called the O'Connell Guards, comprised mainly of Irish railroad workers. He also served in the 17th Virginia Infantry (Army of Northern Virginia) before transferring to the Army of Tennessee.

24 OR 49, pt. 1, 966-967.

attack after dark, he was cautioned not to fire till he reached the works, as <u>Bate's</u> men were there. They were not there and the report was at the time they never were there. . . . <u>I understand</u> that Bate's division did not go to the works at all [emphasis in the original]." Lee asked Hood if he could confirm his information, and then added, "His [Bate's] troops were not at his works when my gallant division got there. Nor if my recollection is correct were many of his dead."[25]

Despite the fact that the Yankee breakthrough occurred along that portion of the line manned by Bate's division on December 16, Thomas Hay blamed the Confederate defeat at Nashville on Forrest's absence (which then made it all Hood's fault). "Forrest's absence from the army was unnecessary and in the end calamitous," argued Hay, who went on to state that Hood's detachment of Forrest to Murfreesboro was "an inexcusable violation of all the rules of war." On December 15, the first day of the battle, Hood's line was about four miles long. After the fighting ended that day, Hood reduced his line to about three miles and improved it considerably. Adding a single cavalry division and small infantry brigade along lines this long would almost certainly have had no impact whatsoever on what occurred at Bate's position on Shy's Hill. No one knew where the attack or breakthrough, if there would be one, would take place. The Confederate army sustained about 1,500 killed and wounded at Nashville (less than five percent of those engaged), but lost about one-half of the army's 100 artillery pieces, which was indeed calamitous. If Hay (and others) believed that "Forrest's absence . . . was unnecessary and in the end calamitous," they have to believe his presence would have either prevented the collapse, or saved much or all of the artillery. Both are highly doubtful. In addition, when Bate's front broke, the Confederate line collapsed so quickly that horses could not be brought forward in time to remove the artillery.[26]

It is also impossible to calculate how many Confederate prisoners taken during the battle and difficult retreat would have been saved by Forrest's presence, but in many cases it would have made no difference whatsoever. Private Sam Watkins wrote that scores of Confederates had "allowed themselves to be captured," and S. A. Cunningham recalled many Tennessee soldiers deserting during the Nashville retreat. In his official report, George Thomas recorded 2,000 Confederate deserters taking the oath of allegiance at

---

25 S. D. Lee letter to John Bell Hood, April 25, 1879, John Bell Hood Personal Papers.

26 Hay, *Hood's Tennessee Campaign*, 141, 168; Horn, *Decisive Battle of Nashville*, 148.

Nashville, although he did not specify how many of these had deserted from Hood's army between December 16 and the end of the Federal pursuit of Hood's army 10 days later. According to Thomas, he ended the Nashville fighting and follow-up with 4,490 prisoners. Because many Confederates were reported to have voluntarily surrendered, it is impossible to estimate the impact Forrest's presence would have had on the number of prisoners Hood lost.[27]

When Hood arrived with his army south of Nashville on December 2, he immediately sought reinforcements from any sector. In fact, his search began even before the army's arrival at Nashville. On November 25, Hood dispatched an officer to Mississippi to gather conscripts for Edward Walthall's division and also asked the Corinth military authorities for 1,000 convalescents to be sent to the Army of Tennessee.[28]

One common and harsh criticism of Hood's invasion of Nashville involves reinforcements from the Trans-Mississippi. In his memoirs, Hood stated his hope that Gen. E. Kirby Smith, commander of Confederate forces west of the Mississippi River, would send troops. The river, however, was completely controlled by the Federals after the fall of Vicksburg and Port Hudson in 1863. It would have been extremely difficult to shift large numbers of men to the river without the enemy knowing it, and then obstruct the crossing. Hood and Beauregard were well aware of this. Historians, however, rarely discussed the fact that an alternative plan was proposed to Smith.

Of all the books written about the Army of Tennessee and Hood's Tennessee Campaign, only Stanley Horn took the time to explain that an alternative plan proposed by Beauregard was in the works. Aware of the difficulties of crossing the river, Beauregard asked Kirby Smith to make a demonstration northward into southeast Missouri simulating a threat to St. Louis. With Smith's Rebel army moving north, the Federals would have but little choice other than to keep a large defending force near that important city, or if Gen. A. J. Smith's corps was en route to Nashville, force its return to Missouri. It was these troops that were being sent as reinforcements to Thomas

---

27 Watkins, *Company Aytch*, 208; Cunningham, *Reminiscences of the 41st Tennessee*, 107; OR 45, pt. 1, 46.

28 Ibid., 1,249.

in Nashville to oppose Hood. A well-played demonstration by Kirby Smith may well have kept A. J. Smith's 15,000-man command from being sent to Middle Tennessee, and may have compelled Washington to divert even more troops to Missouri to supplement Smith's relatively small force. However, Kirby Smith, who often failed to cooperate with coordinated efforts, would not make the demonstration. If A. J. Smith had been held in Missouri, Thomas's army at Nashville would have been smaller by at least 15,000 men (and perhaps more). How that would have played out in the final fighting is anyone's guess.[29]

While Hood's army was gathering below Nashville on December 2, Beauregard was in Montgomery, Alabama, wiring Jefferson Davis about reinforcements for the Army of Tennessee. "Generals Steele and A. J. Smith are reported to be re-enforcing General Thomas at Nashville. Cannot I send General E. Kirby Smith to re-enforce General Hood in Middle Tennessee, or take offensive in Missouri? His assistance is absolutely necessary at this time." Two days later, Davis replied that he concurred with the plan. However, in a stunning admission that Smith was unsuited for his position, the president warned Beauregard that Smith had "failed heretofore to respond to like necessities and no plans should be based on his compliance." Nevertheless, under such dire circumstances, Beauregard, Davis, and by extension, Hood, had little choice but to hope that Smith would comply with so much at stake. Beauregard attempted to appeal to the Trans-Mississippi commander with logic and reason. "You are probably aware that the Army of Tennessee, under General J. B. Hood," began Beauregard, "penetrated into Middle Tennessee as far as Columbia, and that the enemy is concentrating all his available forces, under General Thomas, to oppose him." He continued:

> It is even reliably reported that the forces under Generals A. J. Smith, in Missouri, and Steele, in Arkansas, have been sent to re-enforce Thomas. It becomes, then, absolutely necessary, to insure the success of Hood, either that you should send him two or more divisions, or that you should at once threaten Missouri, in order to compel the enemy to recall the re-enforcements he is sending to General Thomas. I beg to urge upon you prompt and decisive action. The fate of the country may depend upon the result of Hood's campaign in Tennessee. Sherman's army has lately abandoned Atlanta on a venturesome march across Georgia to the Atlantic coast about Savannah. His object is, besides the destruction of public and private property, probably to re-enforce Grant

29 Horn, *The Army of Tennessee*, 406.

and compel Lee to abandon Richmond. It is hoped that Sherman may be prevented from effecting his object, but, should it be otherwise, the success of Hood in Tennessee and Kentucky would counterbalance the moral effect of the loss of Richmond. Hence the urgent necessity of either re-enforcing Hood or making a diversion in Missouri in his favor.[30]

Taken aback by Davis's comment about Smith's anticipated lack of cooperation, Beauregard's adjutant general Col. George W. Brent wrote to Beauregard on December 8: "It would be well to recommend to the Department that General Bragg be sent at once to relieve Smith, and organize and administer Trans-Mississippi, and General R. Taylor to command troops." Brent added that it would "secure prompt action" that Smith was anticipated not to provide. Although there was no way for Confederate authorities to have known, by this date it was too late to help Hood's army at Nashville.[31]

Unmoved by Beauregard's desperate appeal, Smith did not reply until January 6—long after the matter had been settled on the hills south of the Tennessee capital. Writing from his headquarters in Shreveport, Louisiana, Smith informed Adjutant and Inspector General Samuel Cooper:

I have the honor to acknowledge a dispatch from the honorable Secretary of War, received at these headquarters on the 29th ultimo, directing, if practicable, the crossing of troops in aid of General Hood, or a diversion in his favor by a movement into Missouri. The heavy rains which have fallen, unusual even at this season, with the exhausted condition of the country and our limited transportation, make it impossible, before early summer, either to attempt crossing troops or to renew operations against the enemy. I have delayed my reply to this dispatch until views of Lieutenant-General Buckner could be obtained, the matter being then under consideration, a letter previously received from General Beauregard on the same subject having been submitted to him.[32]

Smith wrote to Beauregard that same day, as follows:

Your letter of December 2, from Montgomery, Ala., together with a communication from Colonel Brent, assistant adjutant-general, of the 3rd of the same month, were

---

30 OR 45, pt. 2, 636, 639-640.

31 Ibid., 665.

32 Ibid., 764.

delivered by your aide, Captain Toutant, on the 20th ultimo. Feeling convinced of the utter impracticability of operating during the winter season, I delayed answering your letter until Lieutenant-General Buckner, commanding District of West Louisiana, to whom it had been submitted, could be consulted. I enclose you a copy of his reply. The swamps on the Mississippi are at this season impassable for conveyances, the bayous and streams all high and navigable for the enemy's gun-boats. The country has been so devastated by the contending armies and is so exhausted that the troops would require transportation for supplies for near 300 miles from the interior to the Mississippi.

Appreciating our necessities in your department and ardently desiring the transfer of this army to your aid, I am powerless to assist you either by crossing troops or by operating in North Arkansas and Missouri. The country north of Red River is bare of supplies and is at this season utterly impracticable for the operations of armies and the movement of troops. More than 200 miles of destitution intervenes between our supplies and the enemy's works on the Arkansas, near 500 of desert separate our base on Red River from the productive region of Missouri.

Trusting you appreciate the difficulties under which I labor and believe in an honest desire on my part to assist you, I remain your friend and obedient servant,

E. KIRBY SMITH, General[33]

After having been told that the "fate of the country" depended upon his assistance and knowing Hood's army to be facing a powerful enemy outside Nashville, Smith refused to make even the pretense of a demonstration into Missouri and instead, asked Beauregard to appreciate the difficulties under which he labored. Considering the difficulties under which Hood and the Army of Tennessee had labored from the gates of Atlanta to the fields of Franklin and now in the fortifications south of Nashville; or the suffering of Lee's beleaguered army in the trenches outside Richmond and Petersburg; or the torment endured by the citizens of Georgia under first Sherman's artillery and then his torches, Smith's comment is inexcusable. It also highlights Jefferson Davis's pointed criticism to Beauregard that Smith's cooperation was unlikely.

Thomas Hay wrote of the folly of Hood's vain hope of reinforcements from the Trans-Mississippi, yet told his readers nothing of Beauregard's effort

---

33 Ibid., 765-766.

to convince Kirby Smith to impel—through a mere demonstration—a return of 15,000 Federal troops back to St. Louis from Nashville.[34]

Historians also ignored two important points Hood made in his well-known and oft-cited December 11 letter to Confederate Secretary of War James Seddon. "Some fifteen thousand of the enemy's Trans-Mississippi troops are reported to be moving to reinforce the enemy here," wrote Hood. "I hope this will enable us to obtain some of our troops from that side in time for the Spring campaign, if not sooner." Hood's reference to receiving reinforcements in time for the Spring 1865 campaign season indicates that an attack by Thomas—although probable—was as of December 11 not obviously imminent. Further, Hood's reference may well indicate that he thought it possible Thomas only intended to fortify and hold Nashville, and not attack his army.[35]

More importantly, Hood's statement provided his superiors with yet another alternative method of obtaining reinforcements from the Trans-Mississippi. Knowing that action by Kirby Smith had been requested but not yet answered, Hood (as noted earlier) astutely recognized that sending 15,000 Union troops to Nashville from St. Louis would leave a large portion of the Mississippi River undefended by Federal infantry, and thus create opportunities for the crossing of Trans-Mississippi troops.

Historians who assert that Hood erratically stumbled to Nashville and did nothing but await certain destruction by overwhelming enemy numbers are simply wrong.

On many fronts, historians have had a field day lambasting Hood's march north to the outskirts of Nashville. Thomas Connelly wrote that the move to Nashville was due to the "further deterioration of Hood's mental condition." Hood, continued Connelly, "marched into a trap" at Nashville and—ignoring the circumstances that dictated his decision, and his advance preparations in case of the need to retreat—was "operating with delusions of victory." Of reinforcements from the Trans-Mississippi, Connelly wrote, "Hood had not received the slightest hope from either the government or from Beauregard of any planned reinforcement from Kirby Smith's department." Although true,

34 Hay, *Hood's Tennessee Campaign*, 140.

35 Hood, *Advance and Retreat*, 357-358.

Hood knew that reinforcements had been requested. What he did not know was that Smith had refused to provide reinforcements or make a diversionary movement into Missouri, which could have drawn troops away from Thomas. This is another example of an author holding back the full story from the reader—the alternative plan requested of Smith would have reduced Thomas's total troop strength by at least 15,000.[36]

Wiley Sword also made no mention of Beauregard's efforts with regard to Smith, sharing with his readers only that Hood's movement to Nashville was intended to provide "positive publicity and salve for Hood's injured ego."[37]

Notwithstanding the flurry of desperate attempts to obtain reinforcements or to persuade Smith to make a diversionary movement into Missouri, it must be again noted that neither Beauregard nor anybody in the Richmond high command suggested that Hood withdraw from Nashville.

❧　❧

While awaiting a reply from the uncooperative Smith, and in acknowledgment of Richmond's suggestion that his compliance should not be counted upon, Hood and Beauregard sought reinforcements from other possible sources. On December 6, Hood wired Secretary of War James Seddon, "I respectfully recommend that Major-General Breckinridge, with his forces, either be ordered into Kentucky or to join this army." On the same day, Hood informed Beauregard that the railroad from Pulaski to Nashville was in good condition and, in an effort not to further deplete his army, requested the railroad from Corinth to Decatur be guarded by troops "other than from this army," suggesting reserve troops from Alabama and Mississippi for that purpose.[38]

Hood accelerated his efforts to obtain reinforcements. He wired Beauregard on December 7 asking for additional men and any other soldiers from the Army of Tennessee (not at Nashville) to be sent forward "as soon as possible." Two days later he requested that Beauregard transfer Gen. Joseph H. Lewis's mounted infantry brigade to Nashville. On December 10, Hood turned

---

36　Connelly, *Autumn of Glory*, 506-507.

37　Sword, *The Confederacy's Last Hurrah*, 280.

38　*OR* 45, pt. 2, 653.

to Richard Taylor, appealing for reinforcements from his department, and specifically suggested that garrisons from Huntsville and Corinth be sent to Nashville.[39]

The next day, December 11, Hood sent a dispatch to Secretary Seddon mentioning, among other things, the subject of conscription. This exchange has been completely mischaracterized by Wiley Sword, who claimed that Hood was angry because only 164 recruits had voluntarily joined the invading Southern army. "Hood reacted angrily and resolved 'to bring into the army [by conscription] all men liable to military duty.' If recruits wouldn't voluntarily flock to his standards," Sword wrote, "he intended to bring them in at the point of the bayonet." Sword supported this vitriol by citing a dispatch to Seddon in which Hood wrote only a single sentence on the subject of conscription: "As yet I have not had time to adopt a general plan of conscription, but hope soon to do so, and to bring into the Army all men liable to military duty." Elsewhere in the letter, Hood discussed only routine issues such as railroad repairs and enemy troop strength. Nowhere in the letter is there the slightest hint of anger, nor is there any comment about intending to bring in draftees "at the point of the bayonet." Contrary to Sword's baseless and dramatized depiction, Hood was simply looking to gather conscripts—a common and routine practice by Confederate authorities throughout the South.[40]

On December 13, Hood asked Beauregard to return Gen. Alpheus Baker's Alabama brigade, which had been previously sent to Mobile. Describing the hardships under which his troops were suffering, Hood also requested supplies—specifically clothing and blankets—and again asked Beauregard to assist in the repair of the railroad to Decatur, which Richard Taylor had still not done after almost two months.[41] In an attempt to reinforce and replenish the officer corps, which had been decimated at Franklin, Hood wired the provost office in Corinth, Mississippi, on December 15 asking that officers from the military courts be immediately sent to Nashville.[42]

Hood's unrelenting appeals for assistance proved fruitless. Seven days after the battle of Nashville, during the long hard retreat to Mississippi, Hood

39 Ibid., 669, 700.

40 Sword, *The Confederacy's Last Hurrah*, 315; OR 45, pt. 1, 658.

41 *OR* 45, pt. 2, 685.

42 Ibid., 690.

received this message from Beauregard dated December 23: "I regret to inform you that no re-enforcements can possibly be sent you from any quarter. General Taylor has no troops to spare, and every available man in Georgia and South Carolina is required to oppose Sherman, who is not on a raid, but an important campaign," explained Beauregard. "Should you be unable to gain any material advantage in Tennessee with your present means you must retire at once behind the Tennessee River, and come with or send to Augusta, by best and quickest routes, all forces not absolutely required to hold defensive line referred to."[43]

ಶಿ   ೋ

Many modern-day scholars accuse Hood of concealing the army's depleted condition from Richmond, both after Franklin and even after the retreat from Nashville. These accusations directly conflict with the written historical evidence.

Thomas Connelly wrote that Hood's correspondence with his superiors during the campaign "indicated his clouded thinking—if not his dishonesty," while Wiley Sword—ignoring Hood's prompt and accurate reporting of the loss of 12 generals, 4,500 troops, and 50 cannon, and of the army's later withdrawal from Tennessee—informed his readers that Hood's messages to Richmond "had been without admission of defeat; indeed, they had minimized the army's losses."[44]

Stanley Horn wrote that on January 3, 1865, Beauregard, then in Macon, Georgia, received a telegram from Hood "that must go down in history as a masterpiece of misleading understatement." Horn used only a portion of Hood's telegram, as follows: "The army has re-crossed the Tennessee River without material loss since the battle of Franklin." According to Horn, Hood told Beauregard "nothing of the shocking losses at Franklin; nothing of the disaster at Nashville." This is completely erroneous. In reality, Hood wired Beauregard within 48 hours of Franklin, lamenting "the loss of many gallant officers and brave men," and listed the names of the dozen generals killed, wounded, or captured. An army does not suffer the loss of so many generals without also suffering heavy casualties. While attending to the wounded and burying the dead the day after the battle, Hood issued a circular in an attempt to

---

43 Ibid., 726.

44 Connelly, *Autumn of Glory*, 507; Sword, *The Confederacy's Last Hurrah*, 428.

better ascertain his losses on November 30—which was no easy task given the size of the battle and the numbers of troops involved. On December 11, with his army on the hills south of Nashville, Hood sent a more detailed dispatch to both Secretary of War Seddon and Beauregard describing the actions at Spring Hill and Franklin and informing them of the loss of 4,500 men. On December 17, the day after the fighting ended at Nashville during the retreat to Mississippi, Hood informed Beauregard that his army had been defeated at Nashville and lost 50 cannon and several ordnance wagons.[45]

Like Horn, Sword also attempted to convince his readers that Hood intentionally deceived his superiors. "Beauregard, now at Macon, Georgia read what seemed to be a long-delayed dispatch from Hood about the Nashville battle," explained Sword. "Immediately Beauregard telegraphed the contents to Richmond, noting Hood's claim in an accompanying dispatch dated January 3 that his army had safely re-crossed the Tennessee River 'without material loss since the battle of Franklin.'"[46]

Both authors' statements are factually incorrect. It is difficult to imagine how Sword's assertion could be unintentional—unless he simply copied Horn and did not bother to research the source himself. Here is what the heretofore cited January 3, 1865, dispatch from Hood to Beauregard says in its entirety:

> The army has re-crossed the Tennessee River without material loss *since the battle in front of Nashville* [emphasis added]. It will be assembled in a few days in the vicinity of Tupelo, to be supplied with shoes and clothing, and to obtain forage for the animals.

The difference between what Hood wrote, and what Horn and Sword claimed he wrote, is not only obvious, but compelling and critical to the entire narrative that Hood was lying to or misleading his superiors. The word "Franklin" does not appears anywhere in the telegram. The only thing false or misleading is how Horn and Sword presented it to their readers.

It is also important to revisit Hood's December 17 dispatch to Beauregard and Seddon announcing the army's defeat at Nashville, in which Hood revealed, "We lost in the two days engagements fifty pieces of artillery, with several ordnance wagons." Hood's later message on January 3 ("The army has

---

45 Horn, *The Army of Tennessee*, 421-422; OR 45, pt. 2, 643-644, 699; Hood, *Advance and Retreat*, 355-358.

46 Sword, *The Confederacy's Last Hurrah*, 428.

re-crossed the Tennessee River without material loss since the battle in front of Nashville") accurately informed Beauregard that the army had successfully crossed the Tennessee River without losing more material (artillery and wagons) since what was lost at Nashville—just as he reported in his December 17 telegram. Although highly unlikely, it is possible that Horn was not aware of Hood's informative December 17 dispatch. However, Sword was certainly aware of it because he referred to its contents on pages 425 and 436 (endnote 11) and 428 (endnote 22) of *The Confederacy's Last Hurrah*. Furthermore, Sword cites the *Official Records* (OR 45, pt. 2, 757) that has Hood's January 3, 1865, dispatch in the very same chapter in which he accuses Hood of misleading authorities. It is difficult to explain how Sword could not have known that Hood had accurately informed his superiors of his losses at Nashville.[47]

Another matter to consider is whether Horn intentionally substituted "Franklin" for "Nashville" to make Hood look like a liar, or perhaps misread the *Official Records*. We will likely never know. But if Sword's oversight was unintentional, the only logical way it could have come about is if he copied Horn's quote word-for-word and didn't bother to check it against the readily available *Official Records* or think about what was written elsewhere. If so, this demonstrates yet again how some historians duplicate the work of others (especially the melodramatic) without thinking critically for themselves and researching to verify what they are writing. Tragically, this is how falsehoods and exaggerations become cemented in the public mind and popular history as "truth."[48]

---

47 OR 45, pt. 2, 757, 699; Sword, *The Confederacy's Last Hurrah*, 428.

48 Both Horn and Sword cited OR 45, pt. 2, 768, which is a January 7, 1865, dispatch from Beauregard to Samuel Cooper. That wire states that Hood reported from Corinth, Mississippi, on January 3, 1865, and that the army had re-crossed the Tennessee River "without material loss since [the] battle of Franklin*." The compilers of the *Official Records* put an asterisk after the word "Franklin" and added this at the bottom of the page: "* See dispatch as sent by Hood, p. 757." On page 757 is Hood's correctly written January 3 dispatch to Beauregard and James Seddon stating, "The army has recrossed the Tennessee River, without material loss since the battle in front of Nashville.*" The compilers then added this at the bottom of the page: "* See dispatch as was repeated by Beauregard, p. 768." It is apparent that the compilers of the *Official Records* realized the transcription mistake made by someone on Beauregard's staff and felt obligated to reprint both the erroneous and correct reports—and inserted conspicuous asterisks after the words "Franklin" and "Nashville" to guide readers to both entries. Although it is unknown whether Horn saw and exploited the transcription mistake made by Beauregard's staff, it is difficult to see how Sword could not have known about the correct page 757 entry since he refers to another entry on page 757 elsewhere in his book.

In addition to accurately revealing the condition of the army via correspondence, on multiple occasions Hood asked Beauregard to personally visit the army. On December 7, Hood requested that Beauregard visit the army at Nashville. After the defeat on December 16 and during the retreat south, Hood asked Beauregard on December 25 to meet the army in Bainbridge or Tuscumbia. On the same day, he sent a member of his staff, Col. J. P. Johnson, to Richmond to personally explain the Tennessee Campaign to Confederate officials. On January 3, while in Corinth, Hood again asked to meet with Beauregard, and finally on January 10 and also on January 11, while in Tupelo, Hood requested that Beauregard visit the army to discuss "important matters." If Hood was attempting to deceive his superiors or conceal the condition of the army, he would not have followed the course just outlined.[49]

Beauregard finally arrived in Tupelo on January 13 to meet with Hood, after having left the young commander to his own devices for nearly two months since leaving the Army of Tennessee in Tuscumbia on November 16.[50]

Hood's move to Nashville was rational given the circumstances he faced, the possibility of reinforcements or a diversion to weaken Thomas's army was in play, and when he was driven back in defeat he kept his superiors informed of his situation. Once again, the historical record contradicts many of the leading writers who have asserted otherwise.

---

49 *OR* 45, pt. 2, 731, 778.

50 Roman, *The Military Operations of General Beauregard*, 332.

Chapter 12

"People tend to forget that the word 'history' contains the word 'story.'"

— *Ken Burns*

The Army of Tennessee: Destroyed in Tennessee?

Those versed in Civil War history and literature are well aware of the difficulty of accurately calculating casualties. Contemporary reports are often nonexistent or incomplete, especially on the Confederate side during the last year of the war. Federal and Confederate definitions of "wounded" differed, and prisoners were often exchanged, meaning their loss in most cases was only temporary. Missing soldiers were often killed, their bodies never recovered, while others were taken prisoner. Many wounded troops eventually died of their injuries or were unable to remain in the service. Armies were also depleted by desertions that, whatever the cause, were losses nonetheless.

Contrary to a common conclusion drawn in much of Civil War literature, the Confederate Army of Tennessee was not "destroyed" during the campaign. The *Official Records* and Jefferson Davis's memoirs offer the clearest picture of what actually transpired. Before the Tennessee invasion, on November 6, 1864, the Army of Tennessee's total effective strength stood at 32,859 troops. After the defeat at Nashville and subsequent retreat, the army numbered 18,730 effective infantry and artillery, and 2,306 cavalry, for an effective troop strength of 21,036.[1]

Hood's losses for the entire Tennessee Campaign were reported as 11,823. This sizeable figure, however, was not comprised of just the dead, wounded, and/or captured, but also included losses from desertions. According to S. A. Cunningham, after the retreat ended it was discovered that "nearly all the Tennesseans were gone home. They either had written furloughs or took 'French leave [deserted].'" Federal Gen. James Wilson, in a December 17, 1864, dispatch to George Thomas during his pursuit of Hood's beaten army, confirmed Cunningham's recollection when he informed his commander that Confederate prisoners reported "all the Tennesseans are deserting." Tennessean Sam Watkins elaborated on another form of desertion when he explained that many soldiers "had stopped and allowed themselves to be captured" during the retreat. Thomas himself confirmed reports that many "captured" Rebels were actually looking to desert and go home when he recorded that nearly one-half of the approximate 4,400 prisoners taken during and after Nashville took the oath of allegiance and went home.[2]

Despite access to these (and other) concise and readily available records, historians repeatedly exaggerated Confederate casualties in the Tennessee Campaign. For instance, in *The Confederacy's Last Hurrah*, Wiley Sword inflated Confederate losses by an astounding 11,000 when he wrote, "Hood had suffered during the campaign perhaps 23,500 casualties." Grasping for a forceful superlative, Sword continued, "This appalling loss of nearly two-thirds of a major American army as the result of actual fighting was unprecedented. Never had there been such an overwhelming victory during the Civil War— indeed, never in American military history."[3]

---

1   Cheatham's Corps 10,519, S. D. Lee's Corps 8,632, Stewart's Corps 8,708, cavalry 5,000 (approximate as of November 16 after Forrest's forces had arrived) for a total effective force of 32,859; *OR* 45, pt. 1, 678, 664; Davis, *The Rise and Fall of the Confederate Government*, vol. 2, 491, 579. Although historians almost always offer only an estimate of Nathan Bedford Forrest's troop strength after the Tennessee Campaign, President Davis set it at the very specific number of 2,306.

2   Watkins, *Company Aytch*, 208; Cunningham, *Reminiscences of the 41st Tennessee*, 107; *OR* 45, pt. 2, 238; ibid., 5, pt. 1, 48.

3   Sword, *The Confederacy's Last Hurrah*, 425-426.

Inflating the casualties the army suffered while under Hood's command is a common theme among many writers. Elsewhere, when writing about the Confederate defense of Atlanta, Sword claimed: "Hood had in little over a week squandered nearly 20,000 men in fruitless attacks"—notwithstanding the fact that campaign records report Hood's losses during that period at 9,855, or fewer than one-half of the number Sword reported. The Army of Tennessee totaled 50,414 effectives on July 10, one week before Hood took command, and 40,559 on August 31, after the three battles cited by Sword.[4]

Sword's source for his near-total exaggeration of Hood's casualties in the defense of Atlanta appears to be drawn from Thomas Connelly's *Autumn of Glory*, whose own casualty numbers are bewildering and contradictory. Connelly, who relied upon William T. Sherman's inflated estimates of the battles of Peachtree Creek, Atlanta (Decatur), and Ezra Church, concluded that those casualties "brought Hood's losses thus far in the campaign to over twelve thousand." In the very next paragraph, however, citing the *Official Records* as his source, Connelly contradicted himself when he wrote that Hood's losses in those same battles totaled 8,000. ("By August 10, Hood's total effective strength in both infantry and artillery had slipped to 35,371, a drop of almost 8,000 since the first of July.") Other authors, such as Joseph Wheeler's recent biographer Edward Longacre in *A Soldier to the Last*, regurgitated these mistakes, seems to have ignored official reports, and simply used the higher of Connelly's two unsubstantiated and erroneous figures.[5]

Even more perplexing was Sword's decision to inflate Hood's casualties by using the *sum* of Connelly's two contradictory numbers. After citing the page in Connelly's *Autumn of Glory* that provides both the 12,000 and 8,000 casualty estimates, Sword apparently totaled these two figures and declared that Hood lost 20,000 troops. Although Sword routinely cited the official reports in his books, and in so many ways is a careful and meticulous researcher, he seems to have ignored official reports when calculating Hood's casualties during the Atlanta and Tennessee campaigns in favor of the inflated figures presented by another author—and then inflated even those numbers.[6]

---

4   Ibid., 34.

5   Connelly, *Autumn of Glory*, 455; OR 38, pt. 3, 679, 682-683; Edward G. Longacre, *A Soldier to the Last: Maj. Gen. Joseph Wheeler in Blue and Gray* (Dulles, VA: Potomac Books, 2007), 168.

6   Sword, *The Confederacy's Last Hurrah*, 34; Connelly, *Autumn of Glory*, 455. The only calculation that reaches 20,000 is the addition of the 12,000 and 8,000 numbers.

This trend of relying upon incorrect figures (and other people's work) continues to this day. Producers of the documentary film "The Battle of Franklin" relied heavily on Sword's book and included in its narration the 20,000 casualty number for the Atlanta battles. According to Sword's casualty summation, Hood lost 43,500 troops during his six-month tenure as commander of the Army of Tennessee—an astounding 20,345 more than specified in the *Official Records*.[7]

Sword also appears to have misread the numbers regarding prisoners of war. In *The Confederacy's Last Hurrah*, he included in the casualties suffered by Hood's Army of Tennessee during the Tennessee Campaign all 13,189 prisoners processed by George Thomas during Hood's post-Atlanta tenure (September 7, 1864, through January 15, 1865). For his number to be correct, every Confederate prisoner processed through Nashville during that time frame—whether captured in Kentucky, Tennessee, Mississippi, Georgia, Alabama, or western Virginia—had to have come from Hood's command. Of course, that was impossible. If Sword's number is correct, nearly one-half of the post-Atlanta Army of Tennessee was *captured* during the Tennessee Campaign alone! For his part, Thomas reported 4,462 Confederates captured during the battle at Nashville and the subsequent retreat, with perhaps a few hundred more prisoners taken during the other actions of the campaign.[8]

Historian Eric Jacobson recently discovered that Sword double-counted as many as 3,800 Confederates wounded on November 30. Hood had to leave these injured men at Franklin when he moved the army north to Nashville. Many of these wounded were captured on December 18 when the Federals pursued Hood's retreating army through Franklin. Sword counted these troops as both wounded at the battle of Franklin and among the captured at the battle of Nashville.[9]

Unfortunately, like other genres of history, an error persuasively written and published in Civil War literature is often repeated in subsequent books and magazine articles. Even the most alert academicians can fall prey to these mistakes. For instance, Anne J. Bailey wrote in her otherwise excellent and informative book *The Chessboard of War: Sherman and Hood in the Autumn*

7   *The Battle of Franklin*, Wide Awake Films; Sword, *The Confederacy's Last Hurrah*, 426.

8   OR 45, pt. 1, 48; Sword, *The Confederacy's Last Hurrah*, 426.

9   Jacobson, *For Cause and For Country*, 450.

Campaigns of 1864, "In Tennessee alone, Hood had lost 13,189 men taken prisoners; more than 2,000 deserted to Federal lines, and the killed and wounded totaled about 8,600, a total of 23,789." Bailey's source was not the readily available reports and correspondence in the *Official Records*, but Wiley Sword's inflated numbers published nine years before her own work appeared.[10]

Unfortunately, Bailey is not alone. Many other respected scholars have accepted these erroneous calculations. For the July 20, 1864, battle of Peachtree Creek, Hood's first combat in defense of Atlanta, conscientious scholars Steven Woodworth and Richard McMurry seemed to accept Sherman's inflated estimate of 4,800 total Confederate casualties, even though official battle reports filed by Confederate commanders and the Army of Tennessee medical director put the casualty figure at roughly one-half that oft-cited number. Commanders of four of the six engaged Confederate divisions reported 1,728 casualties. A fifth division under William Bate became lost in dense woods and sustained few if any injuries. The losses sustained by the sixth division, led by Gen. William H. T. Walker, must be estimated because of a lack of contemporary records, but only two of his three brigades were engaged. Even a liberal estimate of 1,000 casualties for Walker's division (500 per engaged brigade) only elevates the total Confederate losses at Peachtree Creek to roughly 2,700.[11]

Sherman estimated Rebel losses for the July 22, 1864, battle of Atlanta at nearly 8,500. This figure has been widely accepted in Civil War scholarship by Woodworth and others. However, official reports suggest Sherman's figure was at least 3,000 too high. General William Hardee, the commander of the most heavily engaged of the two Confederate corps that fought that day, reported his losses at 3,299. Records for the other engaged corps under Gen. Benjamin Cheatham are incomplete, with written reports available for only some of his divisions and brigades. Using specific reports and estimating others, a reasonable approximation of casualties for Cheatham's corps is 2,000. Adding a few hundred casualties for Confederate cavalry and the Georgia militia brings

---

10 Anne J. Bailey, *The Chessboard of War: Sherman and Hood in the Autumn Campaigns of 1864* (Lincoln: University of Nebraska Press, 2000), 168.

11 Davis, "A Reappraisal of the Generalship of John Bell Hood in the Battles for Atlanta," 69; Woodworth, *Civil War Gazette* interview; McMurry, *John Bell Hood and the War for Southern Independence*, 128.

Hood's total losses for the battle of Atlanta to about 5,600—significant, but no where close to the commonly accepted figure of 8,500.[12]

Mistakes also abound related to casualty figures for the July 28 battle of Ezra Church, the third of Hood's major efforts to defend Atlanta. Atlanta Campaign scholars McMurry, William Scaife, Thomas Connelly, James McDonough, and others disregarded more credible records and claimed that the Army of Tennessee incurred about 5,000 casualties—the inflated number reported by Sherman. A close examination of reports filed by the Confederate division commanders engaged in the battle—Brown, Walthall, and Clayton—demonstrate that actual Confederate losses were almost one-half that, or around 2,900.[13]

Reports filed by Army of Tennessee medical director Dr. A. J. Foard corroborated the accounts prepared by Hood's subordinate commanders. For example, Dr. Foard recorded Confederate losses for Peachtree Creek, Atlanta, and Ezra Church of 1,756 killed and 10,267 wounded, for a combined total of 12,023. Sherman, however, estimated Southern losses for these same three battles at 20,000. While the medical corps records did not include captured Confederates, Dr. Foard's reports closely approximated the 11,000 losses reported by Hood's subordinates. It is also important to note that Dr. Foard's report did include all Confederate casualties sustained during the last half of July, even those incurred in other cavalry operations, skirmishing, and the Federal bombardment of Atlanta fortifications unrelated to the three large battles.[14]

No one disputes the fact that the Army of Tennessee was severely depleted during Johnston's long retreat from Dalton, Hood's vigorous defense of Atlanta, and the battles waged in Tennessee. However, it is simply not true to state that the fighting destroyed the army. A large number of cannon were lost at Nashville, but 21,000 effectives returned to Mississippi along with most of

12 OR 38, pt. 3, 877, 883, 895, 902, 931, 938, 942; Benjamin Franklin Cheatham papers, Tennessee State Library and Archives, Nashville.

13 Davis, "A Reappraisal of the Generalship of John Bell Hood in the Battles for Atlanta," 72 (Davis discusses these authors in his essay).

14 Hood, *Advance and Retreat*, 222. Hood reproduced the reports and other sources verbatim in his memoirs.

the army's other equipment and assets. "It is true that we were sadly repulsed at Nashville," wrote surgeon Samuel Thompson of the 41st Tennessee, but Hood "brought off the larger portion of the army with Quartermaster, Commissary, Medical and Ordnance trains."[15]

After Hood's resignation on January 23, 1865, Richard Taylor was placed in temporary command of the Army of Tennessee. Brigades were sent to Alabama and North Carolina, where Joseph E. Johnston was restored to theater command in the Carolinas on February 25, 1865. Johnston, in turn, elevated Gen. A. P. Stewart to lead what was left of the Army of Tennessee, which together with other troops under Johnston's command attacked Sherman at Bentonville, North Carolina, on March 19, 1865, at the cost of more than 3,000 casualties. A comparison of the Confederate orders of battle at Nashville and Bentonville reveals that 23 corps, divisions, and brigades from the Army of Tennessee participated in both battles.[16]

Compared with how they treat other Confederate generals, many historians applied a double standard when analyzing Hood's tenure in command. Few, if any, writers of Civil War history asserted that Kirby Smith or Robert E. Lee destroyed their armies. Smith himself, however, addressing his disintegrated Trans-Mississippi "army" on May 30, 1865, wrote, "I am left a commander without an army, a general without troops." How did this disintegration come about? Surely Kirby Smith was responsible for it? In an April 10, 1865, letter to Jefferson Davis, Lee detailed just how thoroughly the retreat to Appomattox had decimated the Army of Northern Virginia:

> At the commencement of the withdrawal of the army from the lines on the night of the 2d, it began to disintegrate, and straggling from the ranks increased up to the surrender on the 9th. On that day, as previously reported, there were only seven thousand eight hundred and ninety-two (7,892) effective infantry. During the night, when the surrender became known, more than ten thousand men came in, as reported to me by the Chief Commissary of the Army. During the succeeding days stragglers continued to give themselves up, so that on the 12th of April, according to the rolls of those paroled, twenty-six thousand and eighteen (26,018) officers and men had surrendered.

---

15 Cunningham, *Reminiscences of the 41ˢᵗ Tennessee*, 117-118.

16 Johnston's new command encompassed two military departments (South Carolina, Georgia, and Florida and North Carolina and Southern Virginia).

Men who had left the ranks on the march, and crossed James River, returned and gave themselves up, and many have since come to Richmond and surrendered.[17]

If the same logic and statistical interpretations were applied to Lee's final campaign as are routinely applied to Hood's Tennessee Campaign, the Army of Northern Virginia would be defined as "destroyed," and Lee would have been held accountable for destroying his army. After all, fewer than 8,000 troops were on hand when he surrendered the army he had withdrawn from Richmond and Petersburg. Lee lost about seventy-three percent of his troops on his final campaign, a sum that includes deserters, stragglers, captured, and those who voluntarily surrendered.

Historians commonly used the word "defeated" rather than "destroyed" when discussing the final fates of Kirby Smith's and Robert E. Lee's armies. Hood, it seems, has been held to a different standard.

---

17 Lizzie Cary Daniel, *Confederate Scrap Book*, (Richmond, VA: J. H. Hill Printing Company, 1893), 5; Dowdey and Manarin, *The Wartime Papers of Robert E. Lee*, 938.

Chapter 13

"Perhaps in general footnotes should be held guilty
unless proven innocent."

— *James G. Randall*

Did John Bell Hood
Accuse his Soldiers of Cowardice?

$\mathcal{In}$ virtually all the modern books on the Army of Tennessee or the 1864 Tennessee Campaign, John Bell Hood is said to have blamed his failures on others, called the soldiers of the Army of Tennessee cowards or otherwise questioning their bravery. Nowhere in the historical record is there any primary source evidence to support these assertions. Notwithstanding the absence of evidence, these accusations continue. The charges have been repeated so often they are now part of the public consciousness and accepted as fact—not only by amateur Civil War enthusiasts but also by many professional historians.

No one who served with Hood, from the lowly rank of private to the elevated rank of general, ever wrote or claimed that he accused any soldier of cowardice or questioned the bravery of his troops. No diary, letter, or memoir by any soldier, officer, public official, or private citizen contains a word accusing Hood of insulting anyone for lack of valor. Even his rivals and harshest critics claim nothing of the sort. In fact, just the opposite is true.

Contrary to popular belief, and completely ignored by most modern authors, Hood spoke frequently of the valor and gallantry of his fellow soldiers, Confederate and Federal alike. In addition, the man often falsely portrayed as being critical of his own troops was described even by contemporary critics as cordial, congenial, and easily approachable by the rank and file and his fellow officers. Although caricatured during his relatively brief tenure as commander of the Army of Tennessee as rash and vindictive, an unbiased examination of the record reveals something altogether different.

The earliest of the major Tennessee Campaign chroniclers, Thomas Hay, noted Hood's comments in his memoirs about the negative effect Joe Johnston's constant retreating had upon the aggressiveness of the Army of Tennessee. During his account of the Confederate army's movement into Tennessee in the late fall of 1864, Hay made no mention of Hood accusing his army of any cowardice at Spring Hill. Subsequent authors, however, at first subtly and then more blatantly, raised that notion. Embellishment and repetition has cemented that falsehood firmly into place in today's Civil War community.[1]

The myth that Hood accused his troops of cowardice, and therefore ordered the attack at Franklin the next day to teach them a lesson in bravery— or to punish them for dashing his dreams of glory at Spring Hill—seems to have first derived from the pen of Stanley Horn. In his influential *The Army of Tennessee*, Horn made the following claim: "Worst of all, and most unfairly and unjustifiably, he blamed the soldiers." To support this allegation, Horn provided partial quotations from Hood's memoirs about his disappointment that Johnston had embedded a defensive attitude in the army, and that Hood had tried to renew the aggressive spirit of the army through the offensive movement into Tennessee. Hood believed that Johnston's persistent retreating had negatively affected the aggressiveness of the Army of Tennessee, and that this lack of aggressiveness substantially contributed to the successful escape of John Schofield's nearly trapped Federal army at Spring Hill; Horn described Hood's factually accurate recollection as "blather," even though Hood's account was supported by the recorded firsthand observations of his contemporaries.[2]

---

1   Hay, *Hood's Tennessee Campaign*, 95.

2   Horn, *The Army of Tennessee*, 394.

The next major book on the Tennessee Campaign, *Autumn of Glory*, was published several years later by Horn's fellow Tennessean Thomas Connelly, who informed readers that Hood blamed the fall of Atlanta on his subordinates and that he "seriously questioned the army's valor." On the morning of November 30 (the day of Franklin, and the day after Spring Hill), Connelly wrote:

> Probably he [Hood] intended the assault, in his own tormented way, as an exercise of discipline for the army. He later admitted that he utilized frontal assaults for such a purpose, and reveled in the shedding of blood as a booster of morale. For him, the Franklin attack would be a last great effort to mold the army into his image of the Virginia army as he had known it.[3]

Like Horn before him, Connelly source was six pages from Hood's memoirs. The only problem is that there is nothing within those pages that remotely supports Connelly's libelous statements. Hood never accused his soldiers of cowardice or discussed using assaults—frontal or otherwise—to discipline troops. Indeed, Hood could not have admitted to using "frontal assaults" for any purpose for the simple reason that, prior to the afternoon of November 30, 1864, at Franklin, he had never as an army commander ordered a frontal assault (as had Gens. Grant, Burnside, Lee, Bragg, and others). Further, Hood did not write anything that even hinted that he "reveled in the shedding of blood as a booster of morale." It is both perplexing and disturbing that Connelly could read these pages from Hood's own account and make such claims. (For the reader's convenience, the pages from Hood's account are reproduced in Appendix 1.)

Elsewhere in *Autumn of Glory*, Connelly condemned Hood by claiming that he repeatedly "rebuked his own troops for their cowardice," and that the army "knew of Hood's scorn." Not surprisingly given his track record regarding his treatment of Hood, Connelly could not provide a single quote from any "rebuked" soldier, or anyone who recorded Hood's alleged "scorn." If the Army of Tennessee's commanding general had rebuked his own men openly and claimed that they and the army were cowardly (Connelly claimed the men "knew" of Hood's scorn), why hasn't a single diary, journal, letter, or memoir surfaced to substantiate the accusation?

---

3 Connelly, *Autumn of Glory*, 503.

Even if Hood thought the men lacked valor (in fact he unambiguously wrote and stated exactly the opposite), it would have been impossible for his troops to have known it at the time according to the sources Connelly relied upon: Hood's official report of the Tennessee Campaign was written in February of 1865, while his memoir *Advance and Retreat* was published posthumously in 1880. Even if one of Hood's men misinterpreted what he wrote, it could only have occurred after Hood's resignation, and months or in the case of his memoirs, years after the November 30, 1864, march from Spring Hill to Franklin. It is difficult to reach any conclusion other than that Connelly fabricated Hood's supposed scorn for his soldiers, thereby perpetuating and exaggerating Stanley Horn's earlier unfounded implication that Hood considered his soldiers to be cowards.[4]

Unfortunately, as is so often the case when dealing with Hood, these claims by Horn, Connelly, and others have been picked up and repeated ad nauseam by subsequent writers. For example, in 1990, historian Steven Woodworth wrote about Hood's failure at Spring Hill in his acclaimed book *Jefferson Davis and His Generals: The Failure of Confederate Command in the West.* "The failure was unbearable," explained Woodworth, "so Hood convinced himself that he had not failed. His generals—Cheatham, Cleburne and the others—had let him down. They were incompetent and probably cowardly, too. The soldiers, cowardly and afraid to charge an entrenched enemy, had also failed him."[5]

This type of writing claimed detailed and specific insights into Hood's thoughts, his opinion of his soldiers and of specific Confederate commanders, and of his future intentions. Such profound assertions can only come directly from eyewitnesses or reliable written evidence. Dr. Woodworth's source for his clairvoyance, however, was nothing more than Connelly's *Autumn of Glory.* Ironically, when asked in a December 2006 interview if Hood was the recipient of unfair treatment in Civil War literature, Woodworth replied, "I think Hood has received something less than a fair shake from historians, especially from those like [Wiley] Sword."[6]

Sword, a leading John Bell Hood critic, has claimed on more than one occasion that Hood accused his soldiers of cowardice. He did so in his 1992

4   Ibid., 430-431.

5   Woodworth, *Jefferson Davis and His Generals*, 299.

6   Woodworth interview, *Civil War Gazette.*

book *The Confederacy's Last Hurrah: Spring Hill, Franklin, and Nashville*, and again in *Courage Under Fire: Profiles in Bravery from the Battlefields of the Civil War* in 2006. In the latter book, Sword alleged that Hood "sacrificed" men during the defense of Atlanta and that he alleged a "want of courage" in his soldiers when deciding to teach them "a remedial lesson" at the battle of Franklin. In his earlier book, Sword commented extensively on Hood's purported lack of respect for the soldiers of the Army of Tennessee and his intent to "purge their ranks" of their fear of fighting except behind breastworks. In each instance, Sword's source was a single paragraph from Hood's memoirs, in which the general wrote nothing that remotely resembled Sword's interpretation and presentation.[7]

Some Civil War historians feel free to make almost any assertion or assumption and then justify it with an arbitrary source taken out of context, often in reference to something Hood wrote pertaining to another situation entirely. John Lundberg's book *The Finishing Stroke* is further evidence that legends and previous authors' opinions are too often misconstrued as fact. Lundberg presented his own version of events of the morning of November 30, 1864, when he stated that Hood "had the audacity to accuse the men of the army of cowardice." For this incredible assertion he offered no primary source, choosing instead to cite Craig Symonds's *Stonewall of the West*. In the passage cited by Lundberg, Symonds referred to a pair of Hood's subordinates who wrote after the campaign that he was critical of the army's "lack of energy" and its "failure to seize the turnpike." Lundberg somehow took these benign observations by Symonds and twisted them into the affirmative claim that Hood had audaciously called his soldiers cowards. The only one demonstrating audacity was Lundberg, who on the same page claimed the following about the march from Spring Hill to Franklin: "As Hood's charges of cowardice permeated the ranks of the Army of Tennessee, the veterans were offended by the accusations." His support is a reference to an unpublished manuscript by Danny Sessums entitled "Force to be Reckoned With: Granbury's Texas Brigade, C.S.A." If Sessums has discovered a heretofore unknown primary source claiming that Hood called his men cowards and that they knew about it, he would be the first to have done so. The vast majority of the roughly 20,000 Southern officers and men present at Spring Hill survived the Civil War. Not a

---

7   Sword, *The Confederacy's Last Hurrah*, 177-180; Sword, *Courage Under Fire*, 197.

single one is known to have said or written that Hood called them cowards or questioned their valor at any time during the Tennessee Campaign.[8]

Continuing this theme, Lundberg wrote, "[General Hiram] Granbury, like his men, was also bothered by the insult to their honor, and he was no doubt still angry about his exchange with the army commander the next day." There is evidence that a verbal exchange occurred among Hood, Gen. Granbury, and Granbury's immediate superior, Gen. Patrick Cleburne on the previous day during the march from Columbia to Spring Hill, but the subject of the discussion among these commanders was the slow pace of the army's march—not the valor of the soldiers. Granbury's brigade was the vanguard on the march to Spring Hill, and he and Cleburne were complaining to Hood that the rest of the army was not keeping pace.[9]

Regrettably, other authors have mimicked Connelly, Sword, and Lundberg. In his book *It Happened in the Civil War*, Michael W. Bradley described Hood's demeanor on the morning after Schofield's escape at Spring Hill this way: "When General Hood found out what had happened, he blamed everyone but himself, even calling his soldiers and their commanders cowards." If Bradley had more thoroughly researched this subject, or had researched it at all, no incidents of Hood calling anyone a coward would have been included in a book of things that "happened" in the Civil War.[10]

So what, exactly, did Hood write that several authors have cited as justification for declaring that he called his soldiers cowards? These historians either cited another author or relied upon the single paragraph on page 290 of Hood's *Advance and Retreat* describing the failure at Spring Hill. That paragraph reads as follows:

---

8 Lundberg, *The Finishing Stroke*, 85. Lundberg cited a copy of Danny Sessums, "A Force to be Reckoned With: Granbury's Texas Brigade, C.S.A.," in his personal possession.

9 Ibid., *The Finishing Stroke*, 85; Frank H. Smith, "History of the 24th Tennessee," Columbia, TN, March 1904. Smith conveyed the story as told to him by a veteran named Gregory in a section titled, "Hood, Cleburne and Granberry Quarrel": "They halted for dinner at a late hour just south of Blantons Chapel, when there was some more misunderstanding between Hood, Cleburne, and Granberry. Gregory overheard it all but did not pay much attention to it; his present impression is that there were some words between them, as to Cleburne or Granberry being put in the extreme advance and some chafing and dissatisfaction because some of the troops were so slow in coming up."

10 Michael R. Bradley, *It Happened In the Civil War* (Guilford, CT: Globe Pequot Press, 2002), 91.

The best move of my career as a soldier, I was thus destined to behold come to naught. The discovery that the Army, after a forward march of one hundred and eighty miles, was still, seemingly, unwilling to accept battle unless under the protection of breastworks, caused me to experience grave concern. In my inmost heart I questioned whether or not I would ever succeed in eradicating this evil. It seemed to me I had exhausted every means in the power of one man to remove this stumbling block to the Army of Tennessee. And I will here inquire, in vindication of its fair name, if any intelligent man of that Army supposes one moment that these same troops, one year previous, would, even without orders to attack, have allowed the enemy to pass them at Rocky-faced Ridge, as he did at Spring Hill.[11]

Nowhere do the words "fear," "bravery," "cowardice," or "courage" appear in this or any other paragraph relating to this event. All Hood explained was his frustration at the army's apparent unwillingness to accept battle unless from behind breastworks, which he believed was a "stumbling block" instilled by the tactics of the previous commander. Any other reading, especially as portrayed as fact by so many "historians," is grossly inaccurate and completely unwarranted. A full reading of the subject chapter of Hood's memoirs clearly ' demonstrates that he believed the Army of Tennessee was comprised of gallant and accomplished officers, soldiers with great potential whose aggressiveness and ardor had been weakened by the persistent retreating tactics of Joseph Johnston.[12]

Hood served in the Virginia army during the early years of the war, mostly under Robert E. Lee. Almost all of his combat experience included carrying the fight to the enemy, and most of those offensive actions resulted in tactical victories. Eltham's Landing, Gaines's Mill, and Second Manassas in 1862 were significant victories large and small, and all three were won by offensive action. Although the September 17, 1862, battle of Sharpsburg (Antietam) ended in a tactical draw, Hood's aggressive counterattack that morning near the Dunker Church and into the Miller cornfield held off advancing Federals that significantly outnumbered his own command. Although Gen. George McClellan's Army of the Potomac initiated the tactical offensive at Sharpsburg, McClellan did so only after Lee carried the war into Maryland with a bold strategic offensive. In 1863, Lee took the war north yet again, this time through

11 Hood, *Advance and Retreat*, 290-291.

12 Ibid.

Maryland and into Pennsylvania. Ordered to attack the Federal left flank at Gettysburg on July 2, Hood fell wounded while leading his division early in the assault. Later that year after his recovery, Hood was sent to the Western Theater to command a division at Chickamauga in September. There, the Army of Tennessee assumed the tactical offensive and won its first and only major victory of the entire war. Hood had copious firsthand experience that well-planned offensives often led to success (his Virginia battles and at Chickamauga in north Georgia), and had witnessed for himself the stunning offensive capability of the Army of Tennessee. Hood was thusly inspired to believe that the Confederacy's primary Western army, if properly inspired and led, could match the successes of its Virginia counterpart. He had high (but reasonable) expectations for the Army of Tennessee, he knew its soldiers and officers were gallant and courageous, and he attributed any lack of success to the persistent negative influences of some of its leaders (Braxton Bragg, for example, and later and primarily Joseph E. Johnston). As Hood explained after the war in a speech to a reunion of Confederate veterans, "Our soldiers were superior to those of the North . . . in time of battle one Confederate soldier was equal with two or three of the foe. Our Generals likewise as a body were superior."[13]

The single paragraph in Hood's memoir Horn, Connelly, Sword, and others cited as justification for asserting that Hood doubted the valor of his troops is part of a long commentary on the failure at Spring Hill. In the closing pages of that chapter, Hood opined that the army had been negatively influenced by the tactics employed by Johnston—an observation other commanders and enlisted men of the Army of Tennessee also expressed. A careful consideration of Hood's words demonstrate without doubt that he was acknowledging the soldiers' *élan* and aggressive spirit prior to Johnston's assumption of command and the long series of repeated retreats that followed. By simple definition, there is a significant difference between an unnatural lack of aggressiveness on the part of an army and the raw cowardice of its soldiers. An individual soldier or a body of troops can be cautious or defensive in nature and not be cowardly. Hood never mentioned a lack of valor on the part of his soldiers as individuals or the army as a whole. He simply opined that under Johnston, the same men who had invaded Kentucky, fought so hard at Murfreesboro, and scored a stunning victory at Chickamauga had lost their

13 Hood's Oration.

former aggressiveness. The paragraph cited by his detractors merely stated that after the debacle at Spring Hill, he decided to take up the pursuit and make a final effort to catch Schofield's army before it reached Nashville.

Reasonable and unbiased readers of Hood's memoirs realize his observation of the army's lack of initiative and aggressiveness was primarily directed at Johnston and William Hardee. The command structure not only makes and implements all decisions, but also strongly influences its overall nature. The balance of Hood's other 300 pages of *Advance and Retreat* does not offer even the hint of a suspicion of cowardice on the part of the rank-and-file soldiers of the Army of Tennessee. Nor did Hood in any contemporary reports, correspondence, postwar letters, or interviews ever state that his soldiers lacked individual bravery. To the contrary, Hood went to great lengths to praise the gallantry of the individual soldiers of his army.

Hood was not alone in his concern that his predecessor had instilled a lack of aggressiveness in some quarters of the Army of Tennessee. At Spring Hill, cavalry commander Gen. James Chalmers approached Gen. John C. Brown to ask why his division had not attacked the Federals defending the road. When Brown replied that he was awaiting orders from his corps commander Cheatham, Chalmers responded, "General, when I was circumstanced as you are at Shiloh, I attacked without orders." Captain H. M. Neely of Gen. John C. Carter's brigade was also perplexed at Brown's inaction and had implored the hesitant general to attack. "If he would take the responsibility of beginning the attack," Neely recalled telling Brown, "it would be a quick and easy matter to capture and destroy Schofield's corps in its present condition." Brown could not be persuaded to take the initiative, however, and the Federals made good their escape.[14]

Hood's comment on the tentativeness developed by the Army of Tennessee under Johnston is worth consideration. After assuming command of the army, Hood launched four separate attacks in an attempt to repel Sherman and save Atlanta. Those battles, discussed earlier in this book, are known today as Peachtree Creek, Atlanta, Ezra Church, and Jonesboro. Although the first three did not defeat Sherman, they did succeed in delaying the Federal flanking movements intended to encircle the city and cut the Confederate supply lines. In a blistering two-page factually incomplete diatribe, Stanley Horn condemned Hood's heartlessness for allegedly questioning the courage of the soldiers at the

---

14 Young, "Hood's Failure at Spring Hill," *Confederate Veteran*, vol. 16 (January 1908), 34, 35.

battle of Ezra Church: "Hood, assuming an attitude that will forever remain a smirch on his record, attempts to explain away his lack of success here, as well as on subsequent occasions, by unwarranted reflections on the courage of his men." This is patently untrue. In the portion of Hood's memoirs cited by Horn to support this accusation, Hood elaborated extensively on the great potential of the army and his attempts to re-awaken it through successful offensive operations against Sherman. Hood also expressed dissatisfaction with his corps commander William Hardee and commented on the overall negative effect of Hardee's nonaggressive tendencies on the army as a whole. Continuing in his memoirs, Hood stated that in various battle scenarios certain corps and divisions would advance and perform well, but battles were lost when others would not advance in concert. In his discussion of Ezra Church, for example, Hood relied upon the official report of his corps commander Stephen D. Lee, who wrote: "I am convinced that if all the troops had displayed equal spirit, we would have been successful, as the enemy's works were slight, and besides, they had scarcely gotten into position when we made the attack." Hood had remained in Atlanta's defenses with Hardee's corps and the Georgia militia, while Lee's and A. P. Stewart's corps moved west of the city to thwart the Federal flanking movement in that sector. Did Horn think Hood should have objected to or discounted Lee's firsthand assessment when Hood wasn't on site during the battle? Regarding Ezra Church, Hood simply repeated—almost verbatim—what Lee had submitted in his official report. Horn could have informed his readers that Hood was not a witness to the fighting and had relied on Lee's assessment of the Confederate effort at Ezra Church. Unfortunately, and for reasons known only to Horn, he failed to do so.[15]

In discussing the controversy between Hardee and Hood regarding the loss of Atlanta, Eric Jacobson wrote in *For Cause and For Country*, "But Hood went further than simply blaming one of his subordinates. He again accused the troops of performing poorly, if only indirectly, by going so far as to say the attack at Jonesboro on August 31 was 'feeble' because the Confederates suffered only about 1,400 casualties." Jacobson seemed to object to Hood's use of the word "feeble" when it was in fact the *exact* word used by corps leader Stephen D. Lee in his official report to Hood after Jonesboro. Thomas Connelly went a step further, stating that "almost to the point of being psychotic," Hood associated "valor with casualty figures" when the army

---

commander cited the low Southern casualties at Jonesboro. Curiously, Connelly described Hood as being "almost . . . psychotic" for citing the low Confederate casualties at Jonesboro, but S. D. Lee—who made the *identical* report to Hood—somehow evaded Connelly's ire. Was Lee also "almost to the point of being psychotic?"[16]

These authors surely knew that command of the two corps of Lee and Hardee at Jonesboro had been delegated to Hardee, the senior corps commander. Hood, as described earlier, remained in the Atlanta entrenchments with A. P. Stewart's corps and the Georgia militia in case there was a major attack launched against the city. Hardee, who angrily resigned a short time after Jonesboro and was later transferred away from the army, did not submit any after-action reports to Hood, and his own official report of the battle wasn't produced until April 5, 1865, mere days before the demise of the Confederacy. Because of Hardee's indifference, Hood had no facts to report to Richmond from his designated commander at Jonesboro, and thus was forced to rely upon information provided by Lee, who wrote in his official report: "The attack was a feeble one, and a failure, with a loss to my corps of about 1,300 men in killed and wounded," and the assault "was not made with that spirit and inflexible determination that would ensure success." According to Lee, some of the regiments and individuals behaved gallantly, "but generally the troops faltered in the charge" when they encountered enemy breastworks that were only "temporary and informidable." Just as he had with Ezra Church, in order to submit an official report on Jonesboro, Hood was forced to rely upon whatever information was available to him—namely, the assessments of others and the casualty statistics they supplied him. General Francis Cockrell, one of the most distinguished brigade commanders in any army of the entire war, echoed Lee's opinion of his own corps when he wrote to a colleague following the defeat at Jonesboro: "Many attribute the fall [of Atlanta] to the failure of Lee's Corps to fight as was expected of them." Cockrell's use of the word "many" makes it clear that others believed this to be the case.[17]

Regarding Hood's often criticized use of the word "feeble," it should be noted that other senior commanders of the Army of Tennessee used the same

16 Jacobson, *For Cause and For Country*, 31; Connelly, *Autumn of Glory*, 431.

17 Hood, *Advance and Retreat*, 340; F. M. Cockrell letter, September 13, 1864, Letters Sent and Received by the Confederate Secretary of War/Letters Sent and Received Confederate Adjutant and Inspector General, National Archives, 1727-H-1864.

word to describe the occasional lackluster effort of their troops. In addition to Lee at Jonesboro, A. P. Stewart in describing the performance of part of his corps at Nashville reported that some of his troops put up "but feeble resistance" before fleeing the field.[18]

Other Civil War commanders outside the Army of Tennessee also used the term "feeble." After the battle of Sayler's Creek in early April 1865, Confederate Gen. Richard "Dick" Anderson wrote, "The troops seemed to be wholly broken down and disheartened. After a feeble effort to advance they gave way in confusion." Robert E. Lee implicitly, if unknowingly, supported Hood's evaluation of his own Western army when he wrote in an April 10, 1865, letter to Jefferson Davis, "The operations which occurred while the troops were in the entrenchments in front of Richmond and Petersburg were not marked by the boldness and decision which formerly characterized them. Except in particular instances, they were feeble; and a want of confidence seemed to possess officers and men." No reasonable person would ever misinterpret Lee's words as blaming the soldiers of the Army of Northern Virginia for the loss of Richmond and Petersburg or accusing them of cowardice—or that Lee launched the forlorn hope against Fort Stedman at the end of March to punish his troops for their lack of former aggressiveness. And yet, this is precisely what critics and detractors of Hood alleged with startling regularity. The word "feeble" was a commonly used adjective in 19th century military idiom to describe an effort that lacked expected vigor and strength. A basic search in the *Official Records* for the word "feeble" yields numerous results that prove this point.[19]

Hood's comments regarding the Confederate effort at Jonesboro are commonly criticized and cited by authors as justification for contending that he was callous toward his troops. He repeated almost verbatim the words of Stephen D. Lee in his official report: "The vigor of the assault may be in some sort imagined, when only 1,400 were killed and wounded out of the two corps engaged." The obvious point Hood was making by adopting the information Lee provided to him, however, was that losses of about seven percent of the 20,000 Confederate troops involved (two-thirds of the effective infantry of the Army of Tennessee) do not demonstrate the vigor required when tasked with

18 *OR* 45, pt. 1, 709.

19 Ibid., 709; Douglas S. Freeman, *Lee's Lieutenants: A Study in Command* 3 vols. (New York, Touchstone, 1998), vol. 3, 796; Dowdey and Manarin, *The Wartime Papers of Robert E. Lee*, 938.

deciding the fate of the Confederacy's second most important city. In hindsight, the language used (questioning the valor of soldiers by measuring casualties) can be construed as insensitive, especially by modern standards. Such terminology and comparisons, however, were not uncommon during the Civil War era. Joseph Johnston commented on the approximately 3,000 Federal casualties sustained by his adversary William T. Sherman at Kennesaw Mountain: "Such a loss . . . by an army of almost a hundred thousand men, would have been utterly insignificant—too trifling to discourage, much less defeat brave soldiers." Sherman admitted that he was developing an emotional indifference to casualties. In reference to his losses at Kennesaw Mountain, he wrote, "I begin to regard the death and mangling of a couple of thousand men as a small affair, a kind of morning dash." What would Hay, Horn, Sword, or Lundberg have written about Hood if he had described the loss of 3,000 men, either Federal or Confederate, as "utterly insignificant," "a small affair," "trifling," or "a kind of morning dash?"[20]

Hood and Stephen D. Lee were not alone in their opinion of the performance of the Army of Tennessee at Jonesboro. Other sources, both unofficial and official, noted the diminished zeal of the Rebel soldiers during the battle. According to Federal and Confederate accounts, Southern troops who had valiantly assaulted the enemy on so many other battlefields seemed timid and hesitant at Jonesboro. Confederate Gen. Patton Anderson, who was seriously wounded in the attack, reported an incident in which the color bearer of a Louisiana regiment was unsuccessful in attempting to rally forward his retreating comrades. To Anderson's dismay, neither the soldiers nor their officers could be inspired. According to Anderson, the same troops who had previously performed honorably "brought discredit upon a gallant regiment from as gallant a State as shines in the Southern constellation." Likewise Capt. Bushrod Jones of the 58th Alabama Infantry reported that his skirmishers had been sent forward and then, without orders, halted and sheltered themselves behind a pile of fence rails. "The men seemed possessed of some great horror of charging breastworks," wrote Jones, "which no power, persuasion, or example could dispel." Even Gen. William Hardee wrote, "It is true that the attack could scarcely have been called a vigorous one," although he attributed

20 OR 38, pt. 3, 633; Johnston, *Narrative*, 344; William T. Sherman, *Home Letters of General Sherman*, M. A. DeWolfe Howe, ed. (New York: Charles Scribner's Sons, 1909), 299.

the lackluster effort to exhaustion from previous "dear-bought and fruitless victories" ordered by Hood.[21]

Many Federals formed similar opinions. A Yankee officer thought that the explanation for the lethargic Confederate effort at Jonesboro was attributable to exhaustion by a long campaign. "Besides losing a host of men in this campaign," he noted, "the Rebel Army has lost a large measure of vim [vigor], which counts a good deal in soldiering." Major Thomas Taylor of the 47th Ohio was likewise unimpressed with the Rebel attack, calling it "wholly disorganized" and "scarcely respectable," nothing more than "colors advancing after some stragglers with hardly a guard and the remainder of the line straggling after."[22]

Although mischaracterized by historians as a mean-spirited accusation of cowardice, Hood's concern regarding the army's lost aggressiveness was obviously a very real problem, as duly noted by Stephen D. Lee, who joined the Army of Tennessee shortly after Johnston's removal. Lee wrote the following in his official report regarding the army's reluctance to attack the enemy:

> As a corps commander, I regarded the morale of the army greatly impaired after the fall of Atlanta, and in fact before its fall, the troops were not by any means in good spirits. It was my observation and belief that the majority of the officers and men were so impressed with the idea of their inability to carry even temporary breastworks, that when orders were given for attack, and there was a probability of encountering works, they regarded it as reckless in the extreme. Being impressed with these convictions, they did not generally move to the attack with that spirit which nearly always assures success. Whenever the enemy changed his position, temporary works could be improvised in less than two hours and he could never be caught without them.

After noting some exceptions, Lee reported that the feeling of an inability to carry even the slightest of enemy breastworks was so widespread in the army that "anything like a general attack was paralyzed by it." He continued: "These feelings were freely expressed" to Hood.[23]

A similar set of circumstances, wherein a portion of the Army of Tennessee failed to act with expected effort, occurred during the first week of December

21 *OR* 38, pt. 3, 702, 774, 835.

22 Bonds, *War Like the Thunderbolt*, 265; Albert Castel, *Tom Taylor's Civil War* (Lawrence: University Press of Kansas, 2000), 178.

23 *OR* 38, pt. 3, 764; ibid., 39, pt. 1, 810.

1864. The cavalry and infantry force under Forrest was ordered to Murfreesboro by Hood to attack the Federal garrison and to neutralize the effect of the enemy threat to Hood's right flank at Nashville and his supply line leading south into Alabama. In an attack on December 7, two brigades of Confederate infantry in William Bate's division suddenly halted and withdrew. Forrest described the move as "a shameful retreat," in effect calling into question the courage of the soldiers involved in a manner that Hood never did. As mentioned earlier, the cavalryman wrote in his official report: "I seized the colors of the retreating troops and endeavored to rally them, but they could not be moved by any entreaty or appeal to their patriotism." Historians have never accused Forrest of questioning the courage of men under his command, but one can envision what certain historians would have alleged had Hood uttered the very same words.[24]

Hood's counterpart at Atlanta, William T. Sherman, once expounded upon the benefit of aggressive tactics and the "moral effect" on the troops, writing in his official report on the battle of Kennesaw Mountain: "I perceived that the enemy and our own officers had settled down to the conviction that I would not assault fortified lines. . . . An army to be efficient must not settle down to a single mode of offense. . . . I wanted, therefore, for the moral effect to make a successful assault against the enemy behind his breast-works." In a June 18, 1864, letter to Ulysses S. Grant, Sherman expressed his displeasure with the timidity of Gen. George Thomas and his soldiers, writing. "A fresh furrow in a plowed field will stop the whole column, and all begin to entrench." Sherman informed Grant that he had repeatedly urged Thomas to be more aggressive, yet "it seems the whole Army of the Cumberland is so habituated to be on the defensive that, from its commander down to the lowest private, I cannot get it out of their heads." Have any historians ever accused Sherman of calling Thomas and his soldiers in the Army of the Cumberland cowards because he acknowledged the improved morale of an army that assumes the offensive? Have historians asserted that Sherman's attack at Kennesaw Mountain was a vindictive act intended to teach his men a remedial lesson, as many authors have depicted Hood's attack at Franklin?[25]

---

24 Ibid., 45, pt. 1, 755.

25 Ibid., 38, pt. 1, 68; Benson Bobrick, *Master of War: The Life of George H. Thomas* (New York: Simon and Schuster, 2009), 236.

Another common and unjust criticism of Hood stems from a misinterpretation of words he used to express his attempt to renew the morale of the Army of Tennessee. Stating that he was trying to eradicate the "evil" of lost aggressiveness, Hood's words have been twisted to the point that he has been accused of calling the soldiers themselves "evil." As experts in Civil War history, historians, and other authors know or should know there are major differences between 19th and 20th century idiom. The word "evil" was commonly used in the former century to describe a negative or harmful trait or characteristic. For example, on May 10, 1863, Robert E. Lee wrote to Jefferson Davis regarding the reorganization of the Army of Northern Virginia after the death of Stonewall Jackson:

> I have for the past year felt that the corps of this army were too large for one commander. Nothing prevented my proposing to you to reduce their size and increase their number but my inability to recommend commanders. Each corps contains, when in fighting condition, about 30,000 men. These are more than one man can properly handle and keep under his eye in battle in the country that we have to operate in. They are always beyond the range of his vision, and frequently beyond his reach. The loss of Jackson from command of one-half the army seems to me a good opportunity to remedy this *evil* [emphasis added].[26]

Another example is found in an October 8, 1862, letter from the secretary of war to the Confederate Congress: "The subject of the efficiency of the Army is one of paramount importance, and the letter of the Secretary of War herewith submitted has been elicited by correspondence with the generals of our armies in the field, whose practical experience of the *evils* [emphasis added] resulting from the defects in our present system entitles their opinion to great weight." To imply that Hood intended the word "evil" to apply in any way to the personal character of his troops is unreasonable and wholly incorrect.[27]

Among the many examples of officers concerned about the morale and fighting spirit of their commands was Chaplain James McNeilly of Gen. William Quarles's brigade, who recalled Gen. William Loring crying out to his troops during a critical juncture in the Franklin combat, "Great God! Do I command cowards?" Loring's exhortation is never characterized as insulting or

---

26 *OR* 25, pt. 2, 810.

27 Ibid., 4, pt. 2, 110.

as blaming them for the Confederate defeat at Franklin. Historians have never attempted to vilify Loring (as they have Hood) by mischaracterizing the intent of his words.[28]

Other examples abound. After the fall of Vicksburg and Port Hudson, Hardee, then commander of the Department of Mississippi and East Louisiana, distributed public notices in an attempt to convince members of the captured and paroled Confederate garrisons to return to military service by gathering in Enterprise, Mississippi, on August 28, 1863. In the publicly distributed notices, Hardee declared that any soldier who did not return was "a wretch" and that the public would "despise your cowardice." Was Hardee accusing paroled members of the captured Vicksburg and Port Hudson garrisons of being wretched cowards, or was he simply exhorting the soldiers to return to duty by using the language and methods common to that era?[29]

Yet another example is found in Douglas S. Freeman's classic *Lee's Lieutenants*. In a passage dealing with the Army of Northern Virginia's retreat from the lines around Richmond and Petersburg westward to Appomattox, Freeman quoted the postwar memoirs of Gen. William Mahone describing the conduct of Lee's troops during this time. Mahone recalled Lee's effort trying to rally the fleeing men, writing, "At this spectacle Gen. Lee straightened himself in the saddle, and looking more the soldier than ever, exclaimed, as if talking to himself: 'My God! Has the Army dissolved?' . . . I replied, 'No General, here are troops ready to do their duty'; when, in a mellowed voice he replied, 'Yes General, there are some brave men left.'"

In his May 30, 1865, proclamation E. Kirby Smith severely condemned the thousands of deserters melting away from his army. Although he did not directly question their individual courage, he nonetheless called their conduct "unpatriotic" and accused his men of having "voluntarily destroyed our organization and thrown away all means of resistance." Smith has escaped any harsh or extreme interpretation of his language. Is there any doubt that John Bell Hood would have been savaged for stating that the Army of Tennessee had only "some" brave men left during his movement north to Nashville after the Franklin defeat, or during retreat from Nashville after his defeat?

---

28 Stephen Bailes, *Natural Histories: Stories from the Tennessee Valley* (Knoxville: University of Tennessee Press, 2007), 201.

29 Harrison Papers, Southern Historical Collection, University of North Carolina-Chapel Hill.

Unfortunately, this double standard toward Hood has become the norm in Civil War scholarship.[30]

Much of what Hood actually said and wrote about the soldiers of the Army of Tennessee has been omitted from many popular books about the man and his battles. Hood's estimation of the bravery his men demonstrated at Franklin is revealed in his own memoirs *Advance and Retreat*. The men at Franklin, Hood boasted, were "gloriously led by their officers." He went on to discuss "the valor displayed at Franklin," which "deservedly won the admiration of the Federals." Hood praised "the gallantry so conspicuous on that field" and lauded the "courage displayed at Franklin." "Never did troops fight more gallantly," he wrote. He complimented their "extraordinary gallantry" while lamenting the "brave soldiers" of the Army of Tennessee lost in the battle. His praise for his army at that fateful battle was unambiguously given and truly heartfelt. These quotations are explicit evidence of Hood's admiration and high regard for the extraordinary courage and soldierly conduct of his army at Franklin, yet readers of Civil War literature are hard-pressed to find citations of Hood's praise for his men in most of the books cited herein.[31]

Perhaps the greatest offense historians have committed against both Hood and his troops is the omission of his highest tribute, when he compared the Army of Tennessee's performance at Franklin to the efforts of his namesake Hood's Texas brigade—some of Robert E. Lee's most acclaimed soldiers—in what the Texans themselves considered their greatest victory. "The attack [at Franklin], which entailed so great a sacrifice of life, had become a necessity as imperative as that which impelled Gen. Lee to order the assault at Gaines' Mill, when our troops charged across an open space, a distance of one mile, under a most galling fire of musketry and artillery, against an enemy heavily entrenched," wrote Hood. "The heroes in that action fought not more gallantly than the soldiers of the Army of Tennessee upon the fields of Franklin."[32]

Hood could not have paid a greater compliment to the soldiers of the Army of Tennessee than by comparing them to his beloved Army of Northern

---

30 Freeman, *Lee's Lieutenants*, vol. 3, 798; Daniel, Confederate Scrap Book, 5.

31 Hood, *Advance and Retreat*, 140, 296, 297, 317-337. Hood did the same after Nashville. In describing the difficult retreat after his defeat there, Hood wrote: "When the fortunes of war were against us, the same faithful soldiers remained true to their flag, and with rare exceptions followed it in retreat as they had borne it in advance."

32 Ibid., 296.

Virginia. However, this unambiguous praise of the gallantry of his soldiers does not appear in any of the major books on the Tennessee Campaign or the Army of Tennessee.

In a speech before Confederate veterans in Charleston, South Carolina, on December 12, 1875, Hood encouraged the aging heroes to join him in memorializing the valor of the Confederate soldier: "Let us teach the children of the brave men who fought and fell in defense of their homes; what their fathers did . . . for the sake of truth, manhood, and the future, and that the sons may arise worthy of their sires."[33]

☙   ❧

There is no doubt that Hood loved his men, their valor, and their exceptional gallantry—and that the historical record is replete with instances of this admiration. No contemporary evidence exists to the contrary.

33 Hood's Oration.

Chapter 14

"Historians are gossips who tease the dead."

— *Voltaire*

A Callous Attitude:
Did John Bell Hood "Bleed His Boys"?

Many historians and other authors believe John Bell Hood had a callous attitude toward casualties, and routinely and rather nonchalantly sacrificed his troops in battle. Nothing could be further from the truth.

Typical literary portrayals of Hood and his arch rival Joseph Johnston provide a classic example of scholars influenced by a character's historical personage. Historians generally depict Johnston as a commander whose primary concern was the welfare of his men. Hood, in contrast, is portrayed as being careless with the lives of his soldiers. This meme has Hood wasting lives in a hopeless campaign in an attempt to win a war that was already lost, while Johnston—who years later described Hood's decision to attack at Franklin as "useless butchery"—evades censure for his tactical offensive against Sherman at Bentonville in March 1865. Johnston's late-war action cost more than 3,000 Confederate casualties, including approximately 800 killed—which is *more* than the killed and wounded Hood lost in the battle of Nashville. If any Confederate commander can be criticized for wasting lives in a meaningless attack, it is Joe Johnston.

Consider what Johnston wrote about resuming command of the Army of Tennessee during the war's final months:

> I therefore accepted the command . . . with a full consciousness on my part, however, that we could have no other object in continuing the war, than to obtain fair terms of peace; for the Southern cause must have appeared hopeless then, to all dispassionate and intelligent Southern men. I therefore resumed the duties of my military grade with no hope beyond that of contributing to obtain peace on such conditions as, under the circumstances, ought to satisfy the Southern people and their Government.[1]

In a postwar letter to Hood, Johnston's cavalry commander Gen. Matthew C. Butler revealed that Johnston confided to him that he believed the war was a lost cause as early as the spring of 1863. Butler, who served as an escort at Johnston's final surrender meeting with Sherman in North Carolina, wrote, "On our return to camp he [Johnston] told me that he had no confidence in the success of our cause for two years." Butler added, "I then became satisfied that Mr. Davis was correct in his judgment when he relieved him on the previous occasion and made a mistake in restoring him afterwards, for the reason that I could have no faith in an officer in command of an army, in the success of which or the cause he had no confidence."[2]

Hood is almost universally condemned for incurring 11,800 casualties during the Tennessee Campaign in an attempt to liberate Tennessee and destroy a Federal army in November 1864. However, Johnston, who commanded the Army of Tennessee in the spring and summer of 1864 has largely avoided such criticism even though he incurred thousands of casualties that summer, and went on to attack and lose another 3,000 men at Bentonville as late as March 1865—even though in his own words penned after the war, he believed the Confederate cause was already lost some two years earlier. Such is the state of modern Civil War scholarship in the Western Theater.

Hood was influenced and impressed by his aggressive mentors Robert E. Lee and Stonewall Jackson. Jefferson Davis acknowledged that Hood was of the Lee and Jackson school, and placed Hood in command to assume the

---

1   Johnston, *Narrative*, 372.

2   M. C. Butler letter to John Bell Hood, July 18, 1874, John Bell Hood Personal Papers.

offensive at a point in the war when nothing else could turn the tide in the favor of the Confederacy. "Three years of service in Virginia, and one year in the West," Hood recalled after the war, "taught me that a general can acquire sufficient caution by receiving hard blows; but none can acquire boldness; it is a gift from heaven." Hood's military boldness is often described as recklessness, and although there is admittedly a thin line between the two, boldness was more commonly linked to a display of courage in the 19th century. In their influential book *Attack and Die: Civil War Military Tactics and the Southern Heritage*, historians Grady McWhiney and Perry Jamieson argued that aggressiveness was the norm among Confederate officers, and that "Southerners [were] imprisoned in a culture that rejected careful calculation and patience, often refused to learn from their own mistakes." Hood was not atypical. He reflected the regional culture during the antebellum and Civil War period when Southerners felt besieged and occupied by the North, and were willing to sacrifice their lives to defend their homes and way of life.[3]

Although his brigades and divisions suffered horrific casualties at Gaines's Mill, Second Manassas, Sharpsburg, Gettysburg, and Chickamauga, Hood was a subordinate to Robert E. Lee and Braxton Bragg during those battles and dutifully followed the orders of his superiors. Nonetheless, authors asserted that Hood was indifferent to casualties and rarely mentioned that he was a subordinate when his renowned troops were frequently assigned to perform difficult tasks on the battlefields. For example, Thomas Connelly painted Hood as bloodthirsty, declaring that he "pined to repeat" his victories while in Lee's army, which "had been achieved with the shedding of much blood."[4]

Because he frequently incurred staggeringly high losses when called upon by his superiors, Hood is routinely portrayed as responsible for the high casualties. In the documentary film "The Battle of Franklin," the writers introduced Hood by stating that he came west to the Army of Tennessee with an ominous reputation. In a dramatically grim tone, the narrator claimed that Hood, as a commander in Virginia, "bled his boys."[5]

In his study of Spring Hill and Franklin, Eric Jacobson introduced Hood as an aggressive commander and offered William T. Sherman's appraisal of Hood

---

3   Hood's Oration; Grady McWhiney and Perry Jamieson, *Attack and Die: Civil War Military Tactics and the Southern Heritage* (Tuscaloosa: University of Alabama Press, 1984), xv.

4   Connelly, *Autumn of Glory*, 431.

5   The Battle of Franklin, Wide Awake Films.

upon his appointment to command the Army of Tennessee in July of 1864: "[He] is a new man and fighter and must be watched . . . as he is reckless with the lives of his men." Sherman's assessment is ironic because the Federal commander himself often used harsh and cavalier expressions regarding his own casualties. As previously noted, of his losses at the battle of Kennesaw Mountain, Sherman wrote, "I begin to regard the death and mangling of a couple of thousand men as a small affair, a kind of morning dash, and it may be well that we become so hardened. . . . The assault I made was no mistake. I had to do it." Sherman downplayed his casualties at Kennesaw in a letter to Gen. George Thomas immediately following the attack: "At times assaults are necessary and inevitable. . . . Had we broken his line today it would have been most decisive, as it is our loss is small compared with some of those [in the] East." What would modern scholars write about Hood if he had called his losses in Georgia and Tennessee "a small affair, a kind of morning dash," "necessary and inevitable," and "small compared with" Lee's battles in Virginia, Pennsylvania, and Maryland?[6]

In 19th century society, warfare was viewed much differently than it is today. Soldiers were expected to willingly expose themselves to death or injury on the battlefield as a demonstration of courage, honor, and devotion. Colonel W. D. Gale of A. P. Stewart's corps staff has avoided accusations of callousness toward the soldiers even though he described the men of Zachariah Deas's Alabama brigade at Nashville as "utterly lethargic and without interest in battle. I never witnessed such a want of enthusiasm." Referring to Confederate casualties in the defeat at the Nashville in December 1864, Lost Cause founder E. A. Pollard criticized the effort of Hood's soldiers: "Our loss in killed and wounded was disgracefully small." As noted earlier, corps commander Stephen D. Lee likewise complained about the performance of his own corps at the battle of Jonesboro by citing low casualties: "The attack was a feeble one, and a failure, with a loss to my corps of about 1,300 men in killed and wounded." In 19th century warfare, bloodletting was considered a barometer of effort and dedication.[7]

---

6   Jacobson, *For Cause and For Country*, 27; Sherman, Home Letters of General Sherman, 299; *OR* 38, pt. 4, 607.

7   W. D. Gale letter in *Confederate Veteran*, vol. 2 (February 1894), 4; E. A Pollard, *Southern History of the War: The Last Year of the War* (New York: Charles B. Richardson, 1866), 128; Hood, *Advance and Retreat*, 340.

Like most military commanders, Hood maintained strong affection for his men. Although it is rarely revealed in the literature covering his tenure as commander of the Army of Tennessee, Hood demonstrated his affection time and again throughout the war. At Gaines's Mill on June 27, 1862, Robert E. Lee ordered yet another assault against Fitz John Porter's heavily entrenched Federal defenders. Hood's brigade spearheaded this effort. Fulfilling a promise to his old regiment, Hood personally led the 4th Texas Infantry in a frontal charge across a mile of largely open ground, across swampy Boatswain's Creek, and uphill against fortified infantry and artillery positions. Unlike earlier failed attacks, Hood's men broke through; other units followed, and Porter's position unraveled. Hood and his Texas brigade are credited with earning Lee his first tactical victory of the war which, in turn, helped save the imperiled Confederate capital of Richmond. The cost, however, was high. Hood's 4th Texas suffered 50 percent casualties. Every officer in the regiment above the rank of captain was killed or wounded except for Hood, who somehow miraculously escaped without injury. Major James W. Ratchford of Gen. D. H. Hill's staff recalled Hood immediately after the battle openly grieving for his men while wondering aloud why fate had spared him while so many of his soldiers—"every one of them as good as I am"—were dead or suffering. Chaplain Nicholas Davis remembered that Hood was appalled the next day when only a fraction of the men answered the morning's roll call. Their commander rode away weeping. According to Davis, "there was not a soldier in that line but what thought more of him now than ever before."[8]

At Sharpsburg on September 17, 1862, Hood was in temporary command of a small division comprising his Texas brigade under Col. William Wofford and Chase Whiting's brigade of Georgians under Col. Evander Law. When the massive Federal assault against Lee's left flank threatened to break the line early that morning, Hood was ordered to move quickly to the front from his reserve position and counterattack. His vigorous well-directed effort against superior numbers threw back the enemy and temporarily stabilized the line. His leadership impressed Stonewall Jackson, who urged that Hood be promoted to major general. The cost of success, however, was staggering: 532 of 850 men in the Texas brigade were killed, wounded, or captured, as were 427 from Law's

---

8   Dyer, *The Gallant Hood*, 89, 93; Ratchford, Memoirs, 19; Nicholas A. Davis, *Chaplain Davis and Hood's Texas Brigade*, Donald E. Everett, ed. (Baton Rouge: Louisiana State University Press, 1962), 91.

command out of about 1,000. The 1st Texas Infantry suffered 82 percent casualties. When General Lee inquired about his men that evening, Hood answered, "They are lying on the field where you sent them. My division has been almost wiped out." Hood is reported to have "wept as he told Lee of the hundreds of his Texans and Georgians who had fallen that day in the cornfield."[9]

After the battle of Franklin, William Stanton of Granbury's brigade recalled that Hood cried upon learning of the death of Patrick Cleburne. South Carolina artillerist Bryan Bowers described Hood's arrival at the front to inspect the battlefield the morning after the battle: "His sturdy visage assumed a melancholy appearance, and for a considerable time he sat on his horse and wept like a child." Despite a record replete with evidence of his compassion and love for his men, modern historians rarely expounded upon the subject in context.[10]

On May 2, 1864, near Dalton, Georgia, Joseph Johnston presided over what is believed to be the largest mass execution of the Civil War when 14 North Carolina soldiers of the Army of Tennessee were put to death after being convicted of desertion. Johnston's predecessor Braxton Bragg was notorious for executing his soldiers. Few students of the war, however, are aware that there is no known record of any member of the Army of Tennessee being executed after Hood took command of the army in mid-July 1864. In fact, on November 6, 1864, near Florence, Alabama, seven of Hood's soldiers were court-martialed and convicted of desertion, but Hood personally pardoned the men and ordered them returned to duty without punishment. Two soldiers from the 54th Virginia Infantry, three from the 63rd Virginia Infantry, and two from the 58th North Carolina Infantry had been convicted in a court-martial presided over by Col. J. B. Bibb of the 23rd Alabama Infantry. Hood summarily dismissed the charged and ordered the men released from custody and returned to duty without conditions.[11]

---

9   Dyer, *The Gallant Hood*, 138-141; O'Connor, *Hood: Cavalier General*, 117.

10 William Stanton letter to Mary Moody, January 17, 1865, Barker Center Archives, University of Texas at Austin.

11 *North Carolina Troops, 1861-1865: A Roster*, vol. 14, 236-237, 462-463; Army of Tennessee General Order No. 57, November 6, 1864. Typescript provided to the author by David Fraley, in the Carter House files.

Hood further demonstrated his concern for his troops after the defeat at Nashville during the retreat to Tupelo, Mississippi, when he attempted to grant 100-day furloughs to members of the Army of Tennessee. Fearing the men would not return to the army, however, Richmond authorities essentially admonished Hood for making such a proposal. "Repress by all means the proposition to furlough the Trans-Mississippi troops," replied Secretary of War James Seddon. "The suggestion merely is dangerous; compliance would probably be fatal; extinguish, if possible, the idea." Hood's immediate superior, P. G. T. Beauregard, promptly sent Hood a stern reply: "Secretary of War disapproves application relative to your Trans-Mississippi troops. He considers that to grant it would be dangerous, and might be fatal. I agree with him. Discountenance it in full." Persisting on behalf of his troops, Hood replied to Beauregard a few days later: "I am very anxious to see you here in reference to the Trans-Mississippi troops, and also as to some system of furlough for other troops."[12]

Some of the sharpest criticisms of Hood dripped from the pen of Capt. Samuel Foster of Granbury's brigade. It is difficult to find a book, essay, or article about the Army of Tennessee, the Tennessee Campaign, or the battle of Franklin that does not include Foster's bitter condemnations of Hood, as recorded in the captain's diary on December 1, 1864, the day after Franklin. "Gen. Hood has betrayed us," scribbled Foster, because the battle at Franklin "was not the kind of fighting he promised" before the campaign. Franklin, he added, was not a "fight with equal numbers and choice of the ground" that Hood had guaranteed. No other soldier or officer of the Army of Tennessee is known to have recorded that such a pledge was either made or broken by Hood. To the contrary, regimental surgeon Dr. Urban Owen wrote weeks before the battle to his wife on November 5 from Tuscumbia, Alabama, "Our Generals all say we will have to fight a severe fight after we cross the river before we can enter and hold Middle Tenn." Apparently the army didn't mind an upcoming severe battle, because in the same letter Owen added that "our army is buoyant," and on November 19 he confided, "Our whole army is eager to move onward." Nevertheless, Foster's assertion—unsupported and uncorroborated in the recollections of any other member of the Army of Tennessee—was

12 OR 45, pt. 2, 769-770, 778.

evidence enough for modern author Webb Garrison Jr., who cited only Foster when writing, "Hood promised his men that they would face little risk of defeat," and would not attack "a numerically superior foe and he would fight on ground of his choosing."[13]

Even if Foster's dubious claim was accurate, Hood's flanking attempt at Columbia offered clear evidence of the general's attempt to maximize the Confederate advantage. Franklin only became a necessity because of the failure at Spring Hill. Further, if Hood had not attacked at Franklin he would have lost the numerical advantage over Schofield's exhausted Federal defenders and would have been at an even greater disadvantage later at Nashville. In terms of numbers and ground, Franklin was the best situation Hood could have encountered after the Spring Hill fiasco. Thus, even if Hood did promise what Foster later claimed, he did not lie and indeed, he delivered on his promise as best as he could given the circumstances on November 30.

Civil War scholars have rewarded Foster—who literally damned Hood and called him a murderer—by including his tirades in almost all books and articles on the battle of Franklin. The eloquence of Foster's rage seems to exempt him from any examination of his credibility as an observer, yet a close look at his diary suggests that he was a contentious and belligerent man. Foster made statements regarding Jefferson Davis's removal of Joseph Johnston that could easily be interpreted as threatening the life of the president. In conduct clearly unbecoming an officer, Foster bragged of convincing a private to disobey a direct order from Hood after the evacuation of Atlanta. Furthermore, Foster accused Hood of having thousands of men "murdered around Atlanta, trying to prove to the world that he was a greater man than Gen. Johnston." Yet, this same captain also complained about Hood bypassing the Federals at Resaca, Georgia, on October 12; he also complained that Hood did not attack the strongly entrenched Yankee garrison at Decatur, Alabama, on October 29. The malcontent Foster complained when Hood attacked and complained when he did not—and yet Foster's credibility and bias are never questioned by scholars or other authors.[14]

---

13 Foster, *One of Cleburne's Command*, 151; Warwick, *Williamson County*, 179-181; Garrison Jr., *Strange Battles of the Civil War*, 271.

14 Foster, *One of Cleburne's Command*, 107, 133-134, 151, 142.

Chapter 15

"A morsel of genuine history is a thing
so rare as to be always valuable."

— *Thomas Jefferson*

John Bell Hood and
Frontal Assaults

One of the most prevalent suppositions regarding the generalship of John Bell Hood is the persistent belief that throughout his tenure in the Confederate Army he preferred frontal attacks over any other tactic. As with so many claims about Hood's command tenure at the head of the Army of Tennessee, this belief is also untrue and unsupported by the historical record.

"In love or war," wrote historian Thomas Connelly, "Hood's was a simple, naïve code—to attack head on." Of the attack at Franklin on November 30, 1864, Connelly falsely claimed that Hood "later admitted that he utilized frontal assaults" to discipline his troops. Hood never said or wrote any such thing. In its attempt to establish the premise that Hood was too aggressive as a commander, the documentary film "The Battle of Franklin" narrated that the soldiers of the Army of Tennessee knew Hood "likes his men to assault head on," and that as the commander of the Texas brigade in the Army of Northern Virginia, he cared little about his own casualties. Even the website of the Carter

House in Franklin, Tennessee, once declared that Hood was "a firm believer in frontal assaults."[1]

Although Hood was an unapologetic advocate of offensive warfare (as were, among others, Gens. Robert E. Lee and Thomas J. "Stonewall" Jackson), all credible evidence demonstrates Hood's preference for flanking maneuvers rather than frontal assaults. Indeed, his well-known attack at Franklin on November 30, 1864—acknowledged by many contemporaries as a last resort against a trapped enemy after the failed flank attempt at Spring Hill—was the only frontal attack Hood ever ordered as an independent commander.

Hood was a determined Lee and Jackson protégé. The military philosophy of Hood's mentors relied heavily upon wresting the initiative from their adversaries. Jefferson Davis understood how and under whom the young general learned his craft: "Hood had served with distinction under Lee and Jackson, and his tactics were of that school." His experiences under Lee in Virginia molded his military thinking. Hood's small tactical victory at Eltham's Landing and his larger spearhead assault that broke the enemy line at Gaines's Mill in the spring of 1862 were a result of measured aggressiveness. Two months later at Second Manassas in August, Hood once again found himself and his brigade at the tip of the spear in James Longstreet's massive counterattack that swept Gen. John Pope's Federal army from the field. Hood repeated his success at the head of a division at Sharpsburg on September 17, 1862, with a swift and decisive counterattack that repelled the attacking Federals and reestablished Lee's tenuous left flank. One year later at Chickamauga, Hood's attacking division poured through a gap in the enemy lines. His deep and well-led assault helped precipitate the rout of Gen. William Rosecrans's Army of the Cumberland and earn the Army of Tennessee its only major victory of the war.[2]

Although clearly influenced by these aggressive tactical experiences, Hood was not a one-dimensional field commander. At South Mountain on September 14, 1862, where his brigade engaged the enemy at Turner's Gap, Hood counseled Lee to withdraw his brigade from an exposed position. At Gettysburg on July 2, 1863, Hood did his best to avoid shoving his division over the rough ground west of the Round Tops in a direct assault into Federal strength by seeking permission to move around the enemy's left flank. He

---

1   Connelly, *Autumn of Glory*, 322, 504; The Battle of Franklin, Wide Awake Films.

2   Davis, *The Rise and Fall of the Confederate Government*, vol. 2, 488.

tendered his request to corps commander James Longstreet four times, and was rebuffed on each occasion. Hood attacked as ordered, was severely wounded early in the fighting, and his division suffered heavy losses.[3]

Hood joined the Army of Tennessee as a corps commander in the spring of 1864. Although he disapproved of Johnston's Fabian-style retreats during the Atlanta Campaign, he advocated strategic withdrawals in specific instances where circumstances warranted prudence. For example, on May 19 at Cassville, Hood's corps was set to initiate a major attack against part of Sherman's divided command, but Hood wisely halted his advance when an unexpected enemy force of unknown size and composition appeared—and opened fire—on his right flank. Taking appropriate defensive measures, Hood elected not to ignore the threat and discontinued his forward movement. Ten days later at New Hope Church, Hood called off a planned attack after learning that the enemy had repositioned and entrenched during the night. On July 6, Johnston ordered the army to fortify along the north bank of the Chattahoochee River. Hood was instructed to locate his corps at a vulnerable point. "Hood's corps fell to the line of rifle pits," recalled Gen. Francis Shoup, Johnston's chief of artillery, "and General Hood began at once to declare his position unsafe." Shoup, who had designed the fortifications that Sherman described as "one of the strongest pieces of field fortifications I ever saw," conceded that Hood "was right enough, and he ought never to have been put into such a position."[4]

Although Hood's record demonstrates a mixture of cautious, prudent decision-making with a preference for broad flanking maneuvers instead of direct assaults, historians and other writers insisted otherwise. An examination of his battles around Atlanta demonstrates this point of scholarly dissonance. After succeeding Johnston as commander of the Army of Tennessee on July 18, 1864, Hood launched four attacks in an attempt to repel Sherman or halt the Federal envelopment of the city. Each effort involved a flanking movement to some degree, and each was intended to catch the Federals before they could construct defensive fortifications.

The first offensive at Peachtree Creek on July 20 was designed to attack a portion of Thomas's Army of the Cumberland (which was separated from the

---

3 Hood, *Advance and Retreat*, 41, 58-59.

4 Ibid., 120-122; F. A. Shoup, "Dalton Campaign—Works at Chattahoochee River—Interesting History," *Confederate Veteran*, vol. 3 (September 1895), 264; www.comdev.cobb countyga.gov/historic-markers/downloads/appendix.d.pdf.

balance of Sherman's forces) while they were crossing the creek, and before they could entrench on the south bank. The attack was delayed, poorly coordinated by Gen. William Hardee, and ultimately failed. The second major engagement, the July 22 battle of Atlanta (Decatur), was designed as a broad sweeping maneuver into Sherman's left and rear. Once again, Hardee did not get his corps in position on time and attacked piecemeal; when he did attack, he struck a Federal corps that fortuitously found itself in the right place at the right time.

Hood's third engagement at Ezra Church on July 28 was intended to block Gen. Oliver O. Howard's XI corps's move around Atlanta to the west with Stephen D. Lee's corps, and then strike Howard's exposed right flank the following day with A. P. Stewart's corps.[5] Hood delegated independent command of the Ezra Church operation to Lee, who would lead both his own and Stewart's corps. During the movements preceding the July 28 battle, Hood repeatedly instructed Lee and Stewart to exercise caution, and he directed that if an attack was necessary and possible, only to do so *in flank*. Hood remained in the Atlanta fortifications with a single infantry corps and local Georgia militia in case Sherman made a direct attack against the city. At noon on the day of the battle, Hood's adjutant conveyed the following message to Lee: "If the enemy should make an assault on our left the general directs you to strike him in flank." Later that day, Hood ordered Lee to hold the Federals and "do no more fighting than necessary, unless you should get a decided advantage." Instead of following instructions to limit fighting or to strike the enemy in the flank, Lee ignored his superior and ordered frontal assaults. This was Lee's independent action and contrary to Hood's instructions.[6]

The final large scale battle fought around Atlanta at Jonesboro on August 31 and September 1 was a blocking effort by two of Hood's corps, intended to prevent the severing of the last open railroad line into the city. Just as he had done at Ezra Church, Hood delegated independent command to a subordinate, this time William Hardee, who moved south with his own corps and that of S. D. Lee. Hood ordered Hardee to attack the Federals immediately after they had crossed the Flint River and before they could construct defenses. The piecemeal, fitful attacks that followed were largely frontal affairs. Historian Albert Castel blamed Lee for most of the problems: "At 3 P.M. . . . Cleburne's

5   Castel, *Decision in the West*, 435.

6   *OR* 38, pt. 5, 919.

skirmishers start forward. Lee, displaying the same aggressive spirit and talent for blundering that he revealed at Tupelo and Ezra Church, mistakes their fire for the beginning of Cleburne's assault. At once he commands his corps to charge." If the assaults by the Army of Tennessee at Ezra Church and Jonesboro are construed by analysts to be frontal, they must be attributed to S. D. Lee, and not John Bell Hood.[7]

After evacuating Atlanta on September 2, Hood moved the army west of the city to rest and resupply his men. A month later, Hood resumed operations against Sherman's supply lines in northern Georgia, the same area where the two armies had fought six months earlier. Hood was keenly aware of his meager resources when he wrote, "Sherman is weaker now than he will be in future, and I as strong as I can expect to be," and noted the difficulty of obtaining reinforcements or recruits. On October 12, he bypassed the strong Federal positions at Resaca rather than attack them. After capturing the Federal garrison at Dalton on October 13, Hood listened to his subordinates and withdrew the army west, rather than confront enemy reinforcements en route from Atlanta. On October 21, a frustrated Sherman wrote of his adversary's cunning maneuvers in northern Georgia: "To pursue Hood is folly, for he can twist and turn like a fox and wear out any army in pursuit." General James Wilson, George Thomas's cavalry commander who would later resist Hood in the Tennessee Campaign, wrote of his movements after the fall of Atlanta: "The fact is that [Sherman] could neither overtake nor bring that wily and fleet-footed commander [Hood] to an engagement."[8]

During the maneuvering prior to the Tennessee Campaign (as noted earlier in this book), Hood bypassed a heavily outnumbered but defiant Federal garrison at Decatur, Alabama, on October 29. An attack, he explained, would have brought about a "great and unnecessary sacrifice of life."[9]

In the midst of the Tennessee Campaign, two days before the assault at Franklin on November 30, Hood's army intercepted Gen. John Schofield's Federal army at Columbia, Tennessee. Although he outnumbered the Federals by almost 10,000 men, Hood decided to avoid a pitched frontal engagement and instead flank the entrenched defenders. He held Schofield's attention by

---

7 Ibid., 502; McMurry, *Atlanta 1864*, 187.

8 OR 39, pt. 2, 862; ibid., pt. 3, 378; Hood, *Advance and Retreat*, 262-263; Wilson, *Under the Old Flag*, 11.

9 OR 45, pt. 1, 648.

feigning an attack with Lee's corps and the army's artillery, while simultaneously marching Frank Cheatham's and A. P. Stewart's corps on a flanking movement into Schofield's rear at Spring Hill. Schofield was still 40 miles from reinforcements at Nashville, but Hood seized the opportunity of a flanking maneuver—an option he would not have two days later at Franklin. Stanley Horn was the only modern author to recognize Hood's preference for flank attacks when he wrote of Spring Hill, "Here again, as so often in the past, he had recourse to his pet scheme of a flank movement—if he kept trying it, surely it must prevail some time."[10]

Even at Franklin, Hood's vanguard force of Stewart's corps made first contact with the Federal rearguard on the southerly slopes of Winstead and Breezy hills—but did not attack. Instead, Hood diverted Stewart east and successfully flanked the defenders, who withdrew to Schofield's main line at Franklin.

The record is unambiguous. Hood was not an inept and unsophisticated tactician who advocated only reckless frontal attacks. None of his four major battles around Atlanta were intended as such; he bypassed the enemy at Resaca, Georgia, and Decatur, Alabama; and he flanked Schofield at Columbia so successfully that the Confederates came within a whisker of cutting off and destroying Schofield's entire army at Spring Hill.

The only full frontal assault ever ordered by Hood during his entire tenure as commander of the Army of Tennessee was at Franklin, and then it was a last resort. Because of its proximity to Nashville, Franklin was Hood's final opportunity to destroy the trapped Schofield before he reached the relative safety of the Nashville fortifications and joined Thomas's gathering forces. At Franklin, any flanking movement would have required the fording of the rain-swollen Harpeth River and a cross-country march of several miles with only three hours of daylight remaining, resisted the entire way by Federal cavalry, infantry, and artillery.

After Franklin, Hood moved to Nashville and, rather than assault Thomas's entrenched command, entrenched himself, sought reinforcements, and awaited an attack by Thomas. Hood dispatched a cavalry and infantry force to Murfreesboro under Nathan Bedford Forrest to contain the large Federal garrison there and protect his own right flank and logistical lifeline. He again

10 Horn, *The Army of Tennessee*, 384.

demonstrated restraint when he explicitly ordered Forrest not to attack the Federal fortifications, and if attacked, to only drive them back to Murfreesboro.

Author Barbara G. Ellis did not let facts get in the way of her melodramatic writing, despite Hood's documented dislike of frontal assaults and demonstrated preference for flanking maneuvers. Despite experiencing "colossal" casualties in his battles, wrote Ellis, Hood "was of the rash-action school of frontal offensives . . . so beloved because of the potential for heroics."[11]

ȣɣ ɣȣ

On the matter of direct assaults, a careful examination of the historical record upsets the current paradigm. John Bell Hood was not an unthinking careless commander who callously hurled his men against enemy breastworks. In fact, he designed creative strategies to defeat his opponents, and none of his battles (except for Franklin) called for a head-on attack.

---

11 Ellis, *The Moving Appeal*, 290.

Chapter 16

"Historians have powerful imaginations,
which are both essential and dangerous."

— *Robert Stinson*

Hood to His Men:
"Boys, It is All My Fault"

John Bell Hood is often accused of blaming others for his failures and never accepting responsibility for his defeats. Although Hood indeed voiced his displeasure and disappointment with the performance of some of his subordinates—most notably William Hardee in the fighting around Atlanta—he accepted ultimate responsibility for his defeats there and in Tennessee, and praised the common soldiers of the Army of Tennessee. As is typical in the present-day historical portrayal of Hood, his words are often misinterpreted, and in almost every case his praise of his troops is not shared with readers.[1]

Without listing a source, Stanley Horn wrote that on the morning after the failure at Spring Hill, Hood "lashed out viciously at his subordinates, placing the blame everywhere but where it belonged—on himself." Hood, continued

---

1 This chapter is intentionally similar to Chapter 13, "Did John Bell Hood Accuse his Soldiers of Cowardice?", with additional information that required a separate chapter of its own.

Horn, possessed a "strongly developed unwillingness to take responsibility for his own errors." Thomas Connelly picked up on this theme when he wrote, "Although Hood enjoyed imitating Lee's tactics of 1862-63, he did not display that general's willingness to accept blame." According to Nathan Bedford Forrest biographers Daniel Foxx and Eddy Davison, "Hood blamed everyone but himself" for the failure at Spring Hill. Sam Elliott, A. P. Stewart's modern biographer, helped to further cement this idea when he wrote that "Hood was never averse to casting blame." Even the most sympathetic of the modern Hood scholars, Brian Miller, claimed that, "After the war, Hood would blame everyone except himself for the disasters at Franklin and Nashville." For reasons known only to them, these authors consciously decided to ignore evidence to the contrary, including Hood's acceptance of blame when he wrote in his memoirs, "I failed utterly to bring on battle" at Spring Hill.[2]

Hood was not unlike many other Confederate commanders when he engaged in a postwar debate regarding specific defeats and the loss of the war. Examples abound, including Jubal Early versus James Longstreet; Joseph E. Johnston and P. G. T. Beauregard versus Jefferson Davis and Braxton Bragg; Davis versus Louis Wigfall and P. G. T. Beauregard; and of course, Johnston versus Hood. In his postwar writings, Hood placed much of the blame on Hardee for the failure to hold Atlanta, and on Johnston, whose persistent retreating Hood believed negatively affected the offensive effectiveness of the Army of Tennessee. Hood's official report of his operations as commander of that army is often represented as the initial salvo in the Hood-Johnston feud. Oft-ignored evidence suggests otherwise. Hood visited Mary Boynton Chesnut, the famous Southern diarist, in Chester, South Carolina, where she had the time to personally discuss a variety of matters with him. During that visit on April 5, 1865, she wrote in her journal: "He [Hood] calls his report self-defense; says that Joe Johnston attacked him and he was obliged to state things from his point of view." Hood's official report and his memoirs are commonly cited as examples of his placing blame on others for his failures, when in fact they were a part of an ongoing debate with Johnston with each blaming the other for negatively affecting the Army of Tennessee. Commentators were incorrect in asserting that Hood blamed the individual

---

2 Horn, *The Army of Tennessee*, 394; Connelly, *Autumn of Glory*, 430; Davison and Foxx, *Nathan Bedford Forrest*, 358; Elliott, *Soldier of Tennessee*, 234; Miller, *John Bell Hood and the Fight for Civil War Memory*, 239; Hood, *Advance and Retreat*, 287.

soldiers of the Army of Tennessee for the defeats at Atlanta and in Tennessee, and in claiming that he did not accept personal responsibility for his defeats.[3]

When casting Hood as an army commander who held others responsible for his failures, critics often overlooked or ignoreed the poor performance turned in by certain units of his army, or the lack of aggressiveness demonstrated by certain regiments and brigades, as noted not just by Hood but by others as well. Hood did indeed blame Johnston and Hardee for negatively influencing the army's aggressiveness, but as detailed elsewhere in this book, he was neither incorrect nor alone in his assessment. Hardee, described by historian Stephen Newton as "the most thorough-going mediocrity and back-stabbing subordinate ever to be nicknamed 'Old Reliable,'" was involved in three of Hood's four major battles around Atlanta; it is difficult to find scholars who describe his performance at any of the battles as praiseworthy. (Likewise, it is virtually impossible to find a commentator who describes Frank Cheatham's performance at Spring Hill as laudable.) An army commander is allowed to point out the failure of a subordinate when the subordinate indeed failed in the field.[4]

In the postwar "blame game," Joe Johnston and William Hardee also cast blame on Hood. Hardee excused his own defeat at Jonesboro by admitting that the loss was due to the lackluster effort of his troops, and then went on to blame Hood for ordering too many attacks after assuming army command. Hardee, who complained that the previous battles were either lost or "dear-bought and fruitless" victories, had been delegated independent command at Jonesboro and deflected guilt to Hood rather than accept responsibility for the defeat that doomed Atlanta. The point, of course, is not whether Jonesboro was a winnable battle for the Confederates; given the heavy disparity in numbers, it likely was not. The issue is that Hardee, as its commander, blamed others for the defeat.[5]

బ్   ✑

As is common in Civil War scholarship and literature, Hood is held to a much harsher standard than other Civil War notables. After the fall of Atlanta,

---

3   Chesnut, *A Diary from Dixie*, 376.

4   Newton, "Overrated Generals," *North and South*, 15.

5   *OR* 38, pt. 3, 702.

Hood told Jefferson Davis in a brief letter, "According to all human calculations, we should have saved Atlanta had the officers and men of this army done what was expected of them." That sentence in Hood's letter often appears in Civil War literature. What historians routinely excluded are the words that followed, which as we will later see, distorts the context of the oft-repeated sentence: "It has been God's will to be otherwise. I am of good heart and feel that we shall yet succeed." In a letter to James Seddon on Sept 21, 1864, after expressing confidence in his army and his plan to force Sherman out of Atlanta and "give me battle," Hood accepted personal responsibility for the loss of the important city, admitting simply, "I lost Atlanta."[6]

It is important to understand that expressions such as the one Hood penned to President Davis were common during the Civil War. Robert E. Lee said of George McClellan's impending escape near the end of the 1862 Peninsula Campaign, "Yes, he will get away because I cannot have my orders carried out." Lee wrote this immediately after the failure to catch the Union Army of the Potomac while in motion at Glendale/Frayser's Farm. Lee may have been referring, at least in part, to Stonewall Jackson's poor performance on June 30. After the surrender at Appomattox in April of 1865, Lee wrote to Davis, "The operations which occurred while the troops were in the entrenchments in front of Richmond and Petersburg were not marked by the boldness and decision which formerly characterized them. Except in particular instances, they were feeble; and a want of confidence seemed to possess officers and men." No reasonable person would misinterpret Lee's words as blaming the soldiers of the Army of Northern Virginia for McClellan's escape in 1862, or for the loss of Richmond and Petersburg in 1865. Unfortunately, such misinterpretations are promulgated with noticeable regularity by Hood's many detractors.[7]

William T. Sherman also eluded criticism for blaming subordinates for his defeats. Here is what Sherman wrote about his bloody repulse at Chickasaw Bayou in Mississippi during the Vicksburg Campaign: "I have always felt that it was due to the failure of General G. W. Morgan to obey his orders, or fulfill his promise made in person." Sherman added that a Federal victory would have

---

6   Ibid., 38, pt. 5, 1,023; John Bell Hood letter to James Seddon, September 21, 1864, Compiled Service Records, A. P. Mason, National Archives.

7   Dowdey and Manarin, *The Wartime Papers of Robert E. Lee*, 938; Emory Thomas, *Robert E. Lee: A Biography* (New York, NY: W. W. Norton & Company, 1995), 241.

been attained, "had he [Morgan] used with skill and boldness one of his brigades."[8]

Some of Hood's own subordinates occasionally held each other culpable for poor performances, and some blamed Hood; they, too, evade the disparagement of historians. Corps commander A. P. Stewart, for example, blamed Hood for the failure at Spring Hill by claiming repeatedly after the war that Hood was in command and should have personally ensured that his orders had been obeyed. Cavalry commander James Chalmers openly criticized infantry general John C. Brown for the lost opportunity at Spring Hill, while Nathan Bedford Forrest faulted multiple commanders—but never himself. Nor is Hood's division commander William Bate condemned for criticizing Chalmers's weak attack against the Federal right at Franklin, or his complaint that Forrest's cavalry failed to support his flanks at Murfreesboro. Forrest, in turn, criticized Bate's infantry at Murfreesboro. Neither Forrest, Bate, nor Chalmers have been accused of blaming others for the failures at Spring Hill, Franklin, and Murfreesboro.[9]

S. D. Lee, another of Hood's senior officers, strongly criticized the performance of his own corps during the defense of Atlanta; rarely is he condemned for blaming his own commanders for his failures. Lee wrote in his official report, "The majority of the officers and men were so impressed with the idea of their inability to carry even temporary breastworks, that when orders were given for attack, and there was a probability of encountering works . . . they did not generally move to the attack with that spirit which nearly always assures success."[10]

One of the most unfair and disappointing aspects of the modern literary portrayal of Hood is the almost complete absence of the unambiguous praise he heaped upon his troops. Since Hood's words of respect and appreciation for his soldiers reside in the same body of historical evidence commonly cited by scholars and other authors, it is difficult to argue that the absence of his laudatory words is unintentional.

8   Sherman, *Memoirs of General William T. Sherman*, vol. 2, 224.

9   Elliott, *Soldier of Tennessee*, 234; Young, "Hood's Failure at Spring Hill," *Confederate Veteran*, vol. 16, 25-41; OR 45, pt. 1, 743, 746.

10 Ibid., 39, pt. 1, 810.

On December 6, 1864, outside Nashville, for example, Hood issued a general order seeking to recognize and honor the troops for their actions at Franklin: "Commanding officers will forward, with as little delay as possible, the names of those officers and soldiers who passed over the enemy's interior line of works at Franklin, on the evening of the 30th of November, that they may be forwarded to the War Department and placed upon the roll of honor."[11] Two days later on December 8, Hood sent a dispatch to Forrest, who was commanding a detached force at Murfreesboro: "General Hood is fully satisfied that you have done all that could be done in the case."[12]

Hood is almost universally criticized for not accepting responsibility for the failure of the Tennessee Campaign, when in fact, he did just that. Near the end of the Nashville retreat on December 21 near Shoal Creek, Alabama, W. G. Davenport of the 10th Texas Cavalry wrote, "General Hood came and looking worn and tired but with kindly words to all, saying to the soldiers, 'Boys, it is all my fault, you did your best.'" In his letter of resignation from the Army of Tennessee, Hood accepted full responsibility for the outcome of the Tennessee Campaign: "I am alone responsible for its conception," and in his memoirs added, "I alone was responsible" for the failed campaign. In an effort to deflect criticism away from his superiors Beauregard and Davis, Hood wrote that the Tennessee Campaign was "my own conception," even though Beauregard and Davis assisted in its planning and approved the invasion.[13]

Mary Chesnut's acclaimed *A Diary From Dixie* mentioned Hood's personal lament and his acceptance of blame. Although authors frequently cited Chesnut on a wide variety of topics, her words of admiration and respect for Hood, as well as his words of contrition, are rarely reproduced for readers. Chesnut, who recalled Hood visiting her home after his resignation as commander of the Army of Tennessee, wrote: "He said he had nobody to blame but himself."[14]

Notably absent in all of the major books on the Army of Tennessee or the Tennessee Campaign is Hood's eloquent tribute to the soldiers who fought at Franklin when he compared them to his namesake Hood's Texas Brigade—

11 Ibid., 45, pt. 2, 654.

12 Ibid., 666.

13 Davenport, *Incidents in the Life of W G Davenport*, 7; OR 45, pt. 2, 805; Hood, *Advance and Retreat*, 287, 310, 311.

14 Foote, *The Civil War*, vol. 3, 760.

some of Robert E. Lee's most accomplished and acclaimed soldiers. "The attack [at Franklin], which entailed so great a sacrifice of life," began Hood, "had become a necessity as imperative as that which impelled Gen. Lee to order the assault at Gaines's Mill, when our troops charged across an open space, a distance of one mile, under a most galling fire of musketry and artillery, against an enemy heavily entrenched. The heroes in that action fought not more gallantly than the soldiers of the Army of Tennessee upon the fields of Franklin."[15]

When considering Spring Hill, his limited options at Franklin, and other challenges, Hood's best explanation for his failure in Tennessee may have appeared in a letter to an acquaintance in 1867: "Accidents however, perhaps beyond human control caused the campaign to fail at a time the fruits of victory were seemingly within our grasp."[16]

---

15 Hood, *Advance and Retreat*, 296.

16 John Bell Hood letter to Sarah Dorsey, March 30, 1867, John Bell Hood Personal Papers.

Chapter 17

"The very ink with which all history is
written is merely fluid prejudice."

— *Mark Twain*

John Bell Hood and
Words of Reproach

Although reasoned criticisms of John Bell Hood's
military decisions are appropriate, some
authors seem also compelled to insult his character. Few Civil War figures have
received the volume and depth of personal attacks as has Hood.

Hood's harshest critic is Wiley Sword, who used his considerable literary
talents to literally assail Hood from cradle to grave in his books *The Confederacy's
Last Hurrah* and *Courage Under Fire*. He began by challenging Hood's pedigree.
"In the beginning," posited Sword, "there was little in John Bell Hood's
background to suggest that he would become one of the more influential
generals of the Civil War." How Sword reached such a conclusion is puzzling.
Both of Hood's grandfathers were veterans of the American Revolution and
the French and Indian War. Hood was surely influenced by these grandfathers,
for his own father, Dr. John W. Hood, spent many months away from his
family during his frequent visits to Philadelphia, where he studied and later
taught medicine. For Sword to conclude that there was "little" in his
background given Hood's ancestry was strange indeed. Thankfully, more recent

military writers did not affirm this bizarre conclusion. Eric Jacobson, for example, wrote in *For Cause and Country* that "John Bell Hood was born to be a soldier and the Civil War gave him every opportunity to unleash his instincts." Biographer Brian Miller concurred, writing in *John Bell Hood and the Fight for Civil War Memory* that Hood "had a family lineage rich in military history."[1]

Sword described Hood as "an ill mannered hellion" who grew up "with a streak of wildness and nonconformity about him," adding that he was "frequently in trouble." The author's sole source for the allegation is *The Gallant Hood,* John Dyer's 1950 biography. There is no historical record whatsoever of any legal problems or issues of being "frequently in trouble" during John Bell Hood's younger years. The absence of facts did nothing to stop Dyer from claiming that Hood proudly proclaimed that he had led other youths into trouble. Dyer's only source is an oral statement made by one of Hood's distant relatives, who was interviewed by the author a century after Hood's childhood. A single-source oral description of Hood's adolescent personality, corroborated by no historical evidence of illegal, destructive, or rebellious conduct by Hood during his entire life—from infancy to adulthood, in his military and civilian affairs—is less than credible. Yet, both Dyer and Sword used it as a basis to draw bold and unflattering conclusions.[2]

Sword also alleged that Hood's father lacked confidence in his son, repeating the unverifiable word-of-mouth legend of Dr. Hood telling the boy, "If you can't behave, don't come home [from West Point]. . . . Go to the nearest gate post and butt your brains out." There is no contemporary credible source to back this statement. Sword also failed to share with his readers that Hood was called home from Fort Mason, Texas, in March of 1856 to oversee the financial and personal affairs of his ailing father. At that time Dr. Hood's wife, a daughter, and two other sons—one older and one younger than John Bell—were still in Montgomery County, Kentucky. Why would the senior Hood insist that his disruptive and irresponsible middle son, who was then serving in the army 1,500 miles away, seek leave and travel all the way back to Kentucky to administer to his affairs? In requesting the extended furlough in

---

1 Sword, *Courage Under Fire,* 193; McMurry, *John Bell Hood and the War for Southern Independence,* 2-3; Jacobson, *For Cause and For Country,* 35; Miller, *John Bell Hood and the Fight for Civil War Memory,* 2.

2 Sword, *The Confederacy's Last Hurrah,* 6; Sword, *Courage Under Fire,* 194; Dyer, *The Gallant Hood,* 23.

the spring of 1856, Hood explained to Washington authorities, "My father's health is still very distressing. . . . His business is in the greatest confusion and I am the only child he will allow to attend to it for him."[3]

☙ ❧

Many writers portrayed Hood, while a West Point cadet, as undisciplined and lacking in academic ability. Sword claimed that he managed to "prod and squirm his way" through the academy. Hood accumulated 196 demerits during his fourth year, but Sword's research would also have shown that during the most difficult first (plebe) year, Hood accrued a mere 18 demerits—which placed him in the upper quartile of the entire cadet corps. Although he was four demerits short of expulsion by December of his final year, the young Kentuckian did not accumulate a single demerit over the next five months, an outstanding display of conduct and personal discipline.[4]

While at the military academy Hood received demerits for, among other things, a disorderly room, an improperly made bed, improperly folded clothes, absence or tardiness for events, visiting other cadets, using chewing tobacco, visiting the commandant's tent with a cigar in his hat, and wearing the wrong collar to church. Few of his demerits were for military infractions. For example, he was never late for military instruction and never received a demerit for his performance during military drill or training, for having an unclean weapon, or for the "condition of his military equipage." Hood's academic weaknesses were in formal classroom subjects such as mathematics and languages, while he did reasonably well in the military-related curriculum.[5]

In 1860, seven years after graduation, Hood was invited to serve as chief instructor of cavalry at West Point. When he declined the prestigious position, U.S. Adjutant General (and future Confederate general) Samuel Cooper responded, "Mr. Hood, you surprise me. This is a post and position sought by every soldier." Why would the administration of West Point want to subject

---

3   Sword, *The Confederacy's Last Hurrah*, 7; Miller, *John Bell Hood and the Fight for Civil War Memory*, 36.

4   Sword, *The Confederacy's Last Hurrah*, 7; Miller, *John Bell Hood and the Fight for Civil War Memory*, 20; (The author, a graduate of a military academy, Kentucky Military Institute, can personally attest to how difficult it is for a cadet to go five months without receiving a single demerit.)

5   Miller, *John Bell Hood and the Fight for Civil War Memory*, 20.

young impressionable cadets to an allegedly intellectually deficient, "ill-mannered hellion" who had just managed to "squirm and prod" (to quote Sword) his way through the school?[6]

Critics often cite Hood's low class ranking at West Point to support their claim that he lacked intellect. Hood graduated in 1853 in the bottom third of his class (44th out of 52). Additional information authors rarely share with their readers puts Hood's performance at the Academy in proper perspective. In the 19th century, only one-half of all West Point applicants passed the entrance examination. Hood's Class of 1853 began four years earlier with 93 cadets. So of the approximately 200 candidates who attempted to enter the academy in 1849, fewer than half earned admission, and of those who did, 41 cadets either withdrew for personal reasons or were expelled for academic or disciplinary deficiencies during the next four years. To portray any West Point graduate— then or now—as undisciplined or ignorant is both inappropriate and inaccurate, regardless of final class ranking.[7]

Furthermore, class ranking at West Point has never been a fail-safe indicator of postgraduate accomplishment. Many renowned Civil War commanders who graduated from West Point did so in the bottom half of their class. Some of them include: Confederate President Jefferson Davis; Adj. Gen. Samuel Cooper; Gens. William Hardee, W. H. T. Walker, James Longstreet, D. H. Hill, Lafayette McLaws, E. Kirby Smith, Fitzhugh Lee, George Pickett, and Joe Wheeler; and one of Robert E. Lee's personal favorites, Henry "Harry" Heth, who finished dead last in the Class of 1847. West Point "underachievers" also populated the ranks of the Federal army, including: Ulysses S. Grant, Philip Sheridan, Don Carlos Buell, George Custer, Winfield Scott Hancock, George Stoneman, and Alexander McCook. Hood was in good company.[8]

Post-Civil War West Pointers who excelled in combat included Matthias Day, who finished 70th of 76 in the Class of 1877 (and went on to win the Medal of Honor fighting Apaches in 1879), and Powhatan Clarke, who won the Medal of Honor in 1886 despite finishing last in the West Point Class of 1884. Conversely, commanders with a high West Point class ranking, such as Braxton Bragg, G. W. Smith, and P. G. T. Beauregard, enjoyed limited success on Civil

---

6   Ibid., 40.

7   Association of Graduates, *U.S.M.A., Register of Graduates and Former Cadets 1802-1988* (West Point, New York, 1988).

8   Ibid.

War battlefields. Indeed, William Henry Chase Whiting offers one of the finest examples of underachievement on the job. After graduating from Georgetown University at 16, he entered West Point and graduated first in his class in 1845. Whiting performed so poorly at the head of a division of combat troops that Gen. Robert E. Lee replaced him—with John Bell Hood.[9]

Jeb Stuart, West Point Class of 1854, explained that success at West Point was not guaranteed by high intellect, nor did a lack of accomplishment foretell future failure. "For one to succeed here, all that is required is an ordinary mind and application; the latter of which is by far the most important and desirable of the two," explained the brilliant cavalry general. "For men of rather obtuse intellect, by indomitable perseverance, have been known to graduate with honor; while some of the greatest geniuses of the country have been found deficient, for want of application."[10]

George C. Strong, who graduated fifth in the West Point Class of 1857, explained the kind of creative genius that the low-ranked cadets often employed. "It is a favorite idea among many here that it requires an abler man to stand at the foot of the class throughout the course than at the head of it," Strong observed. The "Immortals," as the lower-ranked cadets were called, often would exert only sufficient effort to get by day-to-day, but would then spend "one or two days or nights of intense application" prior to exams to ensure success. Strong added, facetiously, "These are some of the symptoms of that epidemic which is called Genius."[11]

Hood scholar Brian Miller countered criticisms of Hood's low grades at West Point. Miller (a college professor himself) astutely concluded, "In the midst of battle, French, math and English seem inconsequential."[12]

Early writers on the Army of Tennessee were generally respectful of Hood as a person. Thomas Connelly appears to be the first to have assailed the

---

9 James S. Robbins, *Last in Their Class: Custer, Pickett and the Goats of West Point* (New York: Encounter Books, 2006), xii; Association of Graduates, *U. S. M. A., Register of Graduates and Former Cadets 1802-1988.*

10 Ibid., x.

11 Ibid.

12 Miller, *John Bell Hood*, xix.

general's personal integrity. In a vague and nonspecific explanation of the requirements required for an army commander to be effective in the "western command system," Connelly proclaimed that Hood "simply did not have the character that was required," and that "essentially, Hood was untruthful." Connelly's ad hominem attack even challenged Hood's mental and emotional stability by claiming that his "physical handicaps were no less than his emotional ones," and that his "personality had suffered almost as much from his successes as his body had from injuries." Connelly provided no sources for these baseless allegations because there are none. His amateurish attempt at psychoanalysis conflicts with every account recorded about Hood by contemporary physicians, who described him as physically and mentally robust.[13]

Of Hood's critics—wartime, postwar, and modern—Wiley Sword stands out as the one who seized almost any opportunity to diminish the young general. Although famous for his powerful physique and handsome appearance, Hood was said by Sword to have had facial hair that "so elongated his face as to make it appear of outlandish size," and to have looked like a "backwoods lumberjack masquerading in the uniform of a Confederate general." Sword may have lifted and paraphrased the depiction of Hood from Col. J. C. Haskell's memoirs, who wrote that Hood, then a young lieutenant colonel of the Texas brigade, looked like "a raw backwoodsman, dressed up in an ill-fitting uniform." If Sword relied upon Haskell's description, he refrained from informing his readers of Haskell's next sentence: Hood "afterwards filled out and became quite a fine looking man of good address."[14]

Although in and of itself unimportant, Sword's physical description of Hood revealed a strong bias. Countless contemporary sources described Hood's impressive physical appearance, among them Pvt. Philip D. Stephenson of the (Louisiana) Washington Artillery, who wrote:

> Hood's personal appearance was striking and commanding. He was over six feet and of splendid proportions . . . [his] eyes were large and bold. . . . The general effect of his presence was impressive . . . of magnificent and striking appearance. With his yellow

---

13 Thomas Connelly, *Autumn of Glory*, 430, 429.

14 Sword, *The Confederacy's Last Hurrah*, 6; John C. Haskell, *The Haskell Memoirs: The Personal Narrative of a Confederate Officer*, Gilbert E. Govan and James W. Livingood, eds. (New York: G. P. Putnam's Sons, 1966), 16.

waving hair and great tawny beard and big bold blue eyes and Herculean frame he looked like a gigantic old Saxon chieftain come to life again.

Sword's backwoods lumberjack was Stephenson's mythological Greek hero and reincarnated Saxon chieftain. Famous Civil War diarist Louise Wigfall Wright described Hood as "superbly handsome, with beautiful blue eyes, golden hair and flowing beard—broad shouldered, tall and erect," yet Sword, reluctant to say anything positive about Hood, coined a puzzling expression by describing him elsewhere in his book as "almost handsome."[15]

Unique among Civil War authors, Sword also overtly diminished Hood's renowned battlefield successes prior to joining the Army of Tennessee as a corps commander in the spring of 1864. His career offered "a remarkable insight into the incomplete role of physical courage in his life," explained Sword, who went on to write that earlier in the war Hood "seemed endowed with good luck equal to his bravery." Hood, he continued, was a "rising star . . . who just might be destiny's darling" in Robert E. Lee's Army of Northern Virginia. Sword attributed Hood's universally lauded leadership and tactical prowess at the decisive Confederate victories at Gaines's Mill and Second Manassas essentially to good luck. After the battle of Sharpsburg (where Hood's heavily outnumbered brigades played a significant part in holding together Lee's left flank), his "ambition began to burn ever brighter in his mind," claimed Sword. No historical document suggests such a thing at that time, or evidences any obsessive ambition within Hood. But even if this was true, is it not healthy for career soldiers to be ambitious? For that matter, how many professionals in any vocation (including authors and historians) are not ambitious?[16]

At Gaines's Mill (Lee's first victory as commander of the Army of Northern Virginia), Hood fulfilled a promise to his old command, the 4th Texas Infantry, by personally leading his troops during a successful frontal assault that routed Fitz John Porter's heavily entrenched defenders. According to Sword, "Hood, miraculously, was unscathed. Amid the wrecked guns and carnage he looked around. Nearly an entire Federal regiment, the 4th New

---

15 Philip D. Stephenson, *The Civil War Diary of Philip Daingerfield Stephenson, D.D.*, Nathaniel C. Hughes, Jr., ed. (Baton Rouge: Louisiana State University Press, 1998), 209; Wright, *A Southern Girl in '61*, 231; Sword, *The Confederacy's Last Hurrah*, 244.

16 Sword, *Courage Under Fire*, 193, 195; Sword, *The Confederacy's Last Hurrah*, 7-9.

Jersey, had been captured, and fourteen pieces of artillery were taken by his men. It was a sight and thrill he never forgot. . . . Above all else, Hood had gained new confidence. . . . He was a man transfigured." Sword's baseless declaration that Hood was thrilled at these horrendous sights is not only unfounded, it runs counter to eyewitness testimony. Major James W. Ratchford, a Confederate staff officer, left this account after the battle:

> Early in the same night, while I was trying to gather up some of our division that had been scattered in the pursuit [of the Federals], I came upon General Hood sitting on a cracker box. As I approached, he looked up at me, and I could see tears streaming down his cheeks. His brigade had lost heavily, and all about him were the dead and wounded. I spoke to him and he replied brokenly, "Just look here Major, at all these dead and suffering men, and every one of them as good as I am, yet I am untouched."[17]

The young general's grief persisted into the next day. Chaplain Nicholas Davis recalled that Hood attended the next morning's roll call and was appalled that only a fraction of the men were present. As their commander rode away weeping, Davis wrote that "there was not a soldier in that line but what thought more of him now than ever before." And yet, without a credible source, Sword tried to convince his readers that Hood had witnessed "a sight and thrill he never forgot."[18]

Elsewhere, Sword wrote about Hood's attacks on Sherman outside Atlanta. "Hood's recklessly aggressive use of his men clarified the aberration of Gaines' Mill." In an unforgivable insult to the hundreds of Hood's Texans, South Carolinians, and Georgians who fell at Gaines's Mill, Sword labeled their victorious attack (which was ordered by Lee, and not Hood) an "aberration"— in other words, a fluke.[19]

Regarding Hood's role as a division commander at the Confederate victory at Chickamauga, Sword claimed that he had earned public adoration as a Southern war hero "despite the lack of important results in his new command responsibility." This bewildering assertion is baseless, for Hood indeed had enjoyed success as a division leader. He also had earned stunning successes as a brigadier. At the head of his brigade, Hood played a decisive role in tactical

---

17 Ibid., 9; Ratchford, *Memoirs of a Confederate Staff Officer*, 19.

18 Davis, *Chaplain Davis and Hood's Texas Brigade*, 91.

19 Sword, *Courage Under Fire*, 196.

victories at Eltham's Landing, Gaines's Mill, and Second Manassas in Virginia. In the new position to which Sword alludes—that of a division leader—Hood (as noted elsewhere) launched a sharp counterattack at Sharpsburg against heavily superior numbers that knocked back a powerful Federal attack collapsing Lee's left flank. Soon afterward, Hood was promoted to major general by Stonewall Jackson, who wrote, "It gives me pleasure to say that [Hood's] duties were discharged with such ability and zeal as to command my admiration. I regard him as one of the most promising officers of the Army." Hood's next division command was at Gettysburg, where he was wounded at the outset of the fighting. He returned to duty at Chickamauga, where his division played an instrumental role in the Confederate breakthrough around the Brotherton cabin, which began the rout of most of the Federal Army of the Cumberland. For his performance at Chickamauga, Hood was promoted to lieutenant general by his corps commander James Longstreet, who wrote, "I respectfully recommend Major General J. B. Hood for promotion to the rank of Lieutenant General, for distinguished conduct and ability in the battle of the 20th inst. General Hood handled his troops with the coolness and ability that I have rarely known by any officer, on any field." How could any objective historian characterize Hood's outstanding (and in some cases, extraordinary) performances at Gaines's Mill, Second Manassas, Sharpsburg, and Chickamauga as unimportant?[20]

Sword utilized a letter Hood wrote to General Lee while serving in the Army of Northern Virginia in an attempt to persuade his readers that the young commander was overly ambitious and conniving even during the early years of his career. According to Sword, Hood wrote a letter "to his 'friend' Robert E. Lee, suggesting that smaller army corps might be desirable." Sword added suggestively, "Perhaps Lee would favor Hood with such a command?" What Sword failed to inform his readers was that soon after receiving Hood's letter regarding additional but smaller corps of infantry, Lee wrote to President Davis to suggest *exactly* what Hood had proposed. The letter from Hood to Lee cited by Sword was written on April 29, 1863. Just 11 days later on May 10, Lee wrote the following to Davis:

---

20 Ibid., 195; Dyer, *The Gallant Hood*, 144; Hood, *Advance and Retreat*, 65- 66. The original letters of recommendation for promotion from Generals Thomas Jackson and James Longstreet are in the John Bell Hood Personal Papers.

I have for the past year felt that the corps of this army were too large for one commander. Nothing prevented my proposing to you to reduce their size and increase their number but my inability to recommend commanders. Each corps contains, when in fighting condition, about 30,000 men. These are more than one man can properly handle and keep under his eye in battle in the country that we have to operate in. They are always beyond the range of his vision, and frequently beyond his reach.[21]

Readers might well question how Hood, the ignorant West Point under-achiever who had attained battlefield successes only through dumb blind luck, could possibly have conceived an idea on his own that was also held by Robert E. Lee, who thought so much of the concept that he proposed it to the Confederate president in the hope of having it implemented. Sword also believed it was presumptuous and wholly inappropriate for Hood to sign a letter to Lee with "Your Friend." Lee's affectionate reply to Hood dated May 21, 1863—a transcript of which appears verbatim in Hood's memoirs *Advance and Retreat*—was so personal that Lee wrote the letter in his own hand rather than dictate it to a staff member. The letter reads, in part: "Although separated from me, I have always had you in my eye and thoughts. . . . I rely upon you much. . . . I am much obliged to you always for your opinion." Lee closed with, "Wishing you every health and happiness and committing you to the care of a Kind Providence, I am now and always your friend, R. E. Lee." Sword is a skilled researcher. He surely read this letter in Hood's *Advance and Retreat*. Selective disclosure of historical evidence leads readers to incorrectly conclude that Hood and Lee did not have a close personal relationship, and that Hood was simply angling for higher command while trying to ingratiate himself with Lee.[22]

Sword made the following claim in his book *Courage Under Fire* regarding Hood's invasion of Tennessee: "Further, he knew that both his personal career and the fate of the army were at stake. His plight was as obvious as his uncertainty of what to do once he reached the enemy's defenses." Sword's explicit statement that Hood "knew" his own career was at stake when he led his army north to liberate Tennessee was unsupported by any evidence. The claim that Hood didn't know what to do or how to handle enemy defenses was

21 Sword, *The Confederacy's Last Hurrah*, 9; OR 25, pt. 2, 810.

22 Hood, *Advance and Retreat*, 52-53; R. E. Lee letter to John Bell Hood, May 21, 1863, John Bell Hood Personal Papers.

a ludicrous comment considering Hood's previous accomplishments at Gaines's Mill and elsewhere.[23]

Sally Jenkins and John Stauffer described Hood as a "homicidal commander" in their book *The State of Jones*. While that is as extreme as it is utterly false, Sword arguably holds the dubious distinction of having made perhaps the most callous comment of any established writer about a Civil War figure. Hood, he argued, was "a fool with a license to kill his own men." This "fool" of a soldier "with a license to kill" was recommended for promotion to major general by Stonewall Jackson; he was recommended for promotion to lieutenant general by James Longstreet; he was recommended for promotion to full general by President Jefferson Davis, who later wrote in his memoirs, "If he had, by an impetuous attack, crushed Schofield's army, without too great a loss to his own, and Forrest could have executed his orders to capture the trains when Schofield's army was crushed, we should never have heard complaint because Hood attacked Franklin, and these were the hopes with which he made his assault."[24]

Sword described the soldiers of the Army of Tennessee at Nashville as impotent and apathetic in their final battle in Tennessee, but blamed Hood for creating "a bedraggled army, sick and tired of being sacrificed in bizarre tactical efforts." Sword claimed that the retreating Southern troops became "an army running away" from both the enemy and Hood, from whom they had endured "repeated abuse and sacrifice for no sensible purpose." Sword disregards the 2,500 casualties inflicted on Thomas's attacking Federals at Nashville, as well as the facts regarding all of Hood's efforts as commander of the Army of Tennessee, as set forth elsewhere in this book.[25]

"Character," wrote Sword in an attack upon Hood's morality, "the ability to determine and do that which is morally right based upon logic, common sense, and education, may very well be life's ultimate quality." Sword's homily applies equally well to writers and military commanders.[26]

---

23 Sword, *Courage Under Fire*, 196.

24 Sally Jenkins and John Stauffer, *The State of Jones: The Small Southern County that Seceded from the Confederacy* (New York: Anchor Books, 2010), 221; Sword, *The Confederacy's Last Hurrah*, 263; Davis, *The Rise and Fall of the Confederate Government*, vol. 2, 488-489.

25 Wiley Sword, narrative to the painting, The Darkest of All Decembers by Rick Reaves, Collector Historical Prints, Tampa, Florida, 1992.

26 Sword, *Courage Under Fire*, 200.

ॐ   ॐ

The questioning of Hood's personal character does not end with his surrender to Federal authorities in Natchez, Mississippi, on the last day of May 1865. Thomas Connelly wrote of Hood's character and personality, citing, among other sources, Hood's friends Mary Chesnut and Louise Wigfall Wright: "He was a simple man, often tactless and crude, more of a fighter than a general." It is disappointing that Connelly extracted such a conclusion from anything recorded by Chesnut and Wright, who wrote extensively of their love and admiration for Hood. Connelly cherry-picked comments that could be misinterpreted and mischaracterized to appear critical of Hood, while concealing Chesnut's and Wright's repeated references to Hood's integrity and character. Wright wrote of Hood's bravery, patriotism, gallantry, nobility, and "blameless life."[27]

In describing Hood's postwar life in New Orleans near the end of *The Confederacy's Last Hurrah*, Wiley Sword made the most notorious of his many derogatory comments: "As if to refute any inference that he might be a 'lame' lover due to his crippled body, Hood fathered eleven children." This callous and crude statement attempts to reduce John Bell and Anna Marie Hood's many descendants to mere products of a man who sired children only to demonstrate his virility, while discounting the likelihood that Hood—by all contemporary accounts a devoted husband and loving father—wanted the typically large family of that era.

It would be difficult to find anything so insensitive written about another Civil War participant.[28]

---

27 Connelly, *Autumn of Glory*, 322; Wright, *A Southern Girl in '61*, 231.

28 Sword, *The Confederacy's Last Hurrah*, 439.

Chapter 18

"Too many so-called historians are really
"hysterians"; their thinking is more
visceral than cerebral."

— *Thomas A. Bailey*

Words of Praise for
John Bell Hood

Modern books on the Army of Tennessee and Hood's Tennessee Campaign are largely compendiums of criticisms and condemnations targeting John Bell Hood. The intentional suppression of contemporary expressions of respect, sympathy, concurrence, and support for Hood is perplexing.

Some of the harshest words ever written about any Civil War commander were penned by Capt. Samuel Foster, a member of Granbury's Texas brigade. Foster set down his vitriol in his diary immediately after the battle of Franklin: "And the wails and the cries of widows and orphans made at Franklin, Tennessee on Nov. 30, 1864 will heat up the fires of the bottomless pit to burn the soul of Gen. J. B. Hood for murdering their husbands and fathers at that place that day. It couldn't be called anything else but cold blooded murder." Foster added, "He sacrificed those men to make the name of Hood famous." A committed devotee of Joseph Johnston, Foster also condemned Hood's attempt to hold Atlanta—a task Foster himself declared impossible. Foster was an eyewitness, and it is appropriate for historians to record what he wrote—regardless of how angry or malicious his words might be. Indeed, it is difficult to find a study on the Tennessee Campaign that does not include Foster's observations. Context, however, is everything.[1]

Anyone who reads most or all of Foster's diary will discover that he was excessively belligerent by nature, and sometimes insubordinate. The replacement of Johnston with Hood in mid-July 1864 infuriated the captain. He declared his disgust with Johnston's removal by writing, "[I]f Jeff Davis had made his appearance in this army during the excitement he would not have lived an hour." It is not known whether Foster is stating that he personally would have attempted to assassinate Davis or if others were threatening to do so, but he seemed undisturbed by the impropriety of such talk.[2]

After Hood's first three failed attempts to defeat Sherman and drive him away from Atlanta, Foster condemned Hood for attempting to hold the city—the very mission he was assigned by the Confederate government. Foster went on to grossly exaggerate Hood's casualties, writing, "He [Hood] is in a bad fix. And more he has virtually murdered near 10,000 men around Atlanta trying to do what Joe Johnston said could not be done." His willingness to essentially declare Hood a mass murderer for trying to hold one of the South's most important cities is a good illustration of his blind hatred for the commander, while his observation about Johnston's claim suggests the former leader of the Army of Tennessee believed Atlanta could not be held—even though he refused to inform Richmond of his intent to abandon the vitally important city.[3]

Another entry in Foster's diary dated September 27, 1864, demonstrated conduct clearly unbecoming of an officer. According to Foster, Hood ordered that two men from Granbury's brigade return to Atlanta and destroy some equipment that mistakenly had been left intact. One of the men selected for the assignment was Pvt. Jake Eastman, a member of Foster's company. "I told him to not go one foot," declared Foster, "and if Gen. Hood has come out of Atlanta and left two Steam Mills running there, then let him go and burn them himself if he wants it done, and Jake didn't go a step." Foster, the soldier's company commander and thus his immediate superior, instructed an enlisted

---

1   Foster, *One of Cleburne's Command*, 151.

2   Ibid., 107.

3   Ibid., 129.

man to disobey a direct order from his regimental commander that had originated at army headquarters. The mills were left for the benefit of Sherman's occupying army.[4]

During the pre-Tennessee invasion maneuvers, Foster—who had complained of Hood's aggressiveness at Atlanta and would again at Franklin— found fault in Hood's decision to bypass the Federals at Decatur, Alabama, on October 30. Foster complained that Hood bypassed Decatur without attacking the outnumbered but defiant defenders, who "left the U. S. flag flying in full view of us." As discussed earlier, the garrison was strongly defended and Hood saw no reason to shed blood for an inconsequential position.[5]

Context is important. Authors who included Hood-damning cherry-picked sentences penned by Foster without revealing the captain's strong pro-Johnston position, generally belligerent nature, and willingness to defy Hood's orders either did so with a purpose or failed in their effort to fully inform readers. In either case, readers will believe (incorrectly) that most of Hood's troops hated him. The record demonstrates otherwise. S. A. Cunningham of the 41st Tennessee described the army's soaring confidence during the flanking movement to Spring Hill, and as earlier noted, their faith in Hood was "unbounded," so sure were they that a victory would be achieved "that would give us Nashville."[6]

After the war, Dr. Samuel Thompson of Cunningham's 41st Tennessee offered a calm, detached, and balanced view of Hood the military leader:

We regarded him as a brave and daring soldier, and an able division or corps commander, but lacking in ability and experience as an army commander. Many we know, will disagree with us, but we think to calmly and impartially view General Hood's course we will be forced to accord him the highest order and a military commander with but few superiors. . . . What became of General Hood for the remainder of the war we do not know, but if he was removed for failure in Tennessee, he was treated very unjustly. That he did so we believe was no fault of his. He failed simply because he had not the men and supplies to contend with the immense force that was against him.[7]

---

4   Ibid., 133-134.

5   Ibid., 142.

6   Cunningham, "The Battle of Franklin," *Confederate Veteran*, 101-102.

7   Cunningham, *Reminiscences of the 41st Tennessee*, 117-118.

Army of Tennessee Chaplain Dr. Charles T. Quintard agreed: "General Hood deserves well of the country for his bravery, his devotion, his energy and enterprise and he should be honored in all coming time for what he has done. Nor should one word of censure fall upon him for what he has failed to do."[8]

"Still no soldiers' heart but warms when talking of Hood," R. M. Gray of the 3rd Georgia Infantry wrote after the war about his former commander. "[Men] loved the man and officer while condemning his system of tactics. Hold in your heart my son a warm place for the noble, generous and brave Hood whatever verdict the future shall pass upon him."[9]

"Alas for Hood!" wrote Federal cavalry commander Gen. James Wilson in his memoirs. "He passed out [of Tennessee] broken-hearted at last by the weight of his misfortunes. His courage and undoubted ability as a leader and a general deserved better luck."[10]

One of the Civil War's best-known commentators is Pvt. Sam Watkins of the 1st Tennessee Infantry, whose popular memoir *Company Aytch* appears in the bibliography of virtually every book written on the Army of Tennessee and the Western Theater of the Civil War. Watkins was a keen observer and excellent writer, and he had much to say about Hood—some positive, some negative. Rarely, however, do his words of admiration and respect for Hood appear in contemporary books. As previously stated, Watkins elaborated on the affection and respect the army had for Hood's personal character and integrity. Watkins offered a poignant testimony of his admiration for his former commander when he penned the following epitaph in 1884, five years after Hood's tragic death from yellow fever:

> But the half of brave Hood's body molders here:
> The rest was lost in honor's bold career.
> Both limbs and fame he scattered all around,
> Yet still, though mangled, was with honor crowned;

---

8   Elliott, *Doctor Quintard*, 220.

9   Miller, *John Bell Hood and the Fight for Civil War Memory*, 139.

10 Wilson, *Under the Old Flag*, 157.

For ever ready with his blood to part,
War left him nothing whole—except his heart.[11]

B. W. Holcombe of Stovall's Georgia brigade recalled Hood's wit during the retreat from Nashville. Holcombe and his comrades had a fire going by the side of the road. As Holcombe recalled, "Gen. Hood and escort rode up and asked permission to warm, which was granted, he at the same time making the remark that he had only one foot to get cold."[12]

Private Henry A. Morehead of the 11th Mississippi Infantry, who served under Hood in the Army of Northern Virginia, recalled, "Gen. Hood was a brave man, and while he never won the affections of his men as some other commanders did, we may say 'Peace to his ashes,' for he was a good soldier and a true Southern man."[13]

Lieutenant William W. Fergusson, a former member of the 2nd Tennessee Infantry and an engineer with the Army of Tennessee, praised Hood in a postwar letter: "Whose fortunes I shared, whose conduct I applaud, and whose association from the time of taking charge of part of the line of works at Atlanta, to Tupelo, after the ineffectual attempt to redeem Tennessee and revive the lost spirit of the Army of Tennessee."[14]

Texas Senator Louis T. Wigfall, whom Hood succeeded as commander of the Texas brigade in Lee's Virginia army, was one of Jefferson Davis's bitter rivals and thus claimed by many historians, by association, to have disliked Hood. Authors often reproduce Wigfall's well-known slur that Hood "had a fine career before him until Davis undertook to make of him what the good Lord had not done—to make a great general of him." What students of the war rarely read is Wigfall's daughter Louise Wigfall Wright's opinion of the general. She clearly disagreed with her father, and wrote at length about her admiration for Hood the man and the general. It is worth repeating at length:

11 Sam Watkins, *Southern Bivouac*, 2 (May 1884), 399-400. A marble scroll engraved with Watkins's epitaph sits in front of Hood's tomb at Lakelawn/Metairie Cemetery in New Orleans.

12 Yeary, *Reminiscences of the Boys in Gray*, 293-294.

13 Yeary, *Reminiscences of the Boys in Gray*, 539.

14 William W. Fergusson letter to John Bell Hood, February 14, 1867, John Bell Hood Personal Papers.

A braver man, a purer patriot, a more gallant soldier never breathed than General Hood. Aggressive, bold and eager, the "Fabian" Policy of General Johnston was opposed to all the natural impulses of his nature.

He reveled in "a fight," and firmly believed he could lead his troops to a victorious conclusion in the active operations he inaugurated on taking command of the Army of Tennessee. Though, as stated, he remonstrated on General Johnston's being removed from command, yet I have no doubt his soldier's heart beat with eager hope, as he was called to take his place, and he saw in fancy his brave army marching to victory.

He was a man of singular simplicity of character and charm of manner—boyish in his enthusiasm—superbly handsome, with beautiful blue eyes, golden hair and flowing beard—broad shouldered, tall and erect—a noble man of undaunted courage and blameless life.

We made the journey with him homeward when the war was over. I can see him now—we were in a baggage car, seated on boxes and trunks in all the misery and discomfort of the time. He sat opposite, and with calm, sad eyes looked out on the passing scenes, apparently noting nothing.

The cause he loved was lost—he was overwhelmed with humiliation at the utter failure of his leadership—his pride was wounded to the quick by his removal from command and Johnston's reinstatement in his place; he was maimed by the loss of a leg in battle. In the face of his misery, which was greater than our own, we sat silent—there seemed no comfort anywhere. And the ending of his life, years after, was even more somber— dying by the side of his wife with yellow fever and leaving a family of little children to mourn a father, who, though unsuccessful in the glorious ambition of his young manhood, left to them the precious heritage of a stainless name, linked ever with the highest courage and purest patriotism.[15]

Context and balance paints a different picture of people and events we once thought we so fully understood.

---

15 Wilber Jones, *Generals in Blue and Gray: Davis's Generals*, 2 vols. (Mechanicsville, PA: Stackpole Books, 2006), vol. 2, 227; Wright, *A Southern Girl in '61*, 230, 231.

Chapter 19

"Cut-and-paste historians collect all the extant
testimony about a certain limited group of events
and hope in vain that something will come of it."

— *R. G. Collingwood*

John Bell Hood:
Laudanum, Legends, and Lore

Folklore and legends are powerful forces. Stories handed down from generation to generation help keep the past alive. Whether or not they are true is often of little concern to the storytellers. The stories themselves—fabricated, factual, or a mixture thereof—keep us connected to our past. They take on a life of their own with each retelling. As the years pass, certain details are omitted, others added, and "new" evidence surfaces to revitalize an old story. Some well-established and oft-repeated stories about John Bell Hood are so completely devoid of supporting evidence, indeed they are so ridiculous, that it is often difficult to make a persuasive intelligent case against them.

One colorful and entertaining myth concerns the famously pugnacious Nathan Bedford Forrest threatening to "whip" General Hood. Although various versions of the story exist, the most prominent alleges that during a meeting of subordinate commanders at the Harrison house prior to the battle of Franklin, Forrest urged Hood to allow him to attempt a flanking movement around the Federals. When Hood rejected the request, the angry cavalryman left the meeting growling that he would whip Hood "if he wasn't half a man." Not a single written record of this meeting exists, and there is no written evidence that Forrest ever made any such a comment about Hood. The entertainment value of the story, however, ensures its immortality.

అ   ௭

The rumor regarding Hood's use of the painkilling opiate laudanum after his recovery from his grievous Chickamauga wound is one of the most "entrenched" stories to come out of the Civil War. Indeed, it is difficult to find a modern Hood-related book or article, or attend a lecture or tour, where his alleged drug use isn't a subject of discussion. And as with so many stories about Hood, it is completely devoid of substantiating evidence, or indeed, any evidence at all.[1]

According to historian and author Stephen Davis, whose research on this topic was first published in *Blue and Gray* magazine in October 1998, allegations about Hood's use of laudanum did not appear in print until 1940 with the publication of Percy Hamlin's biography *Old Bald Head: General R. S. Ewell.* According to Hamlin's Introduction, Atlanta was lost, a Confederate army destroyed, and Lincoln's reelection assured because "a competent, cautious man was replaced by one who, brave and loyal though he was, had been so crippled by wounds as to make him dependent upon the use of opium." Although Hood was not mentioned by name, there is no doubt as to who replaced Joe Johnston. As Hamlin saw it, the capable and careful Johnston was replaced by Hood, a brave, loyal, crippled opium addict. Hamlin did not provide a source to support his claim, but that made little difference to his readers and future historians. The allegation remained unchallenged and uncontested. And like a cancer it grew.[2]

In his 1972 booklet written for the National Park Service entitled *The Road Past Kennesaw: The Atlanta Campaign of 1864*, Richard McMurry suggested that Hood "may have been taking a derivative of laudanum to ease his pain."

---

1   Davis, "John Bell Hood's Historiographical Journey; or, How Did a Confederate General Become a Laudanum Addict?", 218-232.

2   Ibid.; Percy Hamlin, *"Old Bald Head" (General R. S. Ewell): The Portrait of a Soldier* (Strasburg, VA: Shenandoah Publishing House, 1940), x.

McMurry was not alone in his supposition. Webb Garrison Jr., in his 1995 publication *Atlanta and the War*, guided his readers toward the vague possibility that Hood's overall judgment might have been affected, "perhaps from the use of laudanum to dull his constant pain." Since neither author had any substantiation to back up the claim, both left themselves wiggle room for error, McMurry with the words "may have been," and Garrison with his use of "perhaps." If sufficient evidence existed to make such a claim, equivocal statements would be unnecessary.[3]

Hood's modern critics (there were no contemporary critics who suggested laudanum, just critics in the 20th century) often suggested laudanum as an explanation for the army's embarassing tactical failure on the night of November 29, 1864, at Spring Hill, Tennessee, where the Confederates somehow allowed the hastily retreating columns of John Schofield's Federal army to escape from a well-conceived trap. As described in more detail earlier, Hood and his army rapidly pursued the retreating Federals and were exhausted by the time night fell on the 29th. As we now know, the failure to block the road stemmed from the refusal of some of Hood's subordinates to execute his clear orders to do so.

Authors James McDonough and Thomas Connelly claimed an entirely different reason for the failure in their 1983 narrative *Five Tragic Hours: The Battle of Franklin*. According to their theory, Hood was sound asleep while the Yankees slipped away, "especially if he took any liquor or a drug to relax." Here, for the first time, readers are reminded of Hood's alleged use of drugs, with the added suggestion that the pursuing army's commanding general had taken to the bottle as well. Like Hamlin, McMurry, and Garrison, McDonough and Connelly provided no documentation to support what can only be described as a libelous allegation. Notice also that the whole edifice is supported by one word: "if." Hood was either drinking, or he was not. He was either taking drugs, or he was not. He was either sleeping, or he was not. Despite a complete lack of evidence, McDonough and Connelly planted an entirely new "fact" in Civil War literature by alleging that Hood's drug use had now morphed anew into that of an army commander out of control under the influence of both opium and alcohol. Students of the Civil War now had a new meme: at the most critical

---

3   Davis, "John Bell Hood's Historiographical Journey; or, How Did a Confederate General Become a Laudanum Addict?", 229; Garrison, *Atlanta and the War*, 138.

time in the campaign, Hood decided to "relax" with drugs and a bottle of booze.[4]

Wiley Sword was just as vague in his influential *The Confederacy's Last Hurrah*. According to Sword, after finishing dinner at his headquarters on the night of November 29, Hood retired and "perhaps swallowed some laudanum." Perhaps? Like those preceding him, Sword did not cite any primary source or eyewitness testimony. His only "proof" for this charge was a reference to local legend in William B. Turner's 1955 book *A History of Maury County, Tennessee*.[5]

Regrettably, the dubious character of local legend seems to be the sole origin of a belief that Hood was intoxicated in the vicinity of Spring Hill on the night of November 29, 1864. Historian Stanley Horn also made reference to this local lore, writing in his 1941 work *The Army of Tennessee*, "Old soldiers and old residents around Spring Hill explain all that night's fumbling in blunt terms: 'Hood was drunk.'" This is a grave charge that cannot be verified or dismissed more than a century after the fact. In the same vein, Hood's first biographer Richard O'Connor made reference in 1949 to the power of local legend surrounding the Spring Hill affair in *Hood: Cavalier General*. According to O'Connor, the alcohol use "was a legend of the countryside for many years after that Hood was drunk that night."[6]

Sword's speculation that "perhaps Hood swallowed some laudanum" was kicked up a notch by his publisher in a photograph caption in the same book that "Hood often resorted to laudanum." What was once "legend of the countryside" (alcohol use) or speculated by Hamlin and then others (drug use) evolved into established fact in the mind of Civil War students.[7]

Ronald H. Bailey, in his book *The Battles for Atlanta* (1985), not only dealt with the same falsehood, but elevated it to an entirely new level. "By the accounts of some contemporaries, Hood suffered such intense pain that he was taking laudanum, an opiate that could impair mental judgment." According to Bailey, Hood's contemporaries substantiated what was once mere speculation. The "accounts" that Hood was suffering from "intense pain" as well as the

---

4   Davis, "John Bell Hood's Historiographical Journey; or, How Did a Confederate General Become a Laudanum Addict?", 229.

5   Sword, *The Confederacy's Last Hurrah*, 136.

6   Horn, *The Army of Tennessee*, 392; O'Connor, *Hood*, 232.

7   Sword, *The Confederacy's Last Hurrah*, 244. Whether or not Sword suggested or approved the caption is unknown.

"contemporaries" who claimed as much and referenced his drug use remained unnamed.[8]

Even noted scholar Steven Woodworth fell into this trap. In an essay that appeared in the 1994 book *The Campaign for Atlanta and Sherman's March to the Sea*, Woodworth reported that Hood "at times resorted to alcohol and opium or a derivative of laudanum." His only source is the 1972 booklet written by Richard McMurry, who failed to provide a credible source of his own.[9]

No one ever witnessed Hood taking an opiate or drinking liquor after his return to duty in the spring of 1864. No one is known to have written about it. No historical documentation (letters, journals, diaries, reports, or even receipts or army requisitions) have been discovered to support these claims. So why are modern historians and authors so quick, indeed anxious, to publish such disparaging allegations based upon unsupported speculation?

Stephen Davis suggests the answer to that question rests with the severity of Hood's wounds. As is well known, Hood suffered two major injuries during the war. The first took place on the second day at Gettysburg during the initial fighting late on the afternoon of July 2, 1863. Hood was leading his division into battle when fragments from an artillery shell that exploded overhead ripped into his left arm. Thankfully amputation was not necessary, but the use of his arm was limited to some extent for the rest of his life. Less than three months later, Hood was leading his division when a minie ball struck him in his upper right thigh during the fighting at Chickamauga on September 20, 1863. Unlike his previous wound, this one required amputation. The dangerous surgery was successful, but Hood's chances for a full recovery remained slim. As was customary for general officers during the war, Hood was treated by the army's finest medical officers and recuperated in the most comfortable and sanitary facilities available.

The day after the operation, Hood was carried 15 miles to the home of a staff member's parents and placed under the care of Dr. John T. Darby. By late October, Hood had improved enough to be transported overland to Tunnel

---

8 Ronald H. Bailey, *The Battles for Atlanta* (Alexandria, VA: Time-Life Books, 1985), 91, quoted in Stephen Davis, *Confederate Generals in the Western Theater*, 230.

9 Steven Woodworth, "A Reassessment of Confederate Command Options During the Winter of 1863-1864," *The Campaign for Atlanta and Sherman's March to the Sea*, ed. Theodore Savas and David Woodbury (Campbell, CA: Savas Woodbury Publishers, 1994), 16. Woodworth's description is incorrect, as laudanum is a derivative of opium.

Hill, Georgia, and then by rail to Atlanta.[10] By the first week of November, he was on his way to Richmond. "His stump healed promptly, but remained painful," speculated Jack D. Welsh, M.D., in *Medical Histories of Confederate Generals*, "because an artificial limb was hard to fit."[11]

With an artificial leg and crutches (and only one good arm to manage them, the other partially disabled from his Gettysburg wound), Hood enjoyed limited independent movement, and before long, returned to riding his horse. With his left arm partially paralyzed and in a sling and his entire right leg amputated below the hip, the act of mounting and dismounting required a great deal of effort and exertion. According to the records of Confederate staff officer Joseph B. Cumming, it took three aides to mount the general into his saddle. This included not only seating Hood securely, but also fitting the prosthetic leg into the stirrup while at the same time strapping Hood and his crutches to the saddle. Hood was an accomplished horseman and soon adjusted to the trying situation. He rode regularly after his return to Georgia in February of 1864, where he led an infantry corps in Joe Johnston's Army of Tennessee.[12]

According to Maj. James Ratchford, a member of Gen. Daniel H. Hill's staff who had served with Hood in the Army of Northern Virginia and who later served on Hood's staff in the Army of Tennessee, Hood's injuries did not limit his role in the field. "Though he came to the corps on crutches," explained Ratchford, "he displayed all the energy and activity in attending to the duties of his larger command that had been so noticeable in his care of his Texas brigade, and this never slackened on the campaign with Johnston from Dalton to Atlanta. I was with him in all the fights made during the campaign and wondered at his great activity in his crippled state."[13]

In order to calm apprehensions among the general public concerning his overall comfort, range of mobility, and capabilities in the field, Hood permitted a personal letter he wrote to a friend to be published. "I have been riding all over this country with Gen. Johnston, and have been in the saddle every day enough

10 Dr. John T. Darby's Medical Report of Hood's Chickamauga Wounding and Recovery, John Bell Hood Personal Papers.

11 Jack Welsh, M.D., *Medical Histories of Confederate Generals* (Kent, OH: Kent State University Press, 1995), 106.

12 Stephen Davis, "John Bell Hood's 'Addictions' in Civil War Literature," *Blue and Gray* (October 1998).

13 Ratchford, *Some Reminiscences of Persons and Incidents of the Civil War*, 58.

to have fought two or three battles, without feeling any inconvenience," explained the general. Hood's claim was corroborated by cavalryman Joe Wheeler, who reported that Hood could ride comfortably 14 or 15 miles a day. It is important to note that Hood made no mention of any discomfort or pain associated with his wounds, and nothing to indicate the use of painkillers.[14]

Hood was often in the company of others during the three winter months he spent recuperating in Richmond. Many of those he associated with held important roles in the Confederate government, military, and/or Richmond society. One was Hood's close friend Mary Chesnut, who coincidentally was familiar with laudanum. Chesnut wrote in her diary in July 1861 that she was ill and offered the drug by a friend. She refused the opiate, writing, "I have no intention of drugging myself now. My head is addled enough as it stands, and my heart beats to jump out of my body at every sound." Hood was frequently in her presence following the loss of his leg, and often visited her family in Richmond and South Carolina—before and after his Army of Tennessee command tenure. The alert Chesnut, who recorded everything from gossip to hard news in her journal, did not mention even so much as a whisper about any laudanum use by Hood as he prepared to lead a corps in the Army of Tennessee and ascended to lead the army itself, or after his defeats around Atlanta and in Tennessee.[15]

In a similar tone, Civil War medical historian Dr. Paul Steiner observed that Hood spent a good deal of personal time with Jefferson Davis during the winter of 1863-1864. "Davis," concluded Steiner, "would almost certainly have known of any narcotic addiction." One must conclude that if Davis had knowledge (or a credible suspicion) of drug use, he would have immediately withdrawn Hood's appointment for promotion to lieutenant general. It is also instructive to note that even after Hood's failures around Atlanta and in Tennessee, Davis never wrote about or spoke of any possible drug or alcohol use by Hood.[16]

In spite of a complete lack of evidence, many writers of Civil War history could not resist the temptation to speculate on the degree of pain Hood experienced as a result of his wounds. "His old leg wound may have been

14 Miller, *John Bell Hood and the Fight for Civil War Memory*, 109.

15 Chesnut, *Mary Chesnut's Civil War*, 102; Miller, *John Bell Hood and the Fight for Civil War Memory*, 101.

16 Paul E. Steiner, *Medical-Military Portraits of Union and Confederate Generals* (Philadelphia: Whitmore Publishing Co., 1968), 225, 229.

irritated by the long, damp ride over rough roads," postulated Thomas Connelly in *Autumn of Glory*. Diving headlong into conjecture, James Street Jr., in an article published in *Civil War Times, Illustrated* in May of 1988, wrote freely of Hood's wounds, the pain he suffered, and the obvious need of painkilling drugs to cope with it all. "The pain from the stump of his right leg must have been horrendous when he rode strapped to his saddle," Street speculated without offering any substantiation. "The bouncing and jolting, the abrasive rubbing of the stump against the rough cloth of a dressing or pad could not have been endured without some sort of pain-reliever. An opiate was the standard prescription. The drug would have made Hood sleep at Spring Hill while the Federals escaped his trap." Note that Street claimed firsthand knowledge of the level of pain Hood experienced, when he experienced it, that he needed a painkiller, the type of drug he used, and that it put him to sleep while Schofield escaped at Spring Hill.[17]

Few credentialed academicians appear to have taken the time and energy to determine how other Civil War amputees handled themselves under similar situations. Federal Gen. Daniel Sickles, whose right leg was completely shattered by a solid shot at Gettysburg on the second day of the battle, subsequently underwent amputation at the thigh. Sickles, as would be expected, initially experienced sharp pain in his stump, but remained in the army (although he never served in the field again). He used crutches until his death in 1914. If we apply to Sickles the same line of reasoning applied to Hood, Sickles surely needed opium to cope with the pain. Laudanum (an opiate) was easily accessible and the drug of choice for dulling severe pain. There is nothing in the record to support the fact that Sickles used the drug. Would it be acceptable for historians to claim that Sickles used drugs for the duration of time he was in the army?[18]

Confederate Gen. Richard S. Ewell was kneeling on the Manassas battlefield on August 28, 1862, when a minie ball struck him in the patella and split his tibia. He was found on the field that night in considerable pain and his left leg was amputated just above the knee the next afternoon. Ewell's post-amputation experience was far more traumatic than Hood's. Ewell was so roughly handled while being carried from the battlefield that the severed bone jutted out from the stump. A layer of dead tissue soon covered the wound, and

---

17 Connelly, *Autumn of Glory*, 500; Davis, *Confederate Generals in the Western Theater*, 230.

18 Welsh, M.D., *Medical Histories of Union Generals*, 302, 303.

an inch of bone fell from the femur soon thereafter. After being confined to his bed for several weeks, Ewell learned to support himself with crutches. However, he slipped and fell on the icy streets of Richmond in December of 1862, which ripped apart his stitches, reopened the wound, and lost him another inch of bone.[19]

In addition to these difficulties, Ewell's stump was a peculiar shape and his prosthetic wooden leg did not fit well. Jack Welsh, a doctor who wrote extensively about the medical histories of both Union and Confederate generals, observed that Ewell was often "bothered by abrasions of the skin and by small abscesses" due to his poorly fit wooden leg. Despite these challenges, Ewell returned to duty in May of 1863 and remained in active service until his capture at Sayler's Creek in Virginia on April 6, 1865. Ewell fell from his horse more than once and reopened his wound. On one occasion, Ewell forgot about the loss of his leg while conversing with a fellow officer and tried to walk. He fell to the ground and once again injured his stump. By the autumn of 1863, his injury bothered him enough to require temporary leave from the army.[20]

Ewell's case is germane to our study of Hood because none of Ewell's biographers ever advanced the idea of drug use. As Stephen Davis keenly observed, it is strange logic indeed that Hamlin (Ewell's original biographer) would take for granted the necessity of pain-relieving medication for one amputee (Hood), and ignore that same possibility when writing of his own subject (Ewell), who underwent more agonizing and frequent physical suffering brought about by a similar wound.[21]

Davis also pointed out that it was common for Civil War doctors to liberally dispense opiates, and that over the course of the war, large numbers of soldiers on both sides became addicted to the drug or its derivatives. But as David Courtwright suggested in his book *Dark Paradise: A History of Opiate Addiction in America*, such dispensing and addiction was also attributable to

---

19 Paul D. Casdorph, *Confederate General R. S. Ewell: Robert E. Lee's Hesitant Commander* (Lexington: The University of Kentucky Press, 2004), 209; Welsh, *Medical Histories of Confederate Generals*, 64.

20 Welsh, *Medical Histories of Confederate Generals*, 64.

21 Davis, "Hood's Addictions," *Blue and Gray*. Here is how Davis put it: "How odd that General Ewell's first chronicler, Hamlin, would assume the need for pain medicine in one amputee, Hood, when his own subject suffered more frequent and painful complications of surgery without opium use."

surgeons' prescription of opium for chronic diarrhea and dysentery—not just postoperative pain.[22]

Dr. John T. Darby's detailed medical reports of Hood's wounding and recovery at Gettysburg and Chickamauga, found within the recently discovered cache of Hood's personal papers, indicate, among many things, the physician's concern over the use of opiates. Darby kept a daily record of Hood's wounds and how they healed, as well as his sleep patterns, appetite, energy, moods, and pain levels. He also recorded the precise amount of medication he gave to Hood each day, if any. The fully transcribed Gettysburg report, for example, records that Hood received a 0.50 grain dose of morphine on only one day during the entire five-week period covered by the report. At the time this book went to press, the 16-page, 3,500-word Chickamauga daily log had yet to be completely transcribed, but it does note that on the day after the amputation Hood received a single dose of quinine for nausea brought about by the chloroform used during the operation.

During the entire 67-day recovery period covered in the log (September 20-November 24, 1863)—Darby wrote an entry for each day—the amount of morphine he prescribed for Hood, if any, was carefully recorded. Hood was frequently given 0.25 and 0.50 grain doses, but Dr. Darby was careful to note the opiate was *always* prescribed to help him sleep. Approximately 10 days after the amputation, and on one day only, Hood was given a 1.00 grain dose when intense pain from a complication kept him from falling asleep. In fact, on November 4, 1863, while Hood was in Wilmington, North Carolina, en route to Richmond, Darby wrote, "Slept without morphine for the first time." Entries for subsequent days noted that Hood was sleeping at night without requiring morphine.[23]

In addition to the judicious use of morphine as an anesthetic, Darby carefully recorded the use of other medicinal treatments, including quinine, cold water, and iron, which was prescribed for patients who had lost blood. The only analgesics recorded by Darby were daily "milk punches" (an alcoholic

---

22 David Courtwright, *Dark Paradise: A History of Opiate Addiction in America* (Cambridge, MA: Harvard University Press, 1982), 54.

23 Dr. Darby's Medical Report of Hood's Chickamauga Wounding and Recovery, and Dr. Darby's Medical Report of Hood's Gettysburg Wounding and Recovery, John Bell Hood Personal Papers. A grain equals .065 grams and was a common unit of measure in 19th century medicine. Thanks to Ms. Terry Reimer of the National Museum of Civil War Medicine.

drink similar to eggnog, popular in the South in the 19th century), and on one occasion, Darby recorded that Hood was being given "sherry wine."[24]

As a medical professional, Darby was clearly aware of the addictive nature of opiates, so he prescribed them as little as possible and recorded when their use was discontinued. Although we do not know with certainty whether Hood was aware of the risks of opiates, their addictive effect was common knowledge and his doctor would surely have communicated as much. We do know that Darby recorded on September 26, 1863, a mere six days after the amputation of his entire leg, that Hood "refused morphine."[25]

It is worth noting that not a single Hood biographer—O'Conner, Dyer, or McMurry—ever alluded to the use of opiates in their studies of the general, although each speculates about the effects of his wounds. For example, while offering a glimpse of Hood's physical difficulties, O'Conner quoted Sam Watkins's description of Hood on horseback: "How feeble and decrepit he looked, with an arm in a sling and a crutch in the other hand, trying to guide and control his horse."[26]

Other contemporary descriptions of Hood, however, offer nothing about the commander's mental or physical incapacitation. Although Dr. Urban Owen reported on November 5, 1864, that the army was concerned because Hood was "very sick with pneumonia," he wrote to his wife the following day, "I am glad to inform you that General Hood is again in the saddle." Hood's friend and confidant Dr. Charles T. Quintard, who was both a chaplain and a physician, accompanied the army on the invasion of Tennessee. After noting Hood's excellent "health and spirits" in his diary on November 25, Quintard wrote on November 29 that the general rose at 3:00 a.m. and, when Hood came to tell him goodbye, "I prayed God's blessing, guidance and direction upon him." Hood's reply, as recorded by Quintard: "Thank you, Doctor. That is my hope and trust." While not definitive, none of these descriptions or conversations indicates an intoxicated or hung-over man, and educated observers like Drs.

24 Dr. Darby's Medical Report of Hood's Chickamauga Wounding and Recovery, John Bell Hood Personal Papers. Medicinal use of iron conveyed to the author by Ms. Terry Reimer, National Museum of Civil War Medicine, Nov. 27, 2012.

25 Dr. Darby's Medical Report of Hood's Chickamauga Wounding and Recovery, and Dr. Darby's Medical Report of Hood's Gettysburg Wounding and Recovery, John Bell Hood Personal Papers.

26 O'Connor, *Hood: Cavalier General*, 243.

Owen and Quintard would have recognized signs of drug use or intoxication and commented upon them.[27]

Hood shared a bedroom with Tennessee Governor Isham Harris and another staff officer on the night of November 29, 1864. He received visitors throughout the night, including Gens. Frank Cheatham, A. P. Stewart, and Nathan Bedford Forrest. All of these men survived the war. None of them wrote (or spoke in the presence of another who recorded it) anything suggesting that Hood was in any way impaired during that time frame. Cheatham, one of Hood's most outspoken postwar critics, would have gladly exposed any drug or alcohol use by Hood had he witnessed it.

One justification critics use for assuming Hood took laudanum is the alleged fact that his prosthetic legs came from France, where it was supposedly customary for manufacturers to include a complementary vile of laudanum with a prosthesis. There is no evidence that Hood's "cork legs" came from France. There is, however, evidence that his artificial legs were made in London and were called "Anglesey" legs—state-of-the-art prosthetics in the 19th century named for the Marquis of Anglesey, who was wounded at Waterloo. These were not manufactured out of cork wood, but were called "cork legs" because they were popular and widely used in County Cork, Ireland. An article in the December 1, 1864, Muncie, Indiana, *Delaware Free Press* described the dispatch of a Confederate surgeon to London, where he spent several weeks superintending the manufacture of artificial limbs for wounded Confederate officers, "supplied in sets of two and three each that amid the perils of blockade running one at least should reach its destination in safety." The article went on to state, "On one particular specimen of ingenuity particular care was bestowed and the surgeon took charge of it himself. This was the artificial limb—an Anglesey leg, as it is called—which enabled Gen. Hood to take active service again, and assume command of the army at Atlanta." Even if 19th century French prosthetics manufacturers delivered laudanum in their packaging, Hood's legs were of English design and construction and there is no proof they shipped with an opiate inside.[28]

---

27 Quintard and Elliott, *Doctor Quintard*, 185.

28 *Delaware Free Press* (Muncie, IN: December 1, 1864); Kim M. Norton, "A Brief History of Prosthetics," *In Motion*, vol. 7, Issue 7 (November/December 2007). Special thanks to David Fraley for finding and providing the author with this newspaper article.

Historian Stephen Davis observed an encouraging shift in later scholarship produced by Hood's biographer Richard McMurry, correcting the flawed consensus of Hood's alleged drug use. Ten years following the publication of his 1972 booklet *The Road Past Kennesaw*, in which he indicated that Hood "may have been taking a derivative of laudanum," Dr. McMurry published his biography *John Bell Hood and the War for Southern Independence*. In that influential study, McMurry naturally examined the mental and emotional aspects of Hood's terrible wounds, but refrained from any mention of drug use. Davis wrote, "Richard has reaffirmed to me personally that this non-mention is in effect an admission that in researching his book he found no evidence to support his earlier conjecture."[29]

The historical record is devoid of any evidence of drug or alcohol use by Hood, but Civil War history is permeated with myths, biases, and falsehoods— and change is often a frustratingly slow process. For example, Craig Symonds wrote in *Stonewall of the West*, his award-winning 1997 biography of Patrick Cleburne, that Hood took "an early dinner and a laudanum-induced sleep" on the night before the battle of Franklin. In 2009, Webb Garrison Jr., citing Connelly, McDonough, and Sword in his fittingly named book *Strange Battles in the Civil War*, wrote that Hood "assuaged his pain with laudanum, which affected his judgment." In his 2002 book *The Finishing Stroke*, John Lundberg claimed that Hood was "confused and half asleep" when A. P. Stewart visited him at his Spring Hill headquarters on the night of November 29. Stewart and others present in Hood's room wrote nothing of Hood acting out of the ordinary, let along being "confused and half asleep," yet Lundberg felt compelled to make the assertion. His only citation is Wiley Sword, who himself made the baseless charge that Hood's mind was perhaps "clouded" by laudanum.[30]

A stunning example of the evolution of the drug addiction myth is the 2007 book *Nathan Bedford Forrest: In Search of the Enigma* by Eddy Davison and Daniel Foxx, which elevated Hood's alleged use of laudanum to an altogether new level of abuse. Hood's wounds, claimed Davison and Foxx, should have disqualified him from army command, "not to mention his addiction to alcohol and laudanum." Based upon absolutely nothing, Hood's speculated "possible" and

29 Davis, "Hood's Addiction," *Blue and Gray.*

30 Symonds, *Stonewall of the West*, 254; Garrison Jr., *Strange Battles of the Civil War*, 269; Lundberg, *The Finishing Stroke*, 82.

"occasional" drug and alcohol use had now evolved into a portrayal of Hood as a full-blown drug addict and alcoholic.[31]

Russell Blount, an author generally sympathetic to Hood, carried the myth even further in his recent book *The Battles of New Hope Church*. Hood, argued Blount, "often turns to laudanum and whiskey for relief." Not only did Blount perpetuate the drug and alcohol myth, but apparently discovered that Hood's liquor of choice was whiskey. His source for these assertions is a single page in *Mary Chesnut's Civil War*, in which the famous diarist makes no mention whatsoever of anything akin to laudanum or alcohol use by Hood.[32]

The most preposterous scholarship on the subject appeared in Dr. Barbara G. Ellis's 2003 *The Moving Appeal*, where the toxic mixture of "Hood and drugs" was so prominent that it warranted its own listing in the book's index! Eschewing evidence of any kind, Ellis boldly declared to her readers that Hood's abilities were "increasingly skewed by a growing dependence on opiates," and that Jefferson Davis mistook Hood's look of enthusiasm and resolve on the battlefield as "eyes ablaze with a need for narcotics."[33]

Myths and legends grow easily—and die hard.

If historians and other authors aren't satisfied with accusations that John Bell Hood was a drug addict, alcoholic, and cavorted with prostitutes, we now also "know" that he was a compulsive gambler. According to Thomas Connelly, "By nature Hood was a gambler and the army knew this. There were many tales afloat concerning his gambling habits in the old army, one of which told how he put a thousand dollars on one card in faro game and won." Except for the wild rumor about a one-card bet (which seems more than unlikely given Hood's economic status as an Army officer), Connelly offered no examples of gambling stories supposedly circulating within the Army of Tennessee, and neither do the sources he cited. If they existed, surely at least one of these "many tales" would appear somewhere in the thousands of pages of letters, diaries, and memoirs produced by members of the Army of Tennessee who

---

31 Davison and Foxx, *Nathan Bedford Forrest*, 348.

32 Russell Blount Jr., *The Battles of New Hope Church* (New Orleans: Pelican Publishing, 2010), 47.

33 Ellis, *The Moving Appeal*, 290, 311, 334, 648.

served during Hood's tenure from April 1864 in Dalton, Georgia, until his resignation in Mississippi in January of 1865.[34]

The myth about Hood's gambling provides an excellent illustration of how some authors disregard historical evidence, or the lack thereof. Decades after Connelly's rendition appeared, Douglas Lee Gibboney included his own story of Hood's gambling in his ominously titled book *Scandals of the Civil War*. In this version, Schofield's card game is not at West Point but in Texas when Hood was serving with the U.S. Army. In addition to changing the location, Gibboney added to the story by claiming that Hood was "flat broke" and had borrowed $600 (not Connelly's $1,000) to place the bet. Hood's infamous faro game was changed to poker and the amount rose to $2,500 in Christopher Losson's *Tennessee's Forgotten Warriors: Frank Cheatham and his Confederate Division*.[35]

"But the Gallant Hood of Texas Played Hell in Tennessee"

Numerous books on the Army of Tennessee and the Tennessee Campaign include some variation on a story of the defeated soldiers singing the familiar song "The Yellow Rose of Texas" during the retreat from Nashville, with the final line changed to, "But the gallant Hood of Texas played hell in Tennessee." Like so much about Hood, this too is false.

For support of this claim, most authors cited Bell Wiley's 1943 classic *The Life of Johnny Reb: The Common Soldier of the Confederacy*. Dr. Wiley's source, in turn, was Robert Selph Henry's 1931 book *The Story of the Confederacy*, which included

---

34 Connelly, *Autumn of Glory*, 431. Connelly's $1,000-bet tale was a story purportedly told by John Schofield about how Hood placed a $1,000 bet in a faro (card) game at West Point. The story does not appear in Schofield's memoirs, and readers are expected to believe that a West Point student from rural Kentucky in 1853 would have access to what was in those days a fortune.

35 Douglas Lee Gibboney, *Scandals of the Civil War* (Shippensburg, PA: Burd Street Press, 2005), 132; Christopher Losson, *Tennessee's Forgotten Warriors: Frank Cheatham and His Confederate Division* (Knoxville: University of Tennessee Press, 1989), 173. See also Lawrence Officer, Ph. D. and Samuel Williamson, Ph.D., Measuringworth.com, 2011. Skeptics might consider that $1,000 in 1853 is equal to $29,100 in 2012, and $2,500 in 1859 is the equivalent of $68,000 in 2012. How realistic was it for a 21-year-old West Point student from rural Kentucky to have the modern equivalent of $29,000 to gamble away in 1853, or that a young cavalry lieutenant earning a salary of approximately $64.00 per month, stationed in an adobe and thatch frontier fort in Texas in 1859, had $2,500 cash on hand to be risked in a card game?

the Hood-related lyrics, but did not offer any source to support the change. An exhaustive search for the origin of the revised lyrics suggests that they initially appeared in Judge Frank H. Smith's 1904 book entitled *History of the 24th Tennessee*, and also in W. J. McMurray's *History of the 20th Tennessee Regiment Volunteer Infantry*, published in the same year. It is worth examining each in turn.[36]

Although Judge Smith was a respected jurist and citizen, much of his essay on the 24th Tennessee relied on information provided to him by others. As a result, the accuracy of many of his assertions is questionable. For instance, countless veterans, Federal and Confederate alike, recorded the treacherous condition of the swollen Harpeth River on November 30, 1864, but Smith wrote that a flank movement by Hood would have been "comparatively easy, with the river fordable almost everywhere." This is patently untrue. Smith offered no details or source to support the revised lyrics that Hood "played hell in Tennessee" and the claim that this version became a popular "camp song."[37]

W. J. McMurray provided what appears to be the only eyewitness account of the song being sung with the "played hell in Tennessee" lyric. The author described Hood and his staff riding past some troops south of Pulaski, Tennessee, near the end of the retreat, when a single soldier of the 39th North Carolina Infantry, demonstrating "the spirit, wit and fun there was in the Confederate soldier," sung "The Yellow Rose of Texas" with the words:

> You may talk about your dearest maid
> and sing of Rosalie,
> but the gallant Hood of Texas
> played hell in Tennessee.[38]

Two years later in 1906, B. L. Ridley cited McMurray's earlier book in his memoirs *Battles and Sketches of the Army of Tennessee 1861-1865*: "Dr. McMurray

---

36 Bell Irvin Wiley, *The Life of Johnny Reb: The Common Soldier of the Confederacy* (Baton Rouge: Louisiana State University Press, 2007), 122; Robert S. Henry, *The Story of the Confederacy* (Cambridge, MA: DaCapo Press, 1989), 434.

37 Frank H. Smith, "History of the 24th Tennessee," Columbia, TN, March 1904.

38 W. J. McMurray, *History of the 20th Tennessee* (Nashville, TN: Publication Committee, United Confederate Veterans, 1904), 352.

ought to have given the first part of the parody that the old soldier dwelt on as follows:

> And now I'm going Southward
> for my heart is full of woe.
> I'm going back to Georgia
> to find my Uncle Joe.
>
> You may talk about your dearest maid
> and sing of Rosalie,
> but the gallant Hood of Texas
> played Hell in Tennessee."

It is unclear whether Ridley meant that McMurray had neglected to include the first part of the verse or that the first four lines should have been added to the song being sung by the North Carolinian. It is highly unlikely that Ridley, a member of A. P. Stewart's staff, would have personally heard the song during the retreat (or any other time) since the 39th North Carolina was a part of Cheatham's corps. Ridley was a committed devotee of Joseph Johnston (in his book, opposite the title page, is a portrait of Johnston with the photo caption "General Joseph E. Johnston: The Idol of the Army of Tennessee"), and his memoir is replete with praise for the former commander. It is more than likely that Ridley was facetiously suggesting the addition of those first four lines to the song, and made them up himself.[39]

If any version of the "played hell in Tennessee" version of lyrics was indeed sung by any number of soldiers during the retreat out of Tennessee, proof appears nowhere in the many memoirs, letters, or diaries of the more than 20,000 Tennessee Campaign veterans who survived to tell the tale.

My interest to research such an admittedly trivial historical item was piqued as a result of correspondence I received in 2008 from an active-duty navy captain from Mississippi, who at the time was stationed in Turkey and as of this writing is stationed in Germany. He wrote to me as follows:

> I just happened upon your site on General John B. Hood—the Lion. Two of my great-great grandfathers went north with him to Nashville. The stories were told to me by

---

39 Ridley, *Battles and Sketches*, 439.

my mother's father, whose grandfather was Private George W. Bell of the Third Mississippi Infantry, Featherston's brigade. I don't know how widespread was the army's admiration for General Hood, but I do know they made up a song as they marched south, presumably after Nashville. It was something like this:

They can talk about their Jackson
and sing of General Lee,
but the one-legged Hood
gave 'em Hell in Tennessee.

I have always held that jewel close. It was given to me by my grandfather, Elwin Livingston of Pulaski, Mississippi, a member of the Mississippi Legislature from Scott County. He stated that his grandfather (Private George Bell) had taught him that song. I am afraid I am the only one who still has knowledge of it and I do not want it lost to history.[40]

This stanza about Hood giving them hell ["gave 'em hell"] in Tennessee is of course quite different from the oft-repeated and widely accepted "played hell in Tennessee" version. Although skeptics might question the source (George Bell or Elwin Livingston) of the "gave 'em hell in Tennessee" lyric, its legitimacy is at least equal to that of the famous "played hell" version which, although repeated countless times since 1904, has itself only a single source—an unidentified North Carolinian, as reported by W. J. McMurray.

The earliest major book on the invasion of Tennessee, Thomas Hay's 1929 *Hood's Tennessee Campaign*, made no mention of the "Yellow Rose of Texas" song, nor do more recent books on the campaign, such as Eric Jacobson's *For Cause and For Country* or Thomas Connelly's *Autumn of Glory*. However, many authors not only included the disparaging lyrics—which evidence suggests might have been sung just one time by a single soldier or made up from whole cloth—but also created additional details from thin air. Without citing a source, Stanley Horn crafted new specifics and provided yet another variation of the lyrics in his book *The Army of Tennessee*:

The cold December rain drummed down noisily on the tent, but not noisily enough to shut out the confused babble of an army in retreat. . . . If the heartbroken commander

---

40 Correspondence to author from Captain Randy Stroud, USN, Summerville, SC, 2006, reproduced with permission.

had listened he might actually have heard them singing as they splashed barefoot along the muddy road. The tune they sang was that old favorite, "The Yellow Rose of Texas," but the words they used had been improvised by some camp wit, words that would have seared the wounded heart of Hood:

So now I'm marching southward,
My heart is full of woe.
I'm going back to Georgia
To see my uncle Joe.

You may talk about your Beauregard
And sing of General Lee,
But the gallant Hood of Texas
Played hell in Tennessee.[41]

A few years later in *The Decisive Battle of Nashville*, Horn wrote, "Somewhere along the line some irrepressible wag, with the indestructible *elan* of the Army of Tennessee, had improvised a parody of the popular song 'The Yellow Rose of Texas' [that] he and his sodden, bloody comrades were singing." As with his earlier book, Horn offered no source for his claim, but this time he slightly changed the first two lines of the verse to "So now we're going to leave you, our hearts are full of woe."[42]

James R. Knight chose Horn's version of the lyrics in his recent monograph *The Battle of Franklin: When the Devil Had Full Possession of the Field*. Without citation, the lyrics appeared as the epigraph to a chapter grimly titled "The Death of Hood's Army":

> "You can talk about your Beauregard and sing of General Lee,
> but the gallant Hood of Texas played hell in Tennessee."
>
> — *song reportedly sung to the tune of "Yellow Rose of Texas" by the remnants of the Army of Tennessee as they retreated into northern Mississippi.*[43]

---

41 Horn, *The Army of Tennessee*, 418.

42 Horn, *The Decisive Battle of Nashville*, 153.

43 James Knight, *The Battle of Franklin: When the Devil Had Full Possession of the Earth* (Charleston, SC: The History Press, 2009), 103.

Wiley Sword called upon his fertile imagination for ancillary details of the incident. Citing W. J. McMurray's eyewitness account, Sword accurately related that during the retreat some soldiers had to move to the side of the road to make room for Hood and his staff to pass. Sword added, "As Hood went by he heard the men singing a familiar tune. . . . Only the words seemed somewhat strange. He listened closely." Although he cited McMurray, Sword provided the longer lyrics that appear in Ridley's book, not in McMurray's. In either case, neither McMurray nor Ridley wrote of anyone other than a single North Carolinian singing, and neither author wrote anything about Hood hearing the song, much less listening closely. Taking full advantage of artistic license and thus venturing into the world of fiction, Sword gave his readers details that have no basis in fact but made his portrayal more convincing.[44]

John Lundberg fashioned yet another scene when he described Granbury's brigade crossing the Tennessee River into Alabama on December 26: "As they marched over the pontoons, the Texans sang an altered version [of] "The Yellow Rose of Texas." Lundberg provided the lyrics that appear in Ridley's book, but cited the published diary of Capt. Samuel Foster as his source. Foster, however, mentioned nothing about anyone singing any song on the page cited by Lundberg. The "played hell in Tennessee" lyric appeared only in the notes of the book's editor, who cited Stanley Horn, who provided no source of his own. Lundberg's footnoting created the illusion that the source for the song was a member of Granbury's Texas brigade, when in fact there is *no* evidence that *any* Texan sang the song, let alone wrote about it.[45]

One can reasonably argue that W. J. McMurray's 1904 mention of the modified "Yellow Rose of Texas" established that one soldier sang the altered lyrics at least one time. What is disturbing is the degree to which authors feel free to embellish and fabricate details, creating perceptions and imagery in the minds of readers that have absolutely no factual basis—and then cite sources they must know do not support what they wrote. Such is the level of scholarship when dealing with so many issues related to John Bell Hood.

The great-great-grandson of Pvt. George Bell of the 3rd Mississippi provided an oral—and now written—record of some of Hood's soldiers singing "The Yellow Rose of Texas" with lyrics praising their war-wounded commander's noble efforts to liberate Tennessee. As the decades pass, it will be

44 Sword, *The Confederacy's Last Hurrah*, 422.

45 Lundberg, *The Finishing Stroke*, 119-120.

interesting to see if George Bell's testimony finds its way into Civil War literature.

I suspect it will not.

Nowhere in the genre of Civil War campaign studies is irrelevant titillation and sensationalism on greater display than in Wiley Sword's *The Confederacy's Last Hurrah*. Sword presented as a prominent character Hood's reluctant fiancée Sarah Buchanan ("Sally" or "Buck") Preston, and spun their relationship into and around virtually all of Hood's actions as commander of the Army of Tennessee from July of 1864 until his resignation in January of 1865—and beyond. According to Sword, Hood was obsessed with Preston (who was by all accounts an attractive and flirtatious ideal of a Southern belle) and that all of his major decisions were in some way influenced by how she would interpret and react to his accomplishments or failures as an army commander. The index of Sword's book listed Preston on 13 pages, but numerous other references to her influence over Hood's actions appeared throughout the book. Similarly, Susan Tarleton—Patrick Cleburne's fiancée—was listed in the index on nine pages. By way of contrast, four of the five brigadier generals killed at Franklin—Otho Strahl, John Adams, John Carter, and States Rights Gist—appeared on fewer pages than either Miss Preston or Miss Tarleton, with only the fallen brigadier general Hiram Granbury appearing more times than the two women. In fact, in a book whose subtitle included the epic Franklin combat, Buck Preston, an immaterial woman in Richmond, garnered more attention from Sword than did fallen generals Adams, Gist, and Carter combined![46]

Earlier authors writing on the Army of Tennessee and the Tennessee Campaign gave Preston little attention, and none at all to Tarleton. Thomas Hay and Stanley Horn, for example, made no mention whatsoever of either woman. Thomas Connelly ignored Tarleton completely and found the Hood-Preston courtship important enough to demand only six sentences in a single paragraph—all based on a single source (Mary Chesnut's diary). Influential and acclaimed historians either completely missed the point that Hood was

---

46 Sword, *The Confederacy's Last Hurrah*, index entries: Strahl (six), Carter (two), Adams (four), and Gist (four).

mesmerized by Preston to the point of delirium, or Wiley Sword sought to create melodrama where none existed.

જે   જી

In Ken Burns's acclaimed 1990 PBS documentary film "The Civil War," narrator David McCullough introduced John Bell Hood during the Atlanta portion of the film by saying that Army of Tennessee commander Joseph Johnston was replaced by "Thirty-three year-old John Bell Hood of Texas. His own men called him 'Old Wooden-head,'" an assertion Burns and co-author Geoffrey Ward later repeated in their 1994 book based upon the film. This perception of Hood as "Old Woodenhead" has become so common that the popular Internet sites Wikipedia and *New World Encyclopedia* list John Bell Hood's nicknames as "Sam" and "Old Woodenhead." There is no historical evidence that anyone ever called Hood "Old Woodenhead."[47]

The genesis of this derogatory epithet seems to be Lost Cause historians (and Joseph Johnston devotees) such as E. A. Pollard. As the wartime editorial page editor for the *Richmond Examiner*, Pollard provided no source whatsoever when he wrote in *Southern History of the War* in 1866 that Hood "had the heart of a lion, but, unfortunately, with it a head of wood." In 1914, James C. Nisbet, possibly paraphrasing Pollard, wrote in *Four Years on the Firing Line*: "It has been said of Hood, 'He was a man with a lion's heart, but a wooden head.'" Because of Hood's physical condition, it is likely that some of his men called him "Old Pegleg," but "Woodenhead" seems to have evolved from later writers who combined "Old Pegleg" with the disparaging remark from Pollard and Nisbet.[48]

In typical fashion, authors have been quick to repeat deprecating labels for Hood, while simultaneously ignoring compliments, such as the one offered by Maj. James Ratchford, who praised Hood's military skill and "the great generosity of his nature, which often led to the remark that he possessed a heart as big as that of an ox."[49]

જે   જી

---

47 Ken Burns and Geoffrey Ward, *The Civil War*, Vintage eBooks, Chapter 4.

48 Pollard, *Southern History of the War*, 86; Nisbet, *Four Years on the Firing Line*, 305.

49 Ratchford, *Some Reminiscences of Persons and Incidents of the Civil War*, 56.

Wiley Sword provided one of the best illustrations of how an author's selective use of historical records can alter their true meaning. In his closing chapter of *The Confederacy's Last Hurrah*, Sword persisted in his attack upon Hood's character by providing the general's oft-repeated postwar comment, "They charge me with having made Franklin a slaughter pen, but, as I understand it, war means fight and fight means kill." Sword did not reveal to the reader where Hood's quote came from or the quote's context—both of which are important. Below is the quotation as framed and presented by Sword:

> Hood, ultimately, was a tragic failure, a sad, pathetic soldier whose ambitions totally outstripped his abilities. Essentially, he was an anachronism: an advocate of outmoded concepts, and a general unable to adapt to new methods or technology. Always prone to blame others, and unable to admit his mistakes, to the bitter end Hood never understood his failings. "They charge me with having made Franklin a slaughter pen," he admonished a group of aging veterans, "but, as I understand it, war means fight and fight means kill." Perhaps Hood's own words, written in anticipation of defending his military career, should serve as an epitaph: "To conquer self is the greatest battle of life." Unfortunately for many of his men, that had never occurred.[50]

Sword's readers would have been better served had he not extracted just the 21-word "war means fight and fight means kill" quotation from the eloquent 1,150-word tribute written by others about Hood. Instead, Sword's readers were led to believe that Hood "admonished a group of aging veterans." In fact, the audience was the Army of Tennessee Association of Louisiana, soldiers who had fought under Hood in Georgia and Tennessee, and the tribute was on Hood's behalf—and there wasn't even a suggestion of admonishment in their words. The entire tribute—an epitaph published in a New Orleans newspaper one week after Hood's death—has been reproduced in an appendix in this book. As a convenience to readers, an excerpt presenting the "war means fight and fight means kill" sentence in context is reproduced below:

> An Eloquent Tribute to the Memory of the Late Gen. J. B. Hood

> To his men it mattered not what doubt of success or what intimation of danger might be suggested; those men felt that Hood would make a grand and stupendously bold

---

50 Sword, *The Confederacy's Last Hurrah*, 439-440.

effort, and they could afford to follow his lead and stand by this man of marvelous daring; that even if defeat should follow they would at least have given to the world another example that would excite wonder and approbation and mark the bloody field with indelible and imperishable fame, serving to teach future generations the limit of human effort and human endurance.

As expressed in his own forceful language, when last with us, five short months since; "They charge me with making Franklin a slaughter pen, but, as I understand it, war means fight and fight means kill."

The recollections of his incomparable daring, his eminent skill, his fidelity to duty, his unselfish patriotism, the splendor of his service, his loftiness of purpose, lead us to realize that in the firmament of our military history a brilliant star has suddenly sunk below the horizon of the present; its departure arouses us to what its brightness was, and brings reflections as to how greatly it transcended and differed in glory from other stars, and we stand watching for lights of equal magnitude, wondering if we shall ever look upon its peer.[51]

Context is crucial to understanding meaning. The contrast between Wiley Sword's extract of 21 words and the original source in which they appear drives that point home.

51 *New Orleans Times-Picayune*, September 8, 1879.

Afterword

"Truth will ultimately prevail where there is pains taken to bring it to light."

— *George Washington*

John Bell Hood knew that his career would be open to criticism. He ended the war as a failure, and was acutely aware that some might find him to be the villain. As a man and as a soldier, he was no fool. But there was one thing he wanted above all—to have the truth presented accurately and in context. Hood knew that he had made mistakes. He only wanted the entire truth to be known.

Now, finally, if much of that unvarnished truth has not yet been fully told, it has been set forth in a much brighter light. The control by a select few of the Hood story and that of the Tennessee Campaign of 1864 is over.

So much of what happened during the American Civil War is still being evaluated today, 150 years after the end of that epic conflict. New scholars, writers, and thinkers review the sources, walk the fields, ponder what happened and what could have been, and set pen to paper. Most scrupulously labor to be fair and to let the facts fall where they may. And this is as it should be, for words written today are nearly as important as deeds performed in the past in forming the public understanding or "truth" of the present and the future. As Sophocles stated so well and succinctly, "What people believe prevails over the truth."

Having lived and worked with the historical memory of John Bell Hood for more than two decades, this book is a welcome addition to the ongoing evolution of his story. The facts and accounts presented here have, for the most part, always been readily available. But humans are subjective creatures of habit. Occasionally our own prisms of understanding take root and shove aside facts that conflict with our preconceived notion of what must have happened. And thus, as this book aptly demonstrates over and over again, otherwise good writers and historians neglect facts and sources that conflict with their version of truth. It is easy to go along with a generally accepted story—even if its origins remain murky at best. But as Sam Hood has demonstrated, this approach extracts a historical cost from those who have come before us, and imposes on present readers a false sense of history and what really happened.

Let *John Bell Hood: The Rise, Fall, and Resurrection of a Confederate General* serve as a cautionary tale for those of us who seek to plow the ground of history.

Eric A. Jacobson

Appendix 1

Excerpt from

Advance and Retreat, by Gen. John Bell Hood

(Pages 161, 162, 181, 290, 292, 294 and 297)

Chapter X

SIEGE OF ATLANTA—DIFFICULTIES OF THE SITUATION— BATTLE OF THE 20TH OF JULY.

Notwithstanding the manifold difficulties and trials which beset me at the period I was ordered to relieve General Johnston, and which, because of unbroken silence on my part, have been the occasion of much injustice manifested in my regard, I formed no intention, till the appearance of General Sherman's Memoirs, to enter fully into the details of the siege of Atlanta, the campaign to the Alabama line, and that which followed into Tennessee.

A feeling of reluctance to cause heart-burnings within the breast of any Confederate, who fulfilled his duty to the best of his ability, has, hitherto, deterred me from speaking forth the truth. Since, however, military movements with which my name is closely connected, have been freely and publicly discussed by different authors,

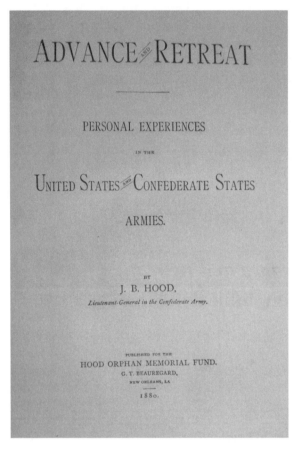

ADVANCE *AND* RETREAT

———

PERSONAL EXPERIENCES

IN THE

UNITED STATES *AND* CONFEDERATE STATES

ARMIES.

BY

J. B. HOOD,

Lieutenant-General in the Confederate Army.

PUBLISHED FOR THE

HOOD ORPHAN MEMORIAL FUND.

G. T. BEAUREGARD,

NEW ORLEANS, LA

1880.

whose representations have not always been accurate, I feel compelled to give an account of the operations of the Army of Tennessee, whilst under my direction.

As already mentioned, the order, assigning me to the command of that Army, was received about II p. m., on the 17th of July. My predecessor, unwilling to await even the dawn of day,

(Page 162)

issued his farewell order that memorable night. In despite of my repeated and urgent appeals to him to pocket all despatches from Richmond, to leave me in command of my own corps, and to fight the battle for Atlanta, he deserted me the ensuing afternoon. He deserted me in violation of his promise to remain and afford me the advantage of his counsel, whilst I shouldered all responsibility of the contest.

I reiterate that it is difficult to imagine a commander placed at the head of an Army under more embarrassing circumstances than those against which I was left to contend on the evening of the 18th of July, 1864. I was, comparatively, a stranger to the Army of Tennessee. Moreover General Johnston's mode of warfare formed so strong a contrast to the tactics and strategy which were practiced in Virginia, where far more satisfactory results were obtained than in the West, that I have become a still more ardent advocate of the Lee and Jackson school. The troops of the Army of Tennessee had for such length of time been subjected to the ruinous policy pursued from Dalton to Atlanta that they were unfitted for united action in pitched battle. They had, in other words, been so long habituated to security behind breastworks that they had become wedded to the " timid defensive" policy, and naturally regarded with distrust a commander likely to initiate offensive operations.

The senior Corps Commander considered he had been supplanted through my promotion, and thereupon determined to resign, in consequence, I have no doubt, of my application to President Davis to postpone the order transferring to me the command of the Army; he however, altered his decision, and concluded to remain with his corps.

The evening of the 18th of July found General Johnston comfortably quartered at Macon, whilst McPherson's and Schofield's Corps were tearing up the Georgia Railroad, between Stone Mountain and Decatur; Thomas's Army was hastening preparations to cross Peach Tree creek, within about six miles of Atlanta; and I was busily engaged in hunting up . . .

(Page 181)

to, at least, create a division. The order was promptly and well executed, and our troops succeeded in taking possession of the enemy's defences in that part of the field. A heavy enfilade fire, however, forced Cheatham to abandon the works he had captured.

Major General G. W. Smith, perceiving that Cheatham had moved out on his left, and having thoroughly comprehended all the orders relative to the battle, moved gallantly forward with his State troops in support of Cheatham's attack, but was eventually forced to retire on account of superiority of numbers in his front. The militia, under his leadership, acted with distinction on this occasion, and Georgia has reason to congratulate herself that her troops were under the command of a soldier of the ability and skill of General G. W. Smith.

Hardee bore off as trophies eight guns and thirteen stands of colors, and, having rectified his line, remained in the presence of the enemy. Cheatham captured five guns and five or six stands of colors.

Notwithstanding the non-fulfilment of the brilliant result anticipated, the partial success of that day was productive of much benefit to the Army. It greatly improved the morale of the troops, infused new life and fresh hopes, arrested desertions, which had hitherto been numerous, defeated the movement of McPherson and Schofield upon our communications, in that direction, and demonstrated to the foe our determination to abandon no more territory without, at least, a manful effort to retain it.

I cannot refrain from mentioning the noble and gallant old hero, Major General W. H. S. Walker, who fell at the head of his division whilst bravely leading it into battle on the 22d of July. He was an officer of the old Army, had served with great distinction in the Mexican war, and was generally beloved by officers and men. On the night of the 21 st, shortly before joining in Hardee's line of march with his troops, he rode by my headquarters, called me aside, and, with characteristic frankness, expressed his appreciation of the grave . . . .

(Page 290)

Headquarters, Six Miles From Nashville" On Franklin Pike, *December 7th, 1864*
Honorable J. A. Seddon.

I withdraw my *recommendation* in favor of the *promotion of Major General Cheatham* for reasons which I will write more fully.

"J. B. HOOD, *General.*"

Headquarters, Six Miles From Nashville " On Franklin Pike, *December 8th, 1864*

Honorable J. A. Seddon, *Secretary of War.* General G. T. Beauregard, *Macon, Ga.*

A good *Lieutenant General* should be sent here at once to *command* the corps now *commanded by Major General Cheatham.* I have no one to *recommend* for the position.

"J. B. HOOD, *General.*"

Headquarters, Six Miles From Nashville" On Franklin Pike, *December 8th, 1864*

Honorable J. A. Seddon.

Major General Cheatham made a failure on the 30th of November, which *will be a lesson to him.* I think it best he should remain in his position for the present. I withdraw my telegrams of yesterday and to-day on this subject.

J. B. HOOD, *General.*"

On the 11th of December I wrote the Hon. Mr. Seddon:

. . . . Major General Cheatham has frankly confessed the great error of which he was guilty, and attaches much blame to himself. While his error lost so much to the country, it has been a severe lesson to him, by which he will profit in the future. In consideration of this, and of his previous conduct, I think that it is best that he should retain, for the present, the command he now holds. . .

The best move in my career as a soldier, I was thus destined to behold come to naught. The discovery that the Army, after a forward march of one hundred and eighty miles, was still, seemingly, unwilling to accept battle unless under the protection of breastworks, caused me to experience grave concern. In my inmost heart I questioned whether or not I would ever succeed in eradicating this evil. It seemed to me I had exhausted every means in the power of one man to remove this stumbling block to the

Army of Tennessee. And I will here inquire, in vindication of its fair name, if any intelligent man of that Army supposes one moment that these same troops, one year previous, would, even without orders to attack, have allowed the enemy to pass them at Rocky-faced Ridge, as he did at Spring Hill.

(Page 292)

CHAPTER XVII

TENNESSEE CAMPAIGN FRANKLIN NASHVILLE RETREAT— TUPELO RETURN TO RICHMOND SURRENDER AT NATCHEZ, MISSISSIPPI.

At early dawn the troops were put in motion in the direction of Franklin, marching as rapidly as possible to overtake the enemy before he crossed the Big Harpeth, eighteen miles from Spring Hill. Lieutenant General Lee had crossed Duck river after dark the night previous, and, in order to reach Franklin, was obliged to march a distance of thirty miles. The head of his column arrived at Spring Hill at 9 a. m. on the 30th, and, after a short rest, followed in the wake of the main body.

A sudden change in sentiment here took place among officers and men: the Army became metamorphosed, as it were, in one night. A general feeling of mortification and disappointment pervaded its ranks. The troops appeared to recognize that a rare opportunity had been totally disregarded, and manifested, seemingly, a determination to retrieve, if possible, the fearful blunder of the previous afternoon and night. The feeling existed which sometimes induces men who have long been wedded to but one policy to look beyond the sphere of their own convictions, and, at least, be willing to make trial of another course of action.

Stewart's Corps was first in order of march; Cheatham followed immediately, and Lieutenant General Lee in rear. . . .

(Page 294)

[Cleburne] expressing himself with an enthusiasm which he had never before betrayed in our intercourse, said, "General, I am ready, and have more hope in the final success of our cause than I have had at any time since the first gun was fired." I replied, "God grant it!" He turned and moved at once toward the head of his Division; a few moments thereafter, he was lost to my sight in the tumult of battle. These last words, spoken to me by this brave and distinguished soldier, I have often recalled; they can never leave my memory, as within forty minutes after he had uttered them, he lay lifeless upon or near the breastworks of the foe.

The two corps advanced in battle array at about 4 p. m., and soon swept away the first line of the Federals, who were driven back upon the main line. At this moment, resounded a concentrated roar of musketry, which recalled to me some of the deadliest struggles in Virginia, and which now proclaimed that the possession of Nashville was once more dependent upon the fortunes of war. The conflict continued to rage with intense fury; our troops succeeded in breaking the main line at one or more points, capturing and turning some of the guns on their opponents.

Just at this critical moment of the battle, a brigade of the enemy, reported to have been Stanley's, gallantly charged, and restored the Federal line, capturing at the same time about one thousand of our troops within the entrenchments. Still the ground was obstinately contested, and, at several points upon the immediate sides of the breastworks, the combatants endeavored to use the musket upon one another, by inverting and raising it perpendicularly, in order to fire; neither antagonist, at this juncture, was able to retreat without almost a certainty of death. It was reported that soldiers were even dragged from one side of the breastworks to the other by men reaching over hurriedly and seizing their enemy by the hair or the collar.

Just before dark Johnson's Division, of Lee's Corps, moved gallantly to the support of Cheatham; although it made a . . . .

(Page 297)

battle of the 20th. He knew also in what manner my orders at Spring Hill had been totally disregarded. After our last brief interview which was followed so quickly by his death, I sought to account for his sudden revolution of feeling and his hopefulness, since he had been regarded as not over sanguine of the final triumph of our cause. I formed the conviction that he became satisfied on the morning of the 30th of November, after having reviewed the occurrences of the previous afternoon and night, and those of the 20th and 22d of July, that I was not the reckless, indiscreet commander the Johnston-Wigfall party represented me; that I had been harshly judged, and feebly sustained by the officers and men; that I was dealing blows and making moves which had at least the promise of happy results, and that we should have achieved decided success on two occasions around Atlanta as well as at Spring Hill. He therefore made a sudden and firm resolution to support me in all my operations, believing that my movements and manner of handling troops were based upon correct principles. It has been said he stated, upon the morning after the affair of Spring Hill, that he would never again allow one of my orders for battle to be disobeyed, if he could prevent it. For these reasons his loss became doubly great to me. The heroic career and death of this distinguished soldier must ever endear the memory of his last words to his commander, and should entitle his name to be inscribed in immortal characters in the annals of our history.

A similar revolution in feeling took place to a great extent among both officers and men, the morning of the day upon which was fought the battle of Franklin; this change —and in a measure the improved *morale* of the Army, which had resulted from a forward movement of one hundred and eighty miles—occasioned the extraordinary gallantry and desperate fighting witnessed on that field.

The subjoined extract from Van Horne's *History of the Army of the Cumberland*, will confirm my assertion in regard.

Appendix 2

Army of Tennessee
Times Picayune, Sept. 8, 1879

An Eloquent Tribute to the Memory of the Late Gen. J. B. Hood

Below is presented an eloquent tribute in the memory of the late Gen. Hood, being the report of the Committee on Resolutions of the Association of the Army of Tennessee, submitted at the meeting held Tuesday night, and were excluded from our morning edition on account of want of space:

Hall of the Association of the Army of Tennessee
Louisiana Division
24 Baronne Street
New Orleans, Sept. 9, 1879

The committee recommends to the association, in view of the death of a member, Gen. John B. Hood, on Saturday, the 30rd of August, 1879, in recognition of his worth and the affection of its members for their former chief, the following memorial:

It having pleased the Great Commander to remove from duty with us our former general and late comrade the heroic John B. Hood, under circumstances that appeal most strongly to our sympathies, and we, deeming it proper at the close of so lofty a career, that we, survivors of his battles and witnesses of his subsequent peaceful vocation among us, should place upon record our appreciation of that noble life, in order that we may not appear unmindful of our loss, as well as that other men may realize the admiration commanded by worth and greatness, do resolve:

That, as former soldiers under his command, we now look back upon his military career as one of the most remarkable known in our day. Graduating from the Military Academy in 1849, he served as an officer of infantry, then of cavalry, and gathered honorable wounds in battle with savages which foreshadowed that brilliant valor which later made him pre-eminent. Promptly at their call he ranged himself in 1861 on the side of the people with whom he was identified. Rapidly promoted through subordinate grades, in March 1862, he was made Brigadier General and placed in command of that devoted band of Texans than whom heroic leader never had more worthy followers. As brigade and as division commander upon fields made glorious by the "incomparable infantry" of the Army of Northern Virginia, Hood shone as one of the most brilliant soldiers about the grand central figure – Lee. Coming to the Army of Tennessee on the eve of one our fiercest struggles, his towering form and gallant bearing, no less then the martial appearance of his veteran division, inspired us with fresh courage; nor can any of us forget his resistless onset and signal success on that bloody field. He emerged from its smoke and carnage a maimed trunk, which inspired by a less lofty soul, had then sought the retirement of the rear or the grave. The command of a corps, at the youthful age of two and thirty, was richly earned reward of almost unexampled valor and devotion. However he fought that corps is known to all who shared in the campaign of Northwest Georgia – when the day's work was fighting, the night's rest entrenching. As general and our commander he delivered staggering blows against the immense army that encircled us at Atlanta, well nigh throwing it back in disastrous flight. Finally, as leader of the "forlorn hope of the Confederacy," in his brilliant and rapid movement of 400 miles into the enemy's rear, he achieved the signal victory of Franklin and spent the expiring but unavailing force of his depleted army against the works of Nashville, having staked all on a final effort, and lost save honor.

That having in four years of constant warfare borne himself with a courage, a devotion and a heroism that have never been excelled: having sacrificed his body, limb by limb to the cause he held so dear; having never despaired, but ever stood firm and steadfast, stoutest when most assailed, strongest when maimed; that in these things John B. Hood has earned the name of hero, and has endeared himself to his survivors in that affectionate regard and respectful homage which are only felt for the noble and the great.

If in this practical age, when all individuality is leveled by the sweeping blade of equality and general education; if after our immortal chieftain Lee, after Albert Sidney Johnston and Stonewall Jackson, there existed a man who on the field, through his great personal prowess, when the hour of battle was approaching, when men desiring to do their utmost in the strife began to look for a stronger arm, a greater mind, a master spirit to uphold their arms, less they themselves might falter; if there was any commander who, riding into the smoke and roar of battle could carry into the ranks a greater sensation of relief, or almost supernatural influence, it was Hood, who rode forward a maimed prodigy of most desperate valor.

To his men it mattered not what doubt of success or what intimation of danger might be suggested; those men felt that Hood would make a grand and stupendously bold effort, and they could afford to follow his lead and stand by this man of marvelous daring; that even if defeat should follow they would at least have given to the world another example that would excite wonder and approbation and mark the bloody field with indelible and imperishable fame, serving to teach future generations the limit of human effort and human endurance.

As expressed in his own forceful language, when last with us, five short months since; "They charge me with making Franklin a slaughter pen, but, as I understand it, war means fight and fight means kill."

The recollections of his incomparable daring, his eminent skill, his fidelity to duty, his unselfish patriotism, the splendor of his service, his loftiness of purpose, lead us to realize that in the firmament of our military history a brilliant star has suddenly sunk below the horizon of the present; its departure arouses us to what its brightness was, and brings reflections as to how greatly it transcended and differed in glory from other stars, and we stand watching for lights of equal magnitude, wondering if we shall ever look upon its peer.

In Fame's eternal volume of the history of war there will always remain one bright, shining page, which neither criticism nor calumny can tarnish or obliterate, on which has been inscribed with his own good sword and trusty right arm, the autograph of John B. Hood.

That as a man we have known him in the trial that have followed our unsuccessful struggle, manifesting as a quiet citizen the same lofty character, the same high principles that had actuated him in more conspicuous places. Modest and unpretentious, courteous and affable, conciliating the love of all who knew him, achieving victories no less renowned than those of war; a man who, having given his youth and his blood for his country, has ended his days among his people in integrity and in honor—a career for the historian to dwell upon; a noble example for posterity to follow.

Geo. A. Williams, Chairman
C.L. Walker
F. L. Richardson
Akfred Bertus
Frank Herron

Appendix 3

Jefferson Davis on Joe Johnston: Excerpt to the Confederate Congress[1]

RICHMOND, VA., March 1, 1865

Col. JAMES PHELAN, Meridian, Miss.:

I received your friendly letter of the 17th of January only about a week ago, and do not see that I can answer it more appropriately than by sending you the annexed copy of a paper which I had prepared for transmission to Congress. As it would, how ever, have been necessary to accompany it, if sent, with a protest against any Congressional interference with the function, exclusively executive, of assigning officers to command, I determined to withhold it rather than, under existing circumstances, to send it to Congress with such a protest as I

---

1 Jefferson Davis's letter to Colonel Phelan, together with the report he wrote to the Confederate Congress regarding Joseph Johnston's war record, can be found in OR 47, pt. 2, 1,303-1,312.

should have felt bound to make. The paper will fully explain my views and Johnston in the matter. I may add that since the accompanying paper was written General Lee has asked that General Johnston should be ordered to report to him for duty, and that I have complied with his wish in the hope that General Johnston's soldierly qualities may be made serviceable to his Country when acting under General Lee's orders, and that in his new position those defects which I found manifested by him when serving as an independent commander will be remedied by the control of the general-in-chief.

Very truly and respectfully, yours,

JEFFN DAVIS

*   *   *

[Enclosure]

The joint resolution of Congress and other manifestations of a desire that General Joseph E. Johnston should be restored to the command of the Army of Tennessee have been anxiously considered by me, and it is with sincere regret that I find myself unable to gratify what I must believe to have become quite a general desire of my countrymen. The expression of this desire has come to me in forms so imposing and from sources so fully entitled to my respect and confidence that I feel it to be due to the people, to justice, and to myself to take the unusual step of discussing matters which would otherwise for public consideration have been passed over in silence and of presenting the reasons which make it impossible for me to assign him again to an important and independent command.

At the commencement of the present war there were few persons in the Confederacy who entertained a more favorable opinion of General Johnston as a soldier than I did. I knew him to be brave and well informed in his profession. I believed that he possessed high capacity for becoming a successful commander in the field. Our relations under the former Government were of a friendly nature and so continued in the new sphere of duty opened to both by the change in the political condition of the country. At different times during the war I have given to General Johnston three very important commands and in each case experience has revealed the fact that with the high qualities above referred to as possessed by him are united defects which unfit him for the conduct of a campaign. When he was relieved from command in July last it was believed that this action on my part would be accepted in its plain and only real significance, as an indication that his conduct of the campaign was disapproved, and that apprehension was entertained that the grave losses already sustained would be followed by still further disasters if he continued in command. Any criticism on this action, however harsh and unjust to me personally, I was prepared to bear in the same silence which the interest of my country has imposed on me, as a duty, in many other instances during the war.

The disclosure of the ground of my conduct it would have been preferable to postpone to a future and more fitting occasion. But it has recently been apparent that there exists in some quarters a purpose, not simply to criticize the past, but to arraign me before the bar of public opinion, and to compel me to do what my judgment and conscience disapproved, or to destroy my power of usefulness by under-mining the confidence of my fellow citizens. It is better to lose that confidence than to retain it at the expense of truth and duty. Yet no man can conduct public affairs with success in a Government like ours unless upheld by time trust and willing aid of the people. I have determined, therefore, now to make the disclosure of the causes which have forced on me the unpleasant duty of declining to gratify the desire of a large portion of the people, as well as the expressed wish of Congress.

General Johnston, on his entering into the Confederate service, was assigned to the command of the Army of the Valley of Virginia, which was then confronted by the enemy in position on the north side of the Potomac. At Harpers Ferry there was a large quantity of materials and machinery for the manufacture of small-arms of the greatest value to the Confederacy. Their removal to places of greater safety was commenced as soon as the necessary arrangements could be made. During the progress of the work General Johnston insisted upon the evacuation of the place, and finally retired from it, as I then thought, and still think, prematurely. The correctness of this opinion is sufficiently shown by the fact that after his withdrawal the working party remained without interruption by the enemy, and removed much valuable property including the heaviest part of the machinery. When General Beauregard was threatened at Manassas by a large column of the enemy, his numerical inferiority and the inactivity of the enemy in the Valley, under General Patterson, evinced the necessity, propriety, and practicability of a prompt march of our Valley army to his aid. General Johnston made serious objections to and expressed doubts as to the practicability of such a movement; and only after repeated and urgent instructions did he move to make the junction proposed. The delay thus occasioned retarded the arrival of the head of his column until after the first conflict had occurred, and prevented a part of his troops from getting into position until the victory had been won. Indeed, we were only saved from fatal defeat at the battle of Manassas by the promptness of General E. Kirby Smith, who, acting without orders, amid moving by a change of direction, succeeded in reaching the battlefield in time to avert disaster. After the battle the forces of General Johnston and General Beauregard remained united. General Johnston, who was in command of the combined forces, constantly declared his inability to assume offensive operations unless furnished with reenforcements, which, as he was several times informed, the Government was unable to supply, and in the fall of 1861 put his troops in entrenched lines covering Centerville.

During the winter he declared that his position was so insecure that it must be abandoned before the enemy could advance, but indicated no other line of defense as the proper one. He was therefore summoned to Richmond in February, 1862, for conference. On inquiry into the character of his position at Centerville he stated that his lines there were untenable, but when asked what new position he proposed to occupy, declared himself ignorant of the topography of the country in his rear. This confession was a great shock to my confidence in him. That a general should have been for many months in command of an army, should have selected a line which he himself considered untenable, and should not have ascertained the topography of the country in his rear, was inexplicable on any other theory than that he had neglected the primary duty of a commander. Engineers were sent by me from Richmond to examine the country and to supply him with the requisite information. General Johnston had announced, however, that his position was favorable as a point from which to advance, if he could be re-enforced. It was, therefore, agreed that he should mobilize his army by sending to the rear all heavy guns and all supplies and luggage, so as to be able to advance or retreat, as occasions might require. The Government was soon afterward surprised by learning that General Johnston had commenced a hasty retreat without giving notice of an intention to do so, though he had just been apprised of the improved prospect of re-enforcing him, and of the hope entertained by me that he would thus be enabled to assume the offensive. The retreat was with-out molestation or even demonstration from the enemy, but was conducted with such precipitation as to involve a heavy loss of supplies. Some valuable artillery was abandoned, a large depot of provisions was burned, blankets, shoes, and saddles were committed to the flames, and this great sacrifice of property was so wanting in apparent justification as to produce a painful impression on the public mind, and to lead to an inquiry by a committee from Congress, which began an investigation into the subject, but did not report before Congress adjourned.

During his retreat General Johnston telegraphed to Richmond to ask at what point he should stop, and afterward admitted at a conference the same want of topographical information previously confessed. When the enemy, instead of pursuing General Johnston in his rapid retreat, changed their base to Fortress Monroe, and made the York River and the Peninsula their line of approach, he was ordered to Yorktown with his army, where General Magruder had for many mouths been actively constructing defensive works to resist an advance up the Peninsula. General Johnston soon pronounced the position untenable, and made another hasty retreat, and with another heavy loss of munitions and armament. He gave notice of his movement, and of the necessity of evacuating Norfolk to the general in command there only after his own retreat had actually commenced. The Secretaries of War and of the Navy had started (the former to Yorktown, the latter to Norfolk) to prevent a hurried evacuation and the consequent loss of the material of war. Too late to restrain General Johnston, they arrived in Norfolk in time to delay General Huger's compliance with his notice until much valuable property was saved. But Norfolk could not long be held after the

Peninsula was in the hands of the enemy, and with it were lost large supplies of all kinds, including machinery which could not be replaced in the Confederacy.

General Johnston halted in his retreat near the Chickahominy, but after spending some days in selecting a position for defense against the advancing enemy, suddenly crossed that stream without notice to the Government and retreated upon Richmond. He remained inactive in front of Richmond, making no entrenchments to cover his position, which might enable him to assume the offensive with the greater part of the army. He again neglected the proper reconnaissance, and failed to have the roads laid down on topographical maps a want of foresight sorely felt by our army, when afterward, under General Lee, endeavoring to cut off McClellan's retreat. He suffered the enemy to bring up their heavy guns, supplies, and troops, without molestation; to build bridges across the Chickahominy, and to cross a portion of their army and make entrenchments, not only without resistance, but without his knowledge of these important military operations. When, on a sudden freshet in the Chickahominy, a body of the enemy's troops was found to be on this side of the stream, an attack was made under the impression that they were cut off by the flood from reinforcements and entirely at our mercy. The battle was disastrous, because the enemy was rapidly re-enforced across bridges the existence of which had not been ascertained by our commander, and because our troops attacked an enemy whom they did not know to be entrenched assailed the front of a position which might have been easily turned by cross-roads which were in constant use by the people of the neighborhood, but which were unknown to our officers. The general fell severely wounded in this engagement, in which he was conspicuous for personal daring. But this gallantry could not redeem the want of that foresight which is requisite for a commander, and the battle was, as I have said, a failure. His wound rendered him unfit for further service in the field for some months, and terminated his first important command, which he had administered in a manner to impair my confidence in his fitness to conduct a campaign for a Government possessed of only very limited material resources, and whose armies are numerically so inferior to those of the enemy as to demand from its generals the greatest vigilance and activity, the best discipline amid organization with careful provision and rigid economy. The loss of supplies during the time he was in command had been great, and our difficulties for the want of them so distressing as to cripple our military operations to a far greater extent than can be appreciated.

On General Johnston's fall General Lee assumed the command of the army. He at once made an entrenched line by which the city could be covered with part of his forces, and was thus enabled to cross the Chickahominy with the main body, and, with the aid of the troops from the Valley, under General Jackson, to attack the enemy in flank and rear, achieving the series of glorious victories in the summer of 1862, which made our history illustrious. As soon as General Johnston reported himself fit for duty he was again entrusted by me with an important command, for, though my confidence in him had been much shaken, it had not yet been destroyed. He had been tested in the immediate command of an army, and in that position had not justified the high opinion

I had previously entertained of him. He was now assigned to a different class of duties to the general supervision and control of several armies, each under an immediate commander, to whom was entrusted the direct duty of organizing, disciplining, and supplying his own troops. His department included the Districts of Tennessee, Alabama, and Mississippi, with power to command in person wherever he should consider his services most needed, and to transfer troops at discretion. He thus controlled the army under General Bragg in Tennessee, those of Generals Pemberton and Gardner at Vicksburg and Port Hudson, and that of General Forney at Mobile and other points in Alabama. The new assignment was of higher grade, and to a more enlarged sphere than the former, embracing within its limits my own home and those of my nearest relatives and friends. It is, therefore, apparent that I felt no disposition to depreciate the merits of General Johnston, or to deprive him of an opportunity of rendering such conspicuous service as would secure military fame for himself if private considerations were needed, in addition to a sense of public duty, in order to insure my earnest support of all his efforts for the good of the country, the motive of personal interest was not absent. Few were exposed to a more total loss of property than myself in the event of his disastrous failure in this new command.

When General Grant made his demonstration on Vicksburg General Johnston failed to perceive its significance and did not repair to that vital point in his department until ordered from Richmond to do so. He arrived, as he reported, too late. He did not proceed to the head-quarters of the forces in the field, but stopped at Jackson and undertook from there to direct the operations of the army, though, as was shown by subsequent events, he was not well informed of the situation. After the investment of Vicksburg, General Johnston remained inactive near Canton and Jackson, stating his inability to attack Grant, notwithstanding very urgent requests to do so. He was thereupon pressed to attack the forces of Banks at Port Hudson and rescue the army of General Gardner, but declined on the ground that he feared Grant would seize the occasion to advance upon Jackson, which place he considered too important to be exposed. Grant was then investing Vicksburg. After both Vicksburg and Port Hudson had been captured without one blow on his part to relieve either, a detachment was sent by General Grant from Vicksburg to capture Jackson. The enemy, it appears, was surprised to find the place held in force, and sent back to Vicksburg for re-enforcements. No attempt was made by General Johnston to improve the opportunity thus presented by attacking the isolated detachment of the enemy in his front. He remained within his lines and permitted Grant again to concentrate a large force against the third and last section of that army. Not once during the entire campaign did he act on the maxim of attacking the foe in detail, a rule peculiarly applicable when an army is contending against an enemy superior in numbers. The familiar historical example of the war conducted by Frederick the Great against three armies, the junction of any two of which would have caused the downfall of his State, illustrates the value of this maxim, and serves to show how much, under the most adverse conditions, may be achieved by a general who, to professional skill, unites genius and energy.

No sooner had the enemy commenced investing Jackson than General Johnston pronounced it untenable. He had been there for many weeks, and to insure the successful defense of the place left Gardner's army at Port Hudson to its fate. Yet when the moment of trial came he decided that the lines of defense had been badly located, and that the works were so imperfect and insufficient as to render the position untenable. Weeks had been passed by the general commanding in the town with an army of between 20,000 and 30,000 men under his orders, and he had neither remedied defective location of lines nor given the works time requisite strength. Jackson was evacuated, and General Johnston withdrew his army to Eastern Mississippi. The evacuation of Jackson, as of Centerville, was marked by one of the most serious and irreparable sacrifices of property that has occurred during the war a loss for which, in my judgment, no sufficient explanation has been given. The railroad bridge across the Pearl River at Jackson had been broken. It was necessary to rebuild it sufficiently to remove cars across, and there was a very large accumulation of rolling-stock on the western side of the stream which, without the bridge, could not be saved if Jackson were evacuated. Under these circumstances General Johnston, with over 20,000 men, suffered this gap to remain without an effort to fill it, although the work could with little difficulty have been completed in a manner to answer the requirements of the occasion. In consequence of this neglect a very large number of locomotives, said to be about ninety, and several hundred cars, were lost. We have never recovered from the injury to the transportation service occasioned by this failure on his part.

General Johnston's second campaign thus closed with the loss of every important position which the enemy had attacked. Not only was Vicksburg forced to surrender, with its garrison, but Port Hudson, with its garrison had been captured when he was able to relieve it, but abstained from making the movement lest he should thereby hazard the safety of Jackson, which, in its turn, was lost with the sacrifice of most valuable property. My confidence in General Johnston's fitness for separate command was now destroyed. The proof was too complete to admit of longer doubt that he was deficient in enterprise, tardy in movement, defective in preparation, and singularly neglectful of the duty of preserving our means of supply and transportation, although experience should have taught him their value and the difficulty of procuring them. It should be added, that neither in this nor in his previous command had it been possible for me to obtain from General Johnston any communications of his plans or purposes beyond vague statements of an intention to counteract the enemy as their plans might be developed. No indication was ever presented to induce the belief that he considered it proper to form combinations for attack as well as defense, and nothing is more certain than the final success of an enemy who with superior forces can continue his operations without fear of being assailed, even when exposing weakness and affording opportunities of which a vigilant adversary would avail himself for attack. I came to the conclusion, therefore, that it would be imprudent to entrust General Johnston with another independent command for active operations in the field. Yet I yielded my convictions, and gave him a third trial, under the following circumstances:

General Bragg, at his own request, was relieved from the command of the Army of Tennessee after the battle of Missionary Ridge, and was succeeded by Hardee, his senior lieutenant general. This officer, distrusting his own ability, earnestly requested the selection of another commander for the army, and a most urgent and general solicitation was made that General Johnston should be assigned to that duty. After relieving General Bragg, of our five generals Lee and Beauregard were the only officers of that grade in the field except General Johnston. Neither of the first two could properly be withdrawn from the position occupied by them and General Johnston thus remained the only officer of rank superior to that of lieutenant-general who was available. The act of Congress authorizing the appointment of general officers with temporary rank had not then been passed. There seemed to be scarcely a choice left, but my reluctance to risk the disasters which I feared would result from General Johnston's assignment to this command could with difficulty be surmounted. Very pressing requests were made to me by members of Congress. The assignment of this commander was said to be demanded by the common voice of the army, the press, and the people; and, finally, some of my advisers in the Cabinet represented that it might well be the case that his assignment with the disasters apprehended from it would be less calamitous than the injury arising from an apparent indifference to the wishes and opinions of the officers of the State governments, of many members of Congress, and of other prominent citizens. I committed the error of yielding to these suggestions against my own deliberate convictions, and General Johnston entered upon his third important command that of the army designed to recover the State of Tennessee from the enemy. In February, 1864, he was informed of the policy of the Government for his army. It was proposed to re-enforce him largely, and that he should at once advance and assume the offensive for the recovery of at least a part of the State of Tennessee. For this purpose he was advised to accumulate as rapidly as possible sufficient supplies for an advance, and assured that the re-enforcing troops should be sent to him as soon as he was prepared for the movement. Until such time it was deemed imprudent to open the country to incursions of the enemy by withdrawing from other positions, or to delay accumulation of supplies by increasing the number of consumers at the front. The winter was dry and mild. The enemy, as it was reported, not expecting any active movement on our part, had sent most of his horses back to Kentucky to be recruited for the spring campaign.

General Hardee had, just before relinquishing the command, reported our army as fully rested and recovered from the effect of its retreat from Missionary Ridge. He represented that there was effectiveness and sufficient supply in the ordnance, quartermasters, and commissary departments; that the artillery was in good condition, the spirits of the troops excellent, and the army ready to fight. General Bragg sent to General Johnston all the information deemed valuable which had been acquired during his continuance of command. The Government spared nothing of men and materials at its disposal. Batteries made for General Lee's army were diverted and sent to General Johnston, and he was informed that troops would be sent to re-enforce him a soon as he had collected supplies in depot for a forward movement. Absentees were rapidly returning to the army when he assumed command. Several thousand men had joined their regiments within the twenty days immediately preceding his arrival at Dalton. Troops were withdrawn from Charleston, Savannah, and Mobile to aid him. The main army of Alabama and Mississippi, under General Polk, was placed at his disposal. Cavalry was returned from East Tennessee to assist him.

General Johnston made no attempt to advance. As soon as he assumed command he suggested deficiencies and difficulties to be encountered in an offensive movement, which he declared himself unable to overcome. The enemy commenced advancing in May, and General Johnston began retreating. His retreat was not marked by any general engagement, nor does he appear to have attempted to cut off any portion or detachment of the enemy while they were marching around his flanks. Little fighting was done by his army, except when attacked in entrenchments. His course in abandoning a large extent of country abounding in supplies, amid offering from its mountainous character admirable facilities for defense, so disheartened and demoralized the army that he himself announced by telegram large losses from straggling and desertion. At Allatoona, his position being almost impregnable, the enemy were compelled to make extensive flank movements which exposed them to attack; but they were allowed by General Johnston, who had marched out of his entrenchments, to interpose themselves between him and the ridge without receiving any assault upon their lengthened and exposed flank. He was then maneuvered out of a most formidable position with slight loss to the enemy. By a repetition of a similar course he was driven, without any apparent capacity to help himself through an entire district of mountain passes and defiles, and across rivers until he was finally brought to the suburbs of Atlanta.

No information was sent to me which tended to dispel the apprehension then generally expressed that Atlanta also was to be abandoned when seriously threatened. Some of those who had most earnestly urged General Johnston's assignment to the command of the army when it was at Dalton now with equal earnestness pressed his prompt removal.

The consequences of changing a commander in the midst of a campaign were regarded to be so embarrassing that, even when it was considered by others too plainly necessary for doubt or delay, I preferred, by direct inquiry of General Johnston, to obtain that which had been too long withheld his plan for future operations. A telegram was sent to him insisting on a statement of his purpose, so as to enable me to anticipate events. His reply showed that he intended leaving the entrenchments of Atlanta under the guard of the Georgia militia, and moving out with his army into the field. This was regarded as conclusive that Atlanta was also to be given up without a battle, and I could perceive no ground for hoping that General Johnston, who had failed to check the enemy's march from Dalton to Atlanta, through a country abounding in strong positions for defense, would be able to prevent the further advance through a level country to Macon, amid the consequent severance of the Confederacy by a line passing through the middle of Georgia. He was therefore relieved. If I had been slow to consent to his assignment to that command, I was at least equally slow to agree to his removal.

I could not discover between the forces of General Johnston and General Sherman any such disparity as was alleged, nor do I believe that our army in any military department since the beginning of the war has been so nearly equal in numbers with the enemy as in this last campaign of General Johnston. His report, dated October 20, 1864, states that he had lost in killed and wounded in infantry and artillery during this campaign, 10,000 men, and from all other causes, principally slight sickness, 4,700. Of his cavalry the losses are not stated. His report, however, omits to state that his returns to the Adjutant-General's Office exhibit a loss of over 7,000 captured by the enemy. His losses, therefore, in infantry and artillery were about 22,000, without including cavalry. Yet, notwithstanding these heavy losses, General Johnston's returns of July 10, a few days before his removal from command, show an aggregate present of 73,849 men, of whom 50,932 are reported to be effective. But his return of the previous month shows that among those not reported as effective were quite 11,000 men performing active service on extra duty, and as non-commissioned staff officers and musicians. The available force present must therefore have been about 62,000 men. The aggregate present of the 10th of March previous (after the arrival of the part of Hardee's corps that had been detached, although too late to aid General Polk in opposing Sherman's raid through Mississippi) was 54,806, and the effective present 42,408. It thus appears that so largely was General Johnston reinforced that after all the losses of his campaign his army had increased about 19,000 men present, and about the same number of men available for active duty.

As the loss in killed and wounded, sick and prisoners, in infantry and artillery alone was 22,000 men, and would probably be swollen to 25,000 by adding the loss in cavalry, and as the force available on the 10th of July was about 62,000, it is deduced that General Johnston had been in command of an army of about 85,000 men fit for active duty to oppose Sherman, whose effective force was not believed to have been much in excess of that number. The entire force of the enemy was considerably greater than the numbers I have mentioned, and so was General Johnston's; but in considering the merits of the campaign it is not necessary to do more than compare the actual strength of the armies which might have joined the issue of battle. When it is considered that with forces thus matched General Johnston was endeavoring to hold a mountainous district of our own country with numerous fortified positions, while the enemy was in the midst of a hostile population and with a long line of communications to guard, it is evident that it was not the want of men or means which caused the disastrous failure of his campaign. My opinion of General Johnston's unfitness for command has ripened slowly and against my inclinations into a conviction so settled that it would be impossible for me again to feel confidence in him as the commander of an army in the field. The power to assign generals to appropriate duties is a function of trust confided to me by my countrymen. That trust I have ever been ready to resign at my country's call, but while I hold it, nothing shall induce me to shrink from its responsibilities or to violate the obligations it imposes.

Bibliography

NEWSPAPERS

Augusta Constitutionalist
Chicago Tribune
Hillsboro Ohio News Herald
Louisville Daily Journal
Mobile Advertiser and Register
Nashville Banner
Nashville Tennessean
New Orleans Daily Picayune
New Orleans Picayune
New Orleans Times
New York Herald
New York Times
New York Tribune
San Antonio Herald

PERIODICALS

Blue and Gray
Century Quarterly
Civil War Gazette

Confederate Veteran
Georgia Historical Quarterly
National Tribune
North American Review
North and South
The Lost Cause, Quarterly Journal of the Kentucky Division (Sons of Confederate Veteran)

NEWSLETTERS

John Bell Hood Historical Society Newsletter

THESIS

Brown, Thomas, "John Bell Hood: Extracting Truth from History." A Thesis Presented to the Faculty of the Department of History, San Jose State University, August 2011.

GOVERNMENT PUBLICATIONS

War of the Rebellion: A Compellation of the Official Records of the Union and Confederate Armies, Series I (Washington, DC, 1880-1901).

Williamson, R.S., Official Report, "Explorations and Surveys for a Railroad Route from the Mississippi River to the Pacific Ocean. Explorations for a Railroad Route from the Sacramento Valley to the Columbia River," U.S. War Department, 1855.

MANUSCRIPTS AND COLLECTIONS

Barker Center Archives, University of Texas, Austin, TX
     William Stanton letter to Mary Moody

Church of Jesus Christ of Latter Day Saints, Salt Lake City, UT
     LDS Church Archives, W.G. Davenport Memoirs

Emory University, Atlanta, GA
     Jefferson Davis Papers

Gilder Lehrman Collection, New York, NY
     Telegram, John Bell Hood to Braxton Bragg

Harvard University, Cambridge, MA
    Joseph Wheeler Papers

Hood Personal Papers (Anonymous)
    John Bell Hood Personal Papers

Ohio Historical Society, Columbus, OH
    Thomas Taylor Letters

Rosanna A. Blake Library of Confederate History, Marshall Univ., Huntington, WV
    Oration of Gen. J. B. Hood, Survivor's Association, Charleston, SC, Dec. 12, 1875

Southern Historical Collection, UNC-Chapel Hill, Chapel Hill, NC
    Virgil Murphey Diary
    John Copley, A Sketch of the Battle of Franklin, Tennessee: With Reminiscences
of Camp Douglas

Tennessee State Library and Archives, Nashville, TN
    Bell Family Papers
    Brown-Ewell Papers

University of Alabama, Tuscaloosa, AL
    Henry Clayton Papers

University of the South, Sewanee, TN
    Leonidas Polk Papers

Wesley Clark Collection, Dallas, TX
    Transcript of Tennessee Senator Gustavus Henry's speech, November 29, 1864

Western Reserve Historical Society, Cleveland, OH
    Braxton Bragg Papers

FILMS

Wide Awake Films, *The Battle of Franklin: Five Hours in the Valley of Death*, Kansas City MO,
2005.

INTERNET

Catton, Bruce. "Rock of Chickamauga," book review of F. F. McKinney's *Education in Violence.* http://home.earthlink.net/~oneplez/majorgeneralgeorgehthomasblogsite.

"Funeral of General Robert E. Lee." www.gdg.org/Research/People/RELEE, Virginia Military Institute Archives, "The Funeral of General Robert E. Lee," 1-2; William Nalle letter, "The Funeral of General Robert E. Lee," March 4, 2011.

BOOKS AND ARTICLES

Ambrose, Stephen, *Duty, Honor Country: A History of West Point.* Baltimore, MD: Johns Hopkins University Press, 1966.

Bailey, Anne J., *The Chessboard of War: Sherman and Hood in the Autumn Campaigns of 1864.* Lincoln, NE: University of Nebraska Press, 2000.

Bailey, Ronald, *The Battles for Atlanta.* Alexandria, VA: Time-Life Books, 1985.

Bales, Stephen, *Natural Histories: Stories from the Tennessee Valley.* Knoxville, TN: University of Tennessee Press, 2007.

Beach, John, *History of the 40th Ohio Volunteer Infantry.* London, OH: Shepard and Craig Printers, 1884.

Benet, Stephen Vincent, *John Brown's Body.* Lanham, MD: Ivan R. Dee Publisher, 1990.

Blight, David W., *Race and Reunion: The Civil War in American Memory.* Cambridge, MA: The Belknap Press of Harvard University Press, 2001.

Blount, Russell Jr., *The Battles of New Hope Church.* New Orleans, LA: Pelican Publishing, 2010.

Bobrick, Benson, *Master of War: The Life of George H. Thomas.* New York, NY: Simon and Schuster, 2009.

Bonds, Russell, *War Like the Thunderbolt: The Battle and Burning of Atlanta.* Yardley, PA: Westholme Publishing, 2009.

Bowden, Scott and Bill Ward, *Last Chance for Victory: Robert E. Lee and the Gettysburg Campaign.* Cambridge, MA: Da Capo Press, 2001.

Bradley, Michael R., *It Happened In the Civil War.* Guilford, CT: Globe Pequot Press, 2002.

Buck, Irving A., *Cleburne and His Command.* Jackson, TN: McCowat-Mercer Press, 1959.

Buell, Thomas B., *The Warrior Generals: Combat Leadership in the Civil War.* New York, NY: Three Rivers Press, 1997.

Burns, Ken, *The Civil War.* Vintage eBooks, Chapter 4.

Burton, Brian K., *Extraordinary Circumstances: The Seven Days Battles.* Bloomington, IN: Indiana University Press, 2001.

Carpenter, Noel, *A Slight Demonstration: Decatur October 1864, A Clumsy Beginning of Gen. John B. Hood's Tennessee Campaign.* Austin, TX: Carol Powell, publisher, 2007.

Casdorph, Paul D., *Confederate General R. S. Ewell: Robert E. Lee's Hesitant Commander.* Lexington, KY: The University of Kentucky Press, 2004.

Castel, Albert, *Decision in the West: The Atlanta Campaign of 1864*. Lawrence, KS: University Press of Kansas, 1992.

Chesnut, Mary, *A Diary from Dixie*, Isabella Martin and Myrta Avary, eds. Avenel, NJ: Gramercy Books, 1997.

Clark, Charles T., *Opdycke's Tigers—125th Ohio, Published by Direction of the 125th OVI Association*. Columbus, OH: Sparr & Glenn, 1895.

Connelly, Thomas, *Autumn of Glory: The Army of Tennessee 1862-1865*. Baton Rouge, LA: Louisiana State University Press, 1971.

——, *The Marble Man: Robert E. Lee and his Image in American Society*. Baton Rouge, LA: Louisiana State University Press, 1977.

——, and Barbara Bellows, *God and General Longstreet: The Lost Cause and the Southern Mind*. Baton Rouge, LA: Louisiana University Press, 1982.

Courtwright, David, *Dark Paradise: A History of Opiate Addiction in America*. Cambridge, MA: Harvard University Press, 1982.

Cox, Jacob D., *Atlanta*. New York, NY: Charles Scribner's Sons, 1882.

Crook, George, *General George Crook: His Autobiography*. Norman, OK: University of Oklahoma Press, 1986.

Cunningham, Sumner A., *Reminiscences of the 41st Tennessee: The Civil War in the West*, John A. Simpson, ed. Shippensburg, PA: White Mane Books, 2001.

Daniel, Larry, *Soldiering in the Army of Tennessee: A Portrait of Life in the Confederate Army*. Chapel Hill, NC: University of North Carolina Press, 1991.

Daniel, Lizzie Cary, *Confederate Scrap Book*. Richmond, VA: J. H. Hill Printing Co., 1893.

Davis, Jefferson, *The Papers of Jefferson Davis: September 1864 – May 1865*. Baton Rouge, LA: Louisiana State University Press, 2004.

——. *The Rise and Fall of the Confederate Government*, 2 vols. New York, NY: D. Appleton and Company, 1881.

Davis, Nicholas A., *Chaplain Davis and Hood's Texas Brigade*, Donald E. Everett, ed. Baton Rouge, LA: Louisiana State University Press, 1962.

Davis, Stephen, *Atlanta Will Fall: Sherman, Joe Johnston and the Yankee Heavy Battalions*. Wilmington, DE: Scholarly Resources, 2001.

——, "A Reappraisal of the Generalship of John Bell Hood in the Battles for Atlanta," in Theodore P. Savas and David A. Woodbury, ed., *The Campaign for Atlanta and Sherman's March to the Sea*, 2 vols. Campbell, CA: Savas Woodbury Publishers, 1992.

——. "John Bell Hood's Historiographical Journey; or, How Did a Confederate General Become a Laudanum Addict?," in *Confederate Generals in the Western Theater, Vol. III, Essays on America's Civil War*, Lawrence Hewitt and Arthur Bergeron, Jr., eds. Knoxville, TN: University of Tennessee Press, 2011.

Davis, William C., *Look Away!: A History of the Confederate States of America*. New York, NY: Free Press, 2002.

Davison, Eddy and Daniel Foxx, *Nathan Bedford Forrest: In Search of an Enigma*. Gretna, LA: Pelican Publishing, 2007.

Dowdey, Clifford and Louis Manarin. *The Wartime Papers of Robert E. Lee*. New York, NY: De Capo Press, 1961.

Dury, Ian, *Confederate Infantryman 1861-1865*. Singapore: Reed International Books, Ltd., 2007.

Dyer, John P., *The Gallant Hood*. New York, NY: Konecky & Konecky, 1950.

Ecelberger, Gary, *The Day Dixie Died: The Battle of Atlanta*. New York, NY: Martin's Press, 2010.

Eicher, David, *The Civil War in Books: An Analytical Bibliography*. Champaign, IL: University of Illinois Press, 1997.

Elliott, Sam Davis, *Soldier of Tennessee: General Alexander P. Stewart and the Civil War in the West*. Baton Rouge, LA: Louisiana State University Press, 1999.

———. *Doctor Quintard, Chaplain C.S.A. and Second Bishop of Tennessee: The Memoir and Civil War Diary of Charles Todd Quintard*. Baton Rouge, LA: Louisiana State University Press, 2003.

Ellis, Barbara, *The Moving Appeal: Mr. McClanahan, Mrs. Dill, and the Civil War's Great Civil War Run*. Macon, GA: Mercer University Press, 2003.

Emory, Thomas M. *Robert E. Lee: A Biography*. New York, NY: W.W. Norton and Company, 1995.

Field, Henry, *Bright Skies and Dark Shadows*. Freeport, NY: Books for Libraries Press, 1970.

Fleherty, S.F., *Our Regiment: A History of the 102nd Illinois Infantry Volunteers*. Chicago, IL: Brewster & Hanscom, 1865.

Foote, Shelby, *The Civil War: A Narrative*, 3 vols. New York, NY: Random House, 1974.

Foster, Gaines, *Ghosts of the Confederacy: Defeat, the Lost Cause and the Emergence of the New South*. New York, NY: Oxford University Press, 1987.

Foster, Samuel T., *One of Cleburne's Command: The Civil War Reminiscences and Diary of Capt. Samuel T. Foster, Granbury's Texas Brigade, CSA*, Norman D. Brown, ed. Austin, TX: University of Texas Press, 1980.

Freeman, Douglas S., *Lee's Lieutenants: A Study in Command*, 3 vols. New York, NY: Charles Scribner's Sons, 1942.

French, Samuel, *Two Wars: An Autobiography of General Samuel G. French*. Nashville, TN, 1901.

Garrison, Webb, Jr., *Atlanta and the War*. Nashville, TN: Thomas Nelson Publishing, 1996.

———, *Strange Battles of the Civil War*. New York, NY: Bristol Park Books, 2009.

Gibboney, Douglas Lee, *Scandals of the Civil War*. Shippenburg, PA: Burd Street Press, 2005.

Gillum, James F., *The Battle of Spring Hill: Twenty-five Hours to Tragedy*. Franklin, TN: James F. Gillum, 2004.

Grant, U. S., *General Grant's Letters to a Friend, 1861-1880*, James Grant Wilson, ed. New York and Boston: T.Y. Crowell and Company, 1897 (1973).

———, *Personal Memoirs of U. S. Grant*, 2 vols., E. B. Long, ed. New York, NY: Charles Webster and Co., 1886.

Groom, Winston, *Patriotic Fire: Andrew Jackson and Jean Laffite at the Battle of New Orleans*. New York, NY: Alfred Knopf Publisher, 2006.

Groom, Winston, *Shrouds of Glory*. New York, NY: Atlantic Monthly Press, 1995.

Hamlin, Percy, *"Old Bald Head" (General R. S. Ewell): The Portrait of a Soldier*. Strasburg, VA: Shenandoah Publishing House, 1940.

Hardesty, Hiram H., *The Military History of Ohio*. New York, NY: H. H. Hardesty, Publisher, 1889.

Haskell Memoirs: *The Personal Narrative of a Confederate Officer*. New York, NY: G. P. Putnam's Sons, 1966.

Hattaway, Herman and Archer Jones, *How the North Won: A Military History of the Civil War*. Champaign, IL: University of Illinois Press, 1983.

Hay, Thomas R., *Hood's Tennessee Campaign*. Dayton, OH: Morningside, 1976.

Henderson, George, *The Science of War: A Collection of Essays and Lectures*. London: Longmans, Green and Co., 1908.

Henry, Robert S., *The Story of the Confederacy*. Cambridge, MA: DaCapo Press.

Hood, John Bell, *Advance and Retreat: Experiences in the United States and Confederate States Armies*. Secaucus, NJ: Blue and Gray Press, 1985.

Horn, Stanley, *The Army of Tennessee*. Norman, OK: University of Oklahoma Press, 1993.

Horn, Stanley, *The Decisive Battle of Nashville*. Baton Rouge, LA: Louisiana State University Press.

Jacobson, Eric A., *For Cause and For Country: A Study of the Affair at Spring Hill and the Battle of Franklin*. Franklin, TN: O'More Publishing, 2006.

Jenkins and Stauffer, *The State of Jones: The Small Southern County that Seceded from the Confederacy*. New York, NY: Anchor Books, 2010.

Johnson, Robert Underwood and Clarence Buell, *Battles and Leaders of the Civil War*, 4 vols. New York, NY: The Century Company, 1884, 1888.

Johnston, Joseph E., *Narrative of Military Operations Directed During the Civil War*. New York: Da Capo Press, 1990.

Jones, Wilmer, *Generals in Blue and Gray*, 2 vols. Mechanicsville, PA: Stackpole Books, 2004.

Jordan, Weymouth T., *North Carolina Troops, 1861-1865, a Roster*. Wilmington, NC: Broadfoot Publishing Company, 1990.

Joslyn, Mauriel, *A Meteor Shining Brightly: Essays on the Life and Career of Major General Patrick R. Cleburne*. Macon, GA: Mercer University Press, 2000.

Knight, James, *The Battle of Franklin: When the Devil Had Full Possession of the Earth*. Charleston, SC: The History Press, 2009.

Livermore, Thomas, *Numbers and Losses in the Civil War in America, 1861-1865*. Boston and New York: Houghton Mifflin and Company, 1900.

Longacre, Edward G., *A Soldier to the Last: Maj. Gen. Joseph Wheeler in Blue and Gray*. Dulles, VA: Potomac Books, 2007.

Losson, Christopher, *Tennessee's Forgotten Warriors: Frank Cheatham and His Confederate Division*. Knoxville, TN: University of Tennessee Press, 1989.

Lowry, Thomas P., *The Story the Soldiers Wouldn't Tell: Sex in the Civil War*. Mechanicsburg, PA: Stackpole Books, 1994.

Lundberg, John, *The Finishing Stroke: Texans in the 1864 Tennessee Campaign*. Abilene, TX: McWhiney Foundation Press, 2002.

McDonough, James L. and Thomas Connelly, *Five Tragic Hours: The Battle of Franklin*. Knoxville, TN: The University of Tennessee Press, 1991.

McKay, John, James Bradford and Rebeccah Pawlowski, *The Big Book of Civil War Sites: From Fort Sumpter to Appomattox, a Visitors Guide to the History, Personalities, and Places of America's Battlefields*. Guilford, CT: Globe Piquot, 2011.

McKinney, Francis F., *Education in Violence: The Life of General George H. Thomas and the History of the Army of the Cumberland*. Chicago, IL: Americana House Inc., 1991.

McMurray, W. J., *History of the 20th Tennessee Infantry Regiment*. Nashville, TN: Publication Committee, United Confederate Veterans, 1904.

McMurry, Richard, *Atlanta 1864: Last Chance for the Confederacy*. Lincoln, NE: University of Nebraska Press, 2000.

——. *John Bell Hood and the War for Southern Independence*. Lincoln, NE: University of Nebraska Press, 1982.

———, *Two Great Rebel Armies: An Essay in Confederate Military History.* Chapel Hill, NC: University of North Carolina Press, 1989.

McNeilly, James H., "With Hood Before Nashville," *Confederate Veteran* (June 1918), vol. 26, 253.

McPherson, James, *Battle Cry of Freedom.* New York, NY: Oxford University Press, 1988.

McWhiney, Grady and Perry Jamieson, *Attack and Die: Civil War Military Tactics and the Southern Heritage.* Tuscaloosa, AL: University of Alabama Press, 1984.

Miller, Brian C., *John Bell Hood and the Fight for Civil War Memory.* Knoxville, TN: University of Tennessee Press, 2010.

Miller, Francis T. and Robert S. Lanier, *The Photographic History of the Civil War*, 10 vols. New York, NY: The Review of Reviews Company, 1912.

Mitchell, Adele H., *The Letters of Major General James E. B. Stuart.* Centreville, VA: Stuart-Mosby Historical Society, 1990.

Morley, Christopher, *Modern Essays.* New York, NY: Harcourt, Brace and Company, 1921.

Mosman, Chesley, *The Rough Side of War: The Civil War Journal of Chesley A. Mosman, 1st Lieutenant, Company D, 59th Illinois Volunteer Infantry Regiment*, Arnold Gatesvol, ed. 59. New York, NY: Basin Publishing Company, 1987.

Muzzey, David S., *The United States of America: Through the Civil War.* Oxford, UK: Ginn & Company, 1922.

Napoleon's Maxims of War. New York, NY: C. A. Alvord Printer, 1861.

Nelson, Larry, *Bullets, Ballots, and Rhetoric: Confederate Policy for the U.S. Presidential Contest of 1864.* Tuscaloosa, AL: University of Alabama Press, 1980.

Nisbet, James Cooper, *Four Years on the Firing Line.* Chattanooga, TN: The Imperial Press, 1914.

O'Connor, Richard, *Hood: Cavalier General.* New York, NY: Prentice-Hall, 1949.

Patterson, Gerard, *Rebels From West Point.* Mechanicsville, PA: Stackpole Books, 2002.

Pollard, Edward A., *Southern History of the War: The Last Year of the War.* New York, NY: C. B. Richardson Publisher, 1866.

Ratchford, James, *Memoirs of a Confederate Staff Officer: From Bethel to Bentonville*, ed. Evelyn Sieburg. Shippensburg, PA: White Mane Books, 1998.

Ratchford, James, *Some Reminiscences of Persons and Incidents of the Civil War.* Austin, TX: Shoal Creek Publishers, 1971.

Register of Graduates and Former Cadets 1802-1988. West Point, NY: USMA Association of Graduates, 1988.

Ridley, B. L., *Battles and Sketches of the Army of Tennessee.* Mexico, MO: Missouri Publishing, 1906.

Robbins, James S., *Last in Their Class: Custer, Pickett and the Goats of West Point.* New York, NY: Encounter Books, 2006.

Roman, Alfred, *The Military Operations of General Beauregard in the War Between the States 1861-1865*, 2 vols. New York, NY: Harper and Brothers, 1884.

Salmon, John S., *Virginia Civil War Battlefield Guide.* Mechanicsville, PA: Stackpole Books, 2001.

Scaife, William R., *The Campaign for Atlanta.* Atlanta, GA: W. R. Scaife, 1993.

Schofield, John M., *Forty-Six Years in the Army.* New York: The Century Company, 1897.

Sherman, William T., *Home Letters of General Sherman*, M. A. DeWolfe Howe, ed. New York, NY: Charles Scribner's Sons, 1909.

———, *Memoirs of General William T. Sherman, by Himself*, 2 vols. Middlesex, UK: The Echo Library, 2006.

Simmons, L. A., *The History of the 84th Regiment Illinois Volunteers*. Macomb, IL: Hampton Brothers, 1866.

Simpson, Harold, *Hood's Texas Brigade*. Fort Worth, TX: Landmark Publishing, 1999.

Smith, Frank H., *History of the 24th Tennessee*. Columbia, TN: United Confederate Veterans, 1904.

Smith, Jean Edward, *Grant*. New York, NY: Simon & Schuster, 2001.

Stanley, David S., *Personal Memoirs of Major-General D. S. Stanley, U.S.A.* Cambridge, MA: Harvard University Press, 1917.

Steiner, Paul E., *Medical-Military Portraits of Union and Confederate Generals*. Philadelphia, PA: Whitmore Publishing Co., 1968.

Stephenson, Philip D., *The Civil War Diary of Philip Daingerfield Stephenson, D. D.*, Nathaniel C. Hughes, Jr., ed. Baton Rouge, LA: Louisiana State University Press, 1998.

Strode, Hudson, *Jefferson Davis: American Patriot, 1808-1861*. New York, NY: Harcourt, Brace and Co., 1955.

Sword, Wiley, *Courage Under Fire: Profiles in Bravery from the Battlefields of the Civil War*. New York, NY: St. Martin's Press, 2007.

———, *The Confederacy's Last Hurrah: Spring Hill, Franklin and Nashville*. Lawrence, KS: University Press of Kansas, 1992.

Symonds, Craig, *A Battlefield Atlas of the Civil War*. Mount Pleasant, SC: Nautical and Aviation Publishing Company of America, 1983.

———, *Joseph E. Johnston: A Civil War Biography*. New York, NY: W. W. Norton and Company, 1994.

———, *Stonewall of the West: Patrick Cleburne and the Civil War*. Lawrence, KS: University Press of Kansas, 1997.

Taylor, Troy, *Spirits of the Civil War*. Chicago, IL: Whitechapel Productions Press, 1999.

Thatcher, Marshall P., *A Hundred Battles in the West: St. Louis to Atlanta, 1861-65*. Detroit, MI: L.F. Kilroy, Printer, 1884.

Thomas, Emory M., *Bold Dragoon: The Life of J. E. B. Stuart*. Norman, OK: The University of Oklahoma Press, 1999.

———. Robert E. Lee: A Biography. New York, NY: W. W. Norton, 1995.

Van Horne, Thomas, *History of the Army of the Cumberland*, 2 vols. Cincinnati, OH: Robert Clarke and Company, 1875.

Walker, Cornelius Irvine, *Great Things are Expected of Us: The Letters of Colonel C. Irvine Walker, 10th South Carolina Infantry, C.S.A.*, William L. White and Charles D. Runion, eds. Knoxville, TN: University of Tennessee Press, 2009.

Warwick, Rick, *Williamson County: The Civil War Years Revealed Through Letters, Diaries and Memoirs*. Nashville, TN: The Panacea Press, 2006.

Wasserman, Paul and Don Hausrath, *Weasel Words: The Dictionary of American Doublespeak*. Herndon, VA: Capital Books, 2006.

Watkins, Sam, *Company Aytch or, A Side Show of the Big Show and Other Sketches*, Thomas Inge, ed. New York, NY: Plume, 1999.

Welsh, Jack, *Medical Histories of Confederate Generals*. Kent, OH: Kent State University Press, 1995.

———, *Medical Histories of Union Generals*. Kent, OH: Kent State University Press, 1996.

Whiteaker, Larry H., *The Tennessee Encyclopedia of History and Culture*. Nashville, TN: Tennessee Historical Society, 1998.

Wiley, Bell Irvin, *The Life of Johnny Reb: The Common Soldier of the Confederacy*. Baton Rouge, LA: Louisiana State University Press, 2007.

Wilson, James Harrison, *Under the Old Flag: Recollections of Military Operations in the War for the Union, The Spanish War, The Boxer Rebellion, etc.*, 2 vols. New York, NY: D. Appleton and Company, 1912.

Winkler, Mrs. C.M., *Life and Character of General John B. Hood*. Austin, TX: Hood's Texas Brigade Association, Draughon and Lambert, 1885.

Woodworth, Steven, *Civil War Generals in Defeat*. Lawrence, KS: University Press of Kansas, 1999.

——, *Jefferson Davis and His Generals: The Failure of Confederate Command in the West*. Lawrence, KS: University Press of Kansas, 1990.

——, *The Chickamauga Campaign*. Carbondale, IL: Southern Illinois University, 2010.

——. "A Reassessment of Confederate Command Options During the Winter of 1863-1864," in *The Campaign for Atlanta and Sherman's March to the Sea*, ed. Theodore Savas and David Woodbury. Campbell, CA: Savas Woodbury Publishers, 1994.

Wright, Louise Wigfall, *A Southern Girl in '61: The War-Time Memories of a Confederate Senator's Daughter*, Mrs. D. Giraud Wright, ed. New York, NY: Doubleday, Page & Company, 1905.

Yeary, Mamie, *Reminiscences of the Boys in Gray, 1861-1865*. Seattle, WA: Morningside Press, Seattle, 1986.

Young, John Russell, *Around the World with General Grant*, 2 vols. New York, NY: The American News Company, 1879.

Index

Diary From Dixie, A, 247
History of Maury County, Tennessee, A, 270
Soldier to the Last, A, 202
Adams, Gen. John, 112, 287
Adams, Pvt. William, 28
Advance and Retreat, xvi-xvii, 50, 144, 178, 211, 213, 216, 225, 258, 293
"all lion, no fox" comment, 14-18
Allatoona, Georgia, 134
Anderson, Gen. James P., 26, 200
Andersonville Prison, 61
Andrew Female Academy, xxxii
Anglesey leg, 278
Army of Tennessee, 9; not destroyed during the Tennessee Campaign, 200, 202-203, 205-206; Hood resigns, 206; Stewart assumes command, 206; Hood did not call his men cowards, 208-209; tentativeness under Johnston, 216
Army of Tennessee, 50, 81, 91
The Army of Tennessee, xxxiv, 127, 149, 155, 209, 270, 284
Army of Tennessee Association, 289
Army of the Cumberland, 9, 54, 161, 222, 236-237
Army of the Tennessee, 54, 56, 61
Army of Tennessee, The: A Military History, 20, 79
Army of Virginia, 8
Atlanta 1864, 57
Atlanta and the War, 269
Atlanta Appeal, 53
Atlanta and West Point Railroad, 90
Atlanta Campaign, xviii, 10, 38, 46, 53, 60-61, 91, 103, 123, 205, 216, 237, 243, 262, 273
Atlanta, Georgia, 12-13, 26-27, 29, 31-32, 34, 41, 48, 62-62n, 63, 69, 75, 82, 90-91, 179
Atlanta, Georgia, battle of, xx, 53, 57, 62-62n, 64-65, 68, 75, 170, 202, 205, 212, 216, 237, 244, 256, 262-263, 294
Attack and Die: Civil War Military Tactics and the Southern Heritage, 229
Augusta Constitutionalist, 54, 59, 91
Augusta, Georgia, 12
Austin, Maj. J. E., 50-51
Authors and Historians: the following is a list of authors and historians mentioned in this book. Page locations for each can be found under individual listings.
Bailey, Anne J.
Blount, Russell
Bonds, Russell
Bradford, James
Bradley, Michael W.
Castel, Albert
Connelly, Thomas
Daniel, Larry
Davis, Stephen
Davis, William C. "Jack"
Davison, Eddy
Dowdey, Clifford
Durham, Walter T.
Dyer, John
Ecelbarger, Gary
Eicher, David J.
Elliott, Sam Davis
Ellis, Barbara G.
Foote, Shelby
Foxx, Daniel
Freeman, Douglas S.
Garrison Jr., Webb
Gibboney, Douglas Lee
Groom, Winston
Hamlin, Percy
Hattaway, Herman
Hay, Thomas
Henderson, George
Henry, Robert Selph
Horn, Stanley
Jacobson, Eric
Jamieson, Perry
Jenkins, Sally
Jones, Archer
Kelly, Dennis
Knight, James R.
Lanier, Robert
Longacre, Edward
Losson, Christopher
Lowry, Thomas
Lundberg, John
Manarin, Louis
McDonough, James
McKay, John
McKinney, Francis F.
McMurray, W. J.
McMurry, Richard
McPherson, James M.
McWhiney, Grady
Miller, Brian C.
Miller, Francis
Muzzey, David S.
Nelson, Larry E.
Newton, Stephen
Nisbet, Col. James C.
Patterson, Gerard

Pawlowski, Rebecca

Pollard, E. A.

Riedel, Len

Roman, Alfred

Scaife, William

Simpson, Harold B.

Smith, Jean Edward

Smith, Frank H.

Stauffer, John

Sword, Wiley

Symonds, Craig

Van Horne, Thomas B.

Wiley, Bell I.

Woodworth, Steven

Autumn of Glory, xxxiv, 74, 91, 128, 202, 210-211, 274, 284

Ayer, Maj., —, 97

Bailey, Anne J., 203-204

Bailey, Ronald H., 270

Bailey, Thomas A., 261

Baker, Gen. Alpheus, 195

Baldwin, James W., 158

Banks, Gen. Nathaniel, 32, 37

Barnes, Lt. Col. Milton, 155

Bate, Gen. William, 31, 57, 59, 98, 113, 186, 204, 222, 246; Spring Hill Affair, 114, 116, 122; Franklin, 145, 188; sent to Murfreesboro, 184-185; Nashville, 186-187

Battle of Franklin, The: Five Hours in the Valley of Death (film), 104

Battle of Franklin, The: When the Devil Had Full Possession of the Field, 285

Battle Cry of Freedom, 17

Battles and Sketches of the Army of Tennessee 1861-1865, 282

Battles for Atlanta, The, 270

Battles of New Hope Church, 280

Beach, John N., 86

Beattie, Col. Taylor, 50

Beauregard, Gen. Pierre G. T., xx, 10, 25, 35, 69, 70-72, 82, 89, 98, 104, 106, 111, 132, 198n, 247; published Hood's memoir, xvii; letter as rationale for Tennessee Campaign, 82-83; rationale for Tennessee Campaign, 84; Military Division of the West, 91-92; first meeting with Hood, 92-93, 105; found it necessary to bypass Taylor, 95, 97; supplies for Hood from Taylor, 95; presses Hood to launch invasion, 96; miscommunication, 100-103; orders Wheeler to resist Sherman, 100; appointed Hood's superior, 104; poor communications, 105; relationship with Hood, 106; arranged for publication of Hood's memoirs, 107; callous treatment by Hood, 107-108; Gadsden meeting letter, 108; logistics, 109; awaits Forrest at Tuscumbia, 110; "barren victory" at Franklin, 176; did not order Hood to withdraw after Franklin, 177; did not think Hood should move on Nashville, 183; seeking help from Kirby Smith, 189-195; Smith refuses to help Hood, 196; Hood retreats into Mississippi, 197; Spring Hill Affair, 197; Hood requests he visit the army, 199; denies Hood's request to furlough troops, 233; West Point, 252; Hood's memoirs, 296; Jefferson Davis to Confederate Congress, 305, 310

Beckham, Col. Robert, 25-26

Bell, Dr. John, 2, 250

Bell, Pvt. George W., 284, 286-287

Benet, Stephen Vincent, 15, 17

Bentonville, North Carolina, battle of, 178, 206, 220, 227-228

Bierce, Ambrose, xxxi

Big Book of Civil War Sites, The: From Fort Sumter to Appomattox, 140

Blair, Gen. Francis, 65

Blair, Montgomery, 65

Blanton, Maj., 116, 118

Blount, Russell, 280

Bonaparte, Napoleon, 19

Bonds, Russell, xxii, 16-17

Bowers, Bryan, 232

Bradford, James, 140

Bradley, Michael W., 213

Bragg, Gen. Braxton, xx, xxxv, 9, 13, 19, 20-24, 31, 59, 91-92, 105-106, 108, 191, 215, 229, 232; Atlanta Campaign, xviii; Johnston commands the department, 37; Chickamauga, 44; West Point, 252; Jefferson Davis to Confederate Congress, 308, 310-311

Breckinridge, Gen. John C., 194

Brent, Col. George W., 191

Bright Skies and Dark Shadows, 166

Broughton, Lt. William, 2n

Brown, A. Whitney, 46

Brown, Gen. John C., 26, 113, 122, 136-138, 142, 144-145, 170-172, 205, 216, 246

Brown, Joseph, 97

Brown, Thomas, xxxiv, 34

Brown's Mill, battle of, 61

Buck, Col. Irving, 65

Buckner, Gen. Simon B., 192

Burns, Ken, 200, 288

Burnside, Gen. Ambrose, 16

Butler, Gen. Matthew C., 32, 59, 228

Butterfield, Gen. Daniel, 48, 51-51n

Byrne, W. J., 29

Campaign for Atlanta, 66

Campaign for Atlanta and Sherman's March to the Sea, The, 271

Carter, Gen. John C., 216, 287

Cassville, Georgia, affair, 46-52, 237

Castel, Albert, 11, 21, 53, 56, 58, 61, 238

Chalmers, Gen. James, xiii, xxi, 116, 124, 153, 216, 246

Chancellorsville, battle of, 8

Cheatham, Gen. Benjamin F., xvi, 26, 71, 110, 166, 185, 211, 216; supports Johnston against Hood, xvi; Spring Hill Affair, 113, 116-118, 120-127, 129-130, 137, 240, 244; letter regarding Spring Hill, 122; refused to allow Johnson to attack, 125; disobeyed orders, 127; promoted his version of Spring Hill, 128; Rippavilla meeting, 136; Franklin, 140, 143, 145, 154, 164, 187; Sword's inflammatory comments about Spring Hill, 142; command meeting at Franklin, 166-167; Hood blames for Spring Hill Affair, 170-171, 173; Nashville, 186; casualty reports, 204; never saw Hood impaired, 278; Hood's memoirs, 295-296, 298

Cherokee Station, Alabama, 93-95, 97

Chesnut, Mary Boynton, 99n, 106, 243, 247, 260, 273, 287

Chessboard of War, The: Sherman and Hood in the Autumn Campaigns of 1864, 204

Chicago Tribune, xix, xxiv

Chickamauga, Georgia, battle of, 9, 44, 174, 229, 236, 256-257, 268, 271, 276

Civil War in Books, The, 51

Civil War, The: A Narrative, 67

Clayton, Gen. Henry, 26, 33, 59, 74, 78, 98, 205

Cleburne, Gen. Patrick, 65, 96, 122, 129, 146, 173, 211, 213, 279, 287; Peachtree Creek, 61; Spring Hill Affair, 113, 116, 123, 144, 169, 171, 174; Franklin, 138, 140, 144-145, 149, 154-155, 156, 158, 169-170, 172, 174-175; Sword's inflammatory comments about Spring Hill, 142; death of, 169, 173, 175, 232; final meeting with Hood, 170; Chickamauga, 174; Jonesboro, 238-239

Clemson, John W., 67

Clifton, Tennessee, 100

Cockrell, Gen. Francis M., 65, 112, 218

Collingwood, R. G., 267

Columbia, Tennessee, 96, 112, 114, 118, 129-130, 133-136, 145, 151, 158, 166, 213, 234, 239-240

Columbus, Mississippi, 92

Comanche Indians, 4

Committee on Resolutions of the Association of the Army of Tennessee, 300

Company Aytch, 264

Confederacy's Last Hurrah, The: Spring Hill, Franklin, and Nashville, xxii, xxv, xl, 11, 16, 21, 91, 127, 142, 147, 159, 198, 201, 203, 212, 249, 260, 270, 287, 289

Confederate Veteran, xv

Confederate Military Units
  Alabama, 17th Infantry, 43, 119, 159; 23rd Infantry, 232; 58th Infantry, 220
  Arkansas, 1st Infantry, 146; 3rd Infantry, 115, 117
  Florida, Florida brigade, 186
  Georgia, 3rd Infantry, 264; 5th Infantry, 123n; 30th Infantry, 28; 63rd Infantry, 28; Marion Light Artillery, 29
  Kentucky, 2nd Infantry, 164; 9th Infantry, 29
  Louisiana, 4th Infantry, 28; 14th Battalion Sharpshooters, 50; Washington Artillery, 254
  Mississippi, 3rd Infantry, 284, 286; 11th Infantry, 14, 265; 23rd Infantry, 181
  North Carolina, 39th Infantry, 282-283; 58th Infantry, 232
  South Carolina, 10th Infantry, 31
  Tennessee, 1st Infantry, 29, 42, 79, 143, 153, 264; 2nd Infantry, 265; 7th Infantry, 118; 12th Infantry, 43; 20th Infantry, 282; 24th Infantry, 282; 41st Infantry, 42, 117, 150, 206, 263; 49th Infantry, 120, 139
  Texas, 1st Infantry, 5, 232; 4th Infantry, xxiii, 6, 231, 255; 10th Cavalry, 98, 247
  Virginia, 17th Infantry, 187n; 54th Infantry, 232; 63rd Infantry, 232

Connelly, Thomas, xl, xxii, xxv, xxxi, xxxiv, xli, 20-23, 41, 49-50, 72, 74, 87, 90-91, 102-103, 106, 108, 128, 139-142, 165, 166, 184, 193, 196, 202, 205, 210-211, 213, 215, 217-218, 229, 235, 243, 254, 260, 269, 274, 279, 280, 281-281n, 284, 287

Cooper, Gen. Samuel, 97, 191, 198n, 251-252

Copley, John, 120, 139

Corinth, Mississippi, 94-95, 105, 111, 189, 195, 199

Courage Under Fire: Profiles in Bravery from the Battlefields of the Civil War, 21, 142, 212, 249, 258

Courtwright, David, 275

Cowper, William, 131

Cox, Gen. Jacob, 66-68

Crook, Gen. George, 3

Cumming, Joseph B., 116, 122, 123-123n, 272

Cunningham, S. A., 42, 117, 150-153, 168, 188, 201, 263

Custer, George A., 252

Dabney, Virginius, xiv

Dalton, Georgia, 27-29, 34, 40, 70, 232, 239, 281, 294

Daniel, Larry, 27

Darby, Dr. John T., 271, 276-277

Dark Paradise: A History of Opiate Addiction in America, 275

Davenport, W. G., 98, 247

Davis vs. Wigfall controversy, 243

Davis, Jefferson, 3, 7, 10, 16, 44, 59, 69, 80-81, 84, 92, 103, 107, 110, 132, 183, 228, 259, 262; Atlanta Campaign, xviii; R. E. Lee's opinion of Hood, 11-12, 14-15, 17; wants a new commander of the Army of Tennessee, 13; Hood not scheming to replace Johnston, 19-20; Hood's first letter to, 20; Hood's correspondence with authorities, 23-24; trying to deny Lincoln's re-election, 32-33; war weariness, 33; distrust of Johnston, 34; early admiration for Johnston, 35; shock at Johnston's ignorance of Virginia topography, 36; Johnston's retreat from Yorktown, 37; Johnston's tight-lipped demeanor, 38; Hardee turns down command, 39; regrets promoting Johnston, 39-40; Sherman's army outnumbered Johnston's, 41; places Hood in command of army, 42-43; removes Johnston, 53; Hood's efforts not useless, 64; letter as rationale for Tennessee Campaign, 83-84; logistics, 99; sanctioned movement to Tennessee, 103; Franklin, 159; conduct of Bates' men, 187; Beauregard seeks help for Hood, 190-191; Army of Tennessee not destroyed during the campaign, 200; R. E. Lee's army destroyed during retreat to Appomattox, 206; Hood's evaluation of his army, 219; army's morale, 223; removal of Joe Johnston, 234; where Hood learned his craft, 236; Hood accepts responsibility, 245; West Point, 252; R. E. Lee's letter regarding Hood's abilities, 257-258; Louis T. Wigfall, 265; Hood spent time with, 273; never saw Hood impaired, 280; Hood's memoirs, 295; Confederate Congress on Joseph E. Johnston, 303-313

Davis, Chaplain Nicholas, 231, 256

Davis, Stephen, xxii, 51, 268, 271, 275, 279

Davis, William C. "Jack," 22, 184

Davison, Eddy, 15, 116-117, 243, 279

Day That Dixie Died, The: The Battle of Atlanta, xl

De Fontaine, Felix, 54

Deal, Pvt. John, 7

Decatur, battle of (See Atlanta, battle of)

Deas, Gen. Zachariah, 230

Decatur, Alabama, 92-97, 109, 234, 239-240, 263, 295

Decision in the West: The Atlanta Campaign of 1864, 11, 21, 50, 56, 58

The Decisive Battle of Nashville, 81, 87, 285

Department of Alabama, Mississippi and East Louisiana, 91, 100

Department of Mississippi and East Louisiana, 224

District of Northern Alabama, 87

District of West Louisiana, 192

Dodd, Capt. W. O., 153

Dorsey, Sarah A., 77

Dowdey, Clifford, 11, 17

Durham, Walter T., 184

Dyer, John, xxxiv, xliii, 8, 250, 277

Early vs. Longstreet controversy, 243

Early, Gen. Jubal A., 12

Eastman, Pvt. Jake, 262

Ecelbarger, Gary, xl

Eicher, David J., 51-52

Elliott, Sam Davis, 115, 143, 243

Ellis, Barbara G., 120-120n, 241, 280

Eltham's Landing, battle of, 6-7, 214, 257

Embrace an Angry Wind: The Confederacy's Last Harrah, xxxiii, xxxiv, xxxviii, xxxix

Ewell, Gen. Richard S., 15, 274-275

Ezra Church, battle of, 27, 58-63, 66-68, 202, 205, 216-218, 238-239

Fabian strategy, xxi, 237, 266

Fergusson, Lt. William W., 265

Field, Henry, 166

Finishing Stroke, The: Texans in the 1864 Tennessee Campaign, 116, 141, 212, 279

Finley, Gen. Jesse J., 186

Fischer, David H., 11

Five Tragic Hours: The Battle of Franklin, 72, 128, 142, 166, 269

Fleherty, S. J., 30

Fleming, L. J., 94-95

Florence, Alabama, 93, 98

Florida brigade, 186

Foard, Dr. A. J., 205

Foch, Field Marshal Ferdinand, 81

Foote, Henry, xxii

Foote, Shelby, 67

For Cause and for Country: A Study of the Affair at Spring Hill and the Battle of Franklin, xxix, 143, 217, 250, 284,

Forney, Gen. John, 37

Forrest, Gen. Nathan B., xviii, 25, 71, 93-94, 100-101, 103, 109, 113, 241, 243, 246-247, 259; Southern Historical Society, xxi; miscommunication, 100-102; Spring Hill Affair, 113-116, 120; Rippavilla meeting, 136; anger about Spring Hill, 139; Franklin flanking maneuver, 146-147, 149-150; could never have flanked Schofield, 150; Franklin, 155, 267; sent to Murfreesboro, 184-186, 188; troop strength, 201n; Murfreesboro, 222, 240; myth about 'whipping' Hood, 267-268; never saw Hood impaired, 278

Fort Granger, Tennessee, 147

Fort Jones, California, 3

Fort Mason, Texas, 4, 250

Fort Monroe, Virginia, 6

Fort Reading, California, 3

Fort Sumter, South Carolina, 5

Foster, Capt. Samuel, 41, 43, 95-96, 233-234, 261-263, 286

Four Years on the Firing Line, 288

Foxx, Daniel, 15, 116-117, 243, 279

Franklin, Tennessee, and battle of, xv, xvi, xvii, xxvi, xl, xliii, 10, 22, 64, 70, 84, 86, 95, 112-113, 119-120, 128-129, 131-134, 136-147, 149, 151-177, 180-183, 187, 192, 196, 203, 209-212, 222, 227, 229, 232-236, 239-240, 243, 246-248, 259, 261, 263, 267, 287, 289, 297

Franklin, Gen. William B., 6, 10

Fredericksburg, battle of, 8, 13

Freeman, Douglas S., 224

French and Indian War, 2

French, Gen. Samuel, 24, 137

Gadsden, Alabama, 85, 92-94, 98, 105, 108

Gaines's Mill, Virginia, battle of, xxiii-xxiv, 8, 14, 146, 214, 229, 231, 236, 248, 255-257, 259

Gale, Col. W. D., 118, 230

Gallant Hood, The, xxxiv, 250

Gardner, Gen. Franklin, 37

Gardner, Washington, 159-160

Garrett, Maj. G. W., 181

Garrison Jr., Webb, 21, 234, 269, 279

Georgia Railroad, 90

Gettysburg, Pennsylvania, battle of, xiv, xv, xx, xxiii, xxiv, xxv, 1, 8, 14, 44, 63, 215, 229, 257, 271-272, 276

Gibbon, Edward, 53

Gibboney, Douglas Lee, 281

Gist, Gen. States Rights, 287

Gordon, Gen. John B., 64, 90

Gorgas, Gen. Josiah, 30

Govan, Gen. Daniel, 115, 170, 173-174

Granbury, Gen. Hiram, 41, 95, 145, 175, 213, 232-233, 261-262, 286-287

Grant, 17

Grant, Gen. Ulysses S., xxvii, 9, 32-33, 37-38, 71, 74-75, 79, 81, 83, 85, 86, 161, 222; treatment of Thomas, xxvi; decides to relieve Thomas, 183; decides to travel to Nashville, 183; impressed by Hood's movement to Nashville, 182; Jefferson Davis to Confederate Congress, 302; West Point, 252

Gray, R. M., 264

Gregg, Gen. David, 12

Groom, Winston, 75, 163

Guntersville, Alabama, 70-71, 93, 98, 101, 105-106

Hood's Tennessee Campaign, 11

Halleck, Gen. Henry, 79, 81, 93

Hamilton, Maj., —, 116, 118

Hamlin, Percy, 268, 275-275

Hancock, Gen. Winfield S., 252

Hardee, Gen. William J., 4, 22-23, 26, 45, 61-62, 111, 204, 217-218, 224; turns down command of the Army of Tennessee, 11, 13, 39; only experienced high level commander, 25; Cassville, 47; Peachtree Creek, 54, 56-57, 238; Ezra Church, 58; requests a transfer, 62n; army's lack of initiative, 216; Jonesboro, 220, 238, 244; Atlanta, 242; army's aggressiveness, 244; West Point, 252; Jefferson Davis to Confederate Congress on Hardee, 310, 311

Harris, Gov. Isham, 113-114, 116-117, 159, 278

Harvie, Col. E. J., 78

Haskell, Col. J. C., 254

Hattaway, Herman, 17

Hay, Thomas, xxxiv-xxxv, xl, xli, xliii, 11, 19-20, 80-81, 87, 91, 98-99, 102, 127, 141, 149, 154, 156-157, 170-171, 173, 181-184, 188, 192, 209, 220, 284, 287

Helms, Pvt. Celathiel, 28

Henderson, George, 79

Hennen (Hood), Anna Marie, xxxii

Henry, Gustavus, 73-73n

Henry, Robert Selph, 281

Heth, Gen. Henry, 252

Hill, Gen. Ambrose P., 15, 173

Hill, Gen. Daniel H., 231, 252, 272

Hindman, Gen. Thomas, 48, 50

History of the 20th Tennessee Regiment Volunteer Infantry, 282

History of the 24th Tennessee, 282

History of the Army of the Cumberland, 177, 299

History of the Twenty-Fourth Tennessee, 43

Holcombe, B. W., 265

Hollow Tree Gap, 147, 150

Hood: Cavalier General, 270

Hood Hospital, xxxii

Hood Relief Committee, 107

Hood, Anna Marie, xviii, 260

Hood, Gen. John Bell, 4, 51, 60, 66, 80, 82, 86, 106, 108, 111, 125n, 150n; criticized Johnston in official report, xii-xiv; destruction of historical memory, xii, xxiv-xxv, xxxiv, xxxviii, xli; Lee Monument Association, xiii; Nashville, battle of, xiii, xxvi, xliii, 297; settled in New Orleans, xiii; Southern Historical Society, xiii, xiv, xix, xx, xxii; Franklin, battle of, xv, xvi, xvii, xxvi, xliii, 162, 243, 247-259, 261, 263, 267, 289, 297; Gettysburg, xv, xxv, 1, 8-9, 14, 237, 257; castigated by Johnston, xvi-xvii; memoirs, xvi, 70, 107, 144, 166, 170, 178, 189, 258, 210-211, 213, 216-217, 225, 293-298; Spring Hill Affair, xvi, xvii, xliii, 22, 62, 112, 114-117, 119, 120-120n, 121, 123-124, 127-129, 130-130n, 134, 136-139, 141-143, 150, 158, 182-183, 209-211, 216, 236, 242, 246, 248, 269, 274, 297-298; Anna Marie, xviii, 260; Atlanta Campaign, xviii, 64, 183, 262; stigmatized by the Lost Cause, xviii; obituary, xix-xx; Tennessee Campaign, xxi, xxxi, 84-85, 87, 89-90, 98, 102, 262, 291-292, 297; blamed for failures by Johnston, xxii; Texas brigade, xxiii, 1, 5-8, 14, 16; death of, xxiv, xxviii, 289; history is improving, xxviii; started a new life after the war, xxviii; tenure with the Army of Tennessee, xxxi; Lost Cause "Hood the butcher," xxxii; married Anna Marie Hennen, xxxii; postwar, xxxiii; rise and fall of, 1; enigmatic career, 1; Owingsville, Kentucky, born in, 1; father John W. Hood, 2; graduates from West Point, 2; nickname "Sam," 2-2n; West Point, 2, 5, 251-253, 258; Fort Jones, 3; Williamson's comment about Hood's departure, 3; Jefferson Barracks, 4; wounded by Comanches, 4; appointed commander of the Texas brigade, 5; declined assignment to West Point, 5; offers services to Magoffin, 5; promoted to colonel, 5; resigns U.S. Army commission, 5; Eltham's Landing, 6-7, 257; Seven Pines, 7; Gaines's Mill, 8, 14, 231, 236, 255-257, 259; Second Manassas, 8, 14, 236, 255, 257; Sharpsburg, 8, 14, 231-232, 257; Suffolk Campaign, 8; Chickamauga, 9, 236, 256-257; promoted to lieutenant general, 9, 257; wounded at Chickamauga, 9, 215, 268, 276, 271; wounded at Gettysburg, 9, 215, 237, 271-272, 276; Nashville, 10, 75, 176-177, 182-183, 189, 191, 195, 240, 243; promoted to full general, 10; recovering from leg amputation, 10; strong relationship with Davis, 10; surrendered at Natchez, 10, 260; R. E. Lee's opinion of, 11-12; opinion of Hood, 13; "All lion, no fox" comment, 14-18; Hood is a bold fighter, 14; R. E. Lee's letter regarding murder of civilians, 14; John Brown's Body poem honors Hood, 15; brave fighter, 16; "Old Woodenhead" label, 17, 288; correspondence with authorities, 19-21, 25; not scheming to replace Johnston, 19-20; ordered to keep Richmond informed, 20; called a "disloyal subordinate" by Sword, 21; "chronic liar" comment, 21; "damaging letter" to Bragg, 22; Franklin, Tennessee, 10, 22, 84, 86-87, 95, 132, 134, 136, 139-141, 150-151, 154-160, 163-166, 168, 170, 172, 182-183, 209-210, 224-225, 227, 232-236, 239; "shamelessly politicked" comment, 22; "damaging letter" to Bragg, 23; disobedience and jealousy of officers, 26-27; outnumbered two-to-one, 26; Confederate deserters, 27-28, 189; troops' decreased fighting spirit, 30; replaces Johnston on July 17, 31, 33, 53-54; letter from G. W. Smith, 40; assigned command of Army of Tennessee, 42-43; soldiers not upset about his appointment, 42; Peter Principle, 44;

successful brigade and division commander, 44-45; James Wilson's letter, 44; Cassville, 48-49, 237; Eicher's accusations, 51n, 52; inherits an impossible situation, 53; Peachtree Creek, 54, 56, 58, 60, 237; Peachtree Creek battle plan, 56; Ezra Church, 58-61, 63, 68, 238-239; plenty of supporters, 59; some officers opposed his replacement of Johnston, 59; open communications with high command, 60; physical condition, 62; Wheeler's raid, 62; a hands-on combat commander, 63; casualties around Atlanta, 63; evacuates Atlanta, 63; Jonesboro, battle of, 63, 220-221, 238-239; blamed only subordinate William Hardee for defeats, 65; largely excused for defeat at Atlanta, 65; poor scholarship about, 66; one-sided portrayal, 69; long account of Tennessee Campaign, 70-72; modern authors oppose, 72, 79; died in New Orleans, 73; Connelly calls a liar, 74; desertions, 75; soldiers poor morale, 77-78; Wolseley's comments, 79; appointed to command Army of Tennessee, 81; Tennessee Campaign not impossible, 81; rationale for Tennessee Campaign, 83-84; logistics, 89-91, 95-97, 99, 109; youngest full general, 89; youngest officer to command an army, 89; kept army well supplied at Atlanta, 91; asks for railroads to be repaired, 92, 96; drawing supplies from Taylor's department, 92; first meeting with Beauregard, 92-93, 105; keen appreciation for logistics, 92; looking for ordnance reserve, 92; plans keep evolving because of various issues, 92-93; anxious to launch the invasion, 94; requests twenty days rations from Taylor, 94; found it necessary to bypass Taylor, 95, 97; Beauregard presses to launch invasion, 96; General Order Number 37, 96; lack of cavalry, 100; miscommunication, 100-102; missing Forrest, 100; Decatur, Georgia, less defended, 101; Forrest's whereabouts unknown, 101; did not disobey orders after Atlanta, 103; accused by Sword of being rash, 104; Beauregard appointed his superior, 104; keeps Richmond informed, 105; poor communications, 105; Wheeler's orders, 105; relationship with Beauregard, 106; Hood Relief Committee, 107; awaits Forrest at Tuscumbia, 109-110; illness at Spring Hill, 116-117, 143; ultimately responsible for Spring Hill, 117; letter regarding Spring Hill, 121; Cheatham's letter, 122; "natural modesty," 123; S. D. Lee's letter, 124-125, 127; Old's letter, 126; accountable for Franklin, 132; Franklin decision explained, 134-135, 147, 149-150; was he upset or angry about Spring Hill, 135; Rippavilla meeting, 136; confident and robust, 143; frontal assault at Franklin comment, 143; similarities to Gaines's Mill, 146; attempting to destroy Schofield, not occupy Franklin, 149; extensive knowledge of the cavalry, 150; Tennessee Campaign official report, 157; troop morale, 151-152; Schofield's "Hood the butcher" comment, 159; dilemma at Franklin, 162; 17 separate attacks rumor, 164; command meeting at Franklin, 165-168; plan to renew the attack at Franklin, 165-166; valor of his soldiers, 165; "wept like a child" comment, 165; "savage in his fury" comment, 166; death of Cleburne, 169, 174-175, 232; did not blame Cleburne for Spring Hill, 169, 172-173; blames Cheatham for Spring Hill, 170-171; final meeting with Cleburne, 170; wept at Cleburne's death, 175; refused to abandon the campaign, 176-177; not trying to conceal anything from Richmond, 177; sends results of Franklin to Beauregard, 177; size of army before Nashville, 178; looking for help from Kirby Smith, 179-180, 189-190, 192, 194; reason to capture Nashville, 179; aware of heavy odds at Nashville, 180; affection by men not lost, 181; movement to Nashville is a problem for historians, 181-182; invades Tennessee, 183; misinformation on Nashville actions, 184; sends Forrest to Murfreesboro, 184-186, 240; seeking reinforcements, 189; conscription, 195; requests Baker's brigade, 195; retreats into Mississippi, 197, 206-207, 233, 247, 265; Nashville losses, 198; requests Beauregard visit the army, 199; Army of Tennessee not destroyed during the campaign, 202-203; casualty reports, 205, 218; resignation, 206; did not call his men cowards, 9, 213, 208-211, 214, 221, 227, 233; official report, 211; Sword is a leading critic, 211-212, 254-260; evaluation of his army, 219; Forrest sent to Murfreesboro, 222; army's morale, 223-224; double standard, 225; loved his men, 226, 231; speech in Charleston, South Carolina, 226; Johnston thought war lost in 1863, 228; Tennessee Campaign losses, 228-229; pardoned deserters, 232; Capt. Foster's criticisms, 233-234, 261-263; wants to furlough troops, 233; generalship, 235; advocate of offensive warfare, 236; joins the Army of Tennessee, 237; where Hood learned his craft, 237; Atlanta, battle of, 238, 256, 262-263; Franklin was last opportunity to destroy Schofield, 240; not a careless commander, 241; always accepted responsibility, 242-247; "I lost Atlanta" comment, 245; accepted responsibility for Tennessee Campaign, 247; compares

Franklin troops to the Texas brigade, 247; resignation, 247; roll of honor for troops at Franklin, 247; large volume of personal attacks, 249; Fort Mason, 250; early writers were respectful, 254; postwar life in New Orleans, 260; modern books, 261; deserves well of the country, 264; Watkins' poem, 264; Louise Wigfall Wright's opinion of, 266; myth about Forrest "whipping" him, 267, 268; stories lack supporting evidence, 267; use of laudanum, 268-280; spent time with Davis in Richmond, 273; Anglesey leg, 278; prosthetics, 278; gambling myth, 281; "The Yellow Rose of Texas," 282-286; Sally Preston, 287; Ken Burn's Civil War series, 288; tribute to, 289, 300-302; knew his career would be open to criticism, 291

Hood: Cavalier General, xxxiv

Hood's Tennessee Campaign (1929), xliii, 87, 91, 127, 141, 181, 284

Hood's Tennessee Campaign (1941), 87

Hooker, Gen. Joseph, 16, 47, 51

Hood, Dr. John W., 2, 249

Hood, Adm. Samuel, 2-2n

Horn, Stanley, xxii, xxv, xxxiv, xl-xli, 20, 49, 63, 81, 84-85, 87, 91, 102, 127, 149, 155, 185, 189, 196-198, 209, 211, 215, 217, 220, 240, 242-243, 270, 284-286

How the North Won the Civil War, 17

Howard, Gen. Oliver O., 57-58, 61, 238

Hudson, Robert, 33

Hunter, Gen. David, 32

Irving, Washington, 169

It Happened in the Civil War, 213

Iverson, Gen. Alfred, 61

Jackson, Gen. Henry R., 186

Jackson, Gen. Thomas J., 8, 15, 65, 78, 115, 173, 223, 228, 231, 236, 245, 259

Jackson, Gen. William H., 100

Jacobson, Eric, xxii, xxix, 22, 72, 81, 130n, 143, 146, 167n, 185, 203, 217, 229, 250, 284, 292

Jamieson, Perry, 229

Jefferson Davis and His Generals: The Failure of Confederate Command in the West, 211

Jefferson Barracks, 4

Jefferson, Thomas, 235

Jenkins, Sally, 259

"John Brown's Body," 15

John Bell Hood and the Fight for Civil War Memory, xxix, xxxiv, 250

John Bell Hood and the War for Southern Independence, xxxiv

John Bell Hood: Extracting Truth from History, xxxiv

Johnson, Gen. Edward, 187, 123-124, 164

Johnson, Herschel V., 64

Johnson, Col. J. P., 199

Johnson's Island, Ohio, prison, 120

Johnston and Beauregard vs. Davis and Bragg controversy, 243

Johnston vs. Hood controversy, 243

Johnston, Gen. Albert Sidney, 4, 173

Johnston, Joseph E., xvii, 6, 10, 23, 24-24n, 33, 66-67, 79-80, 115, 117, 152, 162, 182, 227-228, 268, 283, 288; criticized by Hood in official report, xii-xiv, xvi; Atlanta Campaign, xviii; Southern Historical Society, xxii; memoirs, xxiv; Seven Pines, 7, 34, 37; retreats before Sherman, 10, 40; removed by Davis, 11-12; tactics not working, 13; affection of the army, 16; Hood not scheming to replace, 19; failure to keep authorities informed, 21; timidity, 21; political infighting in army, 25; handling of the army, 27; Confederate desertions, 28; always falling back, xii, 29-30, 209, 214-215, 237; Southerners maintained confidence in, 31; Davis did not trust, 34; Kennesaw Mountain, 34; Pickett's Mill, 34; early admiration by Davis, 35; First Manassas, 35; retreats from Manassas, 36; Yorktown, 36; given command of a department, 37-38; retreats from Yorktown, 37; tight-lipped demeanor, 38, 40; going to abandon Atlanta, 41; his fault he was dismissed from command, 41-42; outnumbered by Sherman, 41; removal upset his soldiers, 42-43; no victories in last 18 months of war, 44; Cassville, 46-52; dismissed as commander, 46; Resaca, 46; removed by Davis, 53-54; some officers opposed Hood, 59; frustrates high command, 60; placed in command of the Army of Tennessee, 69; desertions, 75, 77; poor morale, 77; policy of the government for his army, 82; retreating, 84; logistics, 89-90; Bentonville, North Carolina, 178, 220, 228; long retreat, 205; restored to theater command, 206; army's lack of initiative, 216; thought war was lost in 1863, 228; Dalton, Georgia, 232; largest mass execution of deserters, 232; army's aggressiveness, 244; Foster a devotee, 261-262; Hood's memoirs, 293-295; Jefferson Davis to Confederate Congress, 303-313

Jones, Archer, 17

Jones, Capt. A. C., 115, 117

Jones, Capt. Bushrod, 220

Jones, Franklin P., 69

Jonesboro, Georgia, 62-62n, 63, 90, 216-221, 230, 238-239, 244

Kelly, Dennis, xxi

Kennesaw Mountain, battle of, xxi, 34, 220, 222, 230

Knight, James R., 285

Lanier, Robert, 64

Law, Col. Evander, 8, 231

Leaming, Maj. Henry, 155

Lee Monument Association, xiii

Lee, Gen. Fitzhugh, 12, 252

Lee, Gen. Robert E., xvi, xxv, 1, 4-5, 10, 23, 32, 42, 64, 71, 78, 84, 90, 133, 152, 177-178, 183, 191, 214, 219, 223-224, 228-229, 231-232, 236, 245, 248, 255, 257-258; Lost Cause deity, xv; Texas brigade, xxiii; death of, xxvii-xxviii; appointed commander of the Virginia Army, 7; Seven Day's battles, 8; Johnston's successor, 11; opinion of Hood, 11-12, 17; Hood is a bold fighter, 12; letter to Davis regarding Hood, 12-14; did not reject Hood, 13; Johnston needs to be replaced, 13; letter regarding murder of civilians, 14; Hood's correspondence with authorities, 20, 22-23; asks Davis to reappoint Johnston, 34; no decisive victories after Gettysburg, 44; Franklin, 154; retreat to Appomattox destroyed his army, 206-207; West Point, 253; Jefferson Davis to Confederate Congress, 304, 307-308, 310

Lee, Gen. Stephen D., 25-26, 45, 58, 61, 65, 71, 75, 106, 110, 126, 166, 180, 185, 187, 246; Peachtree Creek, 57; Ezra Church, 58-59, 238-239; Spring Hill Affair, 113, 115, 123, 125, 128, 135; Hood's "natural modesty" comment, 123; text of letter to Hood, 124-125; Franklin, 133, 151, 176, 187; Rippavilla meeting, 136; command meeting at Franklin, 166; death of Cleburne, 169, 174; Cheatham did not want to launch a night attack, 174; complained about Bate's division, 187-188; official report, 217; casualty reports, 218; Jonesboro, 219-220, 230, 238; lost aggressiveness in the army, 221; Hood's memoirs, 298

Lee's Lieutenants, 224

Lewis, Gen. Joseph H., 194

Lexington Gazette, xxvii

Life of Johnny Reb, The: The Common Soldier of the Confederacy, 281

Lincoln, Abraham, 5, 9, 32-33, 65, 68, 74, 79-81, 268

Logan, Gen. John A., 61, 66, 79, 183

Longacre, Edward, 202

Longstreet, Gen. James, xv-xvi, xxix, 8-9, 15, 236-237, 252, 257, 259

Look Away, 22

Lord Acton, 1

Loring, Gen. William W., 26, 144, 223-224

Losson, Christopher, 281

Lost Cause, xiii-xvi, xviii, xx, xxiv-xxv, xxvii-xxviii, xxxii, xxxiv, 230, 288

Love, Cpl. George, 7

Lovejoy's Station, 91

Lowry, Thomas, xl

Lundberg, John, 116, 141-142, 144, 212-213, 220, 279, 286

MacArthur, Col. Arthur, 86, 161
Mackall, W. W., 25, 29, 48-49
Macon and Western Railroad, 56-57, 61, 90
Magoffin, Beriah, 5
Magruder, Gen. John, 36
Mahone, Gen. William, 224
Manarin, Louis, 11, 17
Manassas, First battle of, 35
Manassas, Second battle of, xxiii, 8, 14, 214, 229, 236, 255, 257
Maney, Gen. George, 26, 112
Marietta, Georgia, 29
Martin, Maj. E. L., 123-124, 125-125n
Martin, Maj. Howdy, xxiv
Mary Chesnut's Civil War, 280
Maury, Gen. Dabney, xxxiv
McClellan, Gen. George B., 6, 8, 32, 80, 214, 245
McCook, Gen. Edward, 61
McCullough, David, 288
McDonough, James, xxii, xxv, xxxi, 72, 87, 128, 142, 166, 205, 269, 279
McKay, John, 140
McKinney, Francis F., xxvi
McLaws, Gen. Lafayette, 8, 252
McMicken, Col. M. B., 90-91
McMurry, Richard, xxii-xxxiv, 27-28, 30-31, 48, 51, 57-58, 60, 68, 72, 204-205, 268-269, 271, 277, 279
McMurray, W. J., 282-284, 286
McNeilly, James H., 88, 139, 184, 223
McPherson, Gen. James B., 54, 56-57, 173, 295
McPherson, James M., 17, 72
McWhiney, Grady, 229
Medal of Honor:
  Arthur MacArthur, 86
  Matthias Day, 252
  Powhatan Clarke, 252
Medical Histories of Confederate Generals, 272
Memphis and Charleston Railroad, 92, 95, 98
Merrifield, Pvt. J. K., 161
Military Division of the Mississippi, 85
Military Division of the West, 91, 107
Miller, Dr. Brian C., xxix, xxxiv, 243, 250, 253
Miller, Francis, 64
Mobile Advertiser and Register, 54
Mobile and Ohio Railroad, 93-95, 98
Morehead, Pvt. Henry A., 14, 265
Morgan, Gen. G. W., 245-246
Mosman, Lt. Chesley, 120
The Moving Appeal, 120, 280
Murfreesboro, Tennessee, 184-186, 188, 222, 240-241, 246-247
Murphey, Col. Virgil S., 43, 119-120, 159, 180
Murphree, Sgt. Joel, 31
Muzzey, David S., 79
Nalle, William, xxvii

Nashville Banner, 87-88
Nashville, Tennessee, xxxii, 85, 94, 97, 99, 101, 103, 106, 133, 135, 141, 146-147, 153-154, 156-157, 161, 166, 173, 176, 179-181, 183-184, 190, 193, 197, 216, 240, 247
Nashville, Tennessee, battle of, xiii, xx, xxvi, xliii, 10, 64, 70-71, 74-75, 78-79, 85, 98, 178, 181-182, 185-187, 189, 192-193, 195-198, 201, 203, 205-206, 219, 222, 227, 233-234, 240, 243, 247, 259, 265, 281, 297
Nathan Bedford Forrest: In Search of an Enigma, 15, 279
National Tribune, 67
Neal, Lt. Andrew, 29
Neely, Capt. H. M., 216
Nelson, Larry E., 32
New Hope Church, 237
New Orleans Daily Picayune, xiv, xx
New Orleans Times, xix
New York Tribune, xxvi
Newton, Stephen, 62, 244
Nisbet, Col. James C., 16, 288
O'Connor, Richard, xxxiv, xliii, 270, 277
Old Bald Head: General R. S. Ewell, 268
Old, Maj. William W., 123-124, 126
"Old Wooden-head," 17
Oliver, Capt. Paul A., 51-51n
Opdycke, Col. Emerson, xliii, 152, 161
Orphan Brigade, 29, 164
Orr, A. L., 96
Our Living and Our Dead, xv
Owen, Dr. Urban, 75, 78, 233, 277-278
Owen, Tine, xxiii
Patrick, Pvt. Robert, 28
Patterson, Gerard, 13-14
Pawlowski, Rebecca, 140
Peachtree Creek, battle of, 27, 54, 56-58, 60-61, 62n, 202, 204, 216, 237-238, 295
Pearson, Norman, 89
Pemberton, Gen. John C., 37
Perot, Leopold, 26
Phelan, Col. James, 35, 303
Philadelphia Medical Institute, 2
Pickett, Gen. George, 252
Pickett's Mill, battle of, 34
Polk, Gen. Leonidas, 23, 24n, 26, 39, 47, 70
Pollard, E. A., xxv, 230, 288
Pope, Gen. John, 8
Port Hudson, siege of, 37
Porter, Gen. Fitz John, 146, 231, 255
Presstman, Col. Stephen, 186, 187n
Preston, Sarah Buchanan, xl, xliii, 287-288
Purdy, Tennessee, 110
Quarles, Gen. William A., 88, 184, 223
Quintard, Dr. Charles T., 78, 117, 143, 264, 277-278
Randall, James G., 208
Ranke, Leopold von, 112

Ratchford, Maj. James W., 14, 118, 125, 231, 256, 272, 288
Rebel's from West Point, 13
Resaca, battle of, 30, 46, 134, 234, 239-240
Revolutionary War, 2
Richmond Examiner, xxv
Ridley, B. L., 282-283, 286
Riedel, Len, 25
Rippavilla plantation, 116-117, 136, 170
Road Past Kennesaw, The: The Atlanta Campaign of 1864, 268, 279
Rocky Face Gap, 29
Roddey, Gen. Philip D., 87, 93, 101
Roman, Alfred, 96, 106-107
Rosecrans, Gen. William S., 236
Ross, Gen. Lawrence S., 114-115
Rousseau, Gen. Lovell H., 185-186
Scaife, William, 66, 205
Scandals of the Civil War, 281
Schofield, Gen. John, xxi, xliii, 47, 54, 56, 64, 70, 74-75, 85, 112, 121, 130, 161, 216, 240; Franklin, battle of, xxvi, 259; Franklin, 84, 132, 138, 144, 146-147, 149-151, 153-155, 157, 159, 164, 166, 175, 234, 239; Spring Hill Affair, 116, 118-119, 130n, 133-135, 209, 216, 240, 269, 274; felt he could not hold Franklin, 161; dismisses Hood's critics, 162; Hood's dilemma, 162; memoirs, 162-163; abandoned Franklin, 166-167; casualties at Franklin, 167-167n; safety of Nashville, 178; approved Hood's movement to Nashville, 181; West Point, 281-281n; Hood's memoirs, 295; treatment of Thomas, xxvi; clique to control northern memory, xxvii
Science of War, The, 79
Seddon, James, xvi, 92, 105-106, 177, 193-195, 197, 233, 245, 296
Sedgwick, Gen. John, 6
Sellers, Col. Harry, 9
Sessums, Danny, 212
Seven Day's Battles, 8
Seven Pines, Virginia, battle of, 7, 34, 37
Sharpsburg, battle of, xxiii, 8, 14, 214, 229, 231, 257
Shaw, Lt. Henry, 161
Sheridan, Gen. Philip, xxvii, 3, 252
Sherman, Gen. William T., xii, xvii, xxvii, 24-24n, 26, 29-31, 33, 41, 44-45, 54, 59-60, 63-64, 66, 70-72, 77, 79, 82-84, 86, 90, 93-94, 98, 100-104, 106, 133, 173, 183, 192, 196, 205-206, 216-217, 220, 222, 227, 229-230, 238, 245, 262-263; Atlanta Campaign, xviii, 10; March to the Sea, xxi; death of Thomas, xxvi; Confederate deserters, 27-28; split his army at Cassville, 46-47; Cassville, 47-48; Atlanta, 53; Peachtree Creek, 54; supply

lines, 62; Army of Tennessee not destroyed during the campaign, 202; "To pursue Hood is folly" quote, 239; Hood's memoirs, 293,
Shoup, Gen. Francis, 25-26, 91, 237
Sickles, Gen. Daniel, 1, 274
Sigel, Gen. Franz, 32
Simmons, L. A., 160-161
Simpson, Harold B., xxiii-xxiv
Smith, Gen. Andrew J., 156, 161, 189-190
Smith, Gen. Edmund Kirby, xvii, 10, 35, 179-180, 206-207, 224; refuses to send help to Hood, 189-194; West Point, 252; Jefferson Davis to Confederate Congress, 305
Smith, Frank H., 43, 282
Smith, Gen. Gustavus W., 6-7, 40, 295
Smith, Jean Edward, 17
Soldier of Tennessee, 115
Southern Bivouac, xv
Southern Historical Society Papers, xv, xx, xxix
Southern History of the War, 288
Southern Historical Society, xiii-xiv, xix-xxii, xxv, xxvii, xxxiv
Southern Hospital Association for Disabled Soldiers, xxxii
Spring Hill Affair, xvi-xvii, xliii, 4, 22, 62, 112-114, 116-129, 130n, 133-137, 139, 141-144, 150, 153, 158-159, 169-174, 182, 197, 209-212, 215-216, 229, 234, 236, 240, 242-244, 246, 248, 269-270, 274, 297-298
Spring Hill, Tennessee, 145, 151-152, 154, 156, 162, 164, 211, 213
Stanley, Gen. David, 85-86, 113
Stanton, Edwin M., 79, 81, 175, 232
The State of Jones, 259
Stauffer, John, 259
Steiner, Paul, 273
Stephenson, Pvt. Philip D., 254-255
Stevenson, Gen. Carter, 26, 96
Stewart, Gen. Alexander P., 24, 61, 71, 106, 110, 116, 174, 180, 185, 217-218, 230, 243; new to Army of Tennessee, 25-26; Peachtree Creek, 54, 57-58; Ezra Church, 59, 238; poor morale, 77; Spring Hill Affair, 113-115, 118, 121-123, 240; Franklin, 138, 141, 143-145, 154, 158, 240; command meeting at Franklin, 166-167; death of Cleburne, 175; commands the Army of Tennessee, 206; Jonesboro, 219; blames Hood for Spring Hill, 246; never saw Hood impaired, 278-279; "The Yellow Rose of Texas," 283
Stone, Col. Henry, 177
Stoneman, Gen. George, 61, 252
Stonewall of the West, 138, 172, 212, 279
Stories the Soldiers Wouldn't Tell, The: Sex in the Civil War, xl
Story of the Confederacy, The, 281
Stovall, Gen. Marcellus A., 265

Strahl, Gen. Otho, 287
Strange Battles of the Civil War, 21, 279
Strange, Maj. J. P., 102
Street Jr., James, 274
Strong, Gen. George C., 253
Stuart, Gen. James E. B., 15, 63, 253
Suffolk Campaign, 8, 14
Sunshine Church, battle of, 61
Sword, Wiley, xxii, xxv, xxxi, xxxiii-xxxv, xxxviii,
    xxxix, xl-xli, 11, 16, 21, 25, 84, 87, 90-91, 93,
    95, 99, 103-104, 106-111, 116, 127-128, 142,
    144, 147, 149, 157, 159, 166, 170-173, 194-
    198, 201-204, 211-213, 215, 220, 249, 251,
    254-260, 270, 279, 286-290
Sybel, Heinrich von, 176
Symonds, Craig, 48, 138, 149, 172, 212, 279
Talley, Rev. John, 99, 187
Tarleton, Susan, 287
Taylor, Gen. Richard, 25, 45, 91-93, 97, 100,
    105-106, 111, 179-180, 191, 195, 206;
    complains about Hood to Beauregard, 97;
    fails to notify Forrest of Hood's plans, 100;
    Hood requests 20 days rations, 94; unable to
    supply Hood, 96; logistics, 89, 99; miscom-
    munication, 100-102; poor commun-
    ications, 108; seeking help for Hood, 195;
    Smith refuses to help Hood, 196; supplies
    for Hood, 95
Taylor, Maj. Thomas T., 67-68, 221
Tennessee Campaign, xxxi, xxxiv, xxxviii-xxxix,
    xl, xliii, 43, 69, 70, 72, 74, 79-91, 98, 102-103,
    116-117, 121, 123, 130, 141, 157, 175, 183,
    187-187n, 189, 199, 201-201n, 203, 207-
    211, 213, 228, 233, 239, 247, 261-262, 281,
    283, 287, 291, 297
*Tennessee's Forgotten Warriors: Frank Cheatham and
    his Confederate Division*, 281
Texas brigade, xiii, xix, xxii-xxiv, 1, 6-8, 14, 16,
    146, 225, 231, 235, 247, 254, 265, 272, 286
Texas Brigade Association, xxiii-xxiv
Thomas, Gen. George H., xxv, xxviii, 4, 43, 54,
    70, 74-75, 79, 81, 83-85, 93-94, 102, 119,
    133, 135, 156-157, 162, 179, 184, 190, 193-
    194, 203, 222, 239, 259; Nashville, xxi, 177;
    death of, xxvi-xxvii; legacy, xxvi; response
    to *New York Tribune* letter, xxvi; solid,
    dependable commander, xxvii; Peachtree
    Creek, 54, 56, 237; size of army at Nashville,
    178, 180; gains reinforcements, 180; Grant
    orders to launch an assault, 182-183; attacks
    Hood, 186; Confederate deserters, 188-189;
    Army of Tennessee not destroyed during
    the campaign, 201; Kennesaw Mountain,
    230; Hood's memoirs, 295
Thomas, Rhett, 139
Thompson, Dr. Samuel, 42, 206, 263

Thompson's Station, 113-115, 120
Trans-Mississippi Department, xvii, 179, 189-191,
    193, 206
Tupelo, Mississippi, 10, 199, 233, 239, 265
Turner, William B., 270
Turney, Capt. Daniel, 164
Tuscumbia, Alabama, 94-96, 98, 101-102, 105, 109-
    110, 199, 233
Twain, Mark, 249
United States Military Units
    Illinois, 59th Infantry, 120; 84th Infantry, 160; 88th
        Infantry, 161; 102nd Infantry, 30
    Indiana, 40th Infantry, 155
    New Jersey, 4th Infantry, 256
    New York, 16th Infantry, 7
    Ohio, 40th Infantry, 86; 46th Infantry, 67; 47th
        Infantry, 221; 65th Infantry, 159; 97th Infantry,
        155; 125th Infantry, 152, 161
    U.S. Regulars, 2nd Cavalry, 3-5, 150
    Wisconsin, 24th Infantry, 14, 86, 161
Utoy Creek, battle of, 61
Van Dorn, Gen. Earl, 4
Van Horne, Thomas B., 177, 299
Vancouver, Capt. George, 2n
Vaulx, Maj. Joseph, 137-138
Vicksburg, siege of, 37
Virginia Military Institute, xxvii
Voltaire, 227
Wagner, Gen. George D., 145, 154, 167
Walker, Col. Irvine, 31
Walker, Gen. William H. T., 57, 123n, 252, 295
Walsh, M.D., Jack D., 272
Walthall, Gen. Edward, 26, 189, 205
*War Like the Thunderbolt: The Battle and Burning of
    Atlanta*, 16
The Wartime Papers of Robert E. Lee, 11, 17
Washburn, W. A., 146
Washburne, Elihu, 33
Washington, George, 291
Watkins, Pvt. Sam, 29, 42, 79, 153, 188, 201, 264, 277
Welsh, Jack, 275
Western and Atlantic Railroad, 90
Wheeler, Gen. Joseph, 24, 61-62, 100, 105, 202, 252
Whiting, Gen. William Henry Chase, 6-7, 231, 253
Wigfall, Capt. F. H., 42
Wigfall, Louis T., 20, 51n, 265
Wilcox, Gen. Cadmus, xiii, xx
Wiley, Bell I., 281
Williamsburg, battle of, 6
Williamson, Lt. R. S., 3
Wilson, Gen. James H., 43-44, 65, 85, 118, 135, 147,
    201, 239, 264
Wofford, Col. William, 231
Wolseley, Lord Garnet Joseph, 79
Wood, Gen. Thomas, 155

Woodworth, Steven, xxxv, 53, 56, 58, 62, 140, 204, 211, 271
Wright, Louise Wigfall, 255, 260, 265
Wyatt, Col. J. N., 43
"Yellow Rose of Texas, The," song, 281-286
Yorktown, Virginia, battle of, 6, 36-37
Young, Pvt. J. P., 118-119, 136, 138

Stephen M. Hood

Author

Stephen "Sam" Hood is a graduate of Kentucky Military Institute, Marshall University (BBA, 1976), and a veteran of the United States Marine Corps Reserve. A collateral descendant of Gen. John Bell Hood, Sam is a retired industrial construction company owner, past member of the Board of Directors of the Blue Gray Education Society of Chatham, Virginia, and is a past president of the Board of Directors of Confederate Memorial Hall Museum Foundation in New Orleans.

Sam resides in his hometown of Huntington, West Virginia, and Myrtle Beach, South Carolina, with his wife of thirty-five years, Martha, and is the proud father of two sons: Derek Hood of Lexington, Kentucky, and Taylor Hood of Huntington, West Virginia. He is compiling General Hood's personal papers for publication with Savas Beatie.